ROUTLEDGE LIBRARY EDITIONS:
TRADE UNIONS

Volume 20

CHANGE IN TRADE UNIONS

CHANGE IN TRADE UNIONS

The Development of UK Unions
Since the 1960s

R. UNDY, V. ELLIS,
W. E. J. McCARTHY and A. M. HALMOS

Routledge
Taylor & Francis Group

LONDON AND NEW YORK

First published in 1981 by Hutchinson & Co. (Publishers) Ltd.

This edition first published in 2023
by Routledge
4 Park Square, Milton Park, Abingdon, Oxon OX14 4RN

and by Routledge
605 Third Avenue, New York, NY 10158

Routledge is an imprint of the Taylor & Francis Group, an informa business

British Library Cataloguing in Publication Data
A catalogue record for this book is available from the British Library

ISBN: 978-1-032-37553-3 (Set)
ISBN: 978-1-032-39557-9 (Volume 20) (hbk)
ISBN: 978-1-032-39564-7 (Volume 20) (pbk)
ISBN: 978-1-003-35030-9 (Volume 20) (ebk)

DOI: 10.4324/9781003350309

Publisher's Note
The publisher has gone to great lengths to ensure the quality of this reprint but points out that some imperfections in the original copies may be apparent.

Disclaimer
The publisher has made every effort to trace copyright holders and would welcome correspondence from those they have been unable to trace.

Change in Trade Unions

The development of UK unions since the 1960s

R. Undy, V. Ellis, W. E. J. McCarthy and
A. M. Halmos

Hutchinson

London Melbourne Sydney Auckland Johannesburg

Hutchinson & Co. (Publishers) Ltd
An imprint of the Hutchinson Publishing Group
24 Highbury Crescent, London N5 1RX

Hutchinson Group (Australia) Pty Ltd
30–32 Cremorne Street, Richmond South, Victoria 3121
PO Box 151, Broadway, New South Wales 2007

Hutchinson Group (NZ) Ltd
32–34 View Road, PO Box 40–086, Glenfield, Auckland 10

Hutchinson Group (SA) (Pty) Ltd
PO Box 337, Bergvlei 2012, South Africa

First published 1981

Set in Times

Printed in Great Britain by The Anchor Press Ltd
and bound by Wm Brendon & Son Ltd
both of Tiptree, Essex

British Library Cataloguing in Publication Data
Change in trade unions.
   1. Trade-unions – Great Britain – History – 20th century
   I. Undy, R.
   331.88′0941   HD6664
ISBN 0 09 143880 2

Contents

For Harold Undy and all other local union activists without whom unions could not survive and prosper

Tables

Figures

The authors

R. Undy is Fellow and Senior Tutor of the Oxford Centre for Management Studies. He was previously a maintenance fitter and AUEW(E) Shop Steward before winning a TUC scholarship to Ruskin College, Oxford. He is a member of the AUEW(E) Parliamentary Panel and fought the 1974 general election as a sponsored AUEW(E) candidate.

V. Ellis has lectured in industrial sociology and industrial relations and is currently assistant secretary of a professional union and Research Associate at the Oxford Centre for Management Studies. She is joint author of *Social Stratification and Trade Unions* (1973) and *A Professional Union* (1980).

W. E. J. McCarthy is a Fellow of Nuffield College at the Oxford Management Centre and University Lecturer at Oxford University. He has been an adviser on industrial relations to the Secretary of State for Employment and the Secretary of State for Health and Social Security and has chaired many important inquiries into industrial disputes. He is a member of the TUC's Independent Review Committee and was created a Life Peer in 1975. His publications are numerous and include *Trade Unions* (1970), *Coming to Terms with Trade Unions* (1973) and Wage Inflation and *Wage Leadership* (1975).

A. M. Halmos is a one-time Research Associate at the Oxford Centre for Management Studies. He received a BA degree and did postgraduate research at Wadham College, Oxford, and gained an MA degree in Labour and Industrial Relations at the University of Illinois. He is currently a trade union official.

Preface

This study was made possible by a grant from the Department of Employment to the Oxford Centre for Management Studies. We wish to thank both the Department and the Centre for providing us with the means to carry out the work. We are particularly indebted to Bob Tricker, the past director of the Centre, and to Nigel Forward, who was in charge of the Research and Planning Division of the DE when the grant was agreed. We would also like to thank Fred Bayliss, the present head of the Research and Planning Division, for his encouragement, support and patience.

In the course of the field work we contacted a large number of trade union officials at many levels and in numerous organizations. We need to thank them for giving us so much of their time, and for allowing us access to their records. Since information and opinion were often given on the understanding that it would not be ascribed to individuals, we regret to say that we are unable to mention by name even those who helped us most. We can only hope that those who co-operated will take the view that we have presented their position, and the policies of their union, in a fair and unbiased way.

We also have to thank those who helped us to supplement our own researches by making available to us the results of their own investigations. In particular, we profited by the work of a number of MA students of the Industrial Relations Department of Warwick University. As a result of help from Professor Hugh Clegg we were able to persuade them to direct their MA dissertations towards unions and subjects that interested us. We were also able to make similar arrangements with a number of students taking the Oxford BPhil. in Management Studies at the Management Centre. In this way we were able to obtain data on a much wider basis. We also profited by contacts with Bob Fryer of the Sociology Department of Warwick University, who was undertaking a special study of the National Union of Public Employees during the period of our field work. However, any errors that remain in the book are the sole responsibility of the authors.

Our thanks are also due to the staff of the Oxford Centre, who undertook the task of typing numerous reports and draft chapters with unfailing care and patience – especially Pam Snuggs and Valerie Maggs.

Finally, we feel that we should say a word about the distribution of the work that went into this study and its subsequent presentation for publication. Bill McCarthy was responsible for the overall direction and control of the project.

The greater part of the field work was undertaken by Roger Undy, Valerie Ellis and Tony Halmos. They were most ably assisted by John Terry and John Stirling, who for a time were members of the research team, and we would like to take this opportunity to thank them for their valuable contributions to the final product.

Abbreviations

Unions

ABS	Association of Broadcasting Staff
ABT	Association of Building Technicians
ACTSS	Association of Clerical Technical and Supervisory Staffs (Section of the TGWU)
ACTT	Association of Cinematograph, Television and Allied Technicians
AESD	Association of Engineering and Shipbuilding Draughtsmen (forerunner to DATA)
AEU	Amalgamated Engineering Union
APEX	Association of Professional Executive, Clerical and Computer Staff
APST	Association of Professional Scientists and Technologists
ASB or ASBSBSW	Amalgamated Society of Boilermakers, Shipwrights, Blacksmiths and Structural Workers
ASC&J	Amalgamated Society of Carpenters and Joiners
AScW	Association of Scientific Workers
ASE	Amalgamated Society of Engineers
ASLEF	Associated Society of Locomotive Engineers and Firemen
ASPD	Amalgamated Society of Painters and Decorators
ASSET	Association of Supervisory Staffs, Executives and Technicians
ASTMS	Association of Scientific, Technical and Managerial Staffs
ASW	Amalgamated Society of Woodworkers
ASWcM	Amalgamated Society of Woodcutting Machinists
ATTI	Association of Teachers in Technical Institutions
AUBTW	Amalgamated Union of Building Trade Workers
AUEFW or AEF	Amalgamated Union of Engineering and Foundry Workers
AUEW	Amalgamated Union of Engineering Workers
AUEW(E)	Amalgamated Union of Engineering Workers, Engineering Section

AUFW	Amalgated Union of Foundry Workers
BOG	Bank Officers' Guild
CAWU	Clerical and Administrative Workers Union
CEU	Constructional Engineering Union
CoHSE	Confederation of Health Service Employees
COPOU	Council of Post Office Unions
COPPSO	Conference of Professional and Public Service Organisations
CPSA	Civil and Public Servants Association
CSEU	Confederation of Shipbuilding and Engineering Unions
CWU	Chemical Workers' Union
DATA	Draughtsmen and Allied Technicians Association
EETPU	Electrical, Electronic, Telecommunication and Plumbers Union
EMA	Engineers and Managers Association
EOTA	Engineering Officers (Telecommunications) Association
ETU	Electrical Trades Union
FBU	Fire Brigades Union
FTAT	Furniture, Timber and Allied Trades Union
GHP	Guild of Hospital Pharmacists
GMWU	General and Municipal Workers Union
ISTC	Iron and Steel Trades Confederation
KSSA	Kodak Senior Staff Association
MATSA	Managerial, Administrative, Technical and Supervisory Association (Section of GMWU)
MBSA	Midland Bank Staff Association
MPU	Medical Practitioners Union
NALGO	National and Local Government Officers' Association
NAOP	National Association of Operative Plasterers
NAS	National Association of Schoolmasters
NATSOPA	National Association of Operative Printers, Graphical and Media Personnel
NFA	National Foremen's Association
NFBTO	National Federation of Building Trades Operatives
NGA	National Graphical Association
NUB	National Union of Blastfurnacemen, Ore Miners, Coke Workers and Kindred Trades
NUBE	National Union of Bank Employees (renamed Banking, Insurance and Finance Union, BIFU, 1979)
NUFLAT	National Union of Footwear, Leather and Allied Trades
NUFSO	National Union of Funeral Service Operatives
NUFTO	National Union of Furniture Trade Operatives
NUGSAT	National Union of Gold, Silver and Allied Trades
NUJ	National Union of Journalists

NUM	National Union of Mineworkers
NUPE	National Union of Public Employees
NUR	National Union of Railwaymen
NUS	National Union of Seamen
NUSMWCHDE	National Union of Sheet Metal Workers, Coppersmiths, Heating and Domestic Engineers
NUSW	National Union of Scientific Workers
NUT	National Union of Teachers
NUTGW	National Union of Tailors and Garment Workers
NUVB	National Union of Vehicle Builders
PAT	Professional Association of Teachers
POEU	Post Office Engineering Union
PTU	Plumbing Trades Union
SCMU	Scottish Commercial Motormen's Union
SCPS	Society of Civil and Public Servants
SLADE	Society of Lithographic Artists, Designers, Engravers and Process Workers
SOGAT	Society of Graphical and Allied Trades
TASS	Technical, Administrative and Supervisory Section (of AUEW)
TGWU	Transport and General Workers' Union
TTEG	Telephone and Telegraph Engineering Union
TUC	Trades Union Congress
UCATT	Union of Construction, Allied Trades and Technicians
UIS	Union of Insurance Staffs
UPW	Union of Post Office Workers
URTU	United Road Transport Union
USDAW	Union of Shop, Distributive and Allied Workers
WGSA	Williams' & Glynn's Staff Association

Other abbreviations

ADC	Annual Delegate Conference
AGS	Assistant General Secretary
BAO	Branch Administrative Officer
BDC	Biennial Delegate Conference
CBI	Confederation of British Industry
CIR	Commission on Industrial Relations
CIS	Co-operative Insurance Society
CWS	Co-operative Wholesale Society
DE	Department of Employment
DEP	Department of Employment and Productivity
DES	Department of Education and Science
DGS	Deputy General Secretary

DOE	Department of the Environment
DS	District Secretary
EC	Executive Council
EEF	Engineering Employers' Federation
EPA	Employment Protection Act
FAC	Final Appeal Court
F&GPP	Finance and General Purposes Committee
FTO	Full-Time Official
GC	General Council
GEC	General Executive Council
GS	General Secretary
ICI	Imperial Chemical Industries Ltd
ILEA	Inner London Education Authority
ILO	International Labour Organisation
IRA	Industrial Relations Act
JIC	Joint Industrial Council
LOSC	Labour Only Sub-Contractor
MDW	Measured Day Work
NAG	NALGO Action Group
NBPI	National Board Prices and Incomes
NC	National Committee
NDC	National Delegate Conference
NEC	National Executive Council
NES	New Earnings Survey
NFBTE	National Federation of Building Trade Employers
NHS	National Health Service
NIO	National Industrial Officer
NJC	National Joint Council
NJIC	National Joint Industrial Council
NO	National Organiser/Officer
NPLA	National Power Loading Agreement
PBR	Payment By Results
RFSC	Rank and File Strike Committee
TSB	Trustee Savings Bank
TULRA	Trade Union Labour Relations Act

1 The scope and nature of the study

Uncertainty, in the presence of vivid hopes and fears, is painful, but must be endured if we wish to live without the support of comforting fairy tales.

Bertrand Russell, *History of Western Philosophy*[1]

What this book is not about

The serious student of British trade unions is often asked to prescribe, pronounce and pontificate before he has had time to explain. Those who have never attended a single branch meeting are apt to assume that they already know how unions work and exactly what is wrong with them. What is wanted, one is told, is a blueprint for immediate reform. Otherwise, what is the point of studying trade unions?

It must therefore be admitted at the outset that this substantial volume is without a blueprint of any kind. It is essentially an exercise in understanding and analysis. It sets out to explain the factors that have precipitated and affected change in the major dimensions of union activity – especially those that have influenced the British trade union movement since about 1960.

We believe that there should be the widest possible understanding of the factors that both induce and prevent change in trade unions, if only because in the past misunderstandings and miscalculations have been based on false assumptions about union motivation and behaviour. Yet we have no alternative set of certainties to put in the place of these convictions. What we offer is merely a greater appreciation of the limits and constraints that affect certain kinds of union action. In this way it can be argued that this study has contemporary implications – not least for those who set out to 'reform' the unions from outside.

On the other hand, we would hope that much of what we describe will be of interest to trade unions themselves. Our study challenges several preconceptions about the options open to union leaders and their members. In some ways these are found to be more amenable to deliberate choice and decision than many trade unionists tend to assume. Since unions are as insular as most other well-established British institutions, they do not always learn all they could from each other. Some of our findings indicate that those who wish to effect change in their own organization can learn from the experiences of others.

* Superior figures refer to the Notes on pages 357–81.

We also believe that many of our findings are of interest and significance to those who study trade unions from a more academic point of view. In particular, we feel that many of the concepts and terms employed to analyse union behaviour need to be supplemented and adapted if the process of change is to be understood. After all, we hope that this study will help to dispel at least some of the more persistent and prevailing myths about trade unions – not least the widespread belief that they never change at all.

In the remainder of this introductory chapter we deal briefly with three preliminary matters. We turn first to the origins and problems of the study, as they emerged from the field work. We then present a brief account of the more important concepts and terms used in subsequent chapters. The final section describes the order of the rest of the work and introduces some of its more important themes.

Origins and problems: the changing focus of the study

This study originated in discussions between officials of the Department of Employment and one of the authors – W. E. J. McCarthy. The Research and Planning Division of the DE was interested in sponsoring research into recent developments in trade union policy and behaviour, in the belief that this would reveal a number of 'trends' which could be 'projected' to indicate likely future developments. It was hoped that a study of this kind would help those responsible for advising governments on future policy options.

This seemed to us a worthwhile objective, and we readily agreed to undertake such a project. It was obvious that the resources available would not allow for a detailed examination of more than a dozen or so unions, but we felt that this need not be a major difficulty if the sample was selected with sufficient care, and if all the unions chosen would give us their full co-operation.

We also knew that we ourselves could not hope to investigate all the unions in the sample in sufficient depth; but resources were available to enable us to supplement our own efforts in a number of ways, which are described in the Preface. In broad terms we sought to cover as many different unions as possible – bearing in mind that there were two or three giants who could not be left out.

In the event we encountered few barriers and no significant setbacks; indeed, several organizations threatened to overwhelm us with documents, correspondence and data of all kinds. Because we were interested in overall trends we focused mainly on interviews at national level, although we made several forays into other levels of union organization.

The main problem we encountered was that as our field work proceeded it became more and more obvious that the data we uncovered were not likely to provide us with the basis for reliable and precise extrapolations into the future. The trouble was that they did not appear to fall into any easily discernible pattern. It was true that in each of the major areas examined substantial changes had taken place – often on a more widespread scale than we had supposed; but the form and nature of these changes varied greatly from union to union, and it was often unclear which set of changes we ought to regard as typical or representative. As the study proceeded we became less and less confident of our ability to forecast the likely shape or direction of the future.

Fortunately, we had by this time become even more interested in why it was proving so difficult to discern reliable trends and patterns. We decided that this problem was centrally related to a complex combination of factors which we came to call the 'process of change'. It was easy enough to observe and classify certain *areas of change*, and to group them under three broad heads: those affecting government, job territories, and systems of job regulation. It was also obvious that there were certain common influences at work, which we decided to term the 'agents of change'. They could be broadly classified into those that were *internally* rooted, and those that originated mainly in developments *external* to a given union.

What was much more difficult was to estimate and predict the role likely to be played by two of the more important internal factors – the decision-making structures of a given union, and its existing national leadership. We came to the conclusion that different combinations of these two variables, in different unions at different times, combined to produce widely different forms and degrees of change – even where the external stimulus, in the form of common change agents, appeared to us to be similar or identical.

But if the indeterminacy of our two most important variables made it difficult to predict the likely direction of future change, we were nevertheless able to analyse their processes of interaction and the likely consequences of any particular combination. Indeed, it was possible to construct what we have termed a 'model of change', containing the major factors that are conducive to change in British trade unions.

Thus we would claim that we have been able to analyse, in some detail, that combination of factors that is most likely to produce an innovative union, as against one that may be said to be conservative, or resistant to change. We have also been able to say a great deal about the way in which various combinations of factors produce, or restrict, different movements for change and their consequences. In addition, we have felt able to advance a number of alternative patterns of change, explaining how their relative likelihood depends on the reaction of certain key variables in our model of change to future developments. Thus, although we have not been able to provide many reliable signposts to the route ahead, we can offer our readers a general map of the area.

Of course, it is no part of our argument that change is necessarily desirable in itself – so it cannot be concluded, or assumed, that innovative unions are generally to be preferred to more conservative organizations. As we demonstrate, everything depends on the direction and consequences of change in particular circumstances, and on the observers' point of view. What may be said is that too great a resistance to change, or a total inability to achieve conscious and deliberate change, is likely to produce serious problems for almost any union at some time or another – especially if it finds itself in a competitive job territory and a swiftly changing environment.

We also would not claim to have produced anything in the nature of a general theory of union behaviour; we have focused on change, and a great deal of union activity is essentially repetitive and routine. We have also adopted a view of unions as overall entities. Many of our inquiries were concerned with the attempts of union executives and national leaders to face up to the challenges of the day as they appeared to be presented to them. Other studies, focused on other levels and concerns, would no doubt produce a rather different set of answers.

Our second major problem concerned the absence of an available and recognized set of terms which we could employ to describe and analyse the data we collected. In the chapters that follow therefore we have had to introduce the reader to a rather large number of new concepts, and we can only plead in our defence that we consider them to be essential to the purpose in hand. As each term is introduced it is defined and its use is explained – we hope with simplicity and clarity.

This introductory chapter is not the place to seek to summarize or digest what follows in this respect; but we felt it would help if we were to give a brief indication of the main distinctions we seek to make with our new terminology.

Concepts and terms

Union government

In the area of union government we found that we could make little use of the conventional terminology derived from existing literature. (This employs terms such as 'democratic', 'oligarchic' or 'degree of participation', for the most part imported from classical political theory.) In place of these established terms we have made three distinctions. The first relates to the locus of decision-taking in different unions and marks the extent to which decisions are *dispersed* across different parts of the governmental structure. Two related forms of dispersal are distinguished. One concerns the extent to which decisions are decentralized downwards from the national level, that is, the degree of vertical dispersal; the other relates to the extent to which decisions are concentrated or diffused across a given level of union government – for example, national, regional or local level. This form of dispersal we term 'horizontal dispersal'.

Second, because there is often a significant difference in the way in which union decisions are taken affecting collective bargaining, as against the way a union decides other issues (such as administration and finance), we have advanced a typology of union government that provides for an analysis in terms of *bargaining/non-bargaining* channels. A governmental system where the decision-making process is the same in both channels is termed a 'single-channel' system. Where things are decided differently in the bargaining channel we speak of a 'bifurcated system'.

Third, because union rule books and constitutions are often imperfect guides to the way in which actual decisions are taken, we have imported into our typology the well-known legal distinction between the *de jure* position in union constitutions and the *de facto* position in practice.

Job territories

Our second area of change concerns union job territories. (This term is taken from the works of S. Perlman, and may be defined as that area of the labour market where a union aims to recruit and retain membership.[2]) For the most part the existing literature seeks to classify the job territories of different unions in terms of their approximation to three ideal types – industrial, craft and general unions. More recently H. A. Turner has sought to replace this typology with one of his own.[3] This is based on the extent to which a union pursues 'open' or 'closed' objectives in respect of potential members. In subsequent chapters we give our reasons why we do not regard any of these distinctions as helpful for our purpose. Meanwhile we advance five of our own.

The first distinction relates to the *degree of diversity* among a given union's membership. By 'heterogeneous' unions we mean those with a diverse membership; those who restrict their job territory to a single industry or trade are said to be 'homogeneous'.

Our second distinction relates to *degrees of competition* within a given sector of the labour market. Unions that operate in competition with others are said to be operating in 'exposed' areas; unions enjoying a monopoly within their chosen job territory are described as 'sheltered'.

Our third distinction refers to *union attitudes towards the recruitment and retention of members*. These are classified according to the extent to which unions adopt a positive or passive approach to the question of membership growth. At one end of the spectrum some unions, in some periods, have adopted a restrictive attitude towards recruitment and retention even within the boundaries of their traditional job territories. At other times other unions, or the same unions, have adopted positive policies of expansion, seeking to enlarge their job territory boundaries into those occupied by other unions.

So far as job territory change is concerned our last two distinctions both concern *alternative ways of achieving union growth*. The first marks the distinction between what has been termed 'natural' growth and growth resulting from mergers.[4] Natural growth is often the result of a combination of factors. It may be the consequence of deliberate policies designed to raise membership, or it may result from factors largely outside a union's control – for example an expansion of the labour force in well-organized plants or industries. Thus natural growth need not involve positive and deliberate action on the part of a union that benefits. In contrast to this, the growth that follows from a successful merger is the result of a deliberate and conscious policy on the part of several union leaderships. It requires and presupposes a positive approach to growth as a union objective.

Finally, we have found it useful to distinguish between the objectives of different mergers by the use of a three-fold classification. Thus we refer to *defensive, consolidatory* or *expansionist* mergers, and seek to apply these terms to both the major and minor unions involved in a given merger.

Job regulation

Changes in job regulation are also classified under two main heads – those affecting union character, and those involving what we term 'structural change'. By character changes we mean those that result in a different emphasis being placed on different ways of exerting trade union influence – most notably shifts between reliance on political pressure as against various forms of industrial action. Also involved is a greater, or lesser, readiness to employ various forms of coercive action in pursuit of union goals – what is sometimes termed the 'degree of union militancy'.

By structural change we mean changes in the level of collective bargaining, or the extent to which lay members participate in bargaining decisions. Where bargaining is devolved to a lower level we speak of 'decentralization'; where the participation of lay members is encouraged and extended we refer to the 'diffusion' of the bargaining process.

Major themes and their development

In the chapter that follows we describe in more detail the methodology we have employed to collect and analyse our data. We also develop and illustrate the model of the change process that we use to explain the directions and consequences of change. In Chapters 3–8 this model is employed to explore the process and direction of change in each of our three major areas. Chapter 9 contains our conclusions and aims to describe what we term the 'conditions of change' in British unions.

One of the major themes that emerges in our analysis of every area of change concerns the relative importance of external and internal change agents. In broad terms it may be said that in most cases internal agents appear to be the most important influences at work – especially if one seeks to explain the timing, scope and direction of significant and lasting changes.

Of course, this is not to say that external factors are found to be unimportant – especially when viewed as 'threats' or 'opportunities' from the viewpoint of national leaders and their allies. In this respect we analyse the impact of a wide variety of economic, political and technological developments on union thinking and union action. We discover, for example, that broad movements in the occupational or industrial balance of the labour force had an impact on union government – just as developments in union law and government policy have affected union structure and bargaining priorities.

Nevertheless, and for the most part, it seems to us that these external agents of change have done little more than present union leaders and their allies with additional problems to solve. Such change agents usually allow union leaders a variety of alternative responses, including, on some occasions, the alternative of inaction. And at this point it is the balance and form taken by a number of key internal agents of change that largely determines the response adopted in a given union. This brings us to another major theme that runs through the study.

We have been struck by the way in which a particular combination of factors may be said to facilitate or encourage change in any direction. In effect, two crucial elements are required: first, an innovative, competent, self-confident and more or less united leadership; second, flexible and discretionary decision-making structures – especially those affecting non-bargaining issues.

In the chapters that follow we shall be arguing that a great deal can be explained by reference to the extent to which all or any of these conditions apply in a given union, or section of its membership. They are seen to be the key to the diverse record of unions facing similar external challenges and problems. They also help to explain why it is that union actions and behaviour can be seen to vary through time, and from area to area, without concomitant or complementary developments in the relevant external environment. Indeed, it is our opinion that an understanding of the key conditions of change in British unions is an essential part of the toolkit of any would-be union reformer.

Of course, we are not suggesting that the processes of change within trade unions are all in one direction – from the leadership to the membership. On the contrary, in the chapters that follow, most notably those describing the processes of decentralization and diffusion in the area of job regulation, full weight is given to such factors as rank-and-file pressure for increased participation and the emergence of increased militancy. On the other hand, we do suggest that in respect of many prospective and actual changes – for example those affecting the choice of merger partners, or reactions to technological change – a great deal has depended on how the national leadership used the balance of 'threats' and 'opportunities' facing them at a given time. Moreover, it is another theme of the study that factors of this kind also affect the practicality and desirability of proposals for trade union reform that emanate outside union ranks.

In general, and in conclusion, it may be said that our study has paradoxical implications for the advocate of conscious or deliberate change in British unions. In the first place it indicates that change is by no means unknown and impossible to effect; in the second place it suggests that it is not developing in any easily discernible direction according to a common pattern or trend. Indeed, if anything the government and structure of British unions appear to be more diverse, contradictory and conflicting at the end of our period of study than they were in 1960.

On the other hand, national leaders and their allies appear to have more control over their destiny, and the future direction of their organization, than has sometimes been suggested – for example by academics, who have sought to explain the factors affecting union growth and power. On the other hand, unions often appear to be influenced by extremely narrow and sectional considerations – notably the need of established leaders to ensure their own short-term survival.

In one sense it can be shown that particular attempts to influence union behaviour from outside have made a significant impact – for example changes in the law affecting union mergers, or successive incomes policy criteria. In another sense it is arguable that many of these interventions and inducements have failed to work out as intended, while some have had effects quite contrary to those aimed at by their authors.

As might be expected, it is possible to draw a number of quite different conclusions from this plethora of paradoxes. One can take an extreme or 'radical' view, arguing that lasting and purposive change can be achieved if only one concentrates on persuading or compelling unions to move towards a common framework of rules or decision-making processes – namely, those designed to facilitate 'reform' in the direction desired by the advocate of change.

Against this view one can opt for scepticism or, if one prefers the term, 'conservatism'. Advocates of this view are likely to stress the impossibility of predicting the way in which unions are developing at the moment, coupled with the almost insurmountable problems of predicting how even simple changes in existing rules and constitutions are likely to work out in future. In the final sections of this study we shall return to questions of this kind, and set out our own views.

2 Methodology and model

Our approach

The first point to be made is that we are looking at unions as 'wholes'; we are assuming that a union can be discussed as a single entity. Of course, the degree to which this can be done varies between unions. In many it is difficult to formulate a single strategy, and the more heterogeneous the union membership and the greater the dispersion of decision-making functions within the union, the more difficult this becomes. There may not be a consensus between the competing and conflicting interest groups or between the varying levels at which policy is formulated and implemented within a union. At any particular point in time, therefore, one may simply be describing the ascendant ideology and strategy, which may be subject to change and which may not characterize the activities of all elements within the union. For the most part, therefore, when we speak of the union pursuing this or that strategy we shall be concerned with the existing 'leadership' of that particular union, however that may be defined. The views of the rank and file, except where they are articulated by pressure groups of various kinds within the union, are not our major focus of discussion. The techniques of study that we used did not involve direct consideration of rank-and-file views.

Second, in discussing change we need to steer a course between taking a view that overemphasizes the degree of freedom of decision available to a union, and avoiding the less common view that a union is entirely a 'victim of its circumstances'. The degree to which either of these positions is tenable is a matter for investigation in each case and cannot be assumed *a priori*. The approach adopted in this study seeks to explain change in terms that take account of the degree of discretion that is available to a union, in other words to note the constraints, both internal and external to the union, that specify the limits within which its policies and strategies are formulated. These constraints upon a trade union's actions may be termed the 'logic of its situation'. However, since the union does not necessarily perceive the variety of options that are hypothetically available to it within the constraints of the 'logic of the situation', we need to introduce the notion of the union's 'definition of the situation'. When we come to evaluate the changes that the union has made, however, we may need to point out some of the alternative strategies it could have pursued, had it been less constrained by, for example, internal political factors, or had it been more imaginative in the range of available alternatives that it perceived.

Third, there is the problem of deciding which among the multitude of changes in trade unions may be regarded as significant for our purposes. There is no easy way of deciding what criteria should be applied when selecting the changes to be studied. And in finding a solution to this problem we need to recognize that changes may be of at least two kinds. There are those that arise from positive decisions taken by the union, such as the decision to recruit in a new area of employment, and those that are simply trends of a cumulative or continuous nature, for example the growth or decline in a category of membership. Although we will tend to concentrate on the type of change that results from conscious decisions, these will be analysed against a background of structural trends which form the 'logic of the situation' and provide the context in which those conscious decisions are taken.

The fact that we are focusing on leadership strategies and dealing as far as possible with unions as 'wholes' has also determined the type of research techniques that we have used. We have not employed mass survey techniques, which would have been appropriate had we been trying to gauge the views of the membership at large; nor, partly for that reason, are our hypotheses and conclusions amenable to statistical verifiability or to an exact weighing of the evidence. Instead, we have used a case study approach and a variety of fact-gathering techniques including documentary sources and structured and unstructured interviews with key individuals. As C. Wright Mills has said about the objectives of social research, one has to strike a balance between the significance of the problem chosen for study and the limits of research techniques.

Precision is not the sole criterion for choice of method; certainly precision ought not to be confused, as it so often is, with 'empirical' or 'true'. We should be as accurate as we are able to be in our work upon the problems that concern us. But no method, as such, should be used to delimit the problems we take up, if for no other reason than that the most interesting and difficult issues of method usually begin where established techniques do not apply.[1]

The scope of this study – the changes in trade union job territory, job regulation strategy and internal government – is wide. Most studies of union development in the past have found that to focus on any one of these has been more than sufficient. However, part of our purpose is to link developments in each of these spheres to certain common explanatory variables. Thus the scope must be wide, but in order to make the study more manageable we have focused on a few major unions in depth, although in total they encompass over 60 per cent of TUC affiliated membership. In selecting the sample we have tried to cover a wide range of types and circumstances (see Table 1). Even within this small sample, the TGWU, the AUEW (Engineering Section), the GMWU, NALGO, UCATT, ASTMS and the Post Office Engineering Union have been studied in greater depth than the rest. The minor case studies of the NUM, NUPE, the Boilermakers, NUBE and the NUT have been used to provide additional comparative material.[2]

Table 1 *Structure of the sample of unions*

Union	Sector			Structural type*		
	Public	Private	Craft	General	Indus-trial	White-collar
ASBSBSW	(x)†	x	x			
AUEW	(x)	x	x	(x)		
ASTMS	(x)	x				x
GMWU	x	x		x		
NALGO	x					x
NUBE		x				x
NUM	x				x	
NUPE	x				x	
NUT	x					x
POEU	x		x			
TGWU	(x)	x		x		
UCATT	(x)	x	x		(x)	

* The traditional formulation of structural types has been used purely as a starting point. It does not imply that we think they are the best way of classifying unions or that the position of each union is as ambiguous as the table would suggest.

† (x) indicates secondary classification

The model of change

We have found it helpful to analyse the changes we seek to explain by reference to a series of special terms or concepts. The relationship between these concepts may be termed our 'model of change'. This is set out in diagrammatic form below in Figure 1. The model is not advanced as a sophisticated instrument; it is simply intended as a device for structuring the discussion of the process of change. As such it is used to give the research material a common form. Its utility will therefore be tested by the degree to which it makes the discussion of change in the main areas of union behaviour studied – namely internal government (Chapter 4), job territory (Chapters 5 and 6) and job regulation (Chapters 7 and 8) – manageable and meaningful.

This symmetrical diagram is intended to suggest a multi-directional process of change with several alternative channels of influence. It will be seen that at the top we place the 'change agents', or factors that precipitate change. These are portrayed as making their impact on various parts of the model through a number of arrowed lines. Some of the change agents go straight downwards into the 'decision-making structure'. Immediately below this box we have placed the

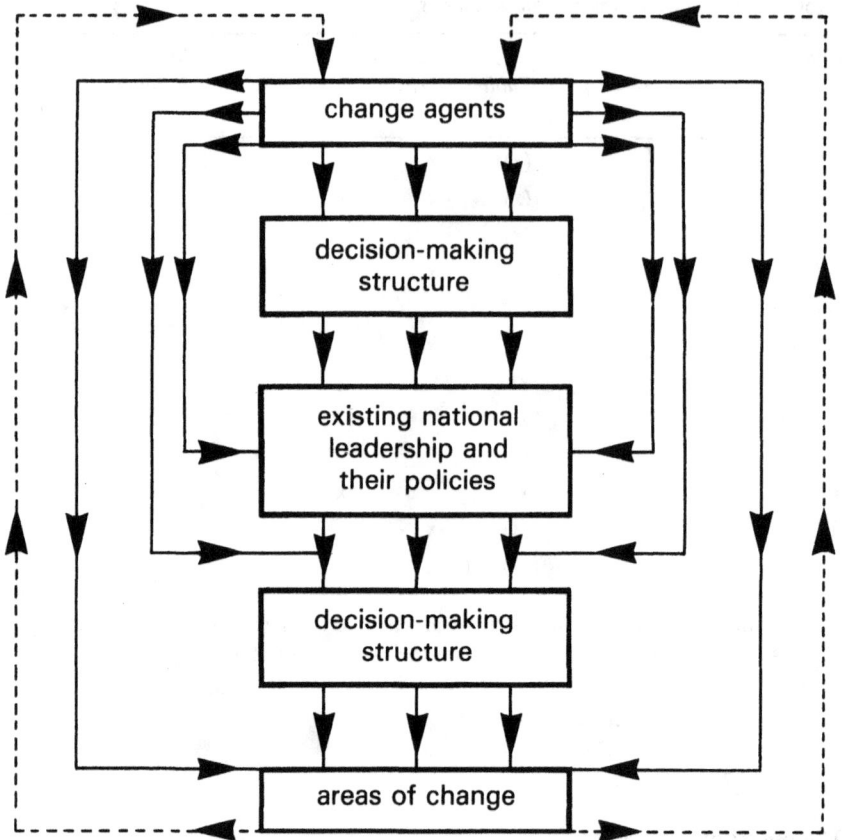

Figure 1   *The model of change*

'existing national leadership and their policies'. This is intended to signify that it is usually the national leadership that is required to act in a positive way if the union is to come to terms with the factors that are acting as agents of change.

Below the national leadership we place once again the union's decision-making structure. This indicates that for the most part the leadership needs to operate through the existing structure of decision-taking within the union. Where they are successful certain aspects of union behaviour are changed, and we describe them in terms of the 'areas of change'.

But the model also illustrates what might be termed the 'shorter' processes of change. These may work through those agents of change that bypass the decision-making structure and make a direct impact on the ideas and perceptions of the national leadership, or bypass both structure and leadership and have a direct influence on particular areas of change. These agents are represented by the initially horizontal lines emanating from the 'change agents' box. Finally, the figure illustrates what might be termed a reverse process of 'upward direction' of change. This occurs when changes in union behaviour involve consequent change in the original change agents. This upward movement is signified by broken lines.

Change agents that bypass both the decision-making structure and the existing leadership are, self-evidently, external to the union's system of government. These external agents can include developments in the labour market, technology, government economic and industrial relations policies, employer organizations and other unions, including the TUC. For example, a union could experience an increase in union militancy, in our terms the equivalent of a change in one aspect of job regulations, as a direct result of a government's restrictive incomes policy. On the other hand, change agents may act directly on the leadership of the union, as is sometimes the case where unions take account of legislation or decisions of the TUC. Also, elements within, or internal to, the union can themselves become change agents. This happens, for instance, when the leadership interprets its role in a new way and sponsors rule changes that alter the union's internal government.

Whether demands are internally or externally precipitated, there will often be several different views on how the union should proceed, of which one will finally emerge as dominant at one particular time (these choices are represented by the vertical lines between 'existing national leadership' and the lower 'decision-making structure' box). The national leadership, in respond to demands, whether direct or mediated through the formal decision-making machinery (upper box), will therefore normally choose between a number of options. Having decided on a strategy, they will still have to ensure compliance within the union, through the lower 'decision-making structure' box, before their decisions can finally emerge and be implemented as an 'area of change'.

The way the model works can be illustrated by the following hypothetical example. Union X organizes skilled textile workers. Certain external factors, including international competition and technical changes introduced in the industry, have combined to reduce both the total number of textile workers and the skilled element within them. These developments have a direct impact on the size of the union (an 'area of change'), bypassing the leadership and decision-making structure. But they also infringe on the consciousness of the leadership directly, through problems of financial viability and a decline in the strategic power of the unions. At the same time, as a result of the external developments, demands may be emerging from the membership for protectionist measures against imports and for resistance to technical change. These latter protests would normally be processed through the upper box labelled 'decision-making structure'.

The leadership faced by these pressures may have several options. These options are represented in our diagram by the three vertical lines linking the 'leadership' to the lower 'decision-making structure' box. The leadership could, for instance, attempt to raise subscriptions to sustain its deteriorating financial position, but this would be likely to meet opposition from members in the light of their declining economic position. Indeed, it may provoke a further loss of members. Other options, such as a merger with another craft union or a larger general workers' union, may also enter the leadership calculator. Such an option would in turn be affected by further change agents, for example, the strategies and policies of the other merger union. (This other union is shown in our diagram entering the process as a change agent between the leadership and the lower decision-making box.) The final decision therefore would need to take these and other variables into account before there was an actual change.

As can be seen from this brief hypothetical example, the interaction between internal and external variables and their process through the decision-making structure can be quite complex. It is to help disentangle the influence of the various factors on changes in union behaviour that we have developed the above model of change. In each of the main chapters studying change, Chapters 4, 5, 6, 7 and 8, we first describe the area of change under examination and then consider and assess the agents and processes of change. By using a common approach in each of these chapters, we hope to provide the reader with a form of analysis that facilitates an appreciation of the relationship between change agents, decision-making structure and leadership. Because the internal decision-making structure is a crucial variable in this relationship, we describe in Chapter 3 the government of each union studied, and also set the scene for the later discussions by introducing our typologies and establishing the unions' positions in or around 1960 in respect of job territory and job regulations. In Chapter 9 we assess the overall adaptability of the different types of unions studied and consider what questions of interest our research raises for the interested parties.

3 Areas of change

The period since 1960 has witnessed some fundamental changes in the structure and character of trade union organization, associated with equally fundamental changes in the environment in which trade unions operate. The changes we have chosen to study fall into three broad categories: changes in internal government, in job territory and in job regulation. These categories do not exhaust all the transformations that have taken place within the unions we have studied; nor within these categories have we explored all the aspects of change. Instead we have focused on certain major developments and challenges that are common to all or several unions and have examined the response of certain unions in detail. For each area of change we have constructed a typology to describe the various dimensions of change and have located individual unions within them. Before dealing with each of these areas, however, we describe some of the broad developments in union behaviour and structure and in the industrial relations environment which form a background against which the changes in individual unions have taken place.

In 1948, of a total workforce of 20,732,000, 9,362,000 were members of trade unions, giving a density of union membership of 45.2 per cent. By 1964 the workforce had risen to 23,706,000 while total union membership had risen to 10,218,000. This represented a slight fall in union density to 43.1 per cent. However, by 1974, while the total workforce had fallen slightly to 23,689,000, union membership had risen to 11,755,000, giving a union density of 49.6 per cent.[1]

These overall figures conceal a number of variations in union membership by occupation, industry and sex which differentially affected the patterns of growth of the major unions (see Table 2). While the public services have grown, many traditional industries, particularly mining, railways and textiles, have declined. White-collar employment has grown at the expense of manual employment, accompanied by a considerable expansion of white-collar unionism, although the overall degree of organization among white-collar employees is lower than among manual workers, particularly those in the declining industries.[2] Female employment grew at the expense of male employment, and as a consequence of the rapid increase of union membership among women the female proportion of total trade union membership rose from 18 per cent in 1948 to 22 per cent in 1963 and 27 per cent in 1974 (Table 3).

Some of the growth accruing to the unions listed in Table 2 was due to

Table 2   *Membership change in unions affiliated to the TUC with membership over 100,000, 1965–75*

Union	Membership 1965	Membership 1975	% change
1 TGWU	1,443,738	1,856,165	+28.6
2 AUEW (E)	1,048,955	1,204,720	+14.8
3 GMWU	795,767	881,356	+10.8
4 NALGO	348,528	625,163	+79.4
5 NUPE	248,041	584,485	+135.6
6 EETPU	282,741	420,000	+43.5
7 USDAW	349,230	327,302	+8.0
8 ASTMS	65,144*	374,000	+474.1
9 NUT	263,000	281,855	+7.2
10 UCATT	347,352†	278,127	−19.9
11 NUM	446,453	261,871	−41.3
12 CPSA	145,775	224,742	+54.2
13 SOGAT	225,046	195,522	−13.1
14 UPW	175,491	185,000	+5.4
15 NUR	254,687	180,429	−29.2
16 CoSHE	67,588	167,200	+147.4
17 AUEW (TASS)	71,707	140,784	+96.3
18 ASBSBSW	122,981	136,193	+10.7
19 APEX	82,564	136,097	+64.8
20 POEU	91,821	124,682	+35.8
21 NUTGW	111,221	109,429	−1.6
22 NGA	84,975	107,441	+26.4
23 ISTC	120,430	104,485	−13.2
24 NUBE	58,444	101,922	+74.4

* combined membership of AScW (21,269) and ASSET (43,875)

† combined membership of ASW (191,620), ASPD (74,064), AUBTW (76,260), ABT (2000) and Packing Case Makers (3408)

Source: TUC Annual Reports (1965, 1975).

amalgamations, although it is difficult to estimate its contribution with precision. The 1960s showed a marked increase over the previous decade in merger activity. The Department of Employment recorded that 35 unions were absorbed by larger unions between 1951 and 1960. By comparison, over the period 1960–70 125 unions were similarly absorbed.[3]

This growth was also accompanied by changes in the character of job regulation, commonly described as increasing 'militancy', but essentially divisible into two distinct developments: a devolution of bargaining to the 'shop floor', in some cases encouraged by the leadership and often associated with

Table 3 *Unionization by sex and major occupational group in the United Kingdom, 1948–74*

	Male				% increase		Female				% increase	
	1948	1964	1970	1974	1948–74	1970–74	1948	1964	1970	1974	1948–74	1970–74
Union membership ('000)												
White-collar	1267	1681	2143	2593	+104.7	+21.0	697	1003	1447	1629	+133.7	+12.6
Manual	6410	6329	6123	5972	−6.8	−2.5	988	1206	1364	1561	+58.0	+14.4
Total	7677	8010	8266	8565	+11.6	+3.6	1685	2209	2811	3190	+89.3	+13.5
Union density (%)												
White-collar	33.8	33.4	40.0	45.5	+10.7	+4.5	25.4	24.9	30.7	32.6	+7.2	+1.9
Manual	59.5	60.0	63.3	64.7	+5.2	+1.4	26.0	32.6	35.2	42.1	+16.1	+6.9
Total	52.9	51.4	55.0	56.9	+4.0	+1.9	25.7	28.6	32.7	36.7	+11.0	+4.0

Source: G. S. Bain and R. Price, 'Union growth and employment trends in the United Kingdom, 1964–70', *British Journal of Industrial Relations*, vol. 10, no. 3 (November 1973).

unconstitutional strikes; and the development of militancy among hitherto quiescent sections of the public sector and among white-collar workers.

A rough measure of some of these developments can be found in the strike statistics. At the time of the Donovan Report it was noted that: 'the typical stoppage involves small numbers of workers and is quickly over – though such stoppages occur comparatively frequently'.[4] Analysis since that period,[5] however, shows a major change in the pattern of strikes. Over the period 1968–71, according to Silver,

Both strike frequency and the number of strikes are nearly double their 'Donovan' average, and the number of days lost has risen enormously – by $3\frac{1}{2}$ times in fact. The 'causes' of strikes have also altered – nearly half now relate to wage claims, compared with about a third earlier on. The industrial composition of strike activity has also undergone a change, as it is only in the current period that the coal industry has finally been deposed as strike leader by the 'un-named' industries. The position of the latter has also been strengthened by the new-found militancy of public employees.[6]

Not only did the number of strikes rise, particularly in the period 1969–70, but they extended to some of the traditionally strike-free industries, notably the public services. Thus, according to Silver, the share of the five industries with the most stoppages outside coal mining (general engineering, construction, motor vehicle, docks, and iron and steel) in the total number of non-mining strikes fell from 62 per cent in 1959 to 54 per cent in 1965 and 49 per cent in 1970.[7]

There was also a significant change in the character of strikes since Donovan. While the frequency and duration of unofficial strikes increased, there was at the same time a significant rise in the number of official strikes whose duration tended to be much longer.

Implied in this is perhaps the most significant change of all, namely the emergence – or in a sense a re-emergence – of the major confrontation as a central focus of industrial conflict. The most dramatic manifestation of this trend was the coal strike in 1972, which alone caused the loss of more working days than all of the 8,931 stoppages which took place during the four years of the Donovan era. . . . The difference today is that the 'Big' disputes have become far more conspicuous – bigger, longer and therefore more severe in their impact. . . .[8]

This pattern continued up to 1974, although the number of stoppages and working days lost were less than the peak achieved in 1970. Between 1974 and 1976, however, there was a steady decline in both indices. The 'new-found militancy' of public employees is manifest in strike statistics over the period 1969–72 (Table 4).

The change in the character of trade unions was not restricted to changes in the tactics and strategy employed within the traditional bilateral collective bargaining context. Relationships with the state also changed dramatically. Indeed, there appears to have been a reversal of the trend towards the institutional isolation of industrial conflict from the rest of society described by Dahrendorf in the 1950s.

Increasingly, the social relations of industry, including industrial conflict, do not dominate the whole of society but remain confined in their patterns and problems to the sphere of industry. Industry and industrial conflict are in post-capitalist society institutionally isolated, i.e. confined within the borders of their proper realm and robbed of their influence on other spheres of society.[9]

Trade unions, via the TUC, have over recent years been drawn deeper and deeper into the area of not only economic but also social planning, particularly during

Table 4 *Working days lost, 1960–73**

	Public services**	Whole public sector excl. mining†	All sectors excl. mining‡	Mining
	(1)	(2)	(3)	(4)
1960	3,000	43,000	2,530,000	494,000
1961	56,000	92,000	2,309,000	737,000
1962	45,000	297,000	5,430,000	368,000
1963	4,000	14,000	1,429,000	326,000
1964	21,000	157,000	1,975,000	302,000
1965	24,000	71,000	2,513,000	412,000
1966	4,000	46,000	2,280,000	118,000
1967	8,000	93,000	2,682,000	105,000
1968	28,000	83,000	4,636,000	54,000
1969	147,000	362,000	5,807,000	1,039,000
1970	374,000	506,000	9,890,000	1,090,000
1971	70,000	6,397,000	13,488,000	63,000
1972	116,000	168,000	13,111,000	10,798,000
1973	361,000	771,000	7,107,000	90,000

* Working days lost are used as the indicator because they reflect both the duration and size of strikes rather than simply the number. This particular index, however, tends to accentuate the influence of strikes in the public sector in comparison with others because they tend to be larger and longer than the majority of strikes in the private sector. Included under the heading 'Public services' are SIC Professional and Scientific workers, in which teachers and nurses predominate, but which also contains other small groups.

** 'Public services' includes national and local government, teaching, and the national health service

† 'Public sector' includes those in col. (1) together with the nationalized industries excluding the National Coal Board and the British Steel Corporation

‡ 'All sectors' includes col. (2) together with the private sector and British Steel Corporation

Source: J. W. Durcan, W. E. J. McCarthy and G. Redman, *Strikes in Britain* (Allen & Unwin forthcoming).

the period of the Social Contract. This in turn has led many unions in the white-collar sector who previously held aloof from the TUC to join the mainstream of trade union activity in the wider sphere and adopt a broader trade union perspective.

Many of these changes were a response to and interacted with changes in the social and economic environment within which unions were operating. The classic description of the changes is to be found in the Donovan Report [10] but is most succinctly described by Allan Flanders:

[The industrial relations] system has been challenged from above and from below. From above by governments acting in response to practical economic difficulties and strong public pressures; and from below in the workplace by the rise of shop stewards and an upsurge of bargaining outside the scope of national regulations.[11]

Flanders described the 'challenge from above' as an important expression of the need for national planning in an area where collective *laissez-faire* was previously the rule. The years since he wrote have seen a radical transformation of the role of the state *vis-à-vis* the industrial relations system in general and trade union activity in particular. As public concern with the general economic decline expressed (particularly in terms of balance of payments difficulties and inflation) increased, so trade unions were identified as the major culprit.

During the period under study, the state has attempted to control the putative effect of trade unions on inflation directly through various forms of incomes policy and indirectly through the institutional reform of both industrial relations procedures and trade union structures, in the abortive *In Place of Strife*, and the Industrial Relations Act 1971.

At the same time, and during the Social Contract, in exchange for control of incomes, the state has increased its role in both the procedural and substantive aspects of industrial relations, for example through the Health and Safety at Work Act, the Equal Pay and Sex Discrimination Acts and the various provisions of the Employment Protection Act and the Trade Union and Labour Relations Act, including the unfair dismissals legislation previously incorporated in the Industrial Relations Act. These have provided certain minimum levels of employee rights and altered the pattern of trade union activity in these areas.

The 'challenge from below' consisted of the growth of workplace bargaining, which, although not a new phenomenon, had previously been largely subsidiary to higher levels, whether local, company or national. As Flanders pointed out,

What stands out about the workplace bargaining of recent years is first that it has developed on a much greater scale than ever before, except under the special conditions of war. But it has also been a spontaneous development with its own independent momentum, so that it lies largely outside the control of trade unions and employers' associations. Far from being subservient to the system of external job regulation, it appears rather to threaten its stability. In other words, it has assumed a form which is not so much an extension of the system as a challenge to it.[12]

Flanders quoted as indicators of the 'challenge from below' the increase in unofficial strikes and the growing phenomenon of earnings drift, that is, the gap between average earnings and official wage rates. He argued that there had been a transformation of power relationships within the workplace.

Neither of the developments Flanders characterizes was entirely new. The tradition of 'voluntarism' was not as pure as Flanders and others would have us believe, nor was the 'challenge from below' restricted to the post-1960 period,[13] as Flanders himself acknowledged. What *was* new was the intensity with which these trends manifested themselves. The Industrial Relations Act was a radical break with tradition; and over the period 1960–76 only four years have been free of incomes policies of one sort or another. Moreover, the incomes policies themselves, particularly during 1966–69, encouraged the devolution of bargaining both because of the emphasis on productivity bargaining and because of the use of 'earnings drift' as a means of overcoming incomes policy restrictions.

Within these broad trends, however, there have been differences in the impact on and response of individual unions. The changes have not been uniform or necessarily unidirectional. Some unions, for example the National Union of Mineworkers (NUM) and Union of Construction and Allied Trades and Technicians (UCATT) have brooked the general trend towards devolution and attempted to strengthen centralized bargaining. While some have joined the general scramble to grow and merge, others have remained resolutely confined, in some cases even though their absolute membership declined.

The rest of this chapter explores each of the areas of change, starting with internal government, then describing changes in union job territories and finally covering alterations in job regulation behaviour.

Change in internal government

Changes in unions' internal decision-making processes, or national systems of government, will be examined in Chapter 4. The main intention here is to identify the theme and unions studied, to describe the state of union government in 1960, and to provide the reader with a typology that will facilitate an understanding of union government and its changes. Furthermore, while examining union government as an *area* of change it must be recognized that it is also a major *agent* of change; hence the inclusion of union government at this early stage in order to facilitate a greater understanding of the workings of the agents of change that affected developments in unions' job territories and job regulations. Finally, in common with other aspects of the study, changes in union government will be viewed primarily from a national perspective. Thus developments in union government below the national level will be considered in depth only where they clearly affected the national level of government.

The theme and the unions studied

The central theme, identified here and further explored in Chapter 4, is concerned with examining the non-bargaining aspects of comparative union government in a period of changing environment. In order to consider in depth those facets of government that influence unions' comparative abilities to change, two unions faced by changing environments but with contrasting systems of government provide the major case studies: the TGWU and the AEU.[14] However, comment on these two unions will be complemented by drawing on material gathered during the studies of the GMWU, ASTMS and the ASW (UCATT).[15] Also, minor references may, where relevant, be made to developments in such unions as NALGO and the NUT. Finally, the model of union government developed in the following discussion will be used to describe briefly all the unions studied.

The process of change in union government at the national level will be explained by examining the interaction between a union's internal structure, its procedures of decision-making and its method of choosing leaders. These aspects of government form the three areas of change in internal government to be examined in Chapter 4. In order to appreciate the nature and degree of change across these three dimensions of union government it is, however, necessary first to have an understanding of the union's position in 1960. Furthermore, as changes in different systems of national government are to be examined, it is helpful to have a typology that assists an understanding of inter-union movements.

A typology of union government

It is common in studies of comparative union government to describe and classify unions according to their democratic or oligarchic tendencies.[16] This practice no doubt predominates owing to unions' own claims to be democratic and the influence of the seminal and pioneering works in this field by the Webbs,[17] Michels[18] and Lipset *et al.*[19] All these studies were centrally concerned with the extent to which unions could claim to be democratic. As a result, the direction of research into union democracy has tended to be almost solely concerned with such matters as participation rates, closeness of elections and the existence of factions or parties.[20]

Little has been written therefore about the quality or effectiveness of the leadership's decisions. In particular, the question of whether a factionalized or party-type system of union government actually contributes anything to the quality of national leadership decision-making has not been fully discussed. Moreover, there has also been an absence of comment in the 'democratic' literature regarding the extent to which a particular system of government allows the 'democratic' or 'oligarchic' national leadership the opportunity to carry out or execute the policy of the union or to achieve its organizational objectives.

There is no discussion, for instance, of the question of whether or not a more or less democratic union survives or grows more effectively than any other union in a changing environment.

Therefore existing theories of union government, with their bias towards participatory aspects of democracy, do not offer any satisfactory methodological guide for a study that seeks to consider both the responsiveness of leaders to members and the comparative effectiveness of systems of government. They do not suggest a method of assessing the relative merits of those constitutional changes that both promote commonly accepted legitimate goals of unionism (for example, growth and hence more bargaining power) and produce a reduction in participatory opportunities. Yet such changes occurred in several small unions that sought defensive mergers with the TGWU if only because such mergers replaced existing elections of full-time officials with appointment on the TGWU model. Also, the ASW and the ASPD, in forming UCATT, changed some full-time officer positions from election to appointment in the hope, ultimately, of strengthening their bargaining opportunities. Yet it is obviously misleading to state that either of the above changes was positively undemocratic purely because they reduced participatory opportunities; for both changes were primarily intended to help the unions concerned achieve goals to which their members generally subscribed.

There are also considerable problems in applying participatory theories of democracy to unions as 'wholes'. These classificatory problems arise because unions may be governmentally divided in a way that makes such definitional generalizations as 'more or less democratic' largely meaningless. A union may, for instance, have two separate or vertically bifurcated channels of decision-making. It may also have different systems of decision-making and methods of choosing leaders at each of several horizontal levels of government. Its decision-making processes may, for example, be constitutionally vertically divided into bargaining and non-bargaining channels. A union could then be highly devolved and participative in the bargaining channel and highly centralized and non-participative in its non-bargaining control. Further, the nature of decision-making may be compounded, yet again, by variations in the location of issues and means of determining issues at national, regional, district, branch and shop floor levels of government. Hence to talk of such unions as 'more or less democratic' in an overall sense is to risk misleading generalizations with little or no concrete meaning.

Thus democratic constructs drawn from wider political theory present serious problems when used in relationship to unions. It is with these thoughts in mind that the following alternative typology is proposed.

Our typology is intended to promote an understanding of both comparative changes in unions' systems of government and the role of national leadership in a changing environment. It provides a means of considering the effectiveness of union government and analysing participatory mechanisms. The typology facilitates these objectives by recognizing that unions' systems of decision-

diffused

concentrated

centralized

national
horizontal
dispersal of
decision-making

X_0

X_1

decentralized

vertical
dispersal of
issues within
government

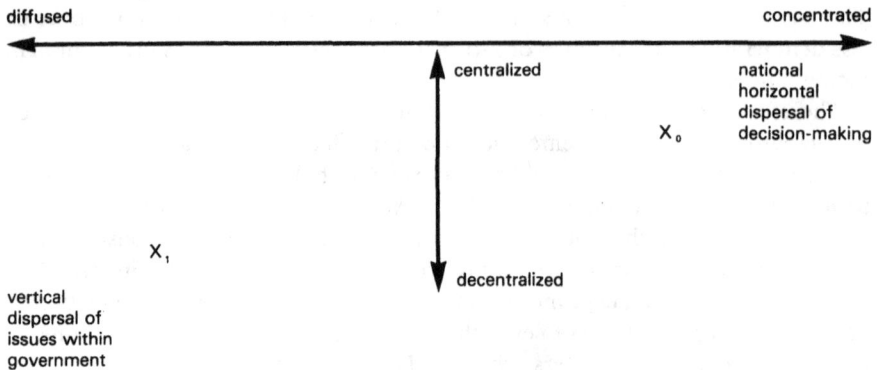

Figure 2   *National union government: vertical and horizontal dispersal
diagram. The hypothetical case of union X is shown. The position X_0
represents the centralized and concentrated non-bargaining decision-
making of the union, while X_1 represents the decentralized and
diffused bargaining decision-making of the union.*

making are composed of different but interrelated parts. In particular, the
typology recognizes this internal division of unions by analysing union decision-
making along two main dimensions, vertical and horizontal (see Figure 2). It will
be seen that the vertical dimension plots positions on a continuum from
'centralized' to 'decentralized'. Along the horizontal dimension we plot a
similar continuum in terms of the degree of 'concentration' and 'diffusion'.

The *vertical dimension* of government refers to the various levels of government within a particular union, for example regional and local (including district
and shop floor) levels of decision-making. Within the vertical structure the
typology distinguishes between those vertical channels of decision-making that
deal primarily with questions of a collective bargaining nature and those that
concentrate on other matters – such as political and administrative issues. Hence
unions are seen as being vertically bifurcated into bargaining and non-bargaining
channels of decision-making. This division is employed primarily for
explanatory purposes. It can however be justified by reference to *de facto* union
practices, although in some unions, for instance the TGWU, it is also written into
their rule books. Thus, as in other spheres of union study, a *de facto* and *de jure*
distinction may be usefully made when referring to either the vertical or
horizontal structures of decision-making. But we also have to note that issues to
be determined within the vertical structure of union government may be
generally dispersed throughout the bifurcated vertical structure or largely
located in any one level of government. In this sense a union can be said to be
'centralized' if it retains a greater degree of national control over a larger number
of issues than other unions with which it is compared. Similarly, a union may be
described as 'decentralized' if it devolves more issues than other unions down to
its lowest levels of decision-making. Finally a union can be said to be

decentralized along one of its vertical channels of decision-making, for example bargaining, yet centralized in its other vertical or non-bargaining channel. For example, union X in Figure 2 is shown as decentralized in the bargaining field X_1, but centralized in its non-bargaining activities X_0.

On the *horizontal dimension* a union can be similarly but less drastically dissected. A union may at each vertical level of government have different horizontal structures. For instance, the national level of government may be composed of a large heterogeneous lay biennial conference, a lay executive, a lay appeal body and appointed full-time officers. It may also be free from factionalism. On the other hand, it may have an elected full-time executive, elected full-time officers and a small homogeneous annual lay conference. It may also be riddled with factionalism. Thus unions may have different concentrations or diffusions of power over decisions taken at the level of government under discussion. The more people/committees actually share in decision-making, the more dispersed the power. Obversely, the fewer people/committees, the more concentrated the power. Thus in Figure 2 union X is shown as diffused in the bargaining field X_1 but concentrated in the non-bargaining field X_0.

Using the same basic approach, an overview of the relative government systems of two or more unions can be presented in the form of a diagram. This is contained in Figure 3. The enclosed area at each level of government represents the relative scope for decision-making. The top level is national government, the middle level represents any appropriate level between district and national level, and the bottom level is composed of district, branch and shop floor levels. A small or large shaded portion at each level represents respectively the relative concentration or diffusion of participation in, and responsibility for, decision-making. For instance, if a relatively large area of government has only a dot, or small shaded area in it, the suggestion is that at that level there is large scope for decision-making but a concentration of power over the relatively large number of issues resolved. It should also be noted that similar diagrams can also be used to show movement through time. They can, for instance, be used to compare the TGWU in 1960 with the TGWU in 1975. (N.B. In all uses of this figure the drawings represent *de facto* situations unless specifically identified as *de jure* descriptions.)

The major unions studied and their relative positions in the typology

The systems of government of the major unions covered by this study, i.e. the AEU, the ASW, the GMWU, the TGWU, ASTMS and NALGO, can now be analysed by reference to the typology outlined above under two heads:
1   the *vertical* structure of government;
2   the *national horizontal* level of government.

The vertical structure of government
Most unions have rules that define reasonably clearly the structures of the non-

non-bargaining | bargaining   non-bargaining | bargaining

national level

regional
or divisional

district, branch and
shop floor levels

Centralized and concentrated in
both non-bargaining and
bargaining activities

Decentralized and diffused in
both non-bargaining and
bargaining activities

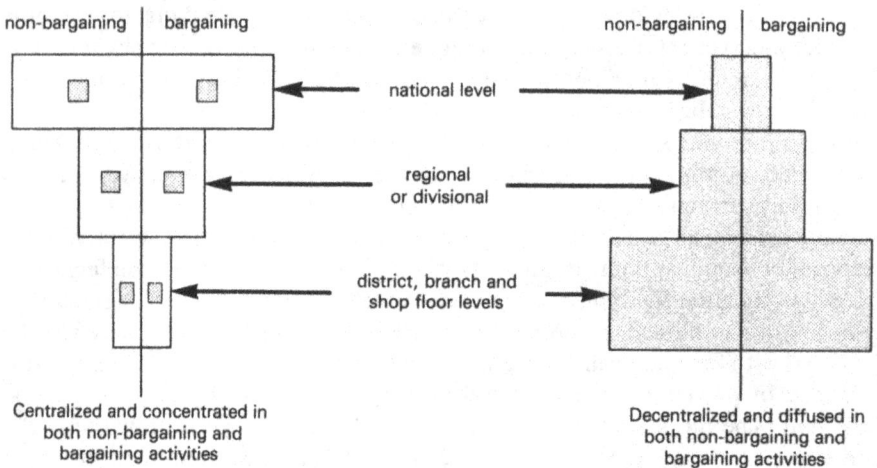

Figure 3   *System of union government showing vertical and horizontal* de
facto *dispersal of decision-making*

bargaining processes of government. These structures in turn shape the general
decision-making processes. On the other hand the bargaining arrangements,
whether in a *de jure* single-channel or a *de jure* bifurcated union, are by no means
so well defined in rule. Moreover, even where bargaining is defined, the *de facto*
bargaining arrangements often bear little relationship to those so prescribed. As
such divergences in *de jure* and *de facto* bargaining processes are discussed
elsewhere (see Chapter 8), they will only be briefly examined here where they
significantly affect the non-bargaining channels of government. The main
emphasis will therefore be on the non-bargaining structure of decision-making.

The TGWU is vertically bifurcated on a *de jure* basis. It has an industrial trade
group bargaining structure of eleven trade groups, running parallel with its
geographically based general policy-making structure. At each level of
government, however, the bargaining independence of the industrial structure is
circumscribed by a rule that confines activities 'to pay, hours and working
conditions'.[21] Where any conflict arises between general policy decisions and
trade group bargaining the overriding authority of the general policy bodies can
be asserted.[22] ASTMS later adopted a somewhat similar vertical structure of
government although it was by no means as highly formalized as that of the
TGWU. NALGO similarly operates a *de jure* vertically bifurcated structure of
government. The AEU, UCATT (ASW) and the GMWU are, on the other hand,
all *de jure* single-channel unions.

Most unions have a three- or four-tier structure of government. ASTMS,
UCATT, the GMWU and NALGO[23] have three-tier structures, that is, branch,
region (or its equivalent in size) and national levels of government. Prior to

joining UCATT in 1971 the ASW was a three-tier union but with a district rather than regional level of organization. The AEU or Engineers Union is now a four-tier structure, with branch, district, division (region) and national levels of government. The Transport Workers is a hybrid three- or four-tier union with district committees in some regions but not in others.

Unions locate issues and therefore powers at different levels of their structure. There is, for instance, no common acceptance that regions rather than districts should be the main source of general policy and administrative decision-making outside of the national level. Below the national level the GMWU, the TGWU, and NALGO (and, after amalgamation, UCATT) placed most reliance for non-bargaining decisions on regional government. In contrast the AEU (and, before UCATT amalgamation, the ASW) preferred to emphasize the role of district committees.

Among unions biased towards regional government the GMWU is the outstanding example of powerful regional organization. It has no district organization and in 1960 had no industrial or trade groupings: branches were grouped only by region. Moreover, many functions that, for instance, are determined at national level in the other major general workers union, the TGWU, are decentralized to the regions in the GMWU. Thus each of the GMWU's ten regions appoint their own officers, whereas in the TGWU the General Executive Council (GEC) control appointment of officers in all their thirteen regions. Furthermore, the ultimate power to appoint officers in the GMWU regions rests with the regional secretary: 'if the Regional Secretary wanted to appoint a man and the Regional Committee turned the Regional Secretary down, the Regional Secretary has the last word'.[24] The GMWU's regional secretary is also responsible for deciding on the size, number, industrial and geographical distribution of branches, and for determining the official relationship between shop stewards and full-time officials in the conduct of negotiations. Hence Figure 4 (page 58) shows the GMWU with a strong regional (intermediate) level of government and a concentration of power in the hands of the regional secretaries for non-bargaining purposes.

By comparison, the TGWU's regional secretaries have much less scope for the exercise of power. However, despite being considerably less influential than their counterparts in the GMWU, the TGWU's regions are still the most powerful part of the TGWU below the national level. Regional committees in the TGWU can, for instance, conduct inquiries into organizational problems in the regions. In the late 1960s some regions chose to show their organizational autonomy by rejecting nationally sponsored calls for an organizational switch at regional level from a trade group to district committee system. Regions 1 (London), 2 (Southern) and 3 (South West) retained their trade groups, while other regions accepted the nationally initiated proposals.

Before the UCATT mergers, the ASW, along with the AEU, maintained traditionally powerful district committees. The common emphasis on district organization is not surprising in the ASW as it was modelled on the ASE, the forerunner of the AEU, in the mid-nineteenth century.[25] As early as 1851 the ASE found that 'ensuring the authority of the Executive Council [over the districts] proved a difficult task'.[26] Similarly in the ASW national-district relations were fraught with difficulty as the national leadership attempted to reduce the autonomy of its district management committees between 1948 and 1960.[27]

By the 1960s, however, the AEU had accepted and guaranteed the district committees a formal major role in government through constitutional safeguards contained in rule 13. In contrast, the ASW's national leadership continued to work towards the limitation of their districts' autonomy, a position that they finally achieved during the formation of UCATT. It was in this merger that the ASW's national leadership successfully promoted rule changes that replaced the district management committees with a regional level of government. Thus the AEU's and ASW's systems of government assumed distinctly different features in the late 1960s. While the ASW favoured the regional level, the AEU continued with a highly autonomous district system of government which, apart from the divisional (regional) committees' role in shaping motions for the AEU's national committee, continues to dominate decision-making below the national level.

It can hence be seen that up to 1960 the GMWU and, to a considerably lesser extent, the TGWU dispersed organizational, administrative and financial decisions to the regions while the AEU and the ASW preferred to emphasize a district level of government.

The manner in which bargaining decisions[28] were actually vertically dispersed followed a similar pattern to non-bargaining decisions in the single-channel AEU and ASW. In these two formerly exclusive craft unions the districts and lay shop floor activists complemented and in some firms supplanted, national officers as the main negotiators of actual wages. In contrast the GMWU, another *de jure* single-channel union, was far more centralized in its bargaining arrangements. Similarly, the TGWU, which contained bargaining within its second and separate industrial trade group channel, was more centralized in the bargaining processes than the ASW and AEU, but less so than the GMWU.

There was therefore in some unions' districts and regions a considerable degree of autonomy in the fields of organization, administration and finance in 1960. In two unions, the ASW and the AEU, districts also played an important part in overseeing shop floor bargaining. In the general policy and constitutional processes of decision-making, however, the lower levels of government were largely restricted to sponsoring motions for consideration and determination by national bodies. They did not have the freedom at local level to determine positively and directly general policy. On the other hand, the lower levels of government could and did thwart national policy by negative inaction. For instance, certain of the AEU's district committees failed to press the national wage claim at local level, as instructed by the National Executive of the union, in 1972.[29] Similarly, as mentioned above, the TGWU's regions did not uniformly comply with the union's nationally sponsored programme of 'districtization'.

Hence, even if districts and regions could not directly determine national policy and constitutional matters, they could negate some such decisions by ignoring them. Thus, the formally prescribed sovereignty of the national level of government in general policy and constitutional matters, to be described below, is not always as absolute as it may appear.

National conference and/or committee motions on general policy can emanate from several parts of the vertical structure of government. In the TGWU, for instance, 'General motions may be moved at the instance of branches, regional trade groups or districts, or national trade groups or sections, regional committees or the General Executive Council'.[30] Unions may however limit the number of motions each branch can submit – a practice accepted by ASTMS and UCATT. In the AEU the district and divisional committees process branch motions before they can be considered by the policy-making National Committee. Generally, however, national bodies' standing orders committees or their equivalents decide what motions should be considered at conference, and the lower levels decide, unhindered by higher level constraints, what motions should be submitted for their consideration.

In summary, there was in the early 1960s no common level to which the unions examined vertically dispersed non-bargaining decision-making. Both the general unions (the TGWU and the GMWU) tended to be relatively more centralized than the two ex-craft unions (the ASW and the AEU). However, the GMWU was far more regionalized than the TGWU in the area of non-bargaining decision-making, while being more centralized than the TGWU in the bargaining processes. Leaving aside for the moment considerations of bargaining development, the unions can thus be placed respectively on a vertical centralization-decentralization continuum, circa 1960, in the following manner: the TGWU, the GMWU, the ASW and the AEU, as shown in Figure 4 (page 58).

Of course, if bargaining is taken into account it is much more difficult to place unions on any single centralization–decentralization continuum. As we have said, a model of union government that mixes non-bargaining with bargaining can be misleading in the case of a bifurcated union. Thus the processes of decision-making are best described separately in a form that allows for the separation of bargaining and non-bargaining features. This is done in Figure 4 below (page 58). In that figure the GMWU is shown, in the bargaining field, as being more centralized than the *de jure* bifurcated TGWU, while the bargaining position of the AEU and the ASW around 1960 resembles that of their non-bargaining decision-making structures. The importance of these vertical differences for the horizontal and national level of government is examined below.

The national horizontal level of government
The first point to stress is that the dispersal of decision-making at this level is influenced very significantly by the nature of a union's vertical dispersal. Clearly, the more centralized the vertical dispersal in the bargaining and non-

bargaining fields, the greater the scope for the exercise of power at national level. Thus there was, around 1960, more potential for the exercise of national leadership in the TGWU and the GMWU than in the AEU and the ASW. Further, it can be argued that *de jure* vertical bifurcation and regional and district devolution of decision-making also influence the degree to which power over issues allocated to the national level of government is concentrated or diffused.

It would appear that *de jure* vertically bifurcated unions have a fundamental structural need for a concentrated form of national government which can effectively unite the various separate bargaining or trade groups in the general policy field of decision-making. Multi-industry unions, such as the TGWU and ASTMS, are reasonably representative of this type of union. They are divided structurally to satisfy both internal trade/occupational demands for bargaining autonomy, and, externally, to attract new merger partners into the union (see Chapter 6). Paradoxically, however, a structure of this kind only succeeds the closer it comes to the situation it seeks to prevent; that is, it provides a high degree of independence to a particular trade, occupational or service grouping, only in order to prevent that group breaking away completely from the parent body. Taken to its extreme, therefore, the multi-industry and *de jure* bifurcated union becomes no more than a federation of smaller bargaining units. Hence it may, because of its structure, have an inbuilt tendency to degenerate into an umbrella organization for virtually autonomous smaller unions unless, in its non-bargaining arrangement, it provides a strong counterbalancing unifying force.

Similar, but less extreme, is the position of the *de jure* single-channel but regionalized union. The GMWU fits this category. Although it was, and is, a multi-industry union, it did not, in 1960, provide its industrial sectors with a separate bargaining structure. But neither did the GMWU attract any significant unions into amalgamation. They did not offer a potential merger partner the opportunity to merge and yet 'retain its identity, and identity is this industrial group problem'.[31] Hence in governmental terms one of the GMWU's concerns was to avoid its structural tendency towards regional rather than industrial federation. A highly regionalized and *de jure* single-channel union thus needs, although not so urgently as the *de jure* bifurcated union, a means of bringing the semi-autonomous regions under the aegis of the national level of government.

On the other hand, the craft-dominated[32] AEU and the ASW in 1960 had no obvious structural need for a concentration of power at the centre. They were not vertically bifurcated or regionalized; they had no major formal structural divisions of an industrial or regional nature. Hence the two unions were not structurally in need of a national unifying force in the early 1960s. Indeed, in contradistinction to the above arguments, the highly decentralized vertical structure in both unions, particularly the devolved bargaining arrangements of the AEU, provided the circumstances in which the AEU's 283 district committees and thousands of constitutionally related shop floor bargainers could develop small local power centres virtually independent of the national government's control; a situation that helped to diffuse decision-making at the lower levels of government seriously threatening the overall sovereignty of the national government in the area of general policy. Moreover, as will be shown below, this local environment suited the growth of factions and parties, which hence also helped further diffuse power over national policy-making. In other words, the AEU, and to a lesser extent the ASW, had vertical structures that, in contrast to the other unions examined, tended to promote diffusion rather than concentration of national power.

Thus, before turning to examine the horizontal continuum of national government, it can be concluded that a *de jure* vertically bifurcated union will, by virtue of its structure, tend to be more concentrated in its general national decision-making processes than single-channel unions. It would appear to need, in order to maintain itself as a union and avoid fragmentation, a 'strong counter-poise at the centre'[33] to bind together the semi-autonomous bargaining groups as in the TGWU and ASTMS; while, in contrast, *de jure* single-channel unions such as the AEU and the ASW will, through the encouragement they give to the formation of independent factions and parties, tend to have a far more diffused system of national government. Finally, somewhere between these extremes will be a union like the GMWU. Such an organization structurally needs to contain its semi-autonomous regions within the bounds of national government to maintain unity of purpose. However, because bargaining is constitutionally re-tained within the one system of government and non-bargaining issues are devolved to the regions, such a union does not normally court the same internal stresses or gain the same growth advantages as the *de jure* bifurcated union. It does not therefore require the same concentration of power at the centre.

Comparison between systems of government
The suggestion made above regarding a union's tendency to concentrate or diffuse its decision-making powers at the national level according to its vertical structure is largely borne out by an examination of systems of national govern-ment in our chosen unions. At this level of government most unions have a national conference, an executive, a rules revision body and an appeals com-mittee[34] or equivalents. General secretaries usually hold the most senior posts. (They hold this position, for instance, in the TGWU, ASTMS, the GMWU, the ASW and NALGO. In the AEU, however, the president is the most influential single figure.) Assistant or deputy general secretaries, national officers or, if full-time, national executive councillors normally hold the next position in the national hierarchy. In the AEU and the ASW (UCATT) these national full-time positions are elected, whereas in the other unions studied they are, apart from the general secretary, nearly all appointed.

Although national positions and bodies are reasonably common across unions, their influence is not. All unions disperse some power constitutionally over several bodies and positions. The degree of concentration or diffusion nationally is influenced heavily, however, by the interaction between vertical structure, discretionary or non-discretionary leadership roles, flexible or non-flexible procedures for decision-making, the methods of choosing leaders and the absence or presence of factions or parties. Obviously, individual leaders are also important. But the extent of this individual influence will, by and large, be constrained by constitutional factors. An individual leader in a union where power is constitutionally concentrated in one position will, *ipso facto*, have potentially more influence on policy than if the same individual were the leader of another union where, *ceteris paribus*, power was more diffused because of a formal system of checks and balances.

Thus the potential for concentration of power, and hence dominance of national decision-making by one leader, will tend to be great in a union that both constitutionally provides such a role and structurally requires a strong figurehead. Such conditions are found in the TGWU. This vertically bifurcated multi-industry union has one elected position at the top of the full-time officer hierarchy, the general secretary. It also provides this position with a highly discretionary decision-making role within flexible national decision-making procedures. Moreover, appointments of all other full-time officials are made under the general secretary's guidance. Further, the lay GEC in the 1960s contained no opposition of any consequence. The TGWU therefore provides a combination of constitutional circumstances suitable for individual dominance, and therefore an extreme concentration of power.

Dominance, even in the TGWU, would however be only potential. Exercise of power would still depend on the abilities of the individual. If an individual is incapable, indolent or disinterested in using the potential for power, he or she is likely to achieve considerably less in terms of influencing policy than a far more able and ambitious person in a more constitutionally constricted role. Therefore a very able national leader in a single-channel and homogeneous union such as the AEU, which had a diffusion of power owing to the opposite consitutional factors – that is, little discretion in any one position, inflexible decision-making processes, election of all full-time National Executive and well developed factions or parties – could still be of some importance in decision-making. However, it would have to be recognized that in most situations the potential for power would be far below that of the leader in a concentrated union.

The unions at the centre of this study thus resemble the two extremes of the national level concentrated–diffused continuum. The TGWU provides its general secretary with the potential for an extremely powerful role at the concentrated end of the continuum, while the AEU, and later the AEUW Engineering section, restricts its president within a far more diffused system of government. Between the two ranging from concentration to diffusion on the non-bargaining power continuum stood, in the 1960s, ASTMS, the GMWU and the ASW (UCATT).

Constitutionally, in 1960 the TGWU was still basically the same union as that formed in the amalgamation of 1922.[35] The thousand-strong regional trade group delegates to the Biennial Delegate Conference (BDC) were and still are constitutionally members of the premier decision-making body. The lay General Executive Council (GEC) was and still is responsible for governing the TGWU between conferences. Regional trade group delegates to the BDC are elected at the branches, and the thirty-nine-strong GEC, which meets quarterly, is composed of regional and national trade group representatives. A further body of major importance in the TGWU is however the eight-strong Finance and General Purposes Committee (F&GPC) elected from within the GEC. The GEC can delegate most of its power to this inner cabinet which meets monthly. It is thus capable of taking virtually all major decisions between meetings of the BDC.

There is, however, within the formal structure of national government of the TGWU, a great deal of procedural flexibility which can enhance the influence of an able general secretary and limit the role of the BDC. Structurally, for instance, the rules in 1960 allowed for the formation, subject to GEC approval, of lay sectional committees to deal with the affairs of a particular section of a trade group. This flexibility was used by the leadership to accommodate and defuse, in a *de facto* and *ad hoc* manner, pressure for more wide-ranging constitutional change which they regularly faced and defeated at the BDCs. Between 1949 and 1965 there were, for instance, ninety-four motions at nine BDCs demanding the formation of separate and hence extra trade groups. The GEC opposed, successfully, all but one of these motions. The exception was a proposal in 1957[36] for an Oil Trade Group to be formed. Yet outside the conference, pressures for formal structural change were absorbed by more minor *ad hoc* and *de facto* adjustments sanctioned by the inner circle of national leaders. The overall structure of the TGWU's government was hence largely left untouched until 1967 despite numerous attempts by lay delegates at BDCs to alter its shape.

Similarly, the formal procedures for decision-making and the methods of appointing full-time officials and electing the general secretary went largely unchanged between 1949 and 1965. This was not due, however, to the absence of membership pressure for change. Various trade groups within the TGWU repeatedly pressed, for instance, for permission at BDCs to hold lay trade group delegate conferences. They were almost equally regularly defeated at the BDCs by the 'platform' (the national leadership). Only the General Road Haulage Section's success in pressing a motion opposed by the platform at the 1953 BDC[37] broke the general rule of platform dominance at BDCs in this particular policy field.

However, apart from these two occasions the platform carried the day at the BDC on all other issues including general policy matters between 1949 and 1965. The national leadership achieved this dominance by making effective use of the concentration of power endowed in them and the General Secretary in particular by the union's constitution. Demands for constitutional change were softened by *ad hoc de facto* concessions and/or were defeated at Conference by bringing the weight of the representative of the 'common good', the general secretary, to bear against sectional demands. Tactically this was often achieved at the BDC not by opposing a motion outright, but by replacing it with what can be termed a 'negative composite', sponsored by the GEC, which, on 'being accepted by Conference, there would be no occasion to move the [original] motion'.[38] On the occasion quoted here it was used and passed to negate an attempt by several trade groups to establish new trade groups and enforce reference-back procedures in negotiations. Such tactics of the platform invariably succeeded. No 'Executive Policy Statement', whether a negative replacement for composite motions or a positive policy statement, was defeated between 1945 and 1965.

The influence of the national leadership in the TGWU was not however always a negative force preventing change. In fact, the best examples of the use of the concentrated power in the TGWU come from examples of change. Moreover, most of these changes came in the TGWU when either the general secretary proposed a change or after the general secretary himself had changed. In 1968, for instance, Frank Cousins, at the end of his period as general secretary successfully proposed a motion to remove the 1949 ban on Communists holding office in the TGWU; the ban had itself been instigated by the former general secretary, Arthur Deakin. Moreover, until Cousins moved against the ban in 1968 it had been repeatedly upheld by the platform despite repeated efforts at Rules Conferences to remove it. Also TGWU policy on the closed shop[39] and collective security[40] was changed under the influence of general secretaries who led the move to change a policy which the union's national leadership had previously constantly supported.

It may be, of course, that the general secretary of the TGWU is successful in promoting policy change because he does not make any proposals to the BDC, GEC or F&GPC that are likely to be defeated. However, the consistency with which the TGWU's general secretaries have successfully sponsored changes that have previously been resisted, and have resisted others that have been repeatedly promoted, makes this appear doubtful. It is rather that the constitutional power endowed in the TGWU's general secretary permits him to innovate and persuade the BDC and other bodies that what he, the only nationally elected officer, proposes represents the union's best and non-sectional interests. It is from this position that he dominates the national non-bargaining decision-making process. Moveover, the procedural arrangements themselves help him to achieve this end. Senior full-time officers and particularly the general secretary speak for the lay GEC in BDC debates. This advantageous position arises at least partly because, according to rule, only three members of the lay GEC can actually attend the BDC in their official capacity. Furthermore, the BDC meets only every two years. It obviously cannot control policy between meetings. Also when it does meet, its size – some 1000 delegates – and its composition – regional trade group representation – militates against the formation of an effective opposition. Organization across like-minded groups is not assisted by the division of delegates according to region and trade group or by the ban (until 1968) on Communists. The BDC is thus highly fragmented and dependent almost solely on the platform for a lead. In practice, on a platform largely without any leading lay members, the general secretary plays the major role provided by his constitutional right to speak on behalf of the lay GEC.

Again, at the lay GEC, the procedures place the general secretary in a predominant position. The GEC was, until at least 1975, largely untouched by effective factionalism. Like the union itself, it is divided by regional and trade group allegiances. Meeting quarterly, it cannot closely monitor, let alone control, day-to-day operations. Moreover, for its operations it relies entirely on a system of detailed reports presented to it, up to 1968, almost solely by national officials. A similar method of business is also used at the inner cabinet, the F&GPC. Hence the general secretary, or other senior full-time officials, initiate most of the work of the national bodies of the TGWU through the constitutional procedures.

Full-time officials are themselves also influenced by the general secretary, if by no other means than through the patronage of that office. This arises through the general secretary's dominant role in the appointment of senior full-time officials. Although in rule the GEC make appointments, the responsibility has, in practice, been delegated to the F&GPC which tends to rely on the general secretary for advice in such administrative matters. Taken to its extreme, the general secretary can also, if he so wished, 'set up' his successor, even though this post is elected. Thus until 1978 all general secretaries had been assistant general secretaries or, in the case of Jack Jones, assistant executive secretary. In the absence of effective factionalism, and weak or non-existent unofficial canvassing, the power of the incumbent, if swung behind one of the contenders for office, can be electorally very influential. Moreover, without an effective oppositional grouping within the TGWU and in the absence of tolerance of unofficial electoral organizations, any official who does step outside the rules restricting canvassing can receive short shrift. Tony Corfield, for instance, found this out to his cost when, following his writing of a pamphlet *Collective Leadership for the TGWU*, which was highly critical of the TGWU's leadership during the election for Cousins's successor in the mid-1960s, he was, in consequence, required to resign his post as secretary of TGWU's Political, Educational and International Department. Thus, not only can the established leadership of the TGWU promote and appoint to key positions within the union, but they can also enforce the rules to reduce the effectiveness of any unofficial opposition within the union.

Thus in the TGWU's national level of government the general secretary is provided, by the constitution, with extensive powers. If the general secretary is capable of exercising such powers he has ample opportunity to dominate the national level of government. The power available can be used to innovate or conserve. The TGWU therefore depends to a great extent for its ability to react to a changing environment on the competence of the general secretary and on whether or not he is an innovator or a conservationist. The changes to be examined in Chapter 4 will show how an innovating general secretary, Jones, used the power inherent in the TGWU to change quite radically the nature of that union.

The ASTMS, as it developed in the late 1960s and early 1970s, is somewhat similar to the TGWU. It is both *de jure* vertically bifurcated and multi-industry. There is also a great deal of flexibility in national government which can be exploited by the general secretary who has, under rule, a large degree of discretionary power. But in contrast to the TGWU, the general secretary of ASTMS is not uniquely legitimized as a unifying force. He is not elected: his post is only one of several full-time appointments made by the National Executive Council of the union. But in common with other unions' general secretaries, the general secretary of ASTMS innovates and persuades and uses the research facilities and journals to formulate objectives and elaborate strategies.

Unlike the general secretary of the longer established TGWU, the premier officer of the new and fast growing ASTMS does not have the TGWU's sophisticated procedures and structures of national government or its highly developed bureaucracy. ASTMS's NEC and its Annual Delegate Conference (ADC) do not always agree. The ADC, in contrast to its counterpart in the TGWU, has on several occasions rejected the NEC, and hence the general secretary's, advice. However the NEC 'formulates the policy of the Association'[41] in co-operation with the ADC. It is therefore not a purely executive body. It is capable of legislative action which compensates it somewhat for its inability consistently to persuade the ADC to accept its advice – although the NEC cannot, with impunity, ignore the wishes of the ADC. In 1972, for instance, when the general secretary and the NEC decided to register under the Industrial Relations Act (IRA), they were prevented from doing so by the ADC which voted for de-registration of the union. Moreover, the rejection of the NEC's recommendation to register owed something to the efforts of appointed full-time officials who mobilized delegates against the NEC and the general secretary. Thus there has not existed in the ASTMS a continuous or consistent domination of the union's conference or full-time officials by the NEC and the general secretary such as occurs in the TGWU.

On the other hand, ASTMS's lay NEC and full-time general secretary do have a large degree of discretion outside of the lay ADC's influence. Moreover, within this considerable sphere of influence, the NEC is heavily dependent on and defers to, the general secretary, who is an *ex officio* non-voting member of the NEC. This may well be because the twenty-two-member NEC is partly a mixture of notables, including a few MPs with no immediate shop floor contact and other largely inexperienced new members of the union. For instance, in 1975 only 7 of the 22 members of the NEC had more than two years' experience on that body. In this respect it is therefore less stable than the GEC of the TGWU, where the 30–40 membership has a turnover of 12–15 members every two years.

However, nascent factionalism can be identified in ASTMS. This may further limit the general secretary's influence in relation to the NEC. Over the 1960–75 period the normally unorganized mix of Labour Party, Communist and Roman Catholic groups has been joined by an ultra-left group of International Socialist (now Socialist Worker Party) origins. It is claimed that this latter faction shows signs of electoral organization.[42] Industrial groupings are also emerging within the union. 'Insurance', with its concentration of members in large offices and closed branches, may signify a potentially high polling capability, and if so it could well upset the existing balance in ASTMS's NEC and ADC.[43]

It can be seen therefore that ASTMS is not as concentrated as the TGWU at the national level. Despite the *de jure* vertical bifurcation, discretionary rule books and flexibility of procedures, ASTMS's general secretary is not as free to innovate and persuade or resist change as his counterpart in the TGWU. ASTMS does not have the organizational features found in the TGWU of highly developed but flexible procedures for dealing with business and selecting lay officials. It also lacks the mix of lay delegates and absence of faction, which underpins the general secretary of that union. The machinery of government that supported the general secretary's position in the TGWU around 1960 is thus somewhat less developed in ASTMS.

Moving towards the diffused end of the continuum but still tending to be a relatively concentrated union, the highly regionalized but *de jure* single-channel GMWU maintains a viable national presence by bringing the key figures in the ten regions, the appointed regional secretaries, directly into national level government. They all sit on the GMWU's highest executive body, the General Council (GC).[44] Half of them sit on its Executive Committee (EC). In practice the EC tends to be more important as a national decision-maker than the GC. In the 1960s regional secretaries shared their national executive functions with the elected general secretary and fourteen regionally elected lay members. Again, in practice, the lay members tend to defer to their regional secretaries on the GC and EC of the GMWU.

At the GMWU's major policy-making body the Annual Congress (AC), regional secretaries again extensively influence the decision-making process. Delegates are elected to the Congress from the regions, by branch voting. These delegates attend regional pre-Congress mandating meetings in which regional secretaries are involved. In the absence of faction and with restrictions on communicating and organizing across branches,[45] the regional secretary is very well placed at mandating meetings to persuade the un-co-ordinated, and hence unorganized, delegates to accept guidance from himself as the acknowledged expert on which motions are worthy of regional support at the Annual Congress. Bearing in mind, as mentioned above, that the GMWU's regional secretaries also have the last word in appointment of other lesser regional officers, it can be reasonably stated that they are thus in an extremely powerful position in the union at regional and national level.

The GMWU's government at the national level is therefore mainly dependent on one major and a number of mini 'general secretaries'. The major figure is the general secretary and the mini-generals are the regional secretaries. The resemblance to the medieval king and barons relationship is sometimes noted by students of the GMWU. Power is not as concentrated nationally as in the TGWU or ASTMS, but it is still spread over individuals rather than factions or parties. The general secretary's job is thus primarily one of balancing the small number of regional interests rather than unifying a large number of fragmented, non-factionalized, and hence relatively powerless interests of the TGWU and ASTMS.

The ASW, by comparison with the above unions, was closest, before the UCATT merger, to the AEU. In common with the AEU, and in contrast to the unions examined above, the ASW elected all its officials. Its rule book was reasonably precise. The area of discretion constitutionally allocated to its senior official, the general secretary, was, by TGWU and ASTMS standards, not very large. Again in contrast to the TGWU, ASTMS and the GMWU, the ASW's Executive Council (EC) was full-time and elected by branch ballot vote, similar to the AEU of the 1960s. This is still the case in respect of UCATT.

However, two factors make the ASW somewhat less diffuse nationally than the AEU. First, the factions in the ASW and in UCATT are considerably less well developed than their counterpart, the parties, of the AEU. The ASW's main-stream establishment faction composed of Labour Party loyalists had a comfortable majority over the left opposition on the five-man EC of the ASW in the early 1960s. 'Rank and File', and later 'The Building Workers' Charter' group, both left-wing Communist-dominated organizations, did not seriously challenge the established leadership's hold in the ASW nationally in the 1960s although they had some impact at the local level, for example the Barbican and Horseferry disputes.[46] Faced by a weaker faction than that found in the AEU, the ASW's general secretary and his supporters on the EC were in a stronger position to influence policy than their engineering counterparts.

Second, the rule book of the ASW allowed, and still allows in UCATT, the EC and general secretary the opportunity to selectively implement the Union's National Conference decisions. Under rule a joint council of the EC and the lay General Council, which is a much less influential body than the EC although it is a lay check on that body's activities, can refer a conference decision to the wider membership before it becomes union policy. This the joint council did, for instance, in 1976 in order to reverse a National Conference decision opposing the 'Social Contract'.[47] Hence the ASW's national leadership does have some important discretionary elements in the decision-making procedures which, as will be shown below, make it less diffused than the AEU. However, the inbuilt system of checks and balances on the EC and general secretary, the election of officers and the existence of factions all combine to make the ASW more diffused than most of the other unions examined.

At the diffused end of the continuum stands the Engineers (AEU 1920–67, AEF 1967–71 and AUEW(E) since 1971). Constitutionally the national government of the Engineers revolves around the president, general secretary, seven-man Executive Council (EC) and fifty-two-member National Committee (NC). The president, general secretary and EC are all full-time elected executive posts. The NC, on the other hand, is a lay legislative body elected annually. In addition, the Rules Revisions Meeting (the NC under another name) and the lay Final Appeal Court also play, periodically, a part in national government of the

Engineers. There is therefore a constitutionally prescribed division of powers between the full-time executive and the lay legislature. Voting for full-time officers took place at the branch until the introduction of postal ballots in 1972. The period of office for each individual position is three years in the first instance and five years thereafter until, 'being 60 years of age or over' and having fought at least two elections, 'he or she shall not be required to seek re-election but shall continue in office until the age of 65 years'.[48] The lay NC by contrast is elected annually and indirectly through the branch, district committee and divisional committee process.

Thus both senior national Engineers' bodies are much smaller than their equivalents in the TGWU. Also, and perhaps more importantly, all positions of importance in the Engineers are elected not appointed. The elected Executive virtually sits on a par with the elected president and in terms of actual decision-making is superior to the general secretary. The president only has, for instance, a casting vote on the EC and, since 1975, no vote at all on the lay NC, which is the major legislating body in the Engineers. Furthermore, the general secretary does not have any kind of vote at either body although he has the major full-time official role *vis-à-vis* the Final Appeals Court. He also controls the official internal communications system and edits the Journal. Hence the formal decision-making processes are, at the national level of the Engineers, considerably diffused. No one position in this craft-dominated, decision-making process has the unique prestige or unifying purpose found in the general secretary of the TGWU. The formal *de jure* system of national government in the Engineers is thus a complex arrangement of checks and balances based on multi-faceted electoral processes.

Underpinning the constitutionally prescribed checks and balances of the Engineers is an unofficial and uninstitutionalized two-party system.[49] The two parties, ideologically divided into left and right electoral organizations, represent, primarily and respectively, Communist and Labour Party divisions within the Engineers. They also enforce the internal formal checks and balances on arbitrary government. Moreover they can act, through their elected supporters, as the co-ordinating agents across the diverse national decision-making bodies. They can hence help to make the union governable by creating a common identity of interest which can unite the major ideological groupings on the disparate parts of national government on controversial issues.

Thus the crucial relationship between national officials and committees in the Engineers, unlike the TGWU, is not primarily affected by a single office. Instead, the Engineers are much more affected by party politics and the interplay between organized groups on the EC and NC and the allegiance of the president and general secretary to either of the unofficial parties. Combinations of, for instance, left-wing president and left-wing NC members or right-wing general secretary and right-wing EC members are normally more important in the Engineers than the abilities or political affiliations of any one isolated individual national official of the union. A politically divided EC at odds with a president may, for example, give the legislating NC more influence within the union than it would otherwise enjoy if a majority of the EC were politically in tune with the president.

Internal divisions of a political nature thus dominate the Engineers' national decision-making processes. The balance of political interests largely determines the extent to which the ability of the president or other senior national officials can be brought to bear on controversial matters. For instance, in 1960 the president, Lord Carron, used his position to limit the impact of the NC at a time when it was under the influence of the so-called 'Progressives' – a predominantly Communist Party and Left Labour alliance. Carron was able to do this because he was backed by a consistent majority of 'moderates' on the EC. At both TUC and Labour Party Conferences Carron adopted what has been termed a 'Janus'-like posture[50] on the question of unilateral nuclear disarmament; this effectively negated the left-wing NC's earlier resolution on the subject.

Somewhat similarly, but obversely, the newly elected left-wing president, Hugh Scanlon, faced in 1968 the first of a series of rebuffs from the more right-inclined NC. Scanlon had urged the NC to sanction industrial action on the 'package deal' negotiated with the EEF. The NC, dominated by the 'right' and backed by a number of EC members of a similar political persuasion, successfully rejected the president's proposals. Later the Labour moderates repeated this treatment. They rejected the proposals from Scanlon and the left on postal ballots in 1971. In 1974 and 1975 they also refused to accept the president's proposals on the re-structuring of the new amalgamation. Thus no one body or official consistently dictates or dominates policy-making in the Engineers; government is, on all politically controversial issues, a party matter, rather than a function of organizational bureaucracy.

Thus, in summary, the Engineers stand at the diffused end of the horizontal continuum. Constitutionally prescribed diffusion and the not-unconnected internal and unofficial two-party system make the Engineers' national government quite distinctly different from that of the concentrated TGWU. Between these two extremes, starting from the concentrated end of the horizontal continuum, stood, in the early 1960s (and for ASTMS the early 1970s), ASTMS, GMWU and ASW (later UCATT).

Other unions and relative positions within the typology

In addition to the unions described above we studied others in rather less detail – mainly from the viewpoint of particular aspects of their job territory and/or bargaining behaviour. As a result we generated much useful information on comparative systems of government, most notably in respect of unions such as the AUFW, the NUM, the ASB, the POEU, NALGO, NUBE, the NUT and NUPE. From this information it is possible to analyse all these unions from the viewpoint of our typology, stating how far they exhibit characteristics similar to, or different from, the unions described above.

Of these unions the AUFW is closest to its craft partner in Engineering, the AEU, while the industrial NUM also has similar internal ideological divisions to the Engineers but with a federal system of government somewhat closer to that of the GMWU. Moving towards the middle ground between the TGWU and the Engineers or the horizontal continuum are the craft-dominated ASB and POEU. The ASB is highly decentralized like the Engineers but without its unofficial party system and hence with considerably more power concentrated in the hands of its leading elected national full-time officials. By comparison, the POEU is highly centralized in both its bargaining and non-bargaining decision-making channels. It is also far less diffused than the Engineers in its national level of government, which is extensively influenced by its appointed officials although the degree of factionalism in the organization is noticeably greater than that in the TGWU. Similarly the *de jure* vertically bifurcated NALGO, with its local government traditions, is also somewhat dependent on its appointed full-time officials although not so reliant as are most other unions who also choose their officials by this process, for instance NUBE, the NUT and NUPE. NALGO was, however, like these other unions in the public sector, highly centralized in 1960 in both its non-bargaining and bargaining channels.

It is possible to present the vertical dispersal of decision-making, and the degree of participation in and division of responsibilities at each level, in the form of a diagram which applies to all the unions referred to in this chapter. This is attempted in Figure 4.[51] It should be noted that *the diagram represents the de facto position* in each union, so far as we are able to determine it on the basis of our investigations. Also, it should be stressed that it is a proximate model of the distribution of power within very different organizations; a heuristic device, the utility of which needs to be judged in use. It should not be taken to imply or assume more similarity between organizations than is necessary for the purpose of analysis and classification in the field of union government: thus we are not suggesting that there is no difference between the NUT, NUBE and NUPE; merely that, for our purposes, they can be usefully grouped together.

Finally, so far as non-bargaining is concerned, we show in Figure 5 the relative position of each of the eight models in Figure 4, by reference to both the vertical and the horizontal planes of government.

Summary and conclusions

In this section we found the democratic typologies commonly used for examining union government unsuitable for our analytical needs. In particular, they were not useful for examining the comparative effectiveness of unions' systems of government. Neither did the existing typologies offer a satisfactory means of separating, for analytical purposes, variations and movements within unions, for instance in the non-bargaining and bargaining channels of decision-making.

Our alternative typology overcomes these difficulties by distinguishing between certain aspects of union decision-making found to be important in our

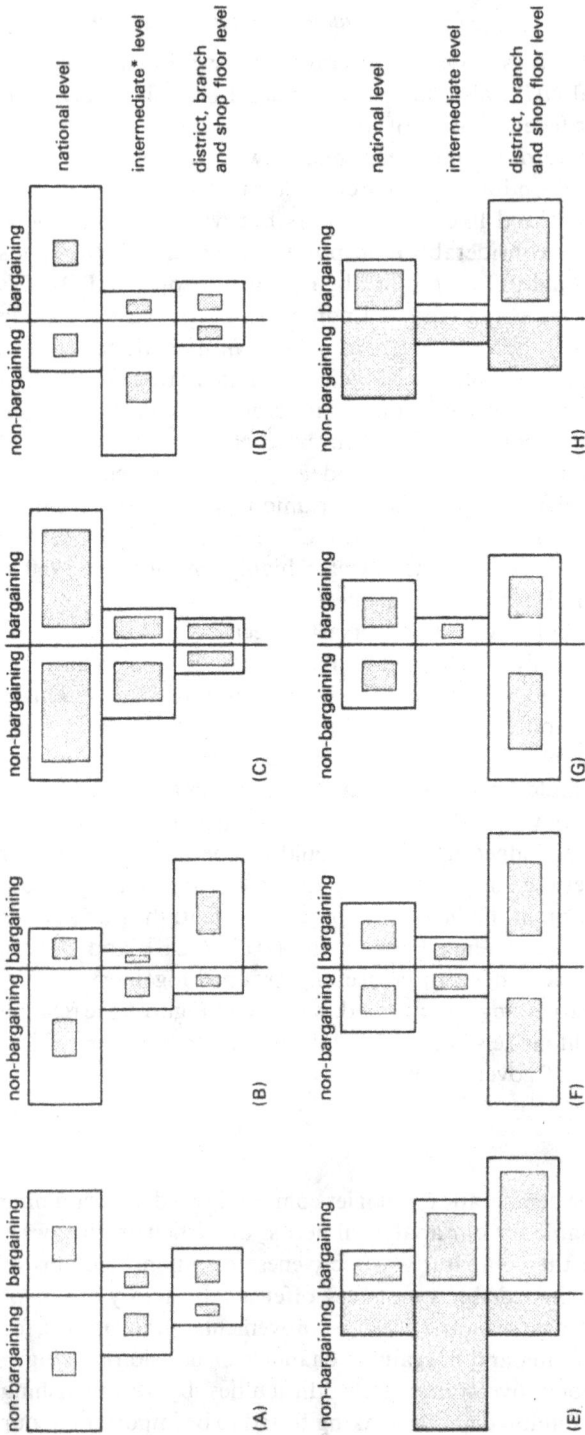

Figure 4 De facto systems of government, circa 1960 (ASTMS 1970). 'Intermediate' level refers to the regional or equivalent level, e.g. AUEW Division. A, TGWU – highly centralized and highly concentrated (the single-channel NUT, NUBE and NUPE, for non-bargaining systems of decision-making, were similar in 1960 to the TGWU; however, their bargaining systems were somewhat different and these are shown individually on page 81, Figure 9); B, ASTMS; C, POEU, and similar to NALGO; D, GMWU – highly regionalized and concentrated; E, NUM – regionalized and diffused; F, ASB; G, UCATT (ASW); H, AUEW(E), and similar to AUFW – decentralized and diffused.

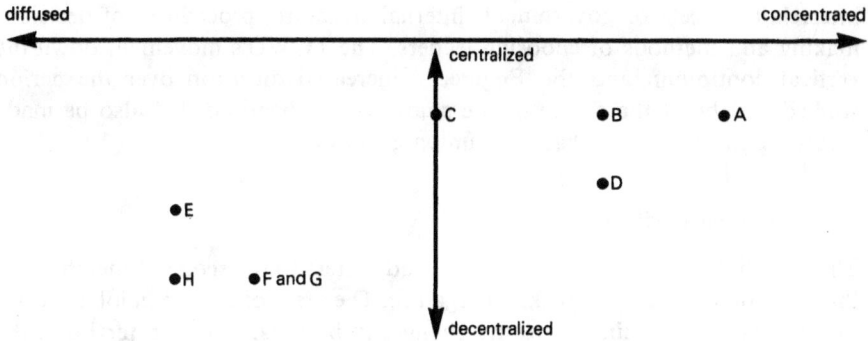

Figure 5   *Relative vertical and horizontal dispersal of unions' systems of non-bargaining decision-making area, 1960 (ASTMS 1970): A–H as in Figure 4.*

case studies of union change. Union government is, in our typology, divided into interrelated parts. The primary division is into vertical and horizontal dimensions of government. Within the vertical continuum unions can be described as being centralized or decentralized, while at each horizontal level of government, within the vertical structure, decision-making can be described according to its concentrated or diffused nature. Second, in order to facilitate an understanding of the separate movements that can take place in a union's non-bargaining and bargaining structures, the vertical continuum is presented as bifurcated. This division, either *de facto* or *de jure*, allows, for instance, separate and contrary movements in the non-bargaining and bargaining continuums of government to be analysed.

The unions studied were found to occupy various positions on the above dimensions of government (as shown in Figures 4 and 5) around 1960. Moreover, there was no necessary correlation between the nature of unions' job territories and certain types of government. The industrially closed and craft-dominated POEU, for instance, stood between the far more 'open' ASTMS and GMWU in terms of non-bargaining type. And the craft-exclusive ASB was considerably less diffused than the more open AEU. The two extreme types, the centralized and concentrated TGWU and the more decentralized and diffused AEU, were also both relatively 'open' unions; and so on. All of which suggests that typologies of government based on the nature of a union's membership were of little value in 1960.

In considering which unions to subject to further in-depth analysis the choice was hence between different combinations of vertical and horizontal dispersals. The two extreme cases were chosen for detailed study in order to contrast the workings of the different types. These unions, fortunately, also happened to be the two largest British unions, the TGWU and the Engineers (AEU).

In Chapter 4 these two unions will be examined across the following three interrelated facets of government: internal structure, procedures of decision-making and methods of choosing leaders. The TGWU's movement down the vertical continuum and the Engineers' increased diffusion over the period studied will be at the centre of the study. Generalizations will also be made regarding the nature of change in union government.

Changes in job territory

The term 'job territory' as used in this study refers to the scope of membership that a union organizes or seeks to organize. The areas of change in job territory that we will be examining are the changes in boundaries of job territory, the absolute and relative growth within and between union job territories and the degree of organization or union density achieved.

We are not, therefore, primarily concerned with the aggregate growth of unionization as analysed in other recent academic studies,[52] although more aggregate patterns of growth do form part of the general context within which the unions in the sample operate. Moreover, the job territory behaviour of individual unions will inevitably have some relevance for aggregate growth.

The scope of recruitment

Scope of recruitment is defined in terms of the diversity of membership, both industrial (horizontal) and occupational (vertical). These two axes are produced in diagrammatic form in Figure 6. The 'ideal types' produced by this two-dimensional intersection would comprise two cases at the extremes of the continuum, 'homogeneous' to 'heterogeneous', and two intermediate cases. Case (b) is the most homogeneous, confined to one occupational level and one industry. Empirical examples of unions that come close to this 'ideal type' include such craft unions as the Association of Pattern Makers and Allied

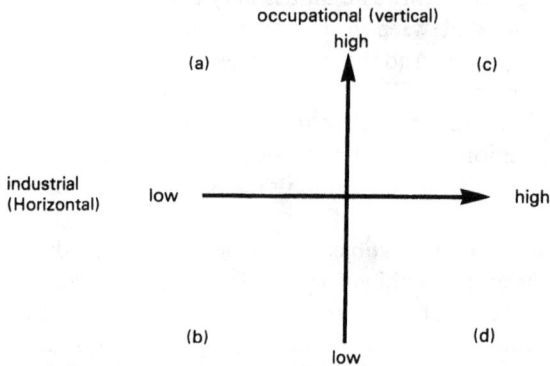

Figure 6 *Degree of diversity of membership*

Craftsmen, and other occupationally restricted unions such as the Associated Society of Locomotive Engineers and Firemen, the British Airline Pilots Association, and the National Union of Teachers.

Case (c), on the other hand, is the most heterogeneous category, comprising those unions that are commonly known as 'general', which recruit in any industry and at any occupational level. The TGWU and GMWU are the only two empirical examples that fully fit this description, although ASTMS comes close to it except that it is confined to the white-collar area in occupational terms.

Case (a) comprises the group commonly known as 'industrial' unions, which organize several occupational levels within a single industrial sector. Empirical examples include the NUM, NUR, ISTC and NUBE. In none of these, however, is the union the sole organizer of all groups within the industry.

Case (d) covers those unions that are relatively homogeneous in the types of occupation covered but organize that occupation in a variety of industries. It is to this 'ideal type' that most of the traditional craft unions approximate. Examples from our own sample include the Engineers, the ASW (in 1960) and the ASB.

In reality few unions fit the 'ideal types' exactly but are ranged along a continuum from homogeneous (b) and heterogeneous (c), or in Turner's terminology from 'closed' to 'open'. The tendency over the period has been for most unions in the sample, with the exception of the NUM and NUT, to move towards the 'open' end of the continuum.

The movement of each union over time is described diagrammatically in Figure 7.

Mergers versus natural growth

The means by which unions achieve changes in job territory can usefully be divided into those that arise through mergers and those that arise through non-merger or 'natural growth'. Although analytically distinct, however, the two are sometimes empirically difficult to disentangle in their cause and effect.

It is, for instance, often difficult to assess the extent to which continuing growth of a union in any one particular sector of industry or occupational group is the result of a previous merger or is due to other trends in factors affecting membership growth.

However, while recognizing that the above interaction of merger and non-merger developments affects unions' job territories, there are still sufficient differences between these two categories of change to make the distinction a valid and useful aid to examining comparative changes in unions' job territories. Mergers, unlike other adjustments in job territories, are legal processes which by their very nature have to be formally dealt with by the established leadership of the unions concerned. They cannot be experienced by the union without a positive act by the national leadership of both merging unions. By comparison, non-merger changes in job territory can happen without the involvement of the national leadership; they can be determined by factors outside the control of the

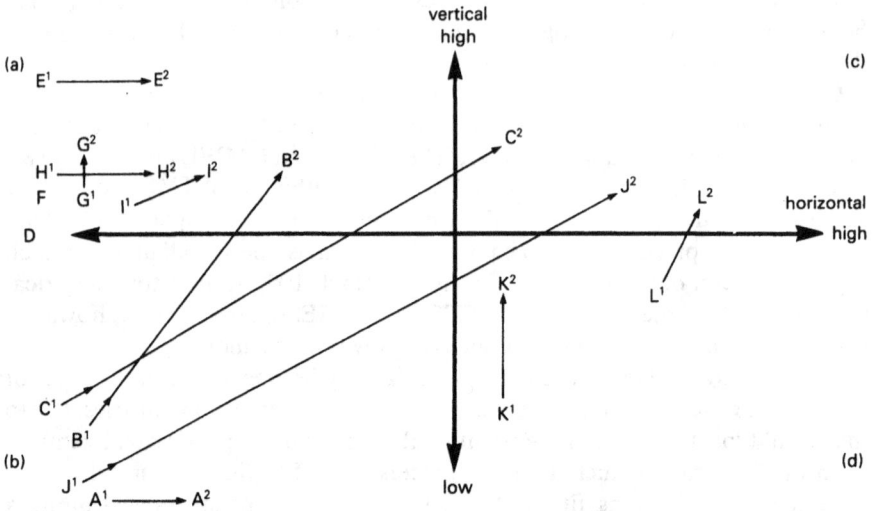

Figure 7   *Degree of diversity of membership, 1960–75. A, Boilermakers; B, UCATT (formerly ASW); C, AUEW (formerly AEU); D, NUM; E, NUBE; F, NUT; G, POEU; H, NALGO; I, NUPE; J, ASTMS; K, GMWU; L, TGWU. The superscript 1 indicates the position in 1960; 2, that in 1975.*

national leaders. Thus, in terms of the model of change, the processes of change and the change agents, merger and non-merger developments can be quite distinctly different. Hence non-merger and merger changes affecting job territories will be examined separately in Chapters 5 and 6.

Before considering the changes in job territory that have occurred within our sample, two major constraints on the pattern of development need to be considered: the characteristics of the membership market and each union's orientation to it.

The membership market

A primary constraint on any union's recruitment strategy is the state of the labour market, particularly if it is operating in a narrowly defined sphere. Such factors account for a substantial part of the growth and decline of unions within our sample, particularly those that are 'closed' either industrially or occupationally. Thus, the decline of the mining industry is largely responsible for the reduction in size of the NUM by 41.3 per cent over the period 1965–75, while the expansion of NUPE (135.6 per cent) and the POEU (35.8 per cent) over the same period is to some extent explained respectively by the expansion of the numbers employed in the public service, and the expansion of the telecommunications sector of the Post Office Corporation. NUBE (74.4 per cent) and NALGO (79.4 per cent) have benefited from the expansion of the white-collar labour force and, in the case of NALGO (like NUPE), the expansion of the public services.[53]

For all these unions, however, unless they make a conscious decision to change the nature of their job territory, the scope for expansion is limited. For the most dramatic changes in the amount and direction of growth we must look to the unions who are or have become more open in their approach to recruitment. The limits to growth in such unions are not defined by the labour market so much as by the activities of other unions; as Turner says, 'sooner or later, any open union extending into a new field of recruitment has encountered another busily ploughing from a different point in the field's periphery'.[54] During the period 1960–75 unions such as the TGWU, the GMWU, ASTMS and to a lesser extent the AUEW were particularly prone to involvement in inter-union competition for members, both with each other and with other unions in more restricted job territories.

The problem of inter-union competition, however, is not limited to relatively 'open' unions. NUBE, UCATT, the NUT and NUPE, although they confine their recruitment to particular industrial sectors, are faced by competition from other unions organizing in their primary sectors. NUPE and UCATT face competition from the two major open unions, the GMWU and the TGWU, among others. NUBE has always had to compete with the internal staff associations for membership. In 1964 NUBE claimed only 37.6 per cent of the total bank employees organized in either NUBE or staff associations. In 1969, immediately following its recognition by the clearing banks, it reached a peak of 49.6 per cent, but fell back again to 43.1 per cent in 1974. Since 1970, however, it has also faced competition from ASTMS and later APEX, a situation exacerbated by NUBE's suspension in 1972 and expulsion in 1973 from the TUC which temporarily removed the protection afforded by the Bridlington procedures.[55]

The NUT faces competition from other teachers' unions and has in fact lost considerable membership to them over the years. Thus, whereas in 1950 the NUT organized 64 per cent of all the teachers in unions,[56] in 1967 the corresponding figure was 50 per cent and in 1973 42 per cent.[57] The major beneficiaries of the decline in the NUT were the National Association of Schoolmasters (NAS) whose proportion increased over the same period from 5 to 9 to 11 per cent and the Joint Four,[58] whose share of the total increased from 10 per cent in 1950 and 1967 to 14 per cent in 1973. Indeed, the NUT declined in absolute terms by 0.30 per cent over the period 1960–73 while the NAS, for example, gained 148.5 per cent over the same period.

Another major element in determining the degree (or density) of trade union organization and to a lesser extent the direction is the employment context. Some areas of employment are notoriously difficult to organize, such as the construction industry where the labour force is highly mobile and fragmented and subject to wide seasonal and cyclical variations. Also important is the attitude of the employer and the pattern of recognition. The role of recognition has been analysed in depth by other authors.[59] In the period covered by this study, the areas that pose particular problems in this respect have been white-collar private sector employment, although some problems remain in the manual private sector, largely in small companies. The public sector has generally settled recognition problems except among white-collar workers in the more recently nationalized steel, aerospace and shipbuilding industries.

As far as the membership market is concerned, the unions studied can broadly be divided into three groups, from the most 'sheltered' to the most 'exposed' in terms of inter-union competition and union security. Among the most sheltered are the Boilermakers, the NUM, the POEU and NALGO, which have a clearly defined job territory in which they have achieved sole recognition. Among the most 'exposed' are the most 'open' unions, ASTMS, the TGWU and the GMWU. ASTMS is the most exposed in that it most often faces a hostile employer and has to compete with other unions – indeed, has actively extended into areas where it does compete. Between these two poles are those unions, UCATT, the AUEW, NUBE, the NUT and NUPE, who have ambitions to be the major or sole union in their sectors of employment but who are exposed to inter-union competition and, in the case of NUBE, UCATT and the AUEW, also to a hostile employer in some areas.

Environmental constraints of the kind mentioned above, though important, are not sufficient in themselves to explain membership developments. For example, within UCATT membership density varies markedly between geographical areas, and in the United States, where the construction industry exhibits similar characteristics, density is much higher. ASTMS and NUBE have faced similar constraints in the finance, banking and insurance sectors, but the former has been rather more successful than the latter where the two are in direct competition. In the GMWU absolute growth in membership and union density varies considerably between regions far beyond that which can be explained by labour market factors. Moreover, the GMWU as a whole has fared worse than NUPE in organizing within the public services and worse than the TGWU, the other 'open' union with which it can most legitimately be compared, in terms of overall expansion. We have, therefore, also to take account of internal factors.

Orientation to the membership market

The pursuit of 'bigness' is not a universal phenomenon, even among unions that are relatively 'open' in their recruitment strategy. Several factors may influence a union's attitude towards the membership market. Different sizes of union may be viable in different situations, and a union may still be effective even if its absolute numbers are declining.

Turner has argued that the major factor that determines a union's recruitment policy is the mode of job regulation, which in turn is related to the 'employment structure within which it [the union] commenced to operate'[60] and its occupational composition. Thus, he argues, whereas unions that operate unilateral controls over labour supply in order to protect their status and remuneration are inevitably restrictionist, regulating those entering the trade and issuing credentials to practise it, 'open' unions, which recruit semi- and unskilled labour which is potentially unlimited in supply, have to rely on collective bargaining, strength of numbers and recruiting the whole of that potential, and are therefore expansionist in outlook.

There are however certain other unions, outside the empirically limited category of those that conform to the exclusive craft union model, for whom job regulation and the employment context are an important factor in determining the scope of recruitment. Thus many unions that confine themselves to a single industrial sector will change their job territory in line with changes in that industry and, as in the case of the NUR and the NUM, even though their membership may be declining will not seek to broaden their job territory unless their strategic position is threatened or they become so small as to be unviable administratively.

Similarly, for example, the POEU's antipathy to amalgamation with the Union of Post Office Workers is based on the view that its present bargaining interests lie in the profitable and expanding telecommunications section of the Post Office rather than in the postal section.

There are other areas too where Turner's simple division into restrictionist and expansionist unions does not apply. There are many cases, particularly in the white-collar public sector area, where the nature of negotiations is such that absolute size or even density have only a marginal effect on the outcome of negotiations. NALGO and the NUT fall into this category, although in the case of the latter its level of organization *vis-à-vis* other teacher unions is crucial in enabling it to dominate the Burnham Committees. The existence of federations will also enable many unions to continue to be viable and to use support services which alone they would be unable to provide, and to benefit from the strengths of a broader front in bargaining while maintaining their autonomy in other spheres.

As an explanatory framework, giving causal primacy to modes of job regulation in producing specific types of union structure, Turner's model is probably more useful when dealing with unions that practise unilateral job regulation. For unions using other forms of job regulation, predominantly various forms of collective bargaining, other factors need also to be considered. As Hugh Clegg has said,

Whereas unilateral regulation demanded certain specific union structures . . . collective bargaining is compatible with almost any union structure. In addition, collective bargaining entails the recognition by employers of the right of unions to represent the employees covered by their agreements. In other words, collective bargaining legitimises the structure of the unions at the time of recognition. Further change does not depend on alteration in methods of regulating terms of employment, but on amalgamation due to the pressures of internal union politics, or to boundary revisions, inspired by doctrines of union organisation.[61]

In fact, union policies in relation to the membership market can best be defined in terms of the extent to which a given union adopts a positive or passive role. Passive unions are not consciously striving to raise the level of membership in the existing or potential membership market; indeed, they may be restrictive in their recruitment aims. Positive unions, on the other hand, may be content with improving their position in the existing market, but they may also wish to expand into new territories.

Thus, for example, the past leadership of the GMWU, which, according to Turner's typology, should, as an 'open' and heterogeneous union, be both positive and expansionist in its orientation to the membership market, has placed as much, if not more, emphasis on the financial stability of the union and on pursuing a 'quiet life'. In pursuit of this objective they have, in the past, been willing to shed more 'militant' members who are seen to be 'expensive' and 'troublesome'. In contrast, ASTMS has pursued a positive and expansionist policy, some would argue with little regard to the logic of job regulation. Many members and officials, for example, viewed the leadership's incursions into the 'city' territory with some misgivings, since they caused considerable extra work for full-time officers (FTOs), possibly to the detriment of its more traditional and strategically powerful areas of organization and possibly because of the less militant character of the 'city' members, to the detriment of ASTMS's militant bargaining posture.

But, of course, attitudes to change in job territory may also vary within a union. For example, in the ASW those craftsmen who worked outside the construction industry would have preferred amalgamation with 'cognate' wood-using trades rather than aiming for an 'industrially' based union which embraced semi- and unskilled workers. Similarly, in DATA there was a long-standing division of opinion as to whether its interests lay with a vertical union in the engineering industry or whether it should expand horizontally to become a broader technicians' union, possibly amalgamating with ASSET and/or the AScW in the process.

There seem therefore to be at least two further dimensions along which orientation to the labour market can be analysed: qualitative and quantitative. The former refers to the occupational and industrial shape that a union has or is prepared to contemplate, and the latter to the importance attached to size or numbers in a union's overall strategy. Turner's continuum 'closed'–'open' could refer to the former, but his term 'expansionist' more appropriately applies to the latter, the opposite of which would not be 'closed' but passive. Thus there could, hypothetically, be a union that had a clearly defined or 'closed' job territory in view, but whose approach to consolidating its own position within that territory was positive. NUPE is a good example. Similarly, there are unions that have an 'open' job territory as in the case of the GMWU, but who do not actively pursue membership growth as a priority.

We have so far identified four continua along which unions can be ranged: homogeneous–heterogeneous in scope of recruitment; sheltered–exposed in

Table 5 *Dimensions of job territory change: the position of each union in 1960*

		Closed	Intermediate	Open
1	Scope of recruitment	ASB, NUBE, NUM NUT, POEU, UCATT (ASW)	ASTMS (ASSET/ AScW) AUEW (AEU) NALGO, NUPE	GMWU, TGWU
		Sheltered	*Intermediate*	*Exposed*
2	Inter-union competition	ASB, NALGO, NUM, POEU, UCATT (ASW)	ASTMS (ASSET/ AScW) AUEW (AEU), NUBE	GMWU, NUPE, NUT, TGWU
		Restrictive–Passive	*Intermediate*	*Positive–Expansionist*
3	Orientation to growth	GMWU, UCATT (ASW), NUM	ASB, ASTMS (AScW), AUEW (AEU), NALGO, NUBE, NUT, POEU	ASTMS (ASSET), NUPE, TGWU

terms of inter-union competition; closed–open in terms of orientation to the scope of recruitment; and passive–positive in terms of their approach to growth. In effect, these four continua can be reduced to three, since homogeneous–heterogeneous and 'open–closed' both refer to the scope of recruitment, and tend to vary together. Although each union could be placed at different points along each continuum, they can for convenience be placed in three categories representing the poles of the continua and a midway or 'intermediate' position. Table 5 shows the broad position of each union in 1960.

In our chapter on natural growth (Chapter 5) we will examine in particular how the GMWU and the TGWU, both, according to the above table, 'open' and 'exposed' unions, varied quite widely in their natural growth primarily because they generally held two different orientations to growth: the GMWU was restrictive–passive while the TGWU was positive–expansionist.

Patterns of union development

The period began in 1960 with a diverse pattern of union membership configurations, and the developments since that date, largely by means of merger, have done little to reduce it, in spite of continued calls by the TUC for a consolidation and rationalization of union structure.[62] Nevertheless, apart from the case of ASTMS's mergers in the financial sector, where a more logical partner for the unions such as the Union of Insurance Staffs and the Midland Bank Staff Association might have been NUBE rather than ASTMS, mergers generally took place between unions whose job territories either met or crossed.

In occupational terms there was a general tendency to continue along established patterns. However, the white-collar/blue-collar divide could be crossed if, for some reason, industrial affinity outweighed occupational considerations. For instance, the Association of Building Technicians joined UCATT and DATA joined the AUEW, becoming the latter's Technical, Administrative and Supervisory Section (TASS) and the draughtsmen in the post office transferred engagements from a white-collar union, the Society of Technical Civil Servants, to a predominantly manual one, POEU.

Moreover, several blue-collar unions, finding their existing potential contracting at the expense of the growth of the white-collar labour force, decided to extend their job territory to include related white-collar occupations, as in the case of the ETU/PTU, or to make a general bid for white-collar workers, as in the case of the GMWU's creation of its MATSA section. Generally, however, the white-collar unions preferred to merge with other white-collar organizations, and there was no attempt by white-collar unions to expand into blue-collar areas independently of the merger context.

Craft considerations were not entirely overlooked in the 1960–74 period. It can, for instance, be argued that UCATT and the AUEW were craft 'aristocracies' which just happened to produce, as a side effect, potential industrial unions. Those unions forming UCATT, except for the small ABT, that is the ASW, the ASPD and the AUBTW, all had craft origins and were all craft-dominated. Similarly, the AUEW was formed out of the AEU, the AUFW, DATA and the CEU, all of which had craft roots and were predominantly officered nationally by craftsmen. Also, the Boilermakers' amalgamation brought three craft unions together.

However, craft identity did appear to be weakening. For instance, the NAOP and the NUVB, both with strong craft origins, chose to join the TGWU in preference to the ASW(UCATT) and the AEU(AUEW) respectively. Although the NAOP and the NUVB did not have the high craft status of, say, the ASW or the AEU, it is interesting that they did choose to merge with an overtly general rather than a craft-dominated union when historically craft unions shunned such mergers.

But most unions did merge with other unions with which they had some industrial or occupational affinity. Thus, the Society of Friendly Boilermakers, which had since its formation in 1834 always been reluctant to extend its organization even to cover related crafts, expanded horizontally by amalgamation to include the Associated Forge and Smithy Workers Society in 1961 and the Shipconstructors and Shipwrights' Association in 1963.

The establishment of UCATT in 1971 fell into a similar category. The three main unions involved also began as exclusive craft unions, tracing their history back to the first half of the nineteenth century when they were generally local or area unions. Since that time there has been a continual movement towards fewer unions, largely through horizontal amalgamation with adjacent trades. The Amalgamated Society of Carpenters and Joiners (ASC&J) was founded in 1860 when 'All branches became governed by the same rules under the control of an Executive Council'.[63] In 1921 the Amalgamated Union of Building Trade Workers (AUBTW) and the ASW were formed out of three builders' unions and two woodworking unions respectively. In 1886 the Sectional Societies of Painters and Decorators amalgamated and a further amalgamation in the same area took place in 1904.

All these amalgamations remained within the context of exclusive craft unions. There were, however, periodic adjustments in the entry requirements. For instance, in 1911 the ASC&J increased its potential membership by agreeing to admit all 'qualified workmen', whereas previously it had recruited only in the shipbuilding and building industries. Moreover, in practice it was the individual branches who determined what constituted a 'qualified workman', as they did also in the AUBTW and later in UCATT. Branches varied in their interpretation and were influenced in their decisions by such external factors as the level of employment. For example, in 1935 the EC of the ASW received complaints about branches admitting into membership men known to have been previously employed as labourers.[64]

The predominantly exclusive craft horizontal movement continued up to 1970. The Scottish masons transferred to the AUBTW during the Second World War. The Scottish Painters fused with the Amalgamated Society of Painters and Decorators (ASPD) in 1963 and the National Union of Packing Case Makers etc., transferred engagements to the ASW in 1965. In theory this latter transfer should have given the ASW a foothold in the recruitment of unskilled workers, but in practice the local ASW branches had the final say in admitting non-craftsmen and in some areas they exercised this power by refusing to admit labourers who had previously belonged to the National Union of Packing Case Makers, etc. Thus when serious moves towards founding UCATT began, only the AUBTW had a substantial number of non-craft members.[65] The establishment of UCATT marked a move away from an exclusive craft base upwards, taking the Association of Building Technicians (ABT) into the amalgamation, and downwards to recruit the semi-skilled and unskilled workers in the construction trades, in an attempt to become the industrial union for the construction industry.

The AUEW, founded in 1971, was similarly composed of unions with exclusive craft (as in the case of the AUFW, the AEU and the CEU) or occupational (as in the case of DATA) roots. In some ways this amalgamation was the continuation of a much longer process and can be seen in the same light as the 1920 amalgamation of ten unions to form the AEU. Until the merger of the AEU and the AUFW in 1967, however, there had been no significant mergers affecting the AEU since 1920. But there had, in the meantime, been a number of notable shifts in the AEU's composition; for instance, it admitted women into membership in 1943, and also became more active in recruiting semi- and unskilled workers after opening two new sections (V and Va) for this purpose in 1926.[66]

The 'dilution' of the AEU's membership continued throughout the 1920–67 period. Skilled workers declined as a proportion of the membership from approximately 75 per cent of all members in 1920 to approximately 50 per cent in 1960.[67] Thus the AEU, unlike UCATT, was already moving towards becoming a more general union for the engineering industry long before its amalgamations in the late 1960s and early 1970s.

Mergers, however, even when they involved unions with industrial interests in common, did not always produce a movement towards industrial unionism. The existence of general recruiting unions such as the GMWU, the TGWU and ASTMS makes a comprehensive rationalization of union structure on industrial lines extremely unlikely. For instance, the NAOP, which organized a distinct craft, opted to merge with the TGWU, which had a minor interest in the construction industry, thus pre-empting UCATT's ambition of organizing the whole of the construction industry. Similarly the Midland Bank Staff Association (MBSA), a non-TUC-affiliated union, transferred its membership in 1974 to the general white-collar union ASTMS, thus preventing NUBE from achieving full consolidation within the banking sector. Thus, although there were some notable moves, such as the UCATT amalgamation, to create industrial unions, there were also some significant mergers that further restricted, by extending the recruitment territory of general unions, the development of a comprehensive structure of industrial unionism.

The GMWU has been less of a threat in this sense than the TGWU and ASTMS. For, although, since its formation in 1924 by an amalgamation of the National Union of Gasworkers (founded in 1889 as the National Union of Gasworkers and General Labourers of Great Britain and Ireland), the National Amalgamated Union of Labour (founded in 1889 as the Tyneside and General Labourers' Union) and the Municipal Employees Association (founded in 1894), it had always been a 'general' or 'open' union, there are some industries, usually those organized by sectoral or quasi-industrial unions, where it has virtually no membership. Its main strength has always been in engineering and shipbuilding and in local government, which together in 1973 formed 44.5 per cent of its total membership. Since the formative amalgamation in 1924 it has been involved in no major amalgamations. Moreover, since 1960, a period when amalgamations were developing apace in many other unions, apart from small transfers of engagements such as the 500 members of the Manchester Warehousemen's Association, the only significant amalgamation was with the 4000-member National Union of Waterworks' Employees in 1972. Nor has the pattern of recruitment shifted significantly, except for the establishment of a separate white-collar section, the Managerial, Administrative Technical and Supervisory Association (MATSA) in 1972 in the hope of encouraging white-collar workers to join the union. Moreover, its general approach to membership growth was until the late 1960s predominantly passive. ASTMS and the TGWU, on the other hand, are both open and aggressively expansionist.

The TGWU was formed in 1922 by the amalgamation of eighteen separate unions, giving the new organization a membership of 297,460. By December

1975, as a result of both natural growth of its membership and the amalgamation with it of sixty-three further unions, this had risen to 1,856,165. The growing diversity of the membership is illustrated by the growth in trade groups that encompassed the major areas of membership. In 1922 the six trade groups were: docks; waterways including fishing; administrative clerical and supervisory; passenger road transport; commercial road transport; and general workers. The power workers' group was formed in 1926 with the amalgamation of the National Amalgamated Union of Engineers, Firemen, Motormen, Mechanics and Electrical Workers. A separate trade group was established in 1931 for engineering workers, and another in 1937 for building trade workers. The government workers' group was established in 1943; in 1945 two new groups followed, one for municipal and one for agricultural workers; and in 1953 the Chemical and Allied Trades group was established. The last six groups drew upon membership that had previously been organized in the 'General Workers' group but indicate a consolidation of membership in each sphere, often by amalgamation. The three major amalgamations within the period 1960–75 were with the Chemical Workers' Union in 1971, the National Union of Vehicle Builders in 1972 and the National Association of Operative Plasterers in 1969. They had the effect of increasing existing membership in the chemical and vehicle building fields and, in the case of the NAOP, constituted the TGWU's first break-through into the skilled craft territory.

ASTMS was the product of an amalgamation between the Association of Scientific Workers (AScW) and the Association of Supervisory Staffs, Executives and Technicians (ASSET) in 1968. That date marked a watershed in the development of both unions and became a springboard for establishing ASTMS as a multi-industrial white-collar union, extending far beyond its original engineering base.

ASSET began in 1917 as the National Foremen's Association (NFA) and developed by extending its scope to cover the growing army of technicians who emerged from the gradual differentiation of the supervisory function. The NFA's membership was initially restricted to craft foremen in engineering, shipbuilding and railways, and was heavily dependent on the craft unions' willingness to permit dual membership for supervisory craftsmen. Under the 1927 Trade Disputes Act it lost its members in the government service, but by amalgamation with the Foremen, Managers and Supervisors' Association it gained an entry into the chemical and general manufacturing and allied industries. During the 1930s the increasing rationalization of production led to further differentiation in the foreman's role and a growth in the number of technicians. The NFA therefore changed its name to the Association of Supervisory Staffs and Engineering Technicians in 1942 and extended its sphere of recruitment to include 'allied technicians'.[68] In 1946 the meaning of the ASSET title was changed to conform with the further expansion of membership scope and became the Association of Supervisory Staffs, Executives and Technicians. In 1947 it amalgamated with the Affiliation of Textile Officials' Associations, a union of 2000 members.

Meanwhile, the National Union of Scientific Workers, formed in 1918, restricted its membership to science graduates. The majority of its membership was to be found in the civil service and teaching with a small sprinkling of industrial scientists. In 1924 the newly established industrial section of the union suggested an extension of membership to include ancillary technical staff. Given that NUSW had failed to secure their objective of establishing unilateral professional control over their occupation, it was felt that this was the best way to prevent dilution, to safeguard the interests of graduate scientists, and to gain strength in the industrial sphere. A motion to this effect was passed at conference but never implemented. In 1926 the union changed its name to the Association of Scientific Workers and in 1928 it changed its rules to put it on a similar footing to other professional associations so that it could retain its membership in the civil service after the passing of the Trade Disputes Act in 1927. However by 1933 its civil service rival, the Institution of Professional Civil Servants, had 8000 members within the civil service while the AScW had only 750.

Having almost withered away in the 1930s, the AScW re-registered as a trade union in 1940 and amended its rules to include ancillary technical staff within its scope. This brought it into competition with ASSET, and in 1942 the two unions reached agreement on spheres of influence.[69] The AScW continued to languish, however, and by the time of the amalgamation its small membership of 22,000 was still spread very thinly over a wide area.

Following the formation of ASTMS a further sixteen small organizations transferred engagements to ASTMS by 1974. This took ASTMS both occu-pationally and industrially into new fields such as insurance, banking and finance. At its 1971 conference it made a rule change to include clerical and administrative staff within its membership scope. Thus ASTMS has had the most dramatic transformation of recruitment scope in the sample, and possibly in the trade union movement as a whole.

The rest of the sample were not involved in any major merger activity, nor did they undergo any major changes in scope of membership, although NALGO and NUBE adjusted their territories outwards.

NALGO began in 1905 solely as a local government union. After the Second World War, with the establishment of the health service and the public utilities and the hiving-off of many previously municipal enterprises to them, it retained its existing membership under the new ownership structure. Aside from local government, therefore, NALGO now recruits in some ten different industries. Thus in local government it organizes the whole non-manual workforce, but in the health service and electricity industry, for example, it recruits only the clerical and administrative staff. With its expansion into new areas and the growth of the public sector in general, NALGO has become, with its over 700,000 members, the fourth largest TUC affiliate and claims to be the largest purely white-collar union in the world.

NUBE, which began as the Bank Officers' Guild in 1917, remained within the banking sector until 1971 when, under competitive pressure from both ASTMS and the staff associations, it decided to expand into related areas in the financial field. It made little headway in insurance but had slightly more success in the building societies. Over the period since 1960, therefore, the union has moved horizontally to embrace other areas of the finance industry beyond banking. However, by 1974 the non-banking sector still accounted for less than 5 per cent of the total membership.

Both the NUM and the NUT have faced a declining membership over the period under study, though for different reasons. The NUM, as a result of declining manpower employed in the coal industry, fell from 700,000 in 1958 to 287,200 in 1970–71 but made no attempt to expand horizontally into other areas. The NUT, which began as the National Union of Elementary Teachers in 1870, had, and still has, aspirations to be the only union organizing teachers in schools. However, while the labour force in schools has expanded, membership in this union has declined, largely as the result of breakaways and competition from other teacher unions. It too, however, has made no attempt to move beyond its original job territory.

The POEU, which began in 1896 as the Amalgamated Association of the Postal Telegraph Engineering Department, has been plagued by secessions since its inception.[70] The telegraph mechanics seceded from the union in 1898 to form the Mechanicians Association and the telephone exchange workers broke away in 1922 to form the Telephone and Telegraph Engineering Guild with the explicit intention of becoming a more exclusive craft-based union. The TTEG merged with the Mechanicians Association in 1926, and then in 1927 they opened their ranks to all skilled engineers in the Post Office whether in the exchanges or not. A further secession of 'internal'[71] workers from the POEU to join the TTEG took place in 1929. In 1931 the Guild re-merged with the POEU following changes in the internal governing process of the latter. However, a further secession of skilled 'internal' members to form the Engineering Officers (Telecommunications) Association (EOTA) took place in 1945. The EOTA members maintained that their interests had been neglected by the POEU despite the fact that 'internal' workers formed an absolute majority in the engineering negotiating structure at that time. In 1953 EOTA rejoined the POEU, following further modifications in the latter's constitution. Although there have been no further major secessions since 1953 and the membership over the period under study has expanded as a result of an increase in the labour force, minor amalgamations and a major improvement in organization to the extent that it now has a 98 per cent density, the fear of potential secessions has played a major part in the bargaining policies that have been adopted by the POEU.

Thus unions involved in mergers were influenced in their merger searches by the composition of their own and other unions' membership. Industrial or occupational associations were important for all merging unions. However, it will be argued in Chapter 6 that unions' approaches to mergers can be more meaningfully categorized by reference to their motivation and strategy. In particular, the UCATT merger will be examined to show the *defensive* considerations of many merging unions; while the AUEW merger will be studied as an example of a *consolidatory* merger. Finally, the TGWU's and ASTMS's competitive thrusts into the merger field will be used to show the *aggressive* nature of their merger searches which affected a large number of much smaller unions.

Summary and conclusions

In this section we found Turner's typology of 'open–closed' did not distinguish sufficiently between the various dimensions of development in union job territory. We found three separate dimensions that did not necessarily vary together as Turner's typology assumed. Turner's distinction between 'open' and 'closed' unions has been retained to describe the scope of recruitment either actual or desired. In addition, however, it was found necessary to distinguish different degrees of enthusiasm for growth, between the two extremes of 'passive–restrictionist' and 'positive–expansionist'. Finally, it was thought desirable to distinguish between those operating in a 'sheltered' as opposed to an 'exposed' environment, especially since inter-union competition was a major feature of the period and an important factor in determining the possibility and direction of unions' growth.

A distinction has also been made between 'natural' and 'merger'-generated growth. Although empirically the impact of the two may be difficult to disentangle, the factors influencing the two forms of growth are in some respects different. Mergers have usually been discussed in terms of their impact on trade union structure. In our study, however, we are also concerned with the motivation behind mergers. We argue later, in Chapter 6, that there are basically three types of motivation to merge; the defensive merger, which refers to those cases where a union finds that its present structure is no longer viable and therefore seeks the protection of a larger union; the consolidatory merger, where a union or unions are seeking to strengthen their hold on a particular job territory and to repel marauders; and finally the aggressive merger, where unions are seeking to expand their job territory in competition with others.

In the chapter on natural growth (Chapter 5) the major case studies will be the TGWU and the GMWU, which provide useful comparative studies in that both are 'open' unions recruiting in the most 'exposed' areas of inter-union competition, but with different orientations to growth both within and between them. Secondary comment will also be made on natural change in some other unions, particularly ASTMS which shares many of the attributes of the TGWU. In the merger chapter, on the other hand, the two largest recent mergers, the UCATT and the AUEW, will be the major focus of attention, illustrating the defensive and consolidatory merger respectively. These will be supported by secondary comment on ASTMS and the TGWU, both of which fall into the category of 'aggressive' merger activity.

Job regulation

Job regulation is a broad term which covers one aspect and, we would argue, the major aspect of the trade union function. As far as union functions or goals are concerned, Blackburn *et al.*[72] have made the distinction between 'employment unionateness', which is concerned with collective action relating directly to their employment situation, and 'society unionateness', which refers to identification in the wider society with those who have the status of employee and pursuing redistribution of rewards through political action. Traditionally, the European trade unions have been regarded as 'society-centred', particularly as compared with unions in the United States. Important in this respect is the affiliation of many British trade unions to the Labour Party and the part played by the unions in its initiation. Moreover, for activists and officials within British unions societal objectives are often of major significance and may fundamentally affect the decision-making process within the union.

Such observations, however, should not lead to the conclusion that the primary objectives of British unions are societal in nature. For as Allan Flanders has pointed out, the primary focus of trade unions in Britain is on job regulation, which today is for the most part synonymous with collective bargaining:

As in other industrial countries, trade unions in Great Britain came into being, established themselves on firm foundations and extended their power and social influence mainly as agencies for collective bargaining. This is to say they succeeded as a form of organisation which enabled employees – at first only wage-earners but later also salary earners – to regulate and thus improve their wages and working conditions. All the activities which the trade unions have undertaken and all the other purposes they have acquired must be regarded as a by-product and auxiliary to this their major activity and purpose, since success in it has been the condition for their survival and the basis of their growth.[73]

We are concerned primarily, therefore, with 'employment unionateness' or job regulation, and within that sphere with two types of changes: the 'character' of job regulation, by which we mean the types of strategies and tactics used to pursue employment-centred ends; and the structure of decision-making within unions. The latter is the aspect of internal government that refers to bargaining as opposed to non-bargaining issues.

Empirically, character and structure are closely intertwined, although they can vary independently in the broad direction they take and in the causal relationship between them. Thus, for example, in the case of the TGWU and the AUEW(E) the more liberal attitude taken towards shop floor militancy was closely bound up with the general strategy of devolving bargaining power to the shop floor. At the other end of the spectrum, the centralization of bargaining within the NUM was for one faction at least, part and parcel of a strategy for united and more effective militant action. In the NUT and NALGO, on the other hand, the demand for greater participation by the rank and file in the bargaining process was very much a byproduct of the trend towards greater militancy rather than a crucial developmental feature in its own right.

Character of job regulation

The strategy and tactics or means used in the process of job regulation can be analysed along two dimensions – the type of action used, and the intensity with which that action is pursued.

The traditional distinction usually made in the former case has been between 'political' and 'industrial' action. 'Political' is used in the sense of the use of 'political institutions', such as Parliament, political parties, pressure groups. The distinction is between two types of arenas within which trade union power is exercised – the industrial or the political.

Turner has described two extremes of union strategy as far as the use of political or industrial action is concerned. At one end of the spectrum, the craft union depends largely on unilateral control of the labour supply by strict rules of entry and demarcation of work, reliance on industrial strength to preserve that control, and striving to maintain differentials over the less skilled; and at the other the general union relies on inclusive membership, the establishment of across-the-board increases, the narrowing of differentials, and often the use of political means to underpin minimum wages and conditions. The nearest union to the former model in our sample is the Boilermakers' Amalgamation, and to the latter, the TGWU.

Over the period under study, however, the degree to which unions have relied on industrial rather than political action to achieve their objectives reveals a more complex picture than this. Two of the traditional 'craft' unions, ASB and UCATT, have come to rely much more heavily on state intervention because of trends in their respective industries. At the same time the private sector white-collar unions have taken over the role of the 'new unions' in 1890 of requiring third party support to establish basic procedural rights such as recognition. The rest of the unions have used varying combinations of industrial and political means to achieve their objectives and the relative emphasis on the two elements has varied over time. In fact, as Clegg has pointed out,[74] political action is more usefully seen as complementary rather than as an alternative to collective bargaining. Indeed, Turner has argued that 'of the three classic techniques of trade unionism – "autonomous regulation", collective bargaining and political pressure – the last has become as much a method of avoiding modification in the former two as an alternative route to collective improvements'.[75]

This has been the traditional role of political action among British trade unions as a collectivity, although as we shall see later individually they vary in their use of the weapon. The most recent and dramatic example of such a defensive role has been the trade union response to the attempts, first by the Labour Government by *In Place of Strife* and then, more comprehensively, by the Conservative Industrial Relations Act, to regulate some of the activities of trade unions. Such intervention by the government, together with that on the incomes policy front, has had a general politicizing effect on trade union behaviour. It has made the distinction between 'industrial' and 'political' means and ends much more difficult to draw in the sense that normal industrial conflict has become defined as 'political' when the main partner to the conflict is the state rather than the employer, or when the state is the employer. At the same time, the trade union movement as a whole, particularly during the period of the Social Contract, extended both their objectives and the scope of political influence beyond the purely defensive and employment-centred to involve a wide range of social and economic issues concerning working people as a whole.

As far as the intensity with which action is pursued is concerned, the period has been characterized by a growing degree of 'militancy', particularly within the white-collar area and the public sector, 'militancy' in this context being shorthand for the readiness to take all forms of industrial or political action and 'exploiting fully the use of any criteria',[76] bearing in mind the context in which such tactics are being contemplated. Thus, for example, for a public sector white-collar union that has never had a strike clause within its constitution but then decides to insert one, a significant change has taken place even though such a development could not be measured in strike statistics.

The structure of decision-making in job regulation

The structure of decision-making in bargaining, as for non-bargaining decision-making within trade unions, is analysed along two dimensions. The degree of centralization/decentralization measures the scope of decision-making at the various levels within the organization; and the degree of concentration concerns the degree of participation in the decision-making process at whichever level it takes place. Although the first is often associated empirically with the second, the two can and do vary independently. There are three major levels at which collective bargaining takes place in Britain. The *industry-wide agreement* (often referred to as 'national agreements'), is an agreement between an employer or an employers' association and a trade union or federation of trade unions, covering a whole industry. The *company-wide agreement* takes place between a single employer and one or more unions and covers all plants within a single company. The *workplace agreement* is limited to a particular establishment such as a manufacturing plant, a construction site, a bus garage or commercial office. Bargaining levels are distinct from bargaining units, which refer to the specific group or category of workers covered by a particular agreement or understanding. The structure of bargaining units may differ between levels, as may the substantive bargaining issues. Thus, for example, holidays may be determined for a wide range of different occupations at an industry-wide level, while the actual time at which the holidays were taken would normally be a matter for negotiation with particular groups at workplace level. As far as bargaining levels are concerned, the process of dispersal has two distinct meanings: first, there is the shift of levels at which agreements are made; and, second, there is the scope and importance of various levels of bargaining in a static multi-level bargaining structure.

The other aspect of dispersal with which we are concerned is the degree of participation in bargaining by lay members. This takes two forms. There is the degree of influence that lay members have over the decisions that are made at whatever level these occur, for example, the process whereby draft agreements are submitted to the membership concerned for ratification. There is also the degree to which various lay members, and lay and full-time officials, actually participate in the bargaining process and the degree of autonomy they exercise in doing so.

The two dimensions of centralization and decentralization of bargaining decisions and the degree of concentration and diffusion of power at each level are expressed diagrammatically in Figure 8. This does not exhaust the logical possibilities but it embraces the two logical extremes of the continua and the empirical cases to be found in our sample. This figure and Figure 9 below represent the bargaining aspect of internal government (see Figure 3, page 42).

Thus, in A power is both centralized and concentrated: the majority of collective bargaining decisions are taken at the top and by a single body or office holder. At the opposite pole, D indicates a structure in which the majority of decisions are taken at shop floor level and with the participation of shop floor representatives either working alone or in conjunction with other lay and full-time officials. There are no examples of type A in our own sample. Those unions such as NUPE, the NUM, NALGO, the NUT and the POEU who have at some stage had highly centralized bargaining have also had a degree of delegation of authority at the national level or, as in the case of the NUM, a high degree of autonomy among the areas whose representatives constitute the executive committee. The AUEW(E), the TGWU (after 1960) and ASTMS provide examples of the diffused and decentralized pattern, although the actual form that it takes differs between them.

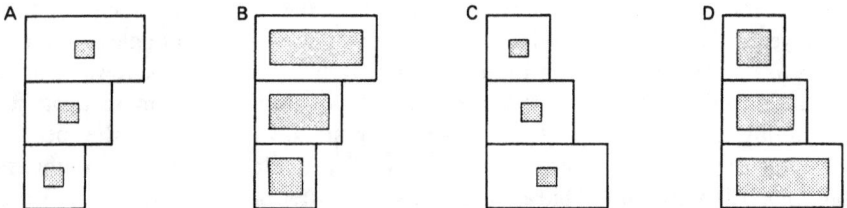

Figure 8   *Some ideal typical forms of decision-making in the bargaining aspects of job regulation. A, high centralization, high concentration; B, high centralization, low concentration; C, low centralization, high concentration; D, low centralization, low concentration. Horizontal spread measures the scope of decision-making at three basic levels in the union: national, intermediate and shop floor. Shading indicates the degree of concentration/diffusion of decision-making.*

Changing patterns of job regulation

Character

The major change in character among the unions studied over the period from 1960 was an increase in militancy, more particularly a growing militancy among the hitherto quiescent areas of the public services and white-collar unions. In the manual unions where there was already a substantial degree of militancy, particularly in coal mining in the public sector and the engineering industry in the private sector, it was not the intensity of militancy but the form that it took that formed the major area of change.

For purposes of the discussion of militancy, therefore, the sample can be divided into two basic groupings: one is the traditionally quiescent area of the public services, and white-collar unions in general; the other comprises most of the manual unions in the sample for whom industrial action in one form or another was not, as it was in the case of many white-collar unions, a new phenomenon.

In 1960 most white-collar unions resorted rarely, if ever, to militant action. By the end of the period under study there were very few that had not taken industrial action in some form or another. In the private sector the growth in militancy, particularly in NUBE, was much bound up with the procedural issue of recognition as well as the pursuit of substantive job regulation objectives. In the public services the problem of recognition had largely been solved, but other factors common to white-collar unions, such as the perceived decline in differentials *vis-à-vis* manual workers, were compounded by the specific factors affecting public sector employees, whether white-collar or manual.

NALGO and NUT have been chosen as the prime examples of changes in character, not only because they combine the white-collar and public services dimension, but also because the trend towards militancy was accompanied by other fundamental changes in their approach to the wider trade union movement, manifest particularly in their affiliation to the TUC. Most of the major private sector-based white-collar unions were already affiliated but the public service white-collar unions had in general held aloof.

In Chapter 7 the focus will be on the white-collar unions in the sample, particularly NUT and NALGO, for it was there that the major qualitative change in character as we have defined it took place. For the majority of manual unions in the sample the pattern of militancy, although mentioned as areas of change within Chapter 7, are subsidiary to and best explained by reference to the major changes that were taking place in the structure of decision-making described in Chapter 8 and to changes that are described in the following chapter on internal government.

The structure of decision-making

It is difficult to attribute changes to individual unions where they cover a multitude of industries and occupations except by a process of inference from the general statistics, and few unions keep their own figures. However, it is possible to characterize the broad outline of the decision-making structure relating to collective bargaining although this may not necessarily include every industry, region or occupation encompassed by each union.

The general tendency over the period from 1960 was towards the dispersal of decision-making in job regulation, although there were some notable exceptions. Some unions were already highly dispersed in 1960, but for the majority power was more centralized and more concentrated in 1960 than in 1975. Before assessing the degree of change that took place, however, we need to know the position of each union in 1960.

The pattern in 1960 of each union in the sample, in terms of the dimensions, centralization–decentralization and concentration–diffusion, is shown in Figure 9, starting with the most centralized and concentrated. NUPE came closest to type A (Figure 8) in 1960, with highly centralized bargaining channels and a concentration of power among full-time officials. A major objective of NUPE during the 1930s had been to achieve industry-wide negotiations for local authority employees; this was first achieved in 1940, although it was not until 1949 that agreement was reached within the NJIC to establish national wage standards and national working conditions for manual workers in local government. National negotiations through the Whitley system were the norm in the NHS from its formation in 1948. Until the mid-1960s the amount of local bargaining in NUPE was negligible.

In 1960 the relationship between full-time officials and lay members was one of full-time officer dominance. Indeed, Bryn Roberts (general secretary until 1962) was firmly opposed to any devolution of collective bargaining responsibilities to the shop floor.[77] Moreover, the degree and effectiveness of lay participation in the largely centralized bargaining process was minimal. The EC, although composed entirely of lay members, was highly dependent on FTOs' advice and strategy, and the links between the EC and their constituencies were tenuous and limited largely to elections. As the Warwick University study commented,

the relationship in rule between Areas and Divisions on the one hand and the Executive Council and National Committees on the other consists virtually of the definition of electoral boundaries only. Relationships with electorates as such, other than once every two years, are not firmly rooted in the on-going structure of NUPE. At present, the Executive Council and National Committee members lack a regular, constitutionally based forum to which they report and from which they can carry information and expectations to national level.[78]

The NUT, NALGO and the POEU, who also had highly centralized negotiating machinery, had a certain degree of diffusion of decision-making functions. Like NUPE, the POEU was committed to centralized negotiations, and this continued after 1960. Unlike NUPE, however, the POEU had effective lay participation in the determination of collective bargaining policy. The annual conference did and still does spend a considerable proportion of its time considering all aspects of bargaining issues and formulating the broad outlines of pay claims.

The structure of occupational committees in the POEU, established in 1954 and composed entirely of lay representatives and serviced by FTOs, ensures that lay members are closely involved in the formulation of policy affecting their occupations. The committees, representing internal engineering staff, external engineering staff, supplies, factory and motor transport staff, have considerable autonomy in determining policy. A two-thirds majority is required on the Executive Council to override an occupational group's decision. Each occupational group has its own annual conference held on one day during the annual conference of the union.

Branch secretaries have traditionally carried on negotiations with management at local level on matters not falling within the scope of national negotiations, and many are seconded full time to union duties. At regional level the POEU has regional councils composed of lay members, to match the equivalent managerial level in the Post Office and the Whitley Council machinery and to take up issues at that level.

Bargaining in NALGO is conducted via the Whitley machinery, actively sought since the First World War although not achieved until the implementation of compulsory arbitration under the wartime emergency order 1305, and as a result of the House of Lords decision against Bolton Corporation in 1942, which made Industrial Court decisions binding on both parties. Under Whitleyism the theory is that the National Joint Council (NJC) should agree the

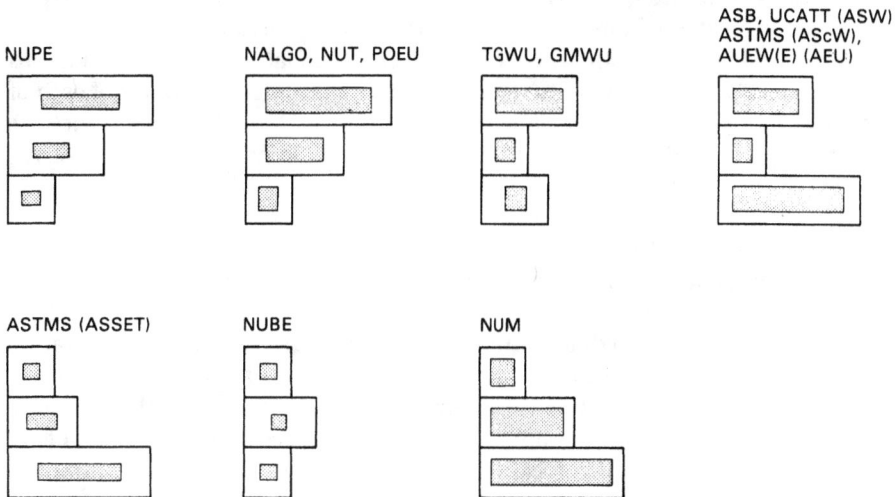

Figure 9   *Patterns of decision-making in the bargaining aspects of job regulation in 1960*

national principles covering a broad range of conditions of service (including salaries, grading, promotion, discipline, recruitment, tenure, hours and leave) and the provincial and local committees should administer the application of these principles at the relevant levels. In practice, however, the precise application of this structure varies between and within the services organized by NALGO. Both in the scope of that which is bargained and the amount of discretion that it leaves to local levels, bargaining under Whitleyism is highly centralized.

Like the POEU, however, NALGO has traditionally allowed for considerable lay participation in collective bargaining even though the activity is highly centralized. The NEC is composed wholly of lay members elected annually and in theory has control over the carrying out of policy between conferences. Although it would be naive to suggest that full-time officials have no ability to sway policy, it is interesting to note that until 1965 the general secretary was not allowed to enter the debate at conference or on the NEC.

Each service represented within NALGO, such as the local government or the National Health Service (NHS), has its own services and conditions committee, composed of lay members, which exercises a high degree of autonomy. The service and conditions structure is formally integrated into the representative structure at branch, district, national and conference level. At branch level the committee (which is normally workplace-based) is involved in local negotiations over service and conditions and each branch executive is encouraged by NALGO's model rules to contain members who are represented on local joint committees or otherwise involved in negotiation. At district level the service and conditions structure is relatively more important. In all districts there are gas, electricity, local government and health service and conditions committees, but not all have transport or water committees. National service and conditions committees in the principal services are composed of a representative of each of the districts, plus three representatives of the NEC.[79] One of the major functions of the service and conditions committees is to appoint the staff sides of the appropriate Whitley Councils.

Beatrice Webb described the constitution of the NUT in 1915 as combining 'in a high degree, local initiative and responsibility with centralised strength for national purposes. . . . The democratic life of the NUT has not militated against the creation of a powerful central Executive.'[80] A whole range of issues that affect teachers are determined at national level to apply to all local education authorities. Since 1920 the teachers' associations, of which the NUT is the major representative, and the national associations of local education authorities have negotiated salaries in the Burnham Committees.[81] Detailed management of the schools is, however, left to local education authorities. The NUT organization mirrors the management structure.

Although pay negotiations in teaching are highly centralized, the NUT has traditionally relied heavily on lay participation. Lay members together with some FTOs are represented on the Burnham Committee as part of the NUT delegation. Moreover, the union has a whole series of standing advisory committees elected by local associations and divisions, which together with EC members, are intended to advise the Executive and 'guarantee that sectional interests are properly safeguarded'.[82]

The NUT has also relied heavily on lay officials to conduct collective bargaining activities on non-pay issues at local level. The key figure within this context is the local association secretary.

In 1960 the GMWU and the TGWU were similar to NUPE in that power tended to be concentrated among full-time officials, irrespective of the level at which bargaining was conducted. However, unofficial movements exercising a high degree of autonomy outside the union machinery did exist in the TGWU, for example in the docks.

To cater for their diverse memberships both the TGWU and the GMWU had national officers responsible for major industrial groups. In the TGWU national trade group policy was and is decided at national trade group committees, and both trade groups and their full-time national secretaries have traditionally exercised considerable autonomy in collective bargaining within their own industries. The general secretary, with one or two notable exceptions such as during the London bus strike of 1958, rarely involved himself directly in day-to-day negotiations either at national trade group or local level. At local level negotiations were normally carried out by the local district officer. Thus, although the situation varied between industries and districts, with some areas, such as vehicles and the docks, characterized by strong workplace and shop steward independence, the predominant relationship was one of lay member and officer dependence on full-time officials both at shop floor and trade group level.

In the GMWU, as in the TGWU, national industrial officers (NIOs) have been traditionally allowed considerable discretion in the conduct of the national negotiations for which they are responsible and all the NIOs interviewed stated that the general secretary would only infrequently intervene in negotiations and would never take over responsibility for those negotiations. This was so during the leadership of the previous general secretary, Lord Cooper. Indeed, the latter remained on holiday and left the organization of the major public sector strikes in 1970 to the national officer concerned.

At national level the NIO, occasionally in consultation with the general secretary, would formulate the initial claim within the 'strategic' guidelines laid down by the NEC, general secretary and/or regional secretaries. In the past each NIO would submit a report on his activities during the previous year and answer questions from delegates at the Annual Congress, but this could not go into the issues in depth. In some JICs provision was made for lay members to sit alongside the FTOs. For example, of the twenty-two GMWU representatives on the Pilkington JIC, fifteen were directly elected from the shop floor, the remaining seven being FTOs. However, there was no clear forum for articulating issues limited to a particular industry, as there was with the trade groups in the TGWU.

The three craft or ex-craft unions – the ASB, the AUEW(E) (AEU) and UCATT (ASW) – were all party to national negotiations covering the majority of their members, the AUEW(E) (AEU) and the ASB through the CSEU and UCATT(ASW) through the NFBTO. For example, since the establishment of the National Wages and Conditions Council in 1920 industry-wide negotiations for the construction industry[83] were conducted between the employers' organization, the National Federation of Building Trade Employers (NFBTE) and the National Federation of Building Trade Operatives (NFBTO). The latter was formed in 1919 with the objective of 'a uniform rate for all building operatives'. Until 1947 the industry-wide negotiations between the NFBTO and the NFBTE set 'the current *standard rate* of wages'.[84] Moreover, 'building employers adhered to the wage structure negotiated at industry level and their standard rates were applied without local additions except where authorised at national level'.[85] After 1947 incentive schemes were widely introduced and various additions to the National Working Rules concerning the application of incentive schemes were made to facilitate their introduction.

By 1960 in all three unions locally or company-based pay determination already formed a considerable proportion of the pay packet. But while in the ASB and the AUEW(E) (AEU) this was usually conducted through negotiations at that level, often directly by shop stewards, in UCATT(ASW) the leadership resisted local negotiations and the introduction of shop stewards. Thus in construction the movements in earnings at local level were often determined either through unofficial workplace shop stewards or by unilateral action by the employer. While the ASB and the AUEW(E) (AEU) accepted that national negotiations were largely concerned with settling certain minimum conditions of employment which could be supplemented by local bargaining, UCATT (ASW) never fully did so.

For ASTMS (ASSET) in engineering and NUBE in the major clearing banks national industry-based negotiations were not an option in 1960 since neither had achieved recognition by the employers at that level. As far as ASTMS (ASSET) is concerned, however, it made a virtue of necessity and has, at least since 1958, been committed to company bargaining as its preferred level of activity. As Clive Jenkins said in 1970,

So we have decided – confidently – to opt for big-company contract bargaining as a central part of all our efforts to get a forward move for the managers, scientists and technicians who bear a great deal of the stress in British Society . . . the 'so-called national bargain' is basically irrelevant to the needs of the firms and the employees, and frequently results in the money going to inappropriate places and groups when viewed in terms of social and economic priorities. Collective bargaining has got to be much more sensitive and closer to the production processes.

Unions in the past may have needed scalps to carry away like a marauding party from the negotiating table. We do not need this any more and we ought to be sensible enough to cope with negotiations at the time and at the point where it seems most appropriate.[86]

NUBE, on the other hand, has always been committed to centralized bargaining. In the absence of recognition in most of the banking sector, union committees and branches were concerned mainly with organization and administration rather than negotiation. Moreover, full-time officers played a dominant role because of the fear of victimization of lay officers by hostile employers.

In 1960 the NUM came closest to the model of a diffused and decentralized union. The most significant bargaining was done at pit level. Traditionally the branch secretary, who is the key lay official, although he is usually paid for union duties for at least some of his working time and in many cases is almost a full-time official, was the key figure in collective bargaining and consultation with management at pit level. It was he who was largely concerned with investigating safety conditions and accidents, and he who advised the sick and injured on the claiming of benefits. His importance and independence was underlined by the fact that area officials were very rarely seen at the pit – 'about once or twice a year' was a typical frequency. Only if there was disagreement between the branch secretary and the pit manager would area officials be called in.

Developments in the structure of decision-making in job regulation since 1960, at least up to 1967, were most classically described by the Donovan Commission Report and associated evidence. The Donovan analysis did not demonstrate any major shift in the formal levels at which collective bargaining was conducted. Indeed, the TUC in its evidence to the Commission, in which it emphasized the importance it attached to industry-wide bargaining,[88] claimed: 'it is certainly not true to say that there has been any major shift away from national bargaining; rather has national bargaining continued slowly but gradually to extend into wider fields'.[89] They did, however, concede that 'the extent to which the significance of national bargaining *vis-à-vis* total earnings or what might be termed supplementary local earnings has changed.'[89]

It was the latter change, whereby the significance of industry-wide bargaining in relation to total earnings was declining compared with the influence of workplace bargaining that concerned the Donovan Commission.

One of the basic measurable indicators of the significance of different bargaining levels is the proportion of the wage packet determined by each level. Donovan produced a series of tables illustrating the position in 1967.[90] Thus, for example, in 1938 the basic time rate for an engineering fitter constituted 91.3 per cent of the average earnings figure for the industry, whereas in 1967 it formed only 51.8 per cent. Similarly, in construction, in 1938 the time rate of the skilled bricklayer was 109.9 per cent of the average earnings in the industry, whereas in 1967 the craftsmen's time rate was only 67.6 per cent of the average earnings in the industry. The Donovan Report also showed that the degree of 'wage drift' increased considerably in the period 1962–67 (see Table 6). The figures from 1968 onwards, however, indicate that the degree of 'wage drift' lessened over the period 1968–76 more so in some industries than others. As Table 7 shows, the proportion of total earnings in all industries and services made up by Payment By Results (PBR) payments decreased from 8.9 per cent in 1968 to 8.0 per cent in

Table 6   *Comparisons of increases in wage rates with increases in earnings in the period October 1962–October 1967*

Industry groups in which manual workers concerned were employed	Percentage increase over the period October 1962–67		
	Average weekly wage rates	Average weekly wage earnings	'Earnings drift' (col. (2) minus col. (1))
	(1) %	(2) %	(3) %
Construction	21.7	35.9	14.2
All metal industries	23.1	32.3	9.2
Food, Drink, Tobacco	23.0	39.5	16.5
Textiles	17.9	37.7	19.8
Paper, Printing, Publishing	22.9	36.5	13.6
Chemicals and Allied Industries	24.8	38.1	13.3
Timber, Furniture, etc.	18.4	35.8	17.4
Bricks, Pottery, Glass, Cement, etc.	25.8	36.7	10.9
Clothing and Footwear	20.6	33.2	12.6
All industries*	23.1	36.4	13.3

* All industries covered by the Ministry of Labour's half-yearly earnings inquiries

Source: derived from Table C in Donovan Report, p. 16.

1976. Within this overall drop, however, there were major differences. Thus, the drop within manufacturing industries was much larger, from 13.2 to 9.0 per cent. Moreover, within manufacturing industry the drop was greatest in Metal Manufacture and Vehicles, reflecting the growth of Measured Day Work (MDW). In mining there was a dramatic drop reflecting the introduction of the National Power Loading Agreement (NPLA), but in construction there has been a significant increase, from 6.1 to 14.1 per cent. Moreover, there was an increase in PBR elements in the predominantly white-collar areas of professional and scientific services, insurance, banking and finance. Significant also was the jump in the public sector, from 1.8 to 13.3 per cent in gas, electricity and water, and from 1.9 to 11.4 per cent in public administration and defence.

Associated with the growing significance of workplace bargaining, according to the Donovan Commission, was the developing independence between the FTOs and lay representatives. On the one hand, at the industry-wide level bargaining was pursued almost entirely by full-time officials, although subject to some influence by annual and biennial conferences; while on the other, workplace bargaining was almost entirely in the hands of workplace representatives, with little reference to full-time officials or to higher levels in the union.

The Donovan remedy for a situation in which, they believed, the 'formal' industry-wide agreements were no longer effective, was not to breathe new life into that level but to institutionalize or 'formalize' the 'informal', by shifting the majority of agreements to lower levels, either company or workplace, and establishing a formal framework of procedures at that level. Under such a system they envisaged a situation whereby lay representatives and FTOs would be jointly involved in company and workplace agreements. This would, they thought, entail a considerable increase in the number of union FTOs to tackle the increased workload.

Table 7 *Proportion of total earnings made up of payment by results, 1968 and 1976*

	1968	1976
	%	%
Agriculture, Forestry, Fishing	7.8	5.9
Mining and Quarrying	11.3	1.6
Food, Drink, Tobacco	3.9	4.7
Chemicals and Allied	5.5	2.7
Metal Manufacture	19.9	13.3
Mechanical Engineering	11.3	9.2
Scientific Instruments, etc.	5.0	3.9
Electrical Engineering	10.3	7.0
Shipbuilding and Marine Engineering	6.6	8.5
Vehicles	21.6	8.1
Metal Goods (not elsewhere specified)	13.7	11.5
Textiles	16.7	10.1
Clothing and Footwear	14.7	18.4
Bricks, Pottery, Glass, Cement, etc.	18.3	15.5
Timber, Furniture, etc.	12.8	13.7
Paper, Printing, Publishing	5.4	5.2
Other Manufacturing	18.8	12.9
Construction	6.1	14.1
Gas, Electricity, Water	1.8	13.3
Transport and Communications	4.8	3.4
Distributive Trades	4.2	4.9
Insurance, Banking, Finance	0.9	3.0
Professional and scientific services	0.5	4.1
Miscellaneous services	3.9	4.6
Public Administration and Defence	1.9	11.4
All industries and services	8.9	8.0
All manufacturing industries	13.2	9.0
All non-manufacturing	4.9	7.1

Source: New Earnings Surveys (1968) and *Department of Employment Gazette* (1976).

Critics of the Donovan Report pointed out that it had over-stated the degree to which collective bargaining had in reality shifted to the workplace, partly resulting from an over-concentration on the engineering industry.[91] Indeed, the Donovan Report itself noted that this was the case:

The informal system has been described mainly in terms of private industry, and not so much in terms of public employment; mainly in terms of manual workers and less in terms of white-collar workers; mainly in terms of men and not women; mainly in terms of organised workers and less in terms of the unorganised.[92]

Certainly our own study of individual unions, covering some 60 per cent of the total TUC affiliated membership, indicates that the devolutionary shift was by no means universal. Moreover, the reasons for those developments, although they owed something to common external forces, reflected diverse internal pressures and leadership strategies that bore little relation to the reforming objectives and concerns of the Donovan Commission.

The overall pattern of development among the unions studied had been a move towards greater dispersal of decision-making in terms of both the level at which bargaining takes place and the degree of concentration of power at each level. The pattern of decision-making in each union in 1975 is shown in Figure 10.

There have been few major shifts in the formal level at which collective bargaining takes place, and of these as many have been shifted upwards as downwards. The major case of an upward shift towards centralization is the NUM. NUBE secured an upward shift when it achieved its long-term aim of

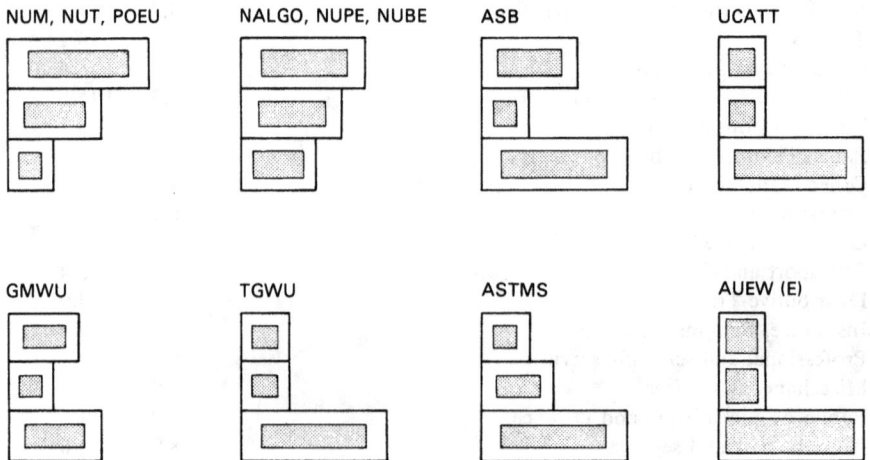

Figure 10   *Patterns of decision-making in the bargaining aspects of job regulation in 1975*

industry-wide bargaining in 1967 when it secured recognition from the clearing banks.

By far the most dramatic shift during the period under study, however, was the temporary abandonment of the National Engineering Procedure encompassing 1.25 million engineering workers, affecting primarily the AUEW(E) but also other unions in the CSEU (the GMWU, the TGWU and the Boilermakers) in December 1971.

As one might expect, shifts in the significance of different bargaining levels tend to follow the same direction as shifts in the formal level. UCATT is the exception to this rule. In its case the re-emphasis of its commitment to industry-wide bargaining has been accompanied by its growing irrelevance as far as 'delivering the goods' is concerned. However, with the exception of the NUM, the NUT and possibly ASTMS, which was already highly devolved, all the unions studied have experienced some increased devolvement of bargaining in terms of the reduced significance of national level negotiations.

As far as the participation of lay members and officers in the negotiation process and their relationship with FTOs is concerned, only in the NUM did power become more concentrated. NUPE and the TGWU were the two unions in our sample to make the most determined effort to widen the degree of participation in decision-making in job regulation.

Summary and conclusions

We have divided the study of changes in job regulation into two parts: changes in 'character' and changes in the structure of decision-making. In the case of 'character' we are concerned primarily with the means used by unions to achieve their job regulation objectives rather than the nature of those objectives. We distinguish between 'industrial' and 'political' means and also the degree of intensity with which these types of activity are pursued.

In terms of union character there was a general increase in militancy over the period. Most notable within this general increase, and largely responsible for the changing pattern of strike activity towards longer, larger, official confrontations as opposed to small, short, unofficial stoppages, was the extension of strike activity to previously quiescent areas such as the public services. Also important was the tendency for the white-collar unions, whether in the public or private sectors, to become more militant. These two trends were combined in the case of NALGO and the NUT, and these two unions will form the major case studies used in the discussion of changes in character in Chapter 7, with NUBE and, to a lesser extent, ASTMS playing supporting roles.

In discussing the decision-making structure in the bargaining activities of unions we use a similar typology to that used when discussing the non-bargaining decision-making structure, namely, on the vertical dimension the degree of centralization or decentralization, and horizontally the degree of diffusion of power at each level.

As far as the structure of decision-making is concerned, the majority of unions dispersed decision-making by both decentralization and diffusion of job regulation activities. The TGWU will be the major case study in the discussion of dispersal, with supplementary evidence from the GMWU, the AUEW(E) and NUPE. UCATT will be the major focus in the discussion relating to unions who 'bucked' the trend to dispersal, with supplementary evidence from the NUM, the POEU and NUBE.

There will, however, of necessity be some overlap between the two sections, 'character' and 'structure' of job regulation, for there is a close relationship in most cases between the two. Thus in the AUEW(E), the TGWU and to a lesser extent the GMWU, the greater leadership encouragement to shop floor militancy was closely associated with the general policy of dispersal of collective bargaining. Similarly, in UCATT the undertaking in 1972 of their first major strike since 1924 was closely related to the leadership's attempt to retain and strengthen centralized control over negotiating activity. In the NUM, too, the issues of militancy and centralization were closely related in the minds of the political factions when determining policy; while in NALGO and the NUT it was the growth of militancy that generated a demand for greater control over the leadership and devolution of power to the 'grass roots'.

Concluding comments

In this chapter we have sought, first, to summarize developments since 1960 in all the major areas of change that will need to be analysed and explained in subsequent chapters; and second, to develop and explain a number of typologies that we shall subsequently employ to describe the broad character of the changes that have taken place since that time.

In the chapters that follow we shall therefore be focusing on the unions that have undergone major changes and shall be looking in more detail at the explanatory factors lying behind them, using the model outlined in Chapter 2. In each chapter detailed comparative studies are made of a small number of unions – often two or three – which have been chosen to provide contrasting or sometimes similar experiences in one of the areas of change examined. This discussion is then usually followed by a much shorter reference to changes in some 'other' unions as a means of supporting and widening the significance of the conclusions. In this way the process of analysing common trends and responses to common circumstances is made more manageable, and the processes in each union can be more easily compared one with another and the major change agents considered. In the final chapter the various changes, change agents and unions will be brought together for comparative analysis.

4 Changes in internal government

As outlined in Chapter 3, our study in this chapter of changes in internal government focuses on changes in the non-bargaining aspects of the governments of the TGWU and the AEU, or its later equivalent the AUEW Engineering Section, although reference will, where relevant, be made to developments in other unions. It was explained in the last chapter that these two unions were chosen for particular study because they stood in 1960 at the opposite extremes of the vertical and horizontal continua of government.[1] Thus an examination of their internal reactions to a changing environment and new national leadership should provide useful insights into the relative effectiveness of different government types.

The model of change, explained in Chapter 2,[2] will be used for analysing the changes in union government. It should be noted however that, in terms of the model of change, union government is significantly different from other areas of change, such as job regulation and mergers, because it appears in different guises at different levels of the model. Thus, for the purposes of this chapter union government appears as an area of change as well as part of the model's 'decision-making structures' and/or 'existing national leadership and policies'. This is because the chapter is essentially a study of how and why unions change themselves in reaction to both internal demands and the external environment.

In studying the TGWU and the AUEW(E) the chapter follows the model of change by outlining the areas of change and then considering the process and agents of change. It concludes by assessing unions' direction of change.

The TGWU

Areas of change

We shall describe the main changes in the national government of the TGWU (and the Engineers) by reference to how they altered three crucial and inter-related aspects of government – structure, procedures for decision-making, and methods of choosing leaders – between 1960 and 1975.

Structure

Between 1960 and 1975 the TGWU altered its structure in several ways. Most, if not all, of these adjustments originated in formal proposals at the 1967 BDC, which called 'upon the GEC to carefully examine the present organisational structure with a view to proposals being presented to the 1968 Rules Conference designed to still further improve and strengthen the organisational efficiency of our great Union'.[3] Following this call the Rules Conference of 1968 accepted proposals to adjust regions and trade groups and encourage the growth of district committees. Changes in existing regions and trade groups tended to affect the horizontal continuum of government. The introduction of district committees affected the vertical structure.

Changes at the regional level of government were of little consequence for national government as they merely involved a redrawing of geographic territories. Unlike the Engineers,[4] the movement of a geographic area does not, in the TGWU, give the leadership the opportunity noticeably to shift political power one way or another. Thus when in 1968 the TGWU reduced its regions from thirteen to eleven by merging its Welsh regions, returning Merseyside to the North West Region and transferring Cumberland and Westmorland to Region 8, centred on Newcastle, it had little effect on national government of the union.

On the other hand, a further administrative change which altered the TGWU's trade groups was of significance for government. In 1968 trade groups in the TGWU underwent two changes. First, as mentioned above, they were reduced in number from thirteen to eleven. The reorganization was administratively quite substantial and among other changes a Vehicle Building and Automotive Trade Group was formed. This was an important factor in later attracting the National Union of Vehicle Builders (NUVB) (see Chapter 6) to the TGWU. Second, changes were made to rule 3 clauses 6 and 7 to allow the establishment of sections, including craft sections, within a particular trade group. Rule 3 clause 6 was changed to read: 'There shall be such other groups and sections, including craft sections. . . .' This was, again, important for the future expansion of the union. It helped the union accommodate, in a largely autonomous section within the Building Trade Group, the predominantly craft-orientated National Association of Operative Plasterers (NAOP) (see Chapter 6).

However, it was in the vertical structure of government that the TGWU made its most radical change, by officially introducing a new system of district committees. District committees were both given official recognition and encouraged to grow, in numbers and activities, by the 1968 changes. The rules were changed to 'recognise the existence of district committees and provide for their extension where required'.[5] Prior to this rule change district committees were an exception to the general rule and regional trade groups were the norm. Following the rule changes the reverse was the case. This resulted in a patchwork organization with Regions 1 (London), 2 (Southern), 3 (South West) and 11 (Ireland) retaining their regional trade groups more or less intact and the other regions moving some way, or completely, to a district committee structure.

Such structural changes made the union more flexible in its form of industrial organization by creating a new category of craft sections while also decentralizing some previous issues from the regional to the district level.

Procedures for decision-making

Developments in the procedures in the TGWU that affected the horizontal and vertical continua of government fall into two categories – *de jure* and *de facto*. Since those who govern the TGWU have a high degree of discretion, many developments of significance did not involve *de jure* changes in rule.

First, the 1968 rule changes introduced a greater flexibility into national level decision-making in respect of regional and trade group boundaries. As a result of these alterations the GEC no longer needed to obtain the approval of the Rules Conference before making adjustments in these fields. After the Rules Conference of 1968, the GEC was given power to 'determine new groups and sections as required'.[6] This clearly resulted in a *de jure* increase in the discretion of the GEC at the expense of the Rules Conference. But, in effect, it increased the general secretary's discretion. For, in practice, the general secretary is the initiator of most rule changes and he no longer needed to persuade both the Rules Conference and the GEC to accept his proposed structural reforms.

Another *de jure* change, affecting rule 15 clause 1 of the TGWU's rules, again increased the discretion of the GEC and therefore further enhanced the *de facto* powers of the general secretary. This alteration to rule replaced a reference to 'assistant general secretary' by 'executive officers'. While the GEC regarded this change as bringing 'the designations more in line with current officering practice',[7] it allowed the GEC to have greater flexibility in the appointment of executive officers. The underlying principle of the change was to ensure that the GEC could appoint and designate executive officers to any special duties that the GEC thought fit; which meant again, in practice, that the general secretary could adjust his executive officer staff to suit his and the unions' requirements. For example, this new flexibility was later used to give leading national officials of merging unions acceptable and appropriate places in the TGWU's hierarchy.

The only other major development that had a significant effect on the degree of concentration or diffusion of national government was the decision by the general secretary to activate the GEC's existing right within rule to present motions to the BDC. Between 1945 and 1971 this opportunity had been used only once. On that one occasion, in 1967, the GEC successfully promoted an anti-incomes policy motion at the BDC. This was in contrast to the GEC's previous practice of either sponsoring normally negative executive policy statements or simply opposing unwelcome motions.

However, following Jones's consolidation of his position as general secretary, the GEC submitted, between 1971 and 1975 (inclusive) nineteen motions to the BDC. All these motions dealt with major issues of policy, including pensions, industrial democracy and the Social Contract. In many ways this initiatory action of the general secretary reflected his ideas of trade union leadership, which were 'Not authoritarian, not dictatorial, not being the Emperor or the boss! not paternalistic, but rather "leadership in ideas" '.[8] The activation in 1971 of the dormant GEC's right openly to promote policy motions at the BDC is thus another example of how the TGWU's general secretary can, if he so chooses, exercise an innovatory influence inside the union. It was also another instance of how, through *de facto* action, the general secretary can significantly adjust the procedure for taking decisions in the TGWU and hence increase the degree of concentration at the national level.

Second, in the case of vertical procedures for decision-making, changes were made which had an impact on the relationship between regional and national levels of government. After 1968 the influence of the regions grew as a result of the movement to decentralize administrative and financial decision-making. A large number of these decisions, such as the hiring of office workers and the buying of office equipment, etc., were passed down from Transport House staff to the regional secretaries. About the same time the regional secretaries were given increased status in other fields by the general secretary's decision to introduce them, complete with reports, to the quarterly meetings of the GEC. (Prior to this the regional secretaries very rarely, if ever, attended a GEC meeting.) Furthermore, Jones instituted regular meetings with all the regional secretaries 'to tell them the Union's policy',[9] and to float his own ideas. In this way he stimulated discussion of future policy among regional secretaries. Subsequently, and no doubt intentionally, some of the ideas floated by the general secretary at the regions reappeared at the GEC as motions originating in the regions. Thus the general secretary[10] was able to decentralize administrative and financial matters to the regions, raise the status of regional secretaries and use them as agents of future change.

These developments interacted with the formal introduction of district committees and the, not unrelated, dispersal of bargaining, to reduce the National Trade Groups secretaries' influence within the union. Bargaining issues previously dealt with by national secretaries were passed to the rapidly expanding numbers of shop stewards (see Chapter 8). Any full-time official who was hesitant or reluctant in complying with these changes in policy must have been reminded by the resignation of Keeley, a National Secretary, of the alternative course of action for those officers who would not conform with TGWU's new decentralized bargaining policy.

Thus national full-time officials, apart from the general secretary and his immediate advisers, generally experienced a decline in bargaining discretion and administrative control. In contrast the general secretary and the regional secretaries enjoyed more discretionary powers in the national and regional levels of government. There was therefore a general weakening of the traditional TGWU national bureaucracy.

Methods of choosing leaders

The formal methods of choosing the leaders of the TGWU changed very little between 1960 and 1975.[11] The general secretary continued to be elected by the total membership in a largely faction free poll, while other full-time officers were appointed. In the appointment of senior full-time officials the general secretary's view was not seriously challenged by the GEC or any group within it. Moreover,

Urwin (deputy general secretary) attended all interviewing panels, for district, regional and national officers, with two members of the Finance and General Purposes Committee. It thus appears that, if the general secretary of the TGWU takes an active interest in the promotion process, he is in a strong position to persuade the lay members of the GEC, or sub-committee, to accept his views regarding the merits of candidates for full-time office.

The numerous elections to lay positions in government are obviously not so easily influenced by the general secretary. On the other hand, neither were they consistently influenced by any organized opposition group of national importance – although absence of such opposition may not be a continuing feature of the TGWU, as the ban on Communists holding office in the union, passed in 1949,[12] was itself repealed in 1968. However, the GEC was given a new 1968 rule under which they could declare any member ineligible to hold office if the organization they owed allegiance to is 'contrary, detrimental, inconsistent or injurious to the policy and purposes of the Union'.[13]

Internal conflicts in the TGWU's elections are therefore predominantly created by industrial or local interests. Some regions, particularly Regions 1 (London) and 5 (Midlands), reflect local pressures in the political composition of their delegates to the BDCs and in elections to regional committee and GEC. However, it is the industrial sectional interest that usually dominates in elections. For instance, the GEC, which has one representative per trade group as well as regional representation, had a disproportionate number of Road Passenger Transport members in the 1950s and mid-1960s, plus an imbalance towards this trade group and the newly formed Chemical and Rubber Trade Group in the 1970s. In 1955 the Road Passenger Transport members had, by far, the largest single representation on the GEC – fourteen seats, or 35 per cent of the total. At this time they accounted for only 16 per cent of the union's total membership. The next largest single representation was the Metal and Engineering group, with seven seats or $17\frac{1}{2}$ per cent of the total. At this time they accounted for $16\frac{1}{2}$ per cent of the total union membership. In contrast, the General Workers group, which was the biggest trade group with $20\frac{1}{2}$ per cent of the total union membership had only four seats or 10 per cent of the representation on the GEC. By 1965 Road Passenger Transport was still the largest single group in the GEC but it had decreased in both representation and membership to 23 and 13 per cent respectively. Later, in 1975, this same group had been replaced as the largest single group by the Chemical and Rubber interests, which had 7.4 per cent of total membership but 21 per cent of GEC seats.

The reasons put forward, in interviews, for this disproportionate GEC representation focused on the interaction between concentration of employment, density of union membership and workplace balloting. It was said that in Passenger Transport members vote in the depots and bus garages during 'stand-down'. In Chemical and Rubber they also ballot at work. By contrast, the other industrial groups tend to work in industries where the membership is not as dense or concentrated. They did not therefore normally hold branch meetings and ballots at the workplace.

However, some regions organize the running of elections so as to prevent industrial domination. Region 1 (London), for instance, divides itself geographically into divisions for election purposes. This practice, it was claimed, prevents the London Busmen and the Ford workers, both highly unionized and concentrated groups, from wielding a disproportionate electoral influence in the region. It is another sign of the flexibility of the TGWU that this practice is by no means common in other regions.

Thus the industrial groups, who appear to have nothing more than sectional industrial axes to grind, were potentially more influential on the GEC of the TGWU prior to 1975 than any other loose collections of politically likeminded members. At no time over the period 1955–75 was there a noticeable change from industrial to political influence on the GEC. However, there was a decline in the number of Busmen's representatives and a rise in the influence of the Chemical and Rubber group on the GEC over this period.

But even assuming the Busmen were influential in 1955, with fourteen of the thirty-nine GEC seats, it is very doubtful if they or the Chemical and Rubber group, with seven and eight seats respectively, are capable of playing a crucial decision-making role on the thirty-nine-strong GEC. In contrast to the political factions in the Engineers, industrial factions within the multi-industry TGWU tended to be very limited in their influence in the period studied. It is not surprising therefore that the general secretary's unifying presence at the GEC was largely unchallenged by industrial factionalism between 1960 and 1975.

The processes and agents of change

There was in the TGWU in the 1950s and 1960s concern over the nature of the union's system of government. The TGWU's lay membership tried many times between 1950 and 1967 to gain a commitment from the national leadership through the constitutional processes to adjust the trade group structure and decentralize decision-making.[14] Over this period ninety-four motions were submitted on the question of new trade groups alone. All ninety-four motions were opposed by the TGWU's GEC and only one was carried. Similarly, numerous unsuccessful attempts were made by delegates at the BDC and Rules Conference to formally move decision-making down the union structure. For instance, in 1957 the BDC debated and rejected a motion calling for more lay representation on 'all bodies on which the Union is entitled to representation'.[15] Thus prior to 1967 the GEC, under the general secretary's guidance, prevented devolutionary and structural motions making progress through the constitutional process by either opposing them or replacing them with negative executive policy statements at the BDC.

The GEC and general secretary's formal rejections at the BDC and Rules Conferences of motions supporting government change did not, however, mean that there were no changes in government prior to 1967. Previous to Jones, general secretaries of the TGWU Deakin and Cousins, for instance, did not on behalf of the GEC merely oppose government change at the union's conferences.

Instead, they tended to make minor *de facto* concessions in order to reduce pressure for wider changes. The first general secretary, Bevin, for example, dealt with a threatened secession by the Croydon no. 2 bus lodge in 1921 with 'a firm hand but recommended the Executive to accept the claim of the London Busmen to be allowed to form a special section within the Passenger Transport Group with their own Central London Bus Committee'.[16] A number of such committees were created in other trade groups by later general secretaries in an *ad hoc* response to demands for more far-reaching changes in government and structure.

Other aspects of government were also changed prior to 1967 by pressures which did not find expression through the union's formal constitutional channels. Change agents that bypassed the 'established leadership', for instance productivity deals (see Chapter 7), also shifted the TGWU's bargaining decision-making downwards. Inquiries such as that of Scamp[17] in the Liverpool docks also further affected the full-time officials'/shop stewards' relations by again reducing the importance of national decision-making and consequently the TGWU's National Trade Group secretary's role in the industry.

Prior to 1967, therefore, external devolutionary pressures altered the TGWU's full-time official/shop steward relations without being processed through the government structure via the 'national leadership'. Thus, despite the GEC's and general secretaries' attempts to manage government change in a piecemeal manner, the internal government relationships between lay and full-time officials were changed in the bargaining field by movements in the external environment. These developments in turn promoted direct pressures from shop stewards – for example, at Ford's and in the docks[18] – for *de jure* recognition of their newly found power.

Generally, however, flexibility of government and discretion in decision-making allowed the GEC and the general secretary to accommodate such pressures by *ad hoc* adjustments. Threats of breakaways and the formation of minor unofficial movements were thus prone to produce marginal rather than major alterations in government. For instance, attempts to form breakaway unions and promote anti-TGWU strikes in the docks were stifled largely because the TGWU made local government concessions to the dissatisfied shop stewards.[19] Thus although the non-constitutional pressure for change developed momentum in the 1960s the TGWU remained relatively unchanged nationally until 1967.

It was change sponsored by the national leadership itself that radically altered the nature of the TGWU's system of government. The fact that the 1967, 1968 and 1969 *de jure* government changes happened as Jones rose to power within the union was not coincidental. Whereas the previous general secretary, Cousins, left the machinery of government largely untouched during his term of active leadership, apart from marginally reducing national officers' role in government, Jones changed it quite markedly in the following decade. It was thus in voting overwhelmingly for Jones[20] for general secretary in 1968, a position more or less guaranteed him by Cousins's support, that the membership indirectly changed the government of their union.

However, Jones's rise to national influence in the TGWU started much earlier than 1968. In 1963 a position of importance dealing with major internal government and administrative problems was created for him in the head office by Cousins. It was from this position that he developed his influence within the union and built up his extensive network of supporters and contacts. As Cousins's chosen successor, Jones was in a good position to inherit the mood of change generated in the union by his predecessor's left-wing stance over such issues as incomes policy and unilateral disarmament. The new left-wing image and the external developments that had already *de facto* decentralized some aspects of government provided an atmosphere within the TGWU quite amenable to extensive government change.

Hence Jones was very well placed both to encourage further proposals for change from branches and regions, and to sponsor changes of his own through the national leadership.

In fact, as far as changes in internal government were concerned, Jones became a major change agent; he used the GEC to sponsor motions at the BDC, introduce regional secretaries to the GEC, decentralized administrative decisions to the regions and so on. In these activities he was particularly ably supported by his assistant, later deputy general secretary, Urwin. Therefore, in order to understand why radical government changes took place in the TGWU at this time it is necessary to understand the leadership's reasons for promoting change.

Jones's drive for national change in the TGWU stemmed from the belief that democracy as a good to be pursued generally, could within the TGWU be advanced by devolutionary policies. He was committed to a 'two-pronged attack. On the one hand there is the move towards the decentralisation and democratisation of decision-making within the Union itself while on the other there is an extension and a widening of the range of subjects being opened up for joint agreement'.[21] This thesis was itself greatly influenced by his previous experience as regional secretary in Region 5 (Midlands).

Region 5 was ideal testing ground for the system of government later practised nationally by Jones. It was, and is, dominated by engineering and vehicle building industries, both of which had long histories of local negotiation and shop steward involvement in negotiations. As Region 5 secretary under a sympathetic general secretary, Jones used his powers to involve the TGWU's shop stewards in decision-making and to encourage the development of district committees. Moreover, in Region 5 he could also assess the effectiveness of such changes in an area where the TGWU, the NUVB and the AEU all pursued competitively aggressive recruiting policies. In the absence of any well organized and hence influential opposition or established faction Jones thus built for himself in Region 5 a populist base by making many of the changes that the lay activists desired. This was, of course, a policy that he later successfully adapted to suit the TGWU's national level of politics.

There were, however, two other major benefits that accrued from Region 5 style of government which influenced Jones: growth and economy. Jones was convinced that 'There is no doubt that membership tends to grow and be consolidated where we develop a good system of local representation based on shop stewards or their equivalent'.[22] It is, of course, difficult to offer conclusive evidence of growth through dispersal (see Chapter 5), but Jones's belief that there was such a correlation was no doubt again influenced by his experience in Region 5, which, with its policy of dispersal, easily outstripped any other region's rate of growth (see Table 8).

Lastly, Jones's experience also showed that the development of shop steward organizations assisted economy. Region 5 consistently maintained a higher ratio of members to full-time officials than any other region (see Chapter 8). Indeed, it had a ratio of members to officials (5471 to 1) twice that of some other regions. Dispersal in Region 5 was therefore seen to be both a more efficient and a cheaper way of boosting membership. Instead of the union paying for more, but less efficient and expensive, full-time officials, the employer could pay for more efficient and cheaper shop stewards.

But in addition to the proven gains made in Region 5 from such policies Jones was also aware of the growth advantage to be gained in the national merger field from changes in the TGWU's trade groups and general devolutionary policy (see Chapter 5). The additional discretion given to the national leadership in altering trade group boundaries was, for instance, important in enabling the TGWU's general secretary to agree to a merger with the NUVB,[23] a union with which he had had major involvement in the vehicle industry in Region 5. Similarly the whole process of dispersal helped the merger with the Chemical Workers Union (CWU). Their general secretary stated that his union found a merger with the TGWU appealing because 'The TGWU had become increasingly accountable to its rank and file. . .',[24] a relationship that 'also characterized the CWU'.[25] Hence the government changes also helped growth by oiling the merger process.

Table 8 *Percentage change in TGWU regional membership, 1950–65*

Region	Change
1	+6.5
2	+26.4
3	+24.6
4	−12.4
5	+58.5
6	+6.8
7	+10.2
8	+20.3
9	+6.8
10	+25.7
11	+14.7

Jones in national office had thus several reasons for thinking that it would be advantageous to run the TGWU nationally on the same lines as Region 5. It would not only promote the altruistic goal of democracy, but it would also strengthen the general secretary's populist base and enable the TGWU to grow faster and be run more economically. Furthermore, with other ex-Region 5 officials – Urwin and Moss Evans – promoted to the head office, he was ably supported in these activities.

By 1968, therefore, the new national full-time officer leadership of the TGWU had clear ideas of how they wished to reform the national government of the union. By placing the weight of their leadership, and particularly that of the general secretary, behind proposals for decentralization and diffusion, they virtually guaranteed the successful passage of pro-dispersal motions at the union's conferences. The execution of the policy decisions, sometimes a problem in the diffused Engineers Union, also created little difficulty in the TGWU. In the absence of a powerful opposition faction there were no groups in the TGWU capable of rejecting a system of government legitimized by the BDC and desired by the general secretary. Furthermore, the general secretary's control of the union's internal communications system enabled him to propagate his philosophy throughout the union. Jones, for instance, used the *Record*, the TGWU's journal, and other union publications to communicate directly with the membership. Union pamphlets including the *Union in Action* series and *Trade Unionism in the Seventies* and *The Right to Participate* by Jones, *Plant and Productivity Bargaining* by Urwin and the *Shop Stewards Handbook* were used, among others, to put the message over to the union's activists. The general secretary did not need to rely therefore on the local full-time officials, whose power he was reducing, for proselytizing his cause.

To summarize, the TGWU's national leadership could, and did in the years before 1967, successfully resist attempts radically to reshape the union's traditionally highly centralized and concentrated form of government. Pressures for change were, in this period, either accommodated by *ad hoc* and *de facto* adjustments, or were opposed. But despite the largely negative responses of the national leadership to constitutionally processed appeals for change, some changes did take place, through external *de facto* developments which bypassed the official processes of government. It was not, however, until the national leadership, therefore, conditioned by previous experience and with clear ideas underwent radical *de jure* alterations. It was only when the new general secretary Jones and his confidants from Region 5 assumed power and sponsored change from the position of national leadership that the *de jure* changes were successfully processed. The membership's choice of leadership in the TGWU was thus more consequential for change in the system of government than their previous efforts to process formal proposals for governmental change. It was the new national leadership, therefore, conditioned by the previous experience and with clear ideas about the changes it wished to promote, that became the major change agent affecting the TGWU's system of government.

The AUEW(E)

Areas of change

Structure

The only major structural changes affecting the government of the Engineers arose from the amalgamation of 1971 (see Chapter 6), when the vertical structure of the AEU was given a new top tier of decision-making. The bodies added to the traditional structure were the Joint Conference and the Joint National Executive Council. The annual Joint Conference is composed of 52 Engineering Section, 7 Foundry, 7 TASS and 3 Construction delegates. The president has, by rule, a casting vote. The Joint National Executive is 13 strong. It includes the president and 7 executive councillors of the Engineers plus 2 members from the Foundry, 2 members from TASS and 1 from the Construction sections. The general secretary of the Engineers acts as general secretary to the whole union. The two new joint bodies thus provide an umbrella organization for the rest of the Union. There was, however, no tradition of strong central organization in any of the larger merging unions which could be taken as a new model for the AUEW. The merger was, therefore, dominated by three highly diffused decision-makers, each of which had and has either a high degree of factionalism or an unofficial two-party system[26] in operation. The AUEW thus went some way towards forming an industrial engineering union with four separate trade groups. It did not however provide the strong counter-poise, or a common national identity, which in the TGWU cements the trade groups into a unitary structure. Indeed, it was stated in the AUEW's 'Instrument of Amalgamation' that 'where there is conflict between ... Rules ... the Rules of that Section shall prevail'. The AUEW was therefore given a federated rather than a unitary structure.

In order to gain the minor unions' agreement to merge, the Engineers accepted disproportionate representation on the two new joint bodies unfavourable to itself. Each of the Engineering Section delegates to the 1971 Joint Conference represented some 23,120 members, and yet the TASS delegate was representing 15,060 members and the other two sections delegates some 9250 members each. If the AUEW Joint Conference had decided controversial issues according to some industrial or craft preference, the proportional imbalance between the sections might not have been a matter of some controversy. But motions at the Joint Conference are reserved by rule for 'issues which affect more than one section ....'[27] Moreover, such decisions are binding on all sections of the union. Thus, at a time when general political issues[28] were of growing importance, a division of issues on general/industrial lines was bound to take from the sections and place at the disposal of the new bodies questions, for instance, on incomes policy and the Social Contract, which had direct effects on sectional wage claims. Furthermore, the factions and unofficial parties were, because of their political nature, able to combine across sections on such general issues. The proportional imbalance, in fact, interacted temporarily with the political divisions to prevent the right-wing majority on the Engineers' delegation (the Moderates)[29] from determining joint policy. For instance, in 1975 thirty of the Engineers' fifty-two delegates voted for the Moderates' proposals and supported the Social Contract at the Joint National Conference. Unfortunately for this moderate contingent, TASS (7), Foundry (7) and Construction (3) delegates all voted against the Social Contract and thus, with the twenty-two dissident Engineers, gave the left's (the Progressives') anti-Social Contract lobby a majority. The Foundry delegates had on this occasion been mandated by their own earlier sectional annual conference to vote against the Social Contract by the casting vote of the chairman.[30]

In taking this mandatory action the Foundry Section set a precedent, the advantages of which were not overlooked by the Engineers' right wing.[31] In 1976 they secured a 29–22 vote at the Engineers' NC in favour of the Social Contract and then mandated all fifty-two delegates to vote accordingly at the later Joint Conference. The Moderates then carried, by use of the mandated vote, a 36–0 majority at the Joint Conference in favour of the Social Contract. However, the motion was passed without opposition purely because of mass protest abstentions by the left and their supporters.

The Joint EC is of less political significance for government of the Engineering Section than the Joint Conference, although there are regular meetings of the Joint Executive which discuss matters of common interest. These matters include items as diverse as the Industrial Relations Act and the union's diaries. But the long-running problem of how to rationalize the existing federated structure of the AUEW dominated much of the Joint Executive's time. On each occasion when proposals to further cement the loose links between the four sections have been presented to the NC of the Engineers (see pages 113–14 below) they have been consistently and successfully rejected by supporters of the right who feared that the left's position inside the AUEW would be enhanced by the Joint EC-sponsored proposals. The inability of the Joint Executive to gain acceptance for these views again emphasizes the degree of diffusion of power in the union.

Therefore the two new national bodies changed very little of substance in the national system of government of the Engineers. The unofficial party and factional organizations prevented the structural additions from fundamentally altering the process of decision-making in the Engineers. Rule changes in the Engineers, even when they involve the creation of two sovereign bodies, are of no great consequence for decision-making if the majority party in the Engineering Section can find some means of maintaining the internal political *status quo*.

However, at the district and divisional levels minor rule changes, which did not seek to add to, or subtract from, the national level of government, did have an effect on this higher level of government. On the face of it these low-level changes were intended to rationalize the local administration to meet an increase in membership and deal with related servicing problems. But because of the unofficial party system each such structural adjustment was perused for political advantage. Whether or not the boundary changes were really motivated by administrative or political reasons is not clear, but they are worthy of a mention because they highlight both the growing role of the unofficial parties in union government in the 1970s and the way in which external legal processes can impinge on decisions to change the structure of the Engineers.

In 1975 the EC recommended, as it had in previous years, that the Rules Revision meeting move districts between different divisional officer divisions. It proposed, first, the movement of Scunthorpe District[32] from Division 13 to Division 12. This was accepted by the narrow and politically divided 27–25 vote at the 1975 Rules Revision meeting. The same meeting agreed to the movement of Banbury District[33] from EC4 to EC5 Division. In both cases the right found ground for complaining that the left were aiming to reduce the Moderates' influence in elections by administrative decisions.

The Banbury District case in particular shows how internal political strife can develop in the Engineers over seemingly innocent administrative adjustments. It also provides a stark contrast with the comments made above on similar administrative boundary changes in the TGWU. The Banbury District saga began innocuously enough in 1975, when the Rules Revision meeting accepted an EC recommendation to transfer Banbury from EC4 to EC5 Division. This alteration to rule was to be operative on 1 January 1976 and was part of the decision to form a new Milton Keynes District. However in 1975 there was an election in EC4 for the Executive; R. Wright, the sitting left-wing member, was opposed by T. Duffy, a Moderate of the right. A victory for Moderates in this election would have altered the political power balance on the EC. It was also believed, mainly because of its past voting record, that Banbury District would cast a substantial vote for the right's candidate. According to the NC decision Banbury was in a position to vote in the EC4 election in October 1975, despite the fact that from January 1976 it would be in the neighbouring EC5 Division. Clearly, it could be argued that this was an administrative anomaly. Yet equally obviously it could be argued that to stop Banbury voting would be both against the express wishes of the sovereign NC and moreover a politically motivated act. At this point the seemingly straightforward administrative decision became the property of the Engineers' unofficial parties.

The EC excluded Banbury from the EC4 election by a narrow margin. This decision was subsequently overturned at a further EC meeting by a 3–2 vote.[34] Finally, a procedural ploy to prevent Banbury voting in the EC4 election was produced by the maverick left-winger on the EC, R. Birch. Somewhat ironically, this rather tortuous ploy was advanced by the proposer to 'avoid argument, legal or otherwise. . .'.[35] It consisted of the suggestion that, as Banbury was to vote in the election, they should also be allowed to nominate a candidate to stand in the election. But in order to allow Banbury to nominate the actual date of the election would have to be deferred until the following March. Of course, by March Banbury, fortunately or unfortunately, depending on the EC members' politics, would have been transferred out of the division and hence unable to vote in the election in question. *Thus the decision to give Banbury the right to nominate in practice prevented Banbury from voting.*

Not surprisingly this convoluted decision led to the Moderate, Duffy, questioning its legality in the High Court. The High Court subsequently prevented the AUEW Engineering Section from deferring the election, thus allowing Banbury to vote. In the election Duffy unseated the sitting member, Wright, from the EC4 position by 45,469 to 20,685 votes. No doubt Duffy benefited from the adverse publicity that Wright received at the hands of the press as a result of the legal action. Thus in the 1970s the development of the Engineers' unofficial party system brought into the political arena questions of an administrative nature.

Procedures for decision-making

Except for the addition of the two joint bodies and the boundary changes commented on above, there were no other rule changes of consequence that affected procedures of decision-making in the Engineers between 1960 and 1975. As noted above the introduction of a Joint National Conference, and to a lesser extent the Joint Executive, led to general issues being taken vertically a stage higher through the joint bodies. At the same level sectional interests remained within the prerogative of sectional committees. In practice the sections' internal factions and unofficial parties sought to manipulate the dichotomy between sectional and joint bodies to their own political advantage.

The left in the Engineering Section, usually in the minority at NC level, attempted to pass politically contentious questions of a general nature from the NC to the floor of the Joint Conference where, with left-wing TASS and Construction support, they had a better chance of a majority. Likewise the right in the Engineers tried to place similar questions before first the NC and then the Joint Conference. By doing this the right hoped to use their majority on the NC to counteract the political advantage of the left at Joint Conference level through the mandating process.

In the decision-making process therefore control of the NC's Standing Orders Committee became an even more tactically important political asset than before, for it was this body that largely determined whether controversial political motions would go before a Joint Conference, biased towards the left, or an NC, biased towards the right. For instance, in 1976 Labour loyalists wanted to place the Social Contract on the NC's agenda. They wished to do this in order to create the opportunity to mandate[36] the NC's delegates to vote in accord with Engineering Section's NC policy at the later Joint Conference of the AUEW. If the Labour group gained a majority at the NC, which was highly likely, they could then gain a majority at the Joint Conference by casting all fifty-two mandated votes for the Social Contract. As things turned out, the manner of deciding the composition of the Standing Orders Committee in 1976 was rather farcical. It hinged, finally, on the toss of a coin after the delegates tied 26–26 in the vote for the final fifth place between two of the best known proponents of the two parties' causes, J. Reid of the left and J. Wheatley of the right. Reid won the toss, but fortunately for the Moderates they already had majority support on the

Standing Orders Committee. The Social Contract was hence placed on the 1976 agenda and subsequently supported by the NC and, later, the Joint Conference (see pages 101–2 above).

Outside of rule changes, the increased activity of the two unofficial parties in the shadow procedures and meetings was the major new influence on the procedure for decision-making between 1960 and 1976. The perusal of every decision-making process by the parties, for party advantage, restricted even further the already limited discretionary aspects of government in the Engineers. Individual and group discretion in politically contentious decision-making areas had to be seen to be exercised under rule. The constitutionally prescribed checks and balances on executive power were fully enforced. A toss of an apolitical coin was therefore preferable to the politically biased president's casting vote.[37]

Methods of choosing leaders

Two changes affecting the Engineers' method of choosing leaders are worthy of examination: first, the *de facto* growth of unofficial party activity; second, the related change to postal balloting in 1972. As unofficial party activities are outside of rule, they have to be explored by reference to both unofficial and official sources of information.[38] Material gathered from these sources will be used to assess the parties' influences on the union's methods of choosing leaders. This will be done by examining full-time officer elections in general and two major left-wing gains in particular.

The first point to note is that any ambitious member of the Engineers seeking full-time office is pressured by the highly competitive electoral system of the union to seek electoral allies. Electoral pressure then combines with an internal ideological left–right division to produce a two-party system. While it is not clear when this two-party system developed, it can be stated with confidence that the left or Progressives started seriously to threaten the *status quo* (that is, the right or Moderates)[39] in the 1960s. In 1959 the right were in a position to agree with 'IRIS' that 'Communists in the . . . AEU have had some severe setbacks in the last couple of years. Now after the defeat of L. Ambrose, the only Communist on the EC is Claude Berridge, he must find it very lonely![40] Out of eleven positions[41] of major national importance in 1960, the right had sympathizers in nine of them and the left in two. By 1973 this situation had altered quite radically. In 1973 the Progressives had some six supporters in these same positions while only five favoured the right. Moreover, one or two of these members were not consistent in their voting. By 1978, however, following the introduction of postal ballots in 1972, the right had restored their supremacy on the Executive and regained the presidency. It was thus during the period 1960–72 that the left-wing Progressives made major electoral gains.

It is possible to identify the success and failure of the Progressives in elections in this period by comparing the information given in unofficial election literature regarding favoured left-wing candidates with the candidates' actual performance in elections. For despite a rule that proscribes the publication of election material,[42] other than the official election address, a number of papers that support the parties' favoured candidates circulate widely within the union. For instance, in the 1960s and early 1970s the 'Voice of the Unions' and 'Engineering Voice' fulfilled this purpose for the Progressives, while 'IRIS' and 'Engineering News and Views',[43] among others, did the same for the Moderates. For the early 1960s, however, 'IRIS' is probably the most reliable source of printed information on both parties. It is certainly the most comprehensive.

A comparison can be made between unofficially favoured candidates and those reaching the second ballot for forty-five elections drawn from the periods 1961–64, 1966–67 and 1971–74. These elections included contests for 2 presidents, 5 general and assistant general secretaries, 4 executive councillors, 11 national organizers, 5 regional organizers, 11 divisional and assistant divisional organizers and 7 district secretaries.

Progressives' nominees reached the second ballot 43 times (96 per cent) and the Moderates' nominee 35 times (78 per cent). There were, on average, 8 candidates in each election. The lower success rate of the right in reaching the second ballot did not, however, signify complete failure on their part in all such elections; for unlike the left, who rarely had more than one supporter in the field, the right often adopted the remaining non-left finalist in the second ballot if their first choice was defeated on the first vote.[44] For instance, in 1962 two national organizer elections ran to a second ballot and in both elections the right's original nominees[45] were eliminated on the first ballot. However, the Moderates switched their vote to the non-progressive in the final ballots. A general sample therefore shows some signs of successful and consistent support for candidates across a wide spectrum of full-time officer positions.

An examination of national elections only[46] between 1962 and 1972 gives further evidence of party activity. Using the same technique of comparing unofficial tickets of favoured party candidates with election results, two distinct national patterns emerge prior to the introduction of postal ballots in 1972.

In those national seats where the incumbent sought re-election under branch ballots both unofficial parties, with one exception, held their positions. On average in these seats in the second ballot the left polled 61.9 per cent fighting nine elections and the right 62.2 per cent fighting seven elections. In contrast, the elections for vacant national positions produced a quite different pattern in the second ballot, as shown below in Table 9.

The year 1962 appears to be an exception to the rest of the table, possibly because the right's favoured nominee and other sympathetic candidates were defeated in the first round. In other elections the electorate were offered a fairly clear choice between candidates. Thus, excluding the exceptional 1962 election, the rest of the figures show a remarkably consistent voting pattern favouring the established right-wing leadership – that is, until the turning point in late 1967, when Hugh Scanlon won the presidential election.

It can be concluded, therefore, regarding national full-time officer elections, that under the branch ballot system of voting between 1960 and 1972 the two

Table 9 *Percentage of votes cast in elections for vacant positions involving the total membership of the AUEW(E)*

	Positions	The right's or moderates' preferred candidates	The left's or progressives' preferred candidates
		%	%
1962	NO	(39.9)	60.1
1962	AGS	64.5	35.5
1962	NO	61.0	39.0
1964	GS	57.0	43.0
1965	AGS	57.0	43.0
1967	NO	58.0	42.0
1967	NO	59.5	40.5
1967	NO	59.2	40.8
1967	President	47.6	52.4
1968	NO	49.1	50.9
1970	NO	39.0	61.0

unofficial parties consistently contested second ballots. They thus extensively influenced the method of choosing the leaders within the Engineers by offering the union's electorate a right-left choice in the final stage of national elections. In contests involving sitting national candidates neither party had much chance of removing the incumbent; however, in elections for vacant positions the opposition – the left – did start to win seats towards the end of 1967.

At the same time as the party balance shifted among the national full-time officials, the lay NC moved in the same left-wing direction. It is not possible, however. to assess this movement in the same 'turning point' manner as that found in 1967 for full-time officials (see Table 9 above). Unfortunately the NC's annual and indirect elections, that is branch to district to division and finally to the NC, do not lend themselves to a similar kind of analysis. Political movements are also difficult to assess on the NC because of their volatility. Both these features lead to a lack of electoral information regarding, for instance, changes in individual districts' political allegiances. But it is possible to show a growing left influence at the NC by reference to the NC's voting figures on politically contro-versial issues. For instance, in 1960 the right of Moderates had a large majority at the NC. In that year, for example, the right-wing president, Carron, included in his address[47] an attack on the Communist Party and the unofficial shop steward movement. The hard-line left could muster only some 20 of the 52 NC votes on controversial issues. By 1965 and the split over the previous year's 'package deal' with the EEF, the delegates were splitting on approximately the same 20–32 basis. And in 1968 the new Progressive president failed to get the NC, with a right majority, to support a strike call over that year's wage claim. It was thus not until the early 1970s that the Progressives radically narrowed the political gap on the NC. Indeed, on some issues in 1972 and 1973 the left did, with the help of one or two floating votes, carry a majority. However, the Progressives did not dominate the NC at this time. For instance, Moderates successfully resisted left-sponsored attempts to dispense with postal ballots and rationalize the structure of the newly formed amalgamated union – both of these rearguard actions being seen by the right as successfully preventing the left from further undermining their power within the Engineers' system of government.

This brings us to an examination of the influence of party organization on the general movement towards the left. Intense political activity surrounded a number of national elections in the mid 1960s leading up to the presidential election in 1967. Following the launching of the 'Voice of the Unions' newspaper in 1963 various meetings, national and regional, were held to publicize and propagate the cause of the left. In 1966 the *AEU Journal*, controlled by the established leadership dominated by the right, ran a full front page and several columns inside with the heading, 'Members be Vigilant'.[48] This article warned against the 'Agitation in the Engineering industry' promoted by 'Voice' publications and their left-wing supporters. The journal then went on to report that the Committee of the Progressives, at a meeting in Birmingham on 14 June 1966, had recommended Hugh Scanlon for the presidency. E. Roberts, Engineers' AGS, further urged members at this meeting to 'analyse the position of union branches in their area and to send men to organise where they lack support'.[49] The intention was that branches with a potentially high poll should be identified and their members persuaded to register a high vote for the left's candidates. Many of those interviewed referred to the effectiveness of the Progressives' campaign in such branches and to the key role high-polling branches played in the presidential and an EC election in Division 5. An 'IRIS' news survey of February 1968 commented at some length on the impact that 'a handful of branches'[50] could have on an election. In the crucial presidential[51] election of 1967 and the vacant EC5 election of 1970 the left won both potitions from the established moderate leadership, even though a majority of those branches that polled average[52] or below-average votes in the British Isles in the two elections gave a majority to the right. This was because the relatively small number of higher polling branches that tended to favour the left played a disproportionate and decisive role in determining the outcome of both the presidential and EC5 elections. Indeed, the 'high' polling branches (over 100 votes cast) that the left's supporters had previously been expressly urged to organize had the most pronounced and disproportionate effect on the elections. For instance, in the presidential election the 9 per cent of 'high' polling branches produced 25 per cent of the total vote and in the EC5 election the 12 per cent 'high' polling branches polled 38 per cent of the total vote. This vote divided in both elections in the Progressives' favour – that is, 56–44 per cent in the presidential and 63–37 per cent in the EC5 election. Moreover, in the EC5 election the left gained 4002 votes from the 12 per cent of high polling branches, while they managed to raise only 2189 votes from the 64 per cent of below-average and average polling branches. In fact, the left in the EC5 election polled the greater part of the above-mentioned

4002 votes in the twenty-seven high polling branches that showed them a preference. Thus the left won both the presidential and the EC5 elections in a small minority of higher polling branches.

A further point of some interest is the geographic distribution of both the vote and the high polling areas in the presidential election. Once again, a few areas had a disproportionate effect on the election. For instance, the left carried a majority in only nine of the union's twenty-six divisional officer divisions. But among these nine were four of the five highest polling divisions in the union, including Manchester, where there was a turnout of 26 per cent, compared with a national average of 11 per cent.

Thus the parties not only placed their candidates into the second ballot, but they also organized a significant part of the vote in the final stage of the election. For while general interest and concern for economic recovery may have raised the national average turnout in the presidential election from $6\frac{1}{2}$ to 11 per cent it is highly unlikely that it could have produced the specific and politically biased voting in the 'high' polling branches and divisions. On the other hand, unofficial party organization of shop stewards and branch officials in potentially high polling branches, as openly prescribed by the left, would have produced a block of politically favourable branch votes as identified above.

Hence by the late 1960s and early 1970s unofficial party organization was influencing and further diffusing the union's method of choosing leaders. Under the branch ballot system the established leadership's or right's chosen or adopted candidate for vacant national seats was successfully challenged by the opposition, or the left's, favoured nominee. The introduction of postal ballots, however, helped swing the political pendulum back in favour of the right.

Postal ballots were introduced in 1972 at the instigation of the lay Rules Revision Committee, despite some full-time official opposition. This change in electoral rule is of significance mainly because it immediately disturbed the parties' organizational activities and hence their electoral fortunes. Broadly, it can be said to have favoured the right, whose supporters sponsored the change, and adversely affected the Progressives, whose followers opposed its introduction.

Postal ballots helped the right by widening the electorate just when the Progressives' party machine was successfully concentrating its activities in a few medium and high polling branches, as described above. With a low national turnout, usually between 6 and 11 per cent, the majority of high polling branches could, if casting votes consistently for one of the parties' candidates, virtually win elections. The postal ballots broke this relationship. At a stroke, they increased the average turnout to between 22 and 50 per cent[53] of the electorate. Furthermore, they shifted the place of voting away from the branch and into the home, where the unofficial parties could not so easily produce voting patterns similar to those that occurred in high polling branches under branch ballots.

The highly developed branch voting machine on the left was thus reduced in effectiveness overnight by the introduction of postal ballots. The left's electoral machine, built around a comparatively small number of key branches, was not an efficient vehicle for mobilizing an electorate four times its previous size, voting in highly fragmented places.

By 1978, following some five and a half years of postal balloting, the Moderates had restored their hold on a number of key positions in the Engineers, with significant victories in elections for national office, e.g. the EC, and the presidency, in which the right, in T. Duffy, defeated the left, in R. Wright. Even incumbents, who as shown above had previously had near security of tenure, were under postal ballots far more prone to defeat, particularly if they were known Progressives. For instance, such left-wing incumbents as L. Dixon, EC, R. Wright, EC, J. Bromley, NO, B. Painter, DS Manchester, P. Farrelly, DO23 and E. Montgomery, DS Barrow and Kendal suffered defeats that would have been unthinkable under branch ballot. In no case was a leading right-wing incumbent beaten in a postal ballot. It may be of course that between 1972 and 1978 the political environment was more conducive to the Moderates' victories than was the 1967–71 period. This, however, appears doubtful. For the environment that was said to favour the left in the late 1960s bears many resemblances to the situation favouring the resurgent right between 1974 and 1978. It is thus unclear how, if at all, rising inflation, narrowing differentials and higher unemployment affects the right and left within the union under a Labour government. It can be stated with some confidence however that in the period examined the environment was of secondary influence compared with the interaction between the activities of the two unofficial parties and the method of voting.

We can therefore conclude that the introduction of postal ballots contributed quite significantly to the changing fortunes of the Engineers' unofficial parties. Moreover, this rule change showed that *de jure* institutional alterations of some consequence for government can be made in the Engineers, provided that, of course, one of the parties has the numbers and ability to exploit the complex rule-making process. But the very introduction of postal ballots also emphasizes the real diffusion of power within the Engineers between the lay NC and the full-time EC. The dominant party on the lay NC, in this case the right, used its position to contain, and reverse, the Progressives' inroads on the full-time EC by changing the rules under which the full-time officials were chosen. A combination of unofficial party activity and the institutionalized system of checks and balances hence keeps the Engineers as highly diffused as its formal system intends.

The processes and agents of change

Unlike the TGWU, the Engineers' national leadership and lay activists broadly accepted that the union's system of government was appropriate to their needs. Even questions regarding the form of the government of the new amalgamated union (see Chapter 6) were more concerned with details of sectional representation than with general views about the nature of government itself. The leadership's and lay activists' major concerns were thus more often with who, and which internal unofficial organization, exercised most influence within the existing system than with radically changing that system.

Developments in the Engineers thus cannot be understood by reference to some declared overall policy or grand strategy of an individual, as in the case of the TGWU. In order to be appreciated, they must be placed within the internal political context and the role of the opposing groups or parties in the processes of change.

In the Engineers' system of government members' formal constitutional motions are processed through the various levels of vertical decision-making until finally decided by either of the two main legislating bodies – the lay NC or the lay Rules Revision[54] meeting. After decisions are taken at this level the EC carry out the policy decisions. This is, of course, a simple description of government, which suggests that the Engineers are somewhat similar to the TGWU and most other unions. There is, however, both constitutionally and in practice, a much clearer division between the legislative and executive decision-making roles in the Engineers than is found in most other unions. Moreover, this distinction is in practice strengthened, like most other checks and balances, by the parties' extra-constitutional activities. By examining one of the changes in methods of choosing leaders, the introduction of the postal ballot, this important and continuing aspect of the Engineers' system of government can be further explored.

The political situation within the Engineers, at the time of the postal ballot saga, was of course very much dominated by the left's election successes. However, these successes were somewhat limited by the left's inability to dominate the lay NC. As the lay NC was indirectly elected, by a different process and for different constituencies to that of the Executive, the left's organizational machine was not able to exploit its full-time officer election tactics in that field. Thus, although the left influenced the political composition of the Executive, it was by no means as successful in influencing the legislature. So when the Moderates or right promoted a proposal in the lay legislative channel for postal ballots to be used in full-time officer elections, the left were faced with a difficult problem.

The arguments advanced by the Moderates in favour of the postal ballot were quite wide-ranging. They were broadly concerned with how external developments had *de facto* reduced the role of, and thus the attendance at, the branch. Indeed, 'IRIS' later produced figures to show that branch attendance had dropped from 8.6 per cent in 1952 to 5.4 per cent in 1972.[55] It was therefore argued that voting should be taken to the members, since the members no longer came to the branch. But, notwithstanding these arguments, postal ballots were also the product of the Moderates' defensive retaliatory action against the Progressives' recent electoral successes.

The Rules Revision meeting[56] in 1970 passed the postal ballot motion by the narrowest of margins, 26–25 with one abstention. An examination of the delegates' voting[57] reveals that the division was largely a political one between the Moderates' and the Progressives' supporters. However, the non-voting Executive, composed of full-time officials including some sympathetic to the Moderates, considered the cost and administrative problems of organizing an electoral roll prohibitive, despite the theoretical political attraction of the scheme. The EC therefore exercised their right to ask a recalled Rules Revision meeting, in 1971, to repeal the 1970 decision. But the Rules Revision meeting again voted for postal ballots, this time by 27–25. This decision did not finish the arguments regarding the postal ballots, however, although the legislature had by now firmly stamped their authority on the proposal.

At this point the new balloting system was implemented but the arguments continued, and the Engineers' Rules Revision meeting in May 1975 was called on again to discuss the question, and again it rejected a move to end postal ballots by a 27–25 vote. The political build-up to this vote started at least as early as February 1975, when the national press carried reports of 'Left-wing calls for the abolition of postal balloting'.[58] At the same time unofficial circulars supporting the Moderates were warning subscribers that the left were going to campaign against the postal ballot.[59] By May the Progressives had further reasons for opposing the postal ballots: they had by then heard the results of the previous October elections.[60] Moreover, they expected more bad news when the results of the March elections were declared. The initial 27–25 vote against removing postal ballots, in which the small number of independents had voted with the Moderates, was thus a major blow to the Progressives' hopes of maintaining their now waning and tentative hold on the EC.

The 1975 27–25 vote for the retention of postal ballots was however only the start of a whole series of votes on the issue at that year's Rules Revision meeting. Following a complaint, the EC considered the credentials of two delegates. It then voted on the question of the delegates' legitimacy and registered a politically divided 3–3 vote. The president's casting vote was then used to disqualify two pro-postal ballot delegates. The vote on the question of postal ballots was then re-taken by the Rules Revision Committee, and not surprisingly tied at 25–25. However, the full-time president and executive official then used another 'casting vote' at the lay NC to carry the motion against postal ballots.

At this point one of the disqualified delegates, following the Engineers' own constitutional process, appealed unsuccessfully to the EC against their previous decision. The disqualified delegate could then have approached the union's own lay Final Appeal Court (FAC) for restitution of his NC place. However, at this time the FAC was also generally considered to be biased towards the left. It had, in fact, recently reinstated a defeated left-wing official to a position held by a more moderately inclined member of the Engineers.[61] (This decision of the FAC was later overturned by the High Court.)[62] The moderate NC delegate could not therefore expect a politically unbiased, or favourably biased, judgement from the FAC. The disqualified delegate thus left the constitutional processes of the Engineers and took the case to the High Court. The rights of the disqualified delegates were finally settled, and the postal ballot consequently saved, by the intervention of Mr Justice Walton, who came to the conclusion that the disqualified delegates' 'credentials were unimpeachable and that the purported act of the National Committee (NC) in revising the voting figures on the proposal to delete the postal ballot rule . . . was totally null and void'.[63] Furthermore, it was also ruled that the president did not have a casting vote at the NC.

Executive power in the Engineers was thus even more firmly delineated by the saga of the postal ballot and the High Court ruling. The success of the left opposition party, in gaining a tentative control of the EC, did not allow them to reshape the government of the union. There was neither sufficient constitutional flexibility nor *de facto* discretion in executive government to allow a narrow left majority on the EC to nullify proposals for government change promoted by a slim Moderate majority on the NC. The majority on the EC needed but did not have a political alliance with a like-minded majority on the other relevant decision-making bodies to be sure of preventing or promoting a change in the system of government. Thus, in clear contrast to the highly concentrated TGWU of the 1960–70 period, the Engineers' decision-making process is dependent not upon one man but upon several combinations of organized votes.

Apart from the combined constitutional and party pressures examined above, the Engineers' national leadership experienced only minor and limited pressure for change from members through the extra-constitutional sources. The abortive breakaway from the Engineers by some Midlands toolmakers in the 1960s, and more recently pressures from similar elite craft groups, brought little *de jure* or *de facto* concessions from the national leadership. Unlike the TGWU of the 1960–75 membership, dissatisfaction and dissent with the Engineers' system of government normally showed itself through the party system rather than in extra-constitutional activity of a different kind.

On the other hand, external pressures for change originating from non-membership sources did somewhat affect changes in the system of government by influencing the AUEW merger.[64] Moreover, the external pressures largely concerning the relative size of the union directed the full-time leadership's attention towards mergers at a time when the wider membership displayed little interest in the matter. Amalgamations, completed by long and complex negotiations between a few people, thus gave leading national members of the Engineers an opportunity to exercise a leadership role. But after the initial arrangements had been agreed, alterations in the amalgamation were not so readily accepted by the NC. In contrast to the original proposals, the EC's later suggested amendments[65] threatened to disturb the Engineers' own structure of government and the balance of internal party power. These politically controversial proposals were presented to the NC or the Rules Revision meeting in 1974, 1975 and, in a slightly amended form, in 1976. They were rejected by the Engineers' lay national leadership on every occasion, by 28–23 in 1974, and 27–24 in 1975 and a tie of 26–26 in 1976 (when the motion was declared not carried in the absence of a presidential casting vote).

Divisions between the two parties in these amalgamation votes were caused mainly by members' perceptions of the internal political consequences of the EC's proposals. It was generally argued that the proposal to enlarge the National Conference to 150 or 300 would enhance the platform's power at the expense of the delegates. More significant, however, was the belief among both parties' supporters that the proportional representation proposed by the EC would assist the progressives and hinder the Moderates. The Moderates had good grounds for thinking that the overwhelming majority of TASS and Construction delegates at the enlarged Conference would combine with the Engineering Section's own progressive minority to form a broad left majority.

Secondary objections by the Engineers' Moderates to the EC proposals focused on the special provisions for TASS. There was particular objection to TASS's full-time officials being allowed to continue in office without facing elections. A successful motion moved at the 1976 NC by opponents of the EC's proposals thus demanded that all TASS officials face elections. The motive for this proposal was again primarily party-political, but also it was generally thought 'unfair' that TASS's officials should be eligible to stand for national office in the wider union from a secure appointed sectional position. Moreover, it was widely believed, and resented, that TASS had appointed a large number of left-wing full-time officials just prior to the presentation of the new merger proposals calling for election of all future officials.

It was not surprising, therefore, that the majority of Moderates on the NC repeatedly threw out the amalgamation deal negotiated by the EC. It was rejected for the same political reasons that led broadly the same delegates to reject attempts to repeal the postal ballot. The NC's stance on both issues is hence best explained by reference to the Engineers' unofficial party system. Both parties believed the repeal of the postal ballots, and the proposed proportional representation on the new National Conference, would favour the Progressives and damage the Moderates. In this situation the right rationally, and successfully, obstructed both proposals.

It is thus clear from the above examination of changes, both actual and abortive, in the Engineers' government that the Engineers' national leadership was far more restricted in its scope for sponsoring change than its counterpart in the TGWU. Without common political majorities on the EC and the NC the Engineers' national leadership found few opportunities for processing politically contentious issues. This does not of course mean that the EC could not use its expertise to deal with administrative details, such as increases in subscriptions. It was rather that each EC proposal, as in the amalgamation, came under the scrutiny of the organized right on the NC which, in the late 1960s and early 1970s, had the power to prevent change.

However, before the rise of the left in the Engineers the EC and the president[66] did successfully lead the NC on a number of issues. This was made possible by the common political cause which by and large bound the EC and NC together at that time. The president, in this case Carron, was able to play a leadership-type

Table 10 *Motions submitted to the NC of the AUEW(E) divided according to whether they were political, industrial or industrial/political*

Year	Total motions	Political	Industrial	Industrial/political
		%	%	%
1954	324	29	66	4
1964	411	33	57	10
1973	517	37	48	16

role in the early 1960s that was not all that dissimilar to that of the general secretary in the TGWU. Therefore parties can be used in the Engineers for positive as well as negative purposes. They can facilitate or restrict change. Indeed, in a union like the Engineers, constitutionally divided into a legislature and executive and bound to observe the division by a series of checks and balances, parties may be said to provide an effective means of co-ordinating activities across the different parts of government.

Furthermore, it can also be argued that the Engineers' unofficial parties, at a time of growing political discussion and diminishing national bargaining (see Chapter 8), constituted an appropriate means of reaching national decisions. Over the 1954–73 period, for instance, NC motions with a political and industrial/political content grew respectively from 29 to 37 per cent and from 4 to 16 per cent of all motions submitted, as Table 10 shows.[67]

Among such motions debated at the NC in 1973, there were many questions regarding industrial relations legislation and incomes policy. Questions of this magnitude could not be determined by the powerful district committees. These and similar motions demanded a national decision. Indeed, in a union approaching 1½ million members, the Engineers' decisions on such issues were significant in the TUC and consequently in talks with the national government. Active members faced with questions of national importance thus found the Engineers' unofficial parties offering them a choice of relevant political options in the unions' elections.

The unofficial parties also tended to guarantee that most of their supporters would, after election, reflect the general left–right division in their voting. Although there was no formal whipping procedure at the NC or EC, the parties' electoral influence helped to maintain some discipline among lay delegates and full-time officials. For instance, after a notable left-wing member from Division 26 failed to vote the left's line at the NC in 1974 on the amalgamation issue, he was replaced at the next election by a more reliable left-wing delegate. Similarly, ambitious full-time officials of either persuasion need to maintain the electoral machines' backing for future national elections. Indeed, under postal ballots even sitting national candidates cannot count on re-election on a personal vote and are thus pushed closer to dependence on the party machines. A voter can hence assume with some confidence that a vote cast for one or other of the parties' favoured candidates will produce a particular kind of stance on controversial political issues. Thus it can be argued that the unofficial parties in the Engineers' system of government influenced most aspects of the decision-making processes, in ways that matched both the needs of the union's constitution and the environment of the late 1960s and early 1970s.

To summarize, change, both actual and abortive, in the Engineers' government was, in the period studied, initiated largely by individuals or parties with vested political interests to protect. The union's general membership showed little interest in any of the changes, including the amalgamation (see Chapter 6). The Engineers therefore experienced few of the piecemeal unofficial pressures for change generated in the TGWU. Such pressures were prevented by the Engineers' traditionally more decentralized and diffused system of government which had long given shop stewards roles in powerful district committees and integrated them into its local system of government. It was of course from these positions of local independence that the two unofficial parties drew their support.

Changes of any importance were thus by and large the property of the union's unofficial parties. Whether they resisted or supported any change generally depended upon its perceived effect on their political positions, although of course other arguments, such as decrying declining branch life during the proposed introduction of postal ballots and proposals for a more efficient amalgamation when wanting to change its governing bodies, etc., were of some considerable influence in swaying the small number of floating voters. But ultimately votes on crucial issues tended to be cast according to political interests decided outside the debating room.

However, as the major decisions taken by the national leadership became more generally political in nature owing to external developments, for instance incomes policy, so the ideologically opposed parties offered the voting membership quite relevant choices in elections. Moreover, the right's party also showed, in the early 1960s, that they could make the highly diffused union more easily governable by co-ordinating activities across the different national executive and legislative bodies; although equally it must be said, that, in the later period studied, the EC found it remarkably difficult to overcome the institutional checks and balances when faced, on the question of amalgamation reform, by a majority on the NC opposed to structural change.

Thus the national leadership in the Engineers is not a homogeneous unit. It is divided constitutionally by rule and unofficially by parties. Hence after the left gained sufficient seats on the EC to make the outcome of its deliberations less politically predictable, there was no common view as to how government should be changed. Proposals by the Engineers' full-time national leadership were therefore, unlike the TGWU, considered with a large degree of political scepticism and, if found politically wanting, were rejected by the lay NC.

Other unions: areas, processes and agents of change

UCATT, in direct contrast to the TGWU, acted to centralize decision-making in the late 1960s and early 1970s, when decision-making was moved from district to regional level. Furthermore, while using its merger negotiations to restructure itself geographically (see Chapter 6), UCATT also introduced an appointed full-time officer position, in 1975.

There were also in 1975 a large number of other rule changes[68] in UCATT. These were primarily intended to rationalize the merger and 'allow the union to compete on better terms with other organisations'.[69] Generally, regional influence was expanded and the branch administrator linked more closely to the shop steward movement. At the national level the size of the Executive was trimmed. A proposal to introduce postal balloting was, however, rejected by the later revision meeting, mainly on the grounds of cost. Indeed, many of the changes made were, as in the merger, concerned with saving money. If, as *The Times* concluded, the changes 'give building militants more power',[70] either at site level or through the 'Charter Group' in regional and national elections, it is more likely to be due accidentally to considerations of cost effectiveness than to political gain.

ASTMS underwent *ad hoc* changes intended to deal with a number of specific problems. Unlike UCATT, they did not propose any major reshaping of government. In particular, ASTMS's national leadership sought to implement piecemeal changes which would streamline and in other ways bureaucratize the rapidly growing union. For instance, several minor procedural changes were introduced at its ever-growing Annual Delegate Conference (ADC) in 1971 and 1975 to enable business to be programmed more effectively. These procedural adjustments did not require a rule change. However, when the national leadership, specifically the Executive tried to change ASTMS's internal structure, it was less successful. Merging staff associations (see Chapter 6) were particularly reluctant to relinquish their autonomy in the interests of a more integrated ASTMS. Moreover the 'closed branch' system, used by ASTMS to attract merger partners, was in turn accentuated by merging staff associations which were completely company-based. ASTMS's national leadership's growth aspirations thus limited their abilities to make the union less of an umbrella organization and more of an integrated whole.

Also, like the Engineers but on a much lower scale, ASTMS experienced a growth in factionalism. This development, coupled with the rise in appointed divisional full-time officers' influence in the union, further weakened the NEC and general secretary's leadership and discretion in national decision-making. The divisional full-time officials, for instance, played a role in 1972 in mobilizing the ADC to vote against the NEC's recommendations that ASTMS should register under the Industrial Relations Act. Following that vote the number of divisional full-time officers with rights to attend conference was radically reduced. The same officers were also subsequently placed within a more hierarchical system of control as part of the NEC's attempt to supervise and control their activities more effectively.

As the NEC sought to control more effectively its full-time officials and to bureaucratize the union, so several political pressure groups of the left developed, intent on democratizing the union. However, the best organized groups in the mid-1970s had industrial affinities. These groups proved themselves capable of wielding significant bloc votes in elections. They included insurance, civil airways and Imperial College membership. Unlike the political factions, such as the International Socialists, they had no particular policies to push. Nevertheless, with the demise of 'notables' on the NEC, particularly the loss of former AScW members and MPs, there may be more scope for pressure group politics, both political and industrial.

NALGO and the NUT, both concentrated and centralized, carried through a few minor changes in government. Both public sector unions marginally adjusted their structures to come more into line with developments in their employing authority. These administrative boundary changes and other alterations had little effect on the nature of government in either union. However, both unions experienced a rise in left-wing factionalism. This took the form of International Socialist-inspired organization – that is, in NALGO, the 'NALGO Action Group' (NAG), and in the NUT the 'Rank and File'. Both these factions had some effect on their respective governments in the late 1960s and early 1970s. They both won a small number of seats on their unions' National Executives.

The regionalized GMWU, on the other hand, remains free of political factions. It did however experience a number of other governmental changes. In 1964 and 1974 respectively it introduced a branch administrative officer (BAO) and a district officer. But neither of these local officers had a significant effect on the hierarchy of government within the GMWU. Structurally the union adopted national and regional industrial conferences in 1969. These bodies were not however incorporated in the GMWU's rule book. They were given an advisory rather than a decision-making function. In 1973 a proposal that 'Congress agrees that the scope and authority of Industrial Conferences be enhanced and that more opportunities be given to the lay members to participate in the formulation of claims and terms of acceptance and agreements'[71] was opposed by the general secretary and heavily defeated.

Changes in the composition of the executive government of the GMWU were proposed at the 1974 Congress.[72] The suggestion, from the floor, was that the national level of government should be composed solely of lay members. This proposal was obviously intended to remove the full-time and politically dominant regional secretaries from the General Council and the National Executive Committee.[73] Such a change would have greatly altered the nature of the regionalized GMWU's system of government. However, changes in the Executive finally implemented in January 1975 had none of these effects. The *status quo* was retained in practice by giving all the regional secretaries places on the new executive along with twenty lay delegates and the general secretary.

Thus, of the 'other' unions studied only UCATT carried through a major restructuring of its system of government. Most unions, in contrast to UCATT, carried through piecemeal adjustments, of the sort normally associated with some particular aspect of government; they were hence treated as individual changes and not seen as contributing to any master plan for change. However, ASTMS, NALGO and the NUT experienced a growth in political factionalism. This was something of a radical change for these unions, all of which were at the concentrated end of the government spectrum in 1960. The national leadership of the TGWU and the GMWU were thus the only ones to remain largely aloof from unofficial opposition movements between 1960 and 1975.

Summary and conclusions: the direction of change

The national leadership of both the TGWU and the AUEW Engineering Section carried through a number of changes that affected both the vertical and horizontal dimensions of union government. The TGWU adjusted its regions and trade groups and introduced, on a wider scale, district committees. Decisions over bargaining and some administrative matters were moved out of the national office and located further down the TGWU's vertical structure. At the same time, the discretion available to the GEC and therefore the general secretary was increased.

The AUEW Engineering Section also marginally adjusted its internal geographic boundaries, but there were no alterations on the scale undertaken by the TGWU. At the higher level the Engineers added two new bodies (that is, the Joint EC and Joint Conference) to its already highly diffused system of national government. But these two additions did not make any great difference to the system of government in the Engineers, largely because the unofficial party system, which developed in importance in the late 1960s and early 1970s, was capable of organizing across the old and new bodies of government and mitigating the importance of the new bodies by various procedural wrangles. It was, however, this unofficial party development that constituted the most significant change in the Engineers. It also, quite clearly, influenced the decision to introduce postal ballots, which in turn had repercussions on the parties' electoral fortunes. A number of the other unions studied also experienced a growth in unofficial opposition movements, but not on the scale of the Engineers.

Following the model of change, the agents affecting union government can be divided into those that emanate primarily from external developments and those that receive their main impetus from internal sources. The external change agents that produced changes of note in a union's system of government tended to be those that affected bargaining or union size. In the case of bargaining change many unions experienced a *de facto* externally determined downwards shift in bargaining levels (see Chapter 8). This decentralization did not itself bring about immediate and direct major *de jure* changes in non-bargaining systems of government. Indeed, most of the unions with highly centralized systems of government similar to that of the TGWU around 1960 tended to make piecemeal and *ad hoc* adjustments in response to membership demands for change stimulated by bargaining developments. This was the standard response, whether or not demands came through constitutional processes or, in the form of strikes, through the non-constitutional channels. The regionalized GMWU's response to certain disputes, partially intended to affect an internal government adjustment in, for instance, the vehicle industry and glass manufacture, also tended to be both *ad hoc* and piecemeal. The entrenched national leadership in the more centralized unions generally contained or localized the influence of bargaining change rather than sponsoring or accepting a more general *de jure* revision of union government.

In the more decentralized unions, on the other hand, there was normally no need for the national machinery to be changed to meet the new bargaining changes. These unions, at least initially, absorbed change at the local level. Thus the *de jure* bifurcated ASTMS, with highly decentralized bargaining institutionalized in 'closed branches' but a centralized non-bargaining channel, experienced no immediate problems from the growth of lower-level bargaining. The Engineers also found the development of their shop stewards' bargaining roles of no real consequence for government. Their traditionally powerful district committees brought key shop stewards into the official system of government while the unofficial parties sought their allegiance as electoral organizers. Changes in bargaining, therefore, as agents of *de jure* change in union government, were marginal in their effect; although in the TGWU in particular the *de facto* decentralization and diffusion of bargaining created an ambience supportive of Jones's later extensive *de jure* changes.

Changes in bargaining levels and attitudes did, however, serve to provide the culture and stimulus for the *de facto* growth of factionalism. Devolution of bargaining in ASTMS and the Engineers gave independence of action to local factional organizations. It was from these sources of independent power that politically ambitious members of opposition groups gained their support. In contrast the centralized unions, such as the NUT and NALGO, experienced a rise in factionalism that was closely associated with the general increase in national militancy. Both the 'Rank and File' in the NUT, and 'NAG' in NALGO grew out of specific internal differences over wage negotiations. In the NUT the left benefited from the Executive's movement to arbitration in 1967, and in NALGO they made capital out of the opposition to a two-year settlement in 1969. In both cases the factions drew their main support from young members in the London area. Hence bargaining and character changes did have a *de facto* effect of some importance on union government.

On the other hand, changes in a union's size, often influenced by external developments, produced change agents of direct and primary importance for *de jure* government change. In particular, as will be shown in Chapter 6, adverse absolute changes of some magnitude in a union's size produced mergers which in turn normally affected a union's system of government. Thus the ASW's membership and financial problems, arising from bargaining difficulties, directly influenced the union's decision to form UCATT and consequently to rationalize its system of government. Moreover, the merger facilitated the introduction of a regional level of government. Similarly, many of the minor unions, which altered their systems of government by joining such expanding unions as ASTMS and the TGWU were moved to adopt these strategies by size considerations (see Chapter 6): they thought their own organizations too small to survive and considered that ASTMS or the TGWU were large enough to provide a secure merger partner. The GMWU's national and regional leadership also re-shaped their national and regional industrial committees, at least partly to make the union more attractive to potential merger partners. Similarly, the AEU offered to merger partners a federated structure of government as an inducement to amalgamation. And even the fast growing TGWU and ASTMS gave themselves yet further advantage in the merger field by extending the discretion of full-time officials in merger operations through rule changes.

Unions that expanded very rapidly were also liable to make *de jure* alterations in government – although these changes were much less drastic than those made by declining unions. ASTMS Annual Delegates Conference (ADC) in 1973, for instance, successfully pressed for an examination of the 'policy-making, administrative and financial structure of the Association'. This motion was motivated by a desire to ameliorate the signs of stress in the organization caused by the unions' leap from 87,000 members in 1967 to 310,000 in 1974. Consequently, in 1975, as mentioned above, some minor alterations were made in these aspects of ASTMS government.

Thus different aspects of changes in size brought unions governed in a variety of ways to reconsider the effectiveness of their own internal decision-making systems in the mid- and late 1960s and early 1970s. Not all types of unions managed to reshape their systems of government in the manner described by the national leadership, however. In the highly diffused Engineers, for instance, internal political considerations overshadowed growth advantages and prevented the merger from developing beyond the initial federated stage.

However, internal change in national leadership led to the most marked re-assessment of the appropriateness of the *de jure* system of government. Unions as disparate as the centralized and highly concentrated TGWU, the regionalized and somewhat less concentrated GMWU and the decentralized and diffused Engineers were all affected by this kind of change agent, although in the former two unions it was a particular general secretary who promoted the changes, while in the Engineers it was the parties and their leading figures who performed this role.

The manner in which the TGWU's new national leadership both processed formal constitutional change and exercised leadership discretion was, as shown above, quite distinctly different to that of the new president of the Engineers and his opponents. In the field of merger change, for instance, the general secretary of the TGWU found it much easier to adjust government and appointment of new officers than did the president of the Engineers.

Differences in the process of change clearly played a major part in distinguishing the TGWU from the Engineers. However, it should not be overlooked that in both unions the agents of change acted to change the system of government for largely internal political reasons. The primary aim was not concerned with the need to achieve any major bargaining or external economic goals.

In formal terms, the new national leaders of the 1960s and 1970s all reached their positions through the prescribed constitutional methods. The various change agents that influenced the choice of leaders were thus ultimately processed through these channels. In practice, however, the election or appointment of a national leader owed most, in the concentrated TGWU, to the existing national leaders' influence and patronage and, in the diffused Engineers, to party activity. Thus, although external economic and political developments obviously affected the choice of national leaders, it was the internal organization factors that primarily determined who actually became the leader of both types of union.

But the established leadership's electoral influence and patronage did not, in concentrated unions, prevent leaders being chosen who were more responsive than their sponsoring predecessors to pressure for change. Indeed, in the environment of the late 1960s, with decentralization of bargaining and merger trends clearly important, the retiring leadership in concentrated unions, and the parties in diffused unions, probably preferred candidates receptive to change, if for no other reason than that they stood a better chance of maximizing support in elections. But in neither union can it be stated that these external facts were primarily instrumental in the choice of actual leaders. This prerogative still rested with internal change agents. So it can be argued that the most powerful change agents within unions were themselves products of the unions they sought to change. The diffused unions, however, which offered the best chance of a political change in the major national leadership positions, tended, paradoxically, because of their division of powers, to give the new leadership the least chance of radically changing the system of government.

It is difficult to generalize about the *direction of change* in government arising from the above developments. While it is clear that the location of some issues on the centralization–decentralization continuum changed, they did not always move in the same direction. However, as will be shown in Chapter 8, *bargaining* decisions tended, with important exceptions, to be decentralized by unions. (The exceptions included UCATT and the NUM.) Decentralization in the *non-bargaining* field was however by no means as general as in the bargaining field. Apart from the TGWU's national leadership's *de facto* and *de jure* attempts to enhance the influence of regions and districts by giving them more to do, it is difficult to identify any other union in our case studies that carried through a similar comprehensive devolutionary policy. Indeed, the only other equally deliberate and comprehensive attempt to move the level of decision-making was by UCATT, which moved decision-making upwards. In fact, in the period studied few unions deliberately chose, or actually achieved, a *de jure* change of any importance in the location of their non-bargaining decision-making. What changes were processed through the constitutions tended, like the Engineers and ASTMS, to be more minor adjustments, made in response to national leadership or lay pressure for piecemeal change. The Engineers' switch to postal ballot, for instance, which further decentralized decision-making from the branch to the home, was clearly no part of any grand devolutionary strategy. In so far as there were other changes in the location of non-bargaining issues, they tended to be the byproduct of some other change; they were produced by mergers, increased national government intervention in industrial relations, growth of factionalism and parties, emerging shop steward organization and the decline in branch attendance, among others.

Mergers, for example, raised the level of national decision-making in the minor merging unions (see Chapter 5) to the much more elevated levels of the major merging unions. Where merger was by amalgamation, as in the AUEW, new higher-level bodies were formed to deal with matters of joint interest to the merger partners. Increased national government intervention in turn gave these new joint bodies and existing national levels of government major new questions for resolution. Industrial relations legislation in particular brought to the attention of national bodies issues of some considerable magnitude during the Labour Government's attempts to gain agreement over their *In Place of Strife* proposals in the late 1960s. Similar responses were produced between 1971 and 1974 as a result of the Conservatives' Industrial Relations Act.

Incomes policy in its various forms also directly added matters of substance to unions' national level debates. In the bifurcated TGWU, for instance, voluntary incomes policies posed particular difficulties. Despite the *de jure* and *de facto* decentralization of bargaining down the vertical bargaining channel, the TGWU's national leadership – general secretary and GEC – found itself having to deal with questions directly related to bargaining at the highest level of the normally non-bargaining channel of government. These issues were generally dealt with by the National Trade Group's committees and secretaries. Such a sideways movement was fraught with difficulty for the TGWU's pro-Social Contract general secretary; for, having promoted a devolutionary bargaining policy that weakened his bureaucratic machinery of control but strengthened his populist base, his attempts to gain acceptance for voluntary incomes restraint struck at his own source of popularity – free collective bargaining by shop stewards. In 1977 this led to Jones's suffering an unprecedented defeat at the BDC on the question of continuing with the Social Contract. Decentralization could not therefore be undertaken with impunity, even by the extremely influential general secretary of the TGWU. Movement in the vertical channels of government could and did weaken the concentration of power at the horizontal level of national government.

The other factors mentioned above as affecting the centralization–decentralization continuum tended to move decisions away from the formal national level of government. Factions, parties, shop stewards' organizations and the decline in branch attendance all tended to shift issues into new channels of decision-making. However, these developments did not necessarily produce decentralizing effects. They bore more of a resemblance to sideways movements. Shop stewards' organizations, factions and parties all tended to take decision-making into shadow, unofficial, channels of government which to some extent compensated for the general decline in participation in the local formal system of decision-making, the branch. Somewhat similarly, but not as effectively, the much weaker factions in the ASW (UCATT), ASTMS, NALGO and the NUT sought to involve members in a shadowy, parallel, system of decision-making.

There was also, in the case of the horizontal continuum, no common direction of movement. However, most of the unions became more diffused at the national level of non-bargaining decision-making owing to the increased influence of parties and factions. The two unions that stood largely aloof from these developments were the TGWU and the GMWU, although, as will be shown later, the changes made in the TGWU appear to have produced circumstances favourable towards the future growth of factionalism.

No union studied, with the possible exception of the NUM, had an opposition that approached the unofficial party organization achieved by the left in the Engineers, although UCATT came somewhat closer to the Engineers' party situation, following the formation of the left-wing and Communist-dominated Building Workers' Charter Group in 1968. This faction gained some notable election victories, for instance in 1975, when their candidate won the Division 3[74] executive seat. However, there did appear among the white-collar unions of the late 1960s a somewhat more rudimentary factionalism.[75] Thus the national leadership of ASTMS, NALGO and the NUT, among others, found themselves faced by a new broad left front dominated by the International Socialists. Most of these groups considered themselves, as NALGO Action Group (NAG) did, 'not a ginger group but a consistent opposition to the present leadership'.[76] In all three unions the new factions had some degree of success. They harried the national leadership on such political matters as incomes policy and industrial relations legislation. They were also universally interested in promoting more open government within their respective unions. In ASTMS, for instance, the new left successfully promoted a motion at ASTMS Annual Delegates Conference (ADC) in 1974 which demanded that details of the NEC's voting should be circulated within the union. The factions also won a small number of elections to executive office in each union. In NALGO this success was further complemented by gaining the right to put their factional title on the ballot sheet.

However, the white-collar factions described above remained rather small. The NUT 'Rank and File' only claimed 800 members in 1975; NAG's unofficial journal in 1973 had a circulation of some 5000. Some of the factions' successes in elections were also very localized – London, in particular, provided NAG with most of its victories. The new white-collar factions did not therefore constitute an immediate danger to the hold of the established national leaderships on their unions. But, like the blue-collar factions, they did further diffuse power within unions. The factions' very presence and scrutiny of official policy helped to keep their unions' national leadership within the constitutionally prescribed checks and balances.

The TGWU, on the other hand, moved even further towards the concentrated end of the horizontal continuum of non-bargaining decision-making between 1960 and 1975. This was due to *de jure* and *de facto* changes in government and to Jones's succession to the position of general secretary. In the absence of factionalism the rule changes that weakened some full-time officials' influence within the TGWU also increased the influence of the general secretary. Moreover, in Jones the TGWU found someone extremely capable of exploiting the new opportunities for individual leadership provided by the changes. By comparison the GMWU, which also avoided factionalism, remained rather more diffused. The introduction of industrial conferences and a reformed executive did little, if anything, to advance the GMWU's new general secretary's position *vis-à-vis* the powerful regional secretaries. The vested political interests of the GMWU's regional secretaries prevented any significant change being successfully sponsored by the new general secretary.

Yet the changes in the TGWU that enhanced the general secretary's position in the short run may have sown the seeds of its future destruction as a position of extreme influence. For the horizontal changes, in conjunction with those on the vertical continuum, probably contributed to the general secretary's first major BDC defeat in 1977 (see Chapter 6). Indeed it could be argued that the TGWU has already made most of the changes that elsewhere have encouraged the growth of an opposition faction (apart from the introduction of elections for full-time officers). In particular, and for the first time, bargaining has been devolved at the same time as the proscription on Communists holding office has been lifted and the power of the local and national officials to control the members reduced. The scenario can thus be seen to unfold where the constitutional changes designed to encourage integrated shop stewards' movements and district committees will be used by the left to promote more independently-minded local organizations.

Such left-wing groups in the new TGWU could not, of course, be expected to accept the sovereignty of the local district official. Moreover, in the absence of locally organized established leadership factions, balloting for lay representatives could also be open to the type of voting patterns seen in the Engineers in the 1960s. In these circumstances, with the general secretary's populist base already showing signs of crumbling, the new general secretary, Moss Evans, may eventually wish that the late 1960s' changes had been somewhat less enthusiastically pursued by his predecessor.

However, movements on the non-bargaining horizontal continuum of government, at least in the short term, did not radically alter the nature of the TGWU's and GMWU's system of government, although, through the growth of

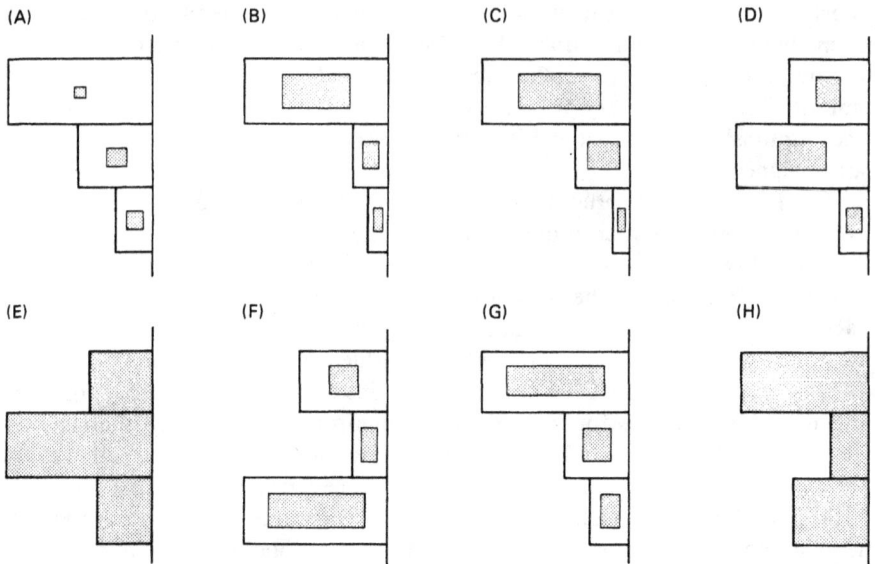

Figure 11   De facto *systems of government (non-bargaining), circa 1976. A,*
TGWU; B, ASTMS, and similar to NUT, NUBE and NUPE (but
these do not have ASTMS's bargaining arrangements); C, POEU,
and similar to NALGO; D, GMWU; E, NUM; F, ASBSW; G, ASW
(UCATT 1976); H, AUEW(E), and similar to the Foundry Section of
the AUEW

factionalism or parties, they did move the rest of the unions more towards the
diffused end of the spectrum.

Vested political interests and/or constitutionally prescribed inertia was thus
sufficient in most unions, in the absence of a dominant and innovating general
secretary, to prevent external developments from producing successful demands
for major reforms of government. Unions did not generally alter their non-
bargaining system of government to meet some external bargaining need; indeed,
they adjusted their governments primarily for internal political purposes.

The typology of government, presented in Chapter 3 and amended here in
Figure 11, therefore shows only marginal change on the non-bargaining side. It
remains for Chapter 8 to explore the other half of the picture – the structure of
collective bargaining within unions.

5   Change in job territory: natural growth

In this chapter and the next we will be concerned with a further exploration of the changes in job territory that were briefly described in Chapter 3. Since our aim is to examine and compare the processes and causes of change by reference to the model of change set out in Chapter 2 we are not primarily concerned with the aggregate growth of unionization as discussed in other recent academic studies.[1] However, it is our intention to draw some conclusions about the relative influence of external and internal factors affecting union growth in different job territories.

Changes in job territory can be usefully divided into those that arise out of 'natural growth' and those resulting from merger activities. By natural growth we mean that increase in membership which occurs without formal links with other unions, involving constitutional change.[2] Of course these two developments are often related and difficult to disentangle, but there are sufficient differences between them to warrant their separate consideration and analysis. Mergers are legal processes which have to be dealt with formally by the established leadership of several independent organizations. They involve deliberate and conscious acts, which often need to be planned and organized over a considerable period. By comparison, non-merger extension into new or related job territories can occur without the direct involvement of national leadership in any union; also, it does not depend upon inter-union co-operation and agreement. Indeed, one union's 'natural growth' activities may be fiercely resented and resisted by its neighbours and rivals; natural growth may all too often result in union disagreement and competition, rather than agreement and co-operation.

For all these reasons this chapter will concern itself solely with the analysis and explanation of changes in natural growth, while Chapter 6 will deal with merger activity and its impact on job territories. Of course the form used for examining both aspects of change is the same – that set out in our model of change in Chapter 2.

The main studies used for this chapter will be those of the TGWU and GMWU. As in previous chapters this material will be supplemented by secondary comment based on other unions studied where significant developments have taken place – for example ASTMS. We have decided to focus on the experiences of the two major general unions because they provide useful complementary studies of 'open' unions recruiting in the most 'exposed'[3] areas of the membership market over a very wide area; yet they adopted radically different policies and approaches to the problems involved; the GMWU was 'restrictive–passive' and the TGWU, 'positive–expansionist' in its orientation to growth.[4] They also began with very different government structures – the TGWU in 1969 was more or less at the extreme end of the concentrated–centralized continuum of government, while the GMWU was highly regionalized.

It should be remembered that in the period under examination there was a substantial overall increase in the density of union members in the UK.[5] Over the period 1964–74 this increased from 45.2 to 49.6 per cent of the total workforce. Within this total however were a number of important general trends, identified in Chapter 3, which affected white-collar workers and women workers in particular. Both groups experienced a far higher national rate of both growth and unionization than average. On the other hand, some industries and occupations contracted. The effect of these and other external developments, and the internal initiatives of the GMWU and TGWU, will be considered below by examining first the GMWU and its areas of change and then its change agents. A second section is concerned with a similar analysis of 'natural change' in the TGWU. The chapter then considers related developments in other unions before summarizing its findings and drawing a number of conclusions.

Growth in the GMWU

Areas of change

Between 1965 and 1975 the GMWU's TUC-affiliated membership rose from 795,767 to 881,356, or 10.9 per cent. Of this increase, however, 11,074 was the direct result of mergers. Thus 'natural' growth contributed some 9.4 per cent of the GMWU's increase in this decade. As Table 2 in Chapter 3 shows, this was, on either count, a relatively low increase compared with most other large unions (compared with the TGWU's total growth of 28.6 per cent or, discounting mergers, 19.3 per cent, it was even less satisfactory).

However, the comparatively low overall growth figure of the GMWU hides some quite significant internal variations. First, the record of the union's ten regions was very uneven, as Table 11 shows. It can be seen that two regions, Northern and Scottish, achieved major increases in size of 28.5 and 29.2 per cent respectively. In contrast three other regions actually experienced a reduction in membership.

Second, within its 10.9 per cent increase the union experienced a major growth in *female* membership. Between 1965 and 1975 female membership rose by 47.7 per cent, from 195,894 to 289,283. Over the same period the male membership of the GMWU fell by 1.3 per cent. Hence the GMWU relied exclusively on female recruitment for any increase in total membership.

Third, the increase in *white-collar* membership of the GMWU appears to have been negligible. Indeed, it was only in 1972 that the GMWU formed a white-collar section, MATSA (Managerial, Administrative Technical and Supervisory

Table 11   *GMWU regional changes in membership, 1965–75*

Region	1965	% of regional total	1975	% of regional total	% of change
London	92,571	12.4	87,987	10.2	–5.0
Lancashire	104,464	13.9	102,367	11.9	–2.0
Northern	79,757	10.6	110,783	12.9	+38.9
Yorkshire	72,272	9.6	83,541	9.7	+15.6
Southern	79,806	10.6	80,229	9.3	+0.5
Scottish	76,043	10.1	101,613	11.8	+33.6
Birmingham	76,539	10.2	96,220	11.2	+25.7
Liverpool	64,911	8.7	79,402	9.2	+22.3
Midlands and East Coast	59,877	7.9	69,659	8.1	+16.3
South Western	43,206	5.8	47,242	5.5	+9.3

Source: GMWU.

Association). In the decade before the founding of MATSA the union gained very little benefit from the national tendency for white-collar workers to join trade unions.

Fourth, over three-quarters of the GMWU's increase in female membership came from increased penetration in three industries – local government, food, drink and tobacco, and engineering. Expansion in local government was by far the most important, accounting for almost half of the total. Apart from the increase in local government, and a general decline of male membership in engineering and shipbuilding, there was no major change in the job territory of the GMWU, as Table 12 reveals.

Fifth and finally, the above areas of change hide, as in most unions, a general flow of members in and out of the GMWU. The union's turnover varied between 12.1 per cent in the Northern Region and 20.5 per cent in London. Nationally the turnover was 15.9 per cent per annum. Hence in order marginally to increase its size in a decade the GMWU had to actually recruit over a million members. This consideration helps to put into perspective the 'net' increase of 74,515 members as a result of non-merger growth.

Agents of change

The model of change[6] shows diagrammatically how change agents can be broadly divided into those that act on areas of change without involving the internal system of decision-making and those that affect a change by being processed through parts of the *internal* decision-making processes. The external factors affecting membership growth will be examined first.

Table 12   *Proportion of total GMWU membership in each industry*

	1963 %	1973 %
Agriculture	0.04	0.08
Mining and Quarrying	1.67	1.35
Food, Drink and Tobacco	4.91	6.85
Coal and Petroleum Products	0.16	0.08
Chemical and Allied	4.67	4.02
Engineering and Shipbuilding	26.16	21.43
Textiles	2.91	2.98
Leather, etc.	0.16	0.08
Clothing and Footwear	0.26	0.33
Bricks, Pottery etc.	3.01	2.55
Glass	1.97	2.16
Timber, Furniture etc.	0.69	0.88
Paper, Printing etc.	0.83	1.07
Other manufacturing industries	4.15	4.53
Construction	2.12	1.72
Public industries	15.51	12.46
Transport, etc.	1.85	1.07
Distributive Trades	0.35	1.28
Business and Finance	—	1.40
Miscellaneous services	0.82	0.96
Hotels and Catering	0.54	0.83
Health services	2.83	2.85
Local Government	19.60	23.10
National Government	2.65	1.74
Trade unions, etc.	—	0.01
Political organizations	—	0.001
Societies	—	0.002
Manual	98.79	96.67
MATSA (estimated figures for 1963)	1.21	3.32
	100.00	100.00

External factors

An obvious external change agent is the level of employment. By analysing changes in industrial employment on a regional basis it should be possible to show whether or not it expanded at a similar rate to the GMWU's regional recruitment. If it can be shown that regional/industrial employment did parallel movements in the GMWU's regional/industrial membership, the argument that employment directly influences membership growth would be worthy of further examination.

Table 13 *Employment and GMWU membership statistics in Engineering and Shipbuilding, 1963 and 1973*

	1963	1973	% change
Northern Region			
GMWU membership	22,152	25,903	+16.9
Membership as % employment	9.17%	10.92%	—
Total employment	241,120	243,839	+ 1.1
Scottish Region			
GMWU membership	10,429	12,839	+23.1
Membership as % employment	3.08%	4.04%	—
Total employment	338,110	317,523	−6.1
Liverpool and Lancashire Regions			
GMWU membership	50,285	32,925	−32.5
Membership as % employment	8.53%	6.10%	—
Total employment	589,380	539,984	−8.5
All other regions			
GMWU membership	111,055	101,384	−8.7
Membership as % employment	3.37%	3.24%	—
Total employment	3,296,470	3,126,483	−5.2
Total			
GMWU membership	193,921	173,051	−10.8
Membership as % employment	4.34%	4.09%	
Total employment	4,465,080	4,227,829	−5.3

Unfortunately, the above comparison can be made directly in only two regions, Scottish and Northern. These are the only regions that have boundaries corresponding with the New Standard Regions used by the Department of Employment. However, by combining the GMWU's membership in Lancashire, Liverpool, North Wales and Irish Region a further comparison can be drawn with North West and Northern Ireland New Standard Regions combined. Thus, by examining movements in employment in engineering and shipbuilding, local government and food, drink and tobacco, some interesting and relevant growth comparisons can be made between GMWU's regional membership and regional industrial employment.

Tables 13, 14 and 15 thus compare GMWU regional membership with total regional employment in the three chosen industries. It can be concluded that changes in employment do not of themselves account for all the variations in regional membership. In three GMWU growth regions/industries the union actually increased its membership quite substantially when employment was falling. In fact, as total employment in food, drink and tobacco fell by 6.6 per cent, the GMWU's membership rose by 52 per cent. Moreover in the Scottish region, in the same industry, employment fell by 3.8 per cent while membership

Table 14   *Employment and GMWU membership statistics in Local Government, 1963 and 1973*

	1963	1973	% change
Northern Region			
GMWU membership	16,226	27,747	+71.0
Membership as % employment	34.33%	55.72%	—
Total employment	47,260	49,800	+ 5.4
Scottish Region			
GMWU membership	25,691	34,459	+34.1
Membership as % employment	3.08%	4.04%	—
Total employment	81,120	95,461	+17.1
Liverpool and Lancashire Regions			
GMWU membership	23,427	30,075	+28.4
Membership as % employment	20.13%	25.77%	—
Total employment	116,390	116,702	+ 0.3
Other regions			
GMWU membership	79,935	94,295	+18.0
Membership as % employment	13.70%	14.06%	—
Total employment	583,360	670,513	+15.0
Total			
GMWU membership	145,279	186,576	+28.4
Membership as % employment	17.54%	20.01%	—
Total employment	828,130	932,476	+12.0

increased by 129.4 per cent. In engineering and shipbuilding the Scottish region yet again achieved an increase in membership against a generally falling employment situation, although the switch from heavy to light engineering was a move in the GMWU's favour. In contrast, the general movement of both membership and employment in local government was similar. Yet even here the Scottish and Northern regions showed a disproportionate increase in membership compared with other regions.

It is therefore apparent that an increase in employment in a particular region/industry was not the major cause of the GMWU's success in increasing its membership in the Northern and Scottish regions. Indeed, the GMWU's two major growth regions gained proportionately more members during a decline in employment, rather than an expansion.

However, as mentioned above, the GMWU did benefit within the three industries[7] examined from the general externally generated swing of female employees towards unionization. Both the Scottish and Northern regions registered high growth rates of female membership; respectively 80.4 and 105.7 per cent, as against the GMWU's national average of 46.4 per cent for the period 1963–73. But, more significantly in overall terms, the Scottish and Northern

Table 15 *Employment and GMWU membership statistics in Food, Drink and Tobacco, 1963 and 1973*

	1963	1973	% change
Northern Region			
GMWU membership	3050	4718	+54.7
Membership as % employment	8.78%	12.79%	—
Total employment	34,740	36,900	+ 6.2
Scottish Region			
GMWU membership	5512	12,647	+129.4
Membership as % employment	5.56%	13.26%	—
Total employment	99,170	95,400	−3.8
Liverpool and Lancashire Regions			
GMWU membership	6319	12,232 *	+93.6
Membership as % employment	3.97%	8.03%	—
Total employment	159,290	152,242	−4.4
All other regions			
GMWU membership	21,507	25,716	+19.6
Membership as % employment	3.86%	5.05%	—
Total employment	557,560	509,604	−8.6
Total			
GMWU membership	36,388	55,313	+52.0
Membership as % employment	4.28%	7.00%	
Total employment	850,760	794,146	−6.6

* Some 5800 of these members were in biscuit manufacturing in the Liverpool area. The GMWU numerically dominated this particular industry in that area.

regions also increased male membership in the same period by, respectively, 9.3 and 12.5 per cent. At the same time the union lost 2.6 per cent of its total male members and London and Lancashire suffered reductions, respectively, of 17.3 and 17.9 per cent. Hence the change agents that enabled the GMWU's growth regions to take advantage of the general trend of female unionization, and to go against the union's general tendency to lose male membership, needs further examination.

Internal factors
The internal factors influencing the diverging growth rates within the GMWU can be divided into two kinds: first, general factors, which mitigated against overall expansion; second, particular factors, which made it possible for the two growth regions to expand at a much faster rate than the rest.

Among general factors we must include the attitude of the national leadership towards membership growth. Union policy at this level was mainly concerned to 'close up' particular industries, where they already had a substantial membership, rather than enter new fields or build on a low membership. In contrast to more growth-oriented unions, such as the TGWU and later ASTMS, the GMWU tended to concentrate nationally on its financial position and not its membership expansion rate. In the terms of one regional secretary, the GMWU in the 1960s was 'benefit-oriented' rather than 'service-oriented' – it was primarily concerned to provide substantial benefits to existing members, such as educational facilities, convalescent and holiday home and friendly benefits, rather than servicing existing or potential membership in the industrial sphere.

At times this benefit-oriented approach led the GMWU to emphasize financial solvency at the expense of membership. Thus, despite a marginal rise in membership, the union's income rose over a ten-year period by 217 per cent, while prices increased by 88 per cent and the total assets of the union increased by 107 per cent. In the light of this approach, members or potential members who threatened to cost substantially more than they contributed were not usually welcome in the GMWU. For instance, the GMWU was not particularly disturbed in 1969 when following a strike at Ford's Halewood plant some 1300 members, including over twenty-five shop stewards, left the GMWU and joined the TGWU, a shift in allegiance largely caused by the GMWU's refusal to make the strike official and hence pay strike benefit. In spite of this clear breach of the TUC's Bridlington procedure, the GMWU made no serious effort to regain these members, largely, it would appear, because they were 'a dead loss economically and financially', costing the GMWU 'more in strike pay than we got in'.[8]

Thus the GMWU's governing attitude towards membership growth in the early and mid-1960s was very largely passive although sometimes restrictionist. The union's national leadership, which included the majority of its regional secretaries was more concerned with balancing the books than trying to extend into unknown job territories; and the recruitment activity of its Organization Department was therefore limited in its scope and effectiveness by the generally cautious manner in which the national leadership approached the whole issue of recruitment and retention.

The attitude of national leadership towards membership further affected recruitment by creating an image in the world of active and prospective trade unionists which was distinctly different from that of its major competitor, the TGWU. Above all, in the early and mid-1960s the GMWU exhibited a strong hostility to militancy. Influenced partly by concern for financial security, and hence its reluctance to pay out strike benefit, it attempted to ensure a strict control over the activities of shop stewards. An illustration of this anti-militant attitude is given by a quotation from the union's *Journal* on the retirement of a national industrial officer in June 1963 who was described as gentle to 'everyone except Communists in the Unions, the so-called intellectuals of the left in the Labour Party and employers who will not stand up to strike-happy shop stewards'. It was as a reaction against the GMWU, and this full-time official in particular, that Ford shop stewards, in the 1950s and early 1960s, refused to hand out recruiting forms for the GMWU, claiming that it was merely a 'company union'.

The final general internal factor that affected the GMWU's relatively low growth rate was the shortage of recruiting agents. By this we mean shop stewards and local full-time officials, rather than special task forces for specific and limited national or regional recruiting campaigns which, within the GMWU itself, were acknowledged to have achieved very little. The Organization Department's recruiting drives in 1956 and 1966, for instance, were not notable for any significant impact on the regions or industries they chose as targets. This was due partly to the local areas' inability to turn the visit of the recruiting team into a sustained recruiting effort, plus difficulties in servicing newly recruited members once national recruiting officers had left the area.

Partly to deal with these manpower problems, branch administrative officers were introduced in 1965. And in 1974, after a commissioned study[9] identified a shortage of local officers as a factor hindering growth, a more growth-conscious general secretary, Basnett, created a new grade of district officers. (Ironically, enough, the faster growing TGWU was by this time moving in the reverse direction. Its general secretary allowed the development of a higher membership – full-time officer ratio – although he also encouraged the development and growth of shop stewards as recruiting and bargaining agents. Such a policy would have been against the traditions of the GMWU – see further below.)

However, change agents in the Northern and Scottish regions went against these general trends. Unlike other regions, which either stagnated or came into life in the latter part of the period examined, the Scottish and Northern regions successfully pursued growth policies from the early 1960s. For the internal government of the GMWU, with its emphasis on regional autonomy and its tendency to concentrate power in the hands of the regional secretary, made possible regional exceptions to the national norms identified above.

Before examining the methods used by Messrs Cunningham and Donnett in the Northern and Scottish Regions respectively, however, mention should be made of certain advantages they enjoyed. The fact was that in both these regions the GMWU was the dominant organization in certain crucial services and trades, most notably local government, engineering and shipbuilding – especially *vis-à-vis* their major competitor, the TGWU. Thus they began with a relatively strong base from which to launch a policy of expansion and development.[10]

In each of the two growth regions the regional secretaries attempted to break away from the GMWU's passive-oriented approach to membership and the union's associated strong hostility to militant industrial action. They made it clear that in their regions they would not always oppose industrial action in all but exceptional circumstances.

Second, they were the first regional secretaries to begin to involve shop stewards, in a systematic way, in actual negotiations. Instead of regarding shop stewards' bargaining as an expedient or an exception to the general rule, stewards were given progressively more of a bargaining function under the Cunningham and Donnett regimes.

Third, Cunningham and Donnett introduced changes in branch structure.

While the average number of members per official was not altered a great deal, a number of extremely large branches, with a membership of 10,000 or thereabouts, were broken up. These were formed into either smaller industry-based branches, or branches covering a particular district or town, with regular sectional meetings for members from different places of work.

The fourth change that took place in these two regions was the direct encouragement by the regional secretaries of recruitment of new members as a matter of regional concern, rather than as a special Organization Department function. Membership growth was not regarded, in their regions, as a secondary objective. Donnett and Cunningham, in contrast to many longstanding full-time officials, did not seek a 'quiet life'. Instead they actively encouraged the officials and shop stewards to be 'membership-oriented', placing a high priority on the achievement of membership growth. Regional officials had previously not seen their role as involving recruitment at all; they had seen themselves mainly as negotiators, a view traditionally encouraged by most of the other regional secretaries and the national hierarchy.

Finally, the two expansionist regional secretaries also involved themselves in recruiting activities. In particular, Cunningham exerted his influence in the field of inter-union competition for members in newly developing industries, attracted to the Northern region by its Development Area status. Indeed, he actively canvassed for membership and closed shop agreements in Midlands and Southern firms considering moving to the North. In such meetings he stressed the advantages of signing a closed shop agreement with the GMWU – if only as a way of keeping out the more militant TGWU.

Later, towards the end of the 1960s, as Lord Cooper grew near to retirement, new regional secretaries took over in Birmingham and West Midlands (1965), Midlands and East Coast (1965), London (1970), Southern (1970) and Liverpool, North Wales and Irish (1970); and the 'package' of alterations initiated by Cunningham and Donnett became more common throughout the GMWU as the new regional secretaries learnt from their example.

Moreover, it was also at this time, in the late 1960s, that the GMWU embraced the check-off method of payment of dues. In February 1967 only 91,000 members (12 per cent of the union's industrial membership) were covered by check-off arrangements; a surprising feature for a union so financially conscious. After 1967, however, the regional secretaries started actively to pursue check-off arrangements as a means of reducing turnover and increasing membership. The number on check-off rose very rapidly to $49\frac{1}{2}$ per cent in 1971 and $68\frac{1}{2}$ per cent in 1973. Further, the internal changes were followed in a number of cases by a reversal of the previously downward trend in regional membership (see Table 16). Also, the reversals in membership decline cannot be easily explained by reference to a reversal in employment trends.[11] Thus it can be tentatively suggested that the new regional secretaries successfully used their discretion to make the GMWU a more effective recruiting machine.

In conclusion, it may be said that, while external change agents provided some

Table 16 GMWU regional membership

Region	1963	1964	1965	1966	1967	1968	1969	1971	1972	1973	% change total	% change male	% change female
London											%	%	%
Total	96,180	94,169	92,571	89,357	86,771	84,487	80,395	84,455	80,684	84,786	-11.9	-17.3	+7.4
Female	21,206	21,200	21,058	21,115	20,696	20,775	20,145	22,226	21,135	22,768			
Lancs.													
Total	105,723	102,937	104,464	102,665	95,927	94,678	94,904	98,463	91,527	90,797	-14.1	-17.9	-2.9
Female	26,732	27,473	28,961	28,097	26,857	28,050	27,039	29,026	26,163	25,959			
Northern													
Total	75,209	76,506	79,757	82,295	83,800	88,747	93,243	100,218	97,483	100,062	+33	+12.5	+105.7
Female	16,466	16,503	20,563	22,055	22,317	24,164	27,934	32,684	31,683	33,863			
Yorks.													
Total	71,227	71,788	72,272	72,287	71,766	74,195	73,457	79,884	76,174	80,019	+12.3	-1.3	+53.4
Female	17,747	18,579	18,930	20,531	20,204	22,557	23,444	26,171	25,113	27,232			
Southern													
Total	80,366	79,048	79,806	79,821	74,788	74,017	72,642	74,804	72,984	74,843	-6.9	-14.5	+27.4
Female	14,693	15,013	15,316	15,494	15,174	15,617	15,149	17,368	17,784	18,712			
Scottish													
Total	72,351	76,143	76,043	78,518	80,580	82,947	85,114	90,229	91,580	95,669	+32.3	+9.3	+80.4
Female	23,365	24,109	25,916	28,275	30,467	32,199	33,420	36,933	38,871	42,150			
Birmingham													
Total	76,782	78,491	76,539	77,610	73,125	74,882	76,787	89,715	87,767	92,082	+19.9	+5.6	+80.1
Female	14,754	15,117	15,390	16,489	15,440	15,833	16,469	22,874	23,009	26,565			
Liverpool													
Total	58,893	63,122	64,911	65,275	60,314	62,714	63,358	71,379	66,880	68,789	+16.8	+7.8	+38.9
Female	17,103	16,351	17,392	17,307	16,663	18,010	20,156	22,412	22,922	23,757			
Midland													
Total	62,232	59,927	59,877	61,420	58,807	58,248	59,828	63,731	64,525	64,987	+4.4	-5.3	+44.8
Female	12,062	11,352	12,181	12,686	13,016	13,535	14,425	16,602	16,639	17,465			
S. Western													
Total	42,118	41,887	43,206	43,996	43,874	43,850	46,692	42,924	43,394	44,402	+5.4	-9.8	+47.5
Female	11,177	12,024	13,201	13,698	13,883	13,951	14,497	14,468	15,671	16,486			
GMWU													
Total	741,181	744,737	750,503	758,837	732,682	742,429	748,900	804,546	782,595	807,675	+8.5	-2.6	+46.4
Female	175,305	177,729	188,930	195,809	194,848	205,150	214,247	241,710	240,145	256,608			

circumstances favourable for the GMWU – with respect to the growth in female and white-collar membership – there were also some counter-movements that did not augur well for the union, for instance the general decline in employment in food, drink and tobacco. But the regional variations in the GMWU growth rate did not fit any of these national external shifts in attitudes or regional adjustments in employment opportunities – that is, apart from a general increase in female membership. And even in the recruitment of women the GMWU's regions revealed distinctly different industrial patterns. Periods of growth thus appear not to have been determined solely, or even largely, by external factors.

It can be reasonably suggested therefore that the GMWU's growth in membership was very largely the result of internal change agents. The nature of decision-making in the union affected the regional variations in growth. Regional secretaries were in a pre-eminent position in the union's hierarchy, equalling and in some respects surpassing the powers of the general secretary. Hence, each regional secretary could, within the confines of his own region, take the decision that made growth a major regional objective. Furthermore, the regional secretary had sufficient discretion in a flexible system of regional government to make changes conducive to growth.

Thus, since at the beginning of the period studied commitment to growth objectives and priorities were confined to two regions, differential rates of growth emerged in those regions. But as more regional secretaries came to accept growth as a priority, and the new general secretary promoted concomitant national changes, such as the introduction of district officers and the encouragement of check-off arrangements, the union began to grow on a national rather than a regional basis.

Growth in the TGWU

Areas of change

Following the formation of the TGWU its membership grew from 297,460 in 1922 to 1,856,165 in 1975 (see Table 17). From 1950 to 1975 the union's total membership grew by 43.5 per cent and from 1965 to 1975 by 25.3 per cent. Considering the period since 1950 in more detail, Table 18 shows the annual average growth of membership in five-yearly periods.

It can be seen from these figures that the TGWU has expanded far more rapidly, particularly since 1965, than the GMWU. However, a significant part of the TGWU growth came from mergers. From 1951 to 1961 no unions merged into the TGWU; but from 1961 to 1975, twenty-one unions merged with the union. Over the 1961–75 period mergers accounted for 29.5 per cent of the total increase in membership. The increasing importance of mergers to growth can be seen from Table 19. Even if the major merger with the NUVB is excluded from the 1970–75 figure, the proportion of growth gained through mergers in that period would still be 35.7 per cent.

Table 17 *TGWU total membership, 1922–75*

Year	Membership
1922	297,460
1930	422,048
1940	743,349
1950	1,293,403
1955	1,328,820
1960	1,340,357
1965	1,481,565
1970	1,638,686
1975	1,856,165

Table 18 *TGWU annual average growth of membership, 1950–75, from all sources*

Year	Annual average growth
1950–55	7,083
1955–60	2,307
1960–65	28,242
1965–70	31,424
1970–75	43,496

Table 19 *Proportion of annual average growth of TGWU membership resulting from mergers, 1950–75*

Year	% accounted for by amalgamations
1950–55	0
1955–60	0
1960–65	2.1
1965–70	13.2
1970–75	59.3

Table 20 *Annual average 'natural' growth of TGWU membership (excluding mergers), 1950–75*

Year	Annual average 'natural' growth of members
1950–55	7,083
1955–60	2,307
1960–65	27,642
1965–70	27,271
1970–75	17,710

Table 21   *Percentage change in the TGWU's regional membership, 1965–75*

Region	% change	Region	% change
1 London	30.2	7 Scotland	46.7
2 Southern	28.5	8 Northern	28.4
3 South West	26.0	9 Yorks	33.8
4 Wales	2.0	10 Humber and East Coast	29.8
5 Midlands	37.6	11 Ireland	0.4
6 North West	34.8		
		Total	25.3

If one excludes immediate growth through mergers, however, the remaining 'natural' growth (19.3 per cent in 1965–75) is shown in Table 20. It can be seen that these 'natural' growth rates are still considerably in excess of those achieved by the TGWU's main competitor, the GMWU. The extent to which these global figures hide diverging patterns of growth by region and sex, as in the GMWU, must now be considered.

Let us first take regional growth. All regions of the TGWU, unlike those in the GMWU, increased their membership over the 1965–75 period. The percentage change in regional membership 1965–75 is shown in Table 21. The figures show that two regions had a noticeably higher growth rate than average – Regions 5 and 7 – and that two other regions, 4 and 11, had a much lower growth rate than average. However, in the case of the faster growing regions, these major deviations from the norm can be explained largely by reference to factors that did not affect the 'natural' growth rate. Regions 5 and 7, in particular, benefited from growth through nationally negotiated mergers. Region 5 gained some 40 per cent of the NUVB's 79,000 members in the merger with the TGWU, an acquisition reflected in the rise in Region 5's Vehicle Building and Automotive Membership of 33,354 between 1969[12] and 1975. The Scottish region also benefited by some 7000 members after the same merger; and it gained approximately 17,600 members from the Scottish Commercial Motormen's Union (SCMU) merger in 1971. If these merger figures are deducted from Regions 5 and 7's membership they both approach the average rate of growth of 25 per cent. Thus only the two low-growth regions are open to further exceptions to the norm. One of these, Ireland, can be excluded from consideration as a special case, since the union is faced with a somewhat different social, economic, industrial and inter-union situation in that country. Region 4, on the other hand, will be discussed later, but it should be stated here that it was a 'new' region in 1969 following an adjustment of regional boundaries. Therefore, although an allowance was made for the reorganization, the membership figures quoted are not as accurate as those for other regions.

Second, female membership of the TGWU made a contribution to the overall growth rate: this changed both in numbers and as a percentage of total membership (see Table 22). Over the period 1960–75 the union's women's

Table 22 *Women's membership of TGWU*

Year	Women's membership	% of total membership
		%
1950	132,644	10.3
1955	155,260	11.7
1960	152,572	11.4
1965	199,573	13.4
1970	222,866	13.6
1975	289,582	15.6

Table 23 *Annual average growth of TGWU's women's membership, 1950-75*

Years	Annual average growth of women's membership (2)	Col. (2) as a % of total annual average growth (male and female)
		%
1950–55	4523	63.9
1955–60	538	—
1960–65	9400	33.3
1965–70	4658	14.8
1970–75	13,343	30.7

membership rose by 89.8 per cent, while the total membership of the union rose by only 38.5 per cent. However, the importance of the growth in women's membership can be seen more clearly from Table 23. As this table shows, the growth of women's membership in the TGWU, while not insignificant, did not account for the bulk of the union's membership growth. Indeed women's membership growth was more rapid in the TGWU in the period of low growth (1950–55) than in the high-growth periods of the 1960s and 1970s. Once again, the TGWU differs from the GMWU in its detailed membership changes.

Third, the TGWU's growth may have stemmed from particular trade groups and industries. Unfortunately for us, as mentioned above the TGWU reorganized its trade groups in 1968. As a result it is very difficult to make useful comparisons over the period 1960–75. Consideration of the growth of particular trade groups will thus be confined to the 1969–75 period. Table 24 shows changes in membership of trade groups over this limited period. If the Vehicle Building and Automotive trade group's growth rate is disregarded, because the NUVB merger accounted for virtually all the growth in this group, three trade groups can be seen to have made a major contribution to the total and 'natural' increase in TGWU memberships from 1969 to 1975 – some 47 per cent of the total. The three trade groups are ACTSS, Public Services and Civil Aviation, and Food, Drink and Tobacco. Public Services and Civil Aviation expanded most markedly, with an increase in membership of 40.2 per cent: this single group contributed 18.4 per cent of the union's total growth in the six-year period.

Table 24   *Changes in TGWU's trade group membership, 1969–75*

Trade group	*Increase in membership* Member-ship change	*% of TGWU's total membership increase*	Trade group	*Decrease in membership* Member-ship change	*% of total decrease*
ACTSS	48,531	13.9	Docks, Waterways, etc.	7,794	32.0
Commercial Services	27,780	8.0	Road and Transport		
Power and Engineering	11,827	3.4	Passenger Services	15,269	62.7
Vehicle Building and			Building Crafts	328	1.3
Automotive	85,092	24.4	Retired members	950	3.9
Building Construction					
and Civil Engineering	12,054	3.5			
Public Services and					
Civil Aviation	64,083	18.4			
Food, Drink and					
Tobacco	50,895	14.6			
Chemicals, Oil, Mining					
and Rubber	18,479	5.3			
General Workers	25,705	7.4			
Free Cards	4,453	1.3			
Total increase	348,899	100.0	*Total decrease*	24,341	100

Finally, as in the GMWU, the TGWU continually experienced a large turnover of membership within the trade groups and regions examined above. In 1961, for instance, the TGWU had an influx of 356,024 new members and an outflow of 338,860 lapsed members. The TGWU therefore suffered the high cost of recruiting a large number of new members in order to obtain a relatively minor increase in total membership; and any action the union took to reduce this turnover could make a major contribution to membership growth.

We must now seek to explain the apparent paradox of the TGWU's growth record – industrial variations alongside general geographic expansion – and to identify why it attained a higher-than-average growth rate and a considerably better record than its main competitor.

Agents of change

External factors
The first point to make is that the growth of female membership was only marginally greater in the TGWU than in the GMWU. Both unions benefited almost equally from the general tendency of women to join unions in the 1960s: the TGWU's female membership rose by 52.9 per cent from 1963 to 1973, as

against 46.4 per cent for the GMWU. But over the same period male membership rose by 22.7 per cent in the TGWU, as against the fall of 2.6 per cent in the GMWU.

The 'natural' growth of the TGWU's predominantly male membership was concentrated industrially in three trade groups largely unaffected by mergers: ACTSS, Public Services and Civil Aviation, and Food, Drink and Tobacco. They accounted for 46.9 per cent of the increase in total membership over the period 1969–75.

The main external factors influencing the ACTSS group were similar to those affecting the growth of white-collar worker employment generally. They combined to make the ACTSS group the fastest growing section of the TGWU, expanding in every British region of the union between 1969 and 1974. The average change per region was 61 per cent, varying from 111 per cent in the South to 29 per cent in Wales. Expansion of white collar membership was particularly marked in Food, Drink and Tobacco and the man-made fibre industries. Yet the proportional increase from 1969 to 1974 was still somewhat limited; ACTSS grew only from 4.6 to 6.1 per cent of total membership in this period. This reflected the fact that ACTSS began as one of the smallest trade groups in 1969, with some 70,300 members, compared with about 248,300 members in the TGWU's largest trade group, Power and Engineering. Nevertheless, the TGWU capitalized far more effectively than the GMWU on the general trend for white-collar workers to join unions.

The Public Services and Civil Aviation trade group was similarly affected by general employment trends. Once again there was a general upsurge in membership throughout all regions, with the exception of Humber and East Coast. In some regions this expansion was clearly linked to a concomitant expansion in employment; for instance, the London region enjoyed the benefits of the increase in employment that occurred at London's Heathrow Airport. However, the trade group's main membership, some 100,000 of the 166,000 in 1973, was in local government, and here the TGWU gained appreciably from the increase in manual employment in the early 1970s.

In contrast to ACTSS and Public Services and Civil Aviation, membership growth in Food, Drink and Tobacco was achieved, as in the GMWU, against the general trend in employment. Employment in Food, Drink and Tobacco dropped from 817,900 in June 1969 to 739,700 in 1974, a reduction of $9\frac{1}{2}$ per cent. Yet the relevant trade group membership rose over the same period by $31\frac{1}{2}$ per cent. Once again, this growth was spread generally over the regions of the TGWU. (Only the Southern Region experienced a fall in Food, Drink and Tobacco over this period.) A small part of the initial growth may have been the result of an internal transfer of membership, following the formation of the new trade group; but this minor bookkeeping adjustment should not be allowed to blur the importance of the increase in new membership in Food, Drink and Tobacco. This trade group, in a falling-employment situation, contributed proportionately more than the ACTSS trade group to total union growth – 14.6 as against 13.9

per cent. It cannot therefore be said that all aspects of the TGWU's remarkable growth record are rooted in favourable employment trends.

On the other hand, it is true that the trade groups that suffered an absolute loss of membership were in declining employment areas, such as Docks and Road Passenger Transport; in the former employment was affected by containerization and other handling developments, while the introduction of one-man buses, and the growth of alternative means of transport, affected Passenger Transport. Similarly Wales, which revealed a much lower growth rate than other regions, suffered from restricted employment opportunities in the above two industries and a loss of jobs in the Chemical, Oil Refining and Rubber trade group.

From the above examination of external developments we can conclude that the TGWU benefited considerably more than the GMWU from factors such as the white-collar movement to unionization and the growth of employment in the public sector. Yet the employment trends, while creating one or two potential growth areas, did not assist the growth of the TGWU in other areas, such as Food Drink and Tobacco. But it was also argued, by union officials responsible for recruiting, that much of the union's extra membership in local government came from increased penetration, rather than a mere receiving of new workers into membership. Similarly, in the miscellaneous, or more correctly General Workers, trade group, growth was again affected by extending membership into areas only previously partially unionized, for instance Metal Box Company. It would appear therefore that, as the TGWU found itself adversely affected by falling employment in its traditionally highly unionized sectors, such as Docks and Buses, it attempted to offset these developments by further penetrating, within its traditional job territory, other lower-density areas of unionization. Hence, in some trade groups scope for growth among existing partially unionized employees was more important for the TGWU's overall expansion than an increase in the total employed in particular trade group territories.

It can therefore be argued that the 'natural growth' of the TGWU in this period was not merely the result of increased membership opportunities of one kind or another: it resulted from a determination to exploit every possible opportunity, including the more effective recruitment of non-members in low-density areas within the union's traditional job territory boundaries. In other words, a large part of the explanation of this union and the GMWU's growth lies in an analysis of internal developments and attitudes.

Internal factors
We noted above that membership growth in the TGWU was spread geographically across almost all regions. We must therefore consider the general internal factors conducive to growth, rather than exceptional geographical developments, as in the case of the GMWU.

The first point to note is that the national attitude of the TGWU towards growth was consistently positive in the 1960s and 1970s. There was no evidence in interviews of the TGWU tending, like the GMWU, to make membership a secondary objective. However it was noticeable from several sources, including interviews, that the TGWU became much more positive and expansionist in its recruiting and merger activities after the succession of Jones to the general secretaryship in 1969; it was after this event that the TGWU experienced a near doubling of its national growth rate over a comparable six-year period.

This more positive attitude revealed itself in various forms. At the 1969 BDC, for instance, the union changed its official policy on the closed shop. Previously the Executive had opposed formal commitment to what it termed 'compulsory trade union membership' – although this did not prevent TGWU members from operating the practice at local level, usually on an 'informal' basis. However, in 1969 the Executive accepted a motion that urged the 'need to obtain and maintain 100% trade union organisation at each place of employment', by 'collective agreements containing 100% membership as a condition of employment clause'.[13] This switch in policy was no doubt extensively influenced by Jones, who since 1963 had been an assistant executive secretary, a post at least partly created to deal with the question of union growth.

Following this policy change determined attempts were made to secure higher membership densities in partially organized areas, and local officials were expected to initiate recruiting drives in suitable places of employment. After 1965[14] increasing stress was placed on the importance of obtaining check-off arrangements – a new development for the TGWU. Since the union in 1966 recruited 387,930 new members but lost 403,833 as a result of 'lapsing', any measures that secured the more effective retention of membership was clearly a way of rapidly increasing the overall size of the TGWU. By 1972 new membership, at 457,861, was in advance of lapsed membership, at 354,761, and on a much higher total membership – 1,746,234 as against 1,465,662.

By 1974 70 per cent of paying membership was on check-off, and we can reasonably assume that this significantly assisted the reduction of turn-over and hence the continual growth of the union.

Success in the recruiting field was also noted and lauded in *The Record*, the TGWU's newspaper. Such headings as 'Garage Drive Gets Ahead in the South East'[15] and 'Welsh Drive Nets Another 800 for T & G'[16] encouraged even greater recruiting efforts. Targets for membership were generated; as one of the speakers from the floor stated in the 1975 BDC debate, 'Give us the tools Jack and we will give you your two million members'. Thus a growth aura was generated at all levels of the union.

Second, over the 1960s the image of the TGWU underwent considerable change in a way that was thought to be conducive to growth. This process began under Cousins's leadership, from 1956 until 1969, when the TGWU assumed a more militant posture than the GMWU on a whole range of issues, including incomes policy. It was against this background that Jones encouraged the development of power and the rapid growth of the shop steward system (see Chapter 8). It was also in this situation that the number of official stoppages attracting dispute benefit increased from 58 in 1960 to 205 in 1974.

But militancy was not encouraged by Jones for its own sake. It was rather a means for ensuring that members and potential members clearly identified increases in wages and improvements in conditions with unionization. Thus the traditional image of the conservative and autocratic TGWU, nurtured under Bevin and Deakin, was transformed in a relatively short period and in a manner that made it clearly identifiable as an alternative to the slower changing GMWU.

Third, and associated with the change in image, a policy to decentralize and diffuse bargaining emerged which directly affected the union's physical recruiting capabilities. Unlike the GMWU, the TGWU did not attempt to introduce a separate and specific recruiting arm or structure staffed by full-time officials. Indeed, although recruitment was clearly identified as the responsibility of local full-time officials and shop stewards, the TGWU actually reduced its number of full-time officials at a time of expanding membership. But the reduction in full-time officials, from 530 in 1968 to 485 in 1974, was more than compensated for, in recruiting terms, by the increase in shop stewards, from some 13,000[17] in 1965 to some 35,000 in 1975.

This increase reduced the ratio of shop steward to members from 1 to 114 in 1965 to 1 to 53 in 1975 during, not coincidentally, a period of rapidly rising membership. Moreover, as Table 25 shows, it was in those fastest growing trade groups of Public Services and Civil Aviation, ACTSS, Food, Drink and Tobacco and the amorphous General Workers that shop stewards were afforded more lay participation than any other trade groups. Thus, in common with the two exceptional growth regions of the GMWU, the TGWU found that encouragement of shop steward activities had a positive effect on membership growth.

Fourth, and once again in contrast to the GMWU, the governmental structure of the TGWU assisted the national leadership in their campaign for greater growth. In particular, the flexibility of the vertical trade group structure helped the TGWU in the inter-union competition for white-collar members. ACTSS is the only trade group in the TGWU organized occupationally. It was founded in 1922, under the name of NACSS (National Association of Clerical and Supervisory Staffs). In 1968 it was given a new name ACTSS (Association of Clerical, Technical and Supervisory Staffs) to assist its further growth. The senior full-time official responsible for administering ACTSS considers that this change added significantly to its appeal as a separate organization not associated in potential members' minds with the 'dockers' union.

The TGWU's concentrated and centralized constitutional arrangements also enabled the general secretary to determine, and gain commitment to, growth policy throughout the union. Thus, when the decision was taken to overturn the union's traditional stance on the closed shop, the general secretary was subsequently able to use his influence to stimulate active support for closed shop agreements and check-off arrangements at every level of the union. He was also able to take the lead in the encouragement of shop steward bargaining, providing the flexible structures and administrative means to support this policy. Above all, perhaps, the general secretary of the TGWU did not have to work through a

Table 25 *Lay involvement in collective bargaining in the TGWU*

Trade groups	Total replies*	1965 compared with 1975†			Present lay composition‡		
		More	Same	Less	All	No	Some
		%	%	%	%	%	%
Docks and Waterways	18	67	22	11	22	—	78
Commercial Transport	29	86	14	—	21	—	79
Passenger Transport	30	50	40	10	10	—	90
Public Service and Civil Air	20	95	5	—	15	—	85
Vehicle	22	91	9	—	20	—	80
Power and Engineering	30	83	17	—	22	—	78
Chemical, Rubber and Oil	25	88	8	4	22	—	78
General Workers	29	97	3	—	14	—	86
Food, Drink and Tobacco	30	90	10	—	10	3	87
Building	21	67	20	4	18	—	82
ACTSS	28	96	4	—	20	—	80

*The numbers in this column vary because some district officials' answers did not cover all trade groups

†'More, Same, Less' refer to lay participation in local negotiations 1965 compared with 1975; for instance, 67% 'More' in Docks and Waterways means that 67% of district officials had more lay participation in negotiations in their district in 1975 than they had in 1965

‡'All, No, Some' refers to proportion in 1975 of lay members on local negotiating bodies; 'Some' therefore means it was mixed lay and full-time officials, 'All' means all lay and 'No' is no lay officials

governmental structure which placed local full-time officials under the direction of semi-autonomous regional secretaries and local regional councils. In effect, the entire full-time officer force of the union could be used, in the late 1960s and early 1970s, to secure compliance with national objectives as laid down by the general secretary.

It can hence be concluded that the geographically general but industrially diverse areas of membership change in the TGWU cannot adequately be explained mainly by reference to external factors. While the TGWU benefited from the same employment and external attitude changes that brought more members into the GMWU, it also sought, unlike the GMWU, radically to increase its own national growth rate by actively recruiting more members within its own partially organized existing job territories. Moreover, the TGWU's internal structures and decision-making processes gave Jones the power to sponsor and effectively execute a growth policy. Thus the TGWU did not just experience a growth in membership owing to external factors: this positively growth-oriented union instead clearly influenced its own growth rate.

Growth in other unions

Areas of change

In the introductory section of this chapter we undertook to supplement our detailed studies of the two main 'open' unions in our sample with complementary data drawn from other organizations. The changes that occurred can best be considered by reference to the extent to which the unions concerned operated in similar or dissimilar job territories – that is, by classifying them according to the extent to which they were exposed to inter-union competition.

At one end of this continuum we find ASTMS, a white-collar union which ended our period almost as 'exposed' as either of the open unions analysed above. In an intermediate position, from the viewpoint of exposure to competition, come a number of occupationally based unions – most notably the AUEW, UCATT, NUBE and the NUT. At the sheltered end of the continuum, enjoying a substantial degree of protection from competition, we find the more industrially 'closed' ASB, the NUM, the POEU and NALGO. In the rest of this section we outline the developments in each of these unions.

Beginning with ASTMS, we find that it was formed in 1968, from ASSET and the AScW. It then grew from a combined membership of 55,649 in 1968 to 351,000 in 1974, an increase of 531 per cent. If growth by merger is discounted ASTMS still recorded an impressive 'natural' increase of 387 per cent over the same six-year period.

Unlike the two exposed blue-collar unions, however, ASTMS concentrated on extending its job territory horizontally. And whereas many unions in search of substantially new horizontal job territory merged with staff associations, or

Table 26   *Distribution of ASTMS membership by industrial sector, December 1974*

Sector	Membership	% membership total
		%
Engineering	160,000	53
Insurance and Banking	35,000	12
Universities	18,000	6
Chemicals, Rubber, Oil	20,000	7
NHS	15,000	5
Construction and Allied Trades	10,000	3
Textiles and Clothing	6,000	2
Potteries	2,000	1
Miscellaneous	30,000–35,000	12
(*of which* Food, Drink and Tobacco	4,000–5,000)	
Total	301,000	

unions already established in the coveted area, to gain a bargaining foothold, ASTMS also opened up new horizontal territory by directly recruiting individual members. For instance, ASTMS deliberately sought to expand horizontally into virgin territory by recruiting white-collar workers in the largely unorganized areas of shipping and building societies and the more unionized banking and civil service sectors in the early 1970s.

Thus by 1974, partly through mergers but also by direct recruiting, ASTMS had moved out of its original engineering, shipbuilding and vehicle base, which amounted to 73 per cent of its membership in 1964, to the extent of having 47 per cent of its membership in other industries. This is demonstrated by Table 26.

But in addition to horizontal moves of this kind, ASTMS also sought to expand vertically – both upwards and downwards. It laid claim to the higher ranks of management (for example by means of advertisements in *The Times* in

Table 27 *Membership of building unions, 1955–71*

Year	ASW	ASPD	Total membership of: AUBTW	ABT	Packing case, etc.
1955	196,020	69,122	93,922	2919	5314
1960	191,726	65,708	83,233	2000	4310
1961	191,685	64,707	82,818	2000	4282
1962	193,851	64,836	83,030	1950	3920
1963	193,708	76,474*	80,363	2000	3861
1964	191,587	78,303	82,194	2000	3408
1965	194,351**	75,861	80,198	2000	—
1966	191,620	74,064	76,260	2000	—
1967	188,114	71,535	73,881†	2000	—
1968	180,229	68,362	70,272	—‡	—
1969	174,285	63,851	68,581‡	—	—
1970	227,287‡‡	—	61,308	—	—
1971	220,895	—	61,097	—	—

December 1971 UCATT Membership§ – 262,610§§

* Scottish Painters Society (12,112) joined the ASPD
** Packing Case Makers, etc., (3402) joined the ASW
† Street Masons (1400) joined the AUBTW
†† ABT went into different TUC group
‡ Amal. Slaters, Tilers, etc., (2012) joined the AUBTW
‡‡ ASPD and ABT (65,851) joined the ASW
§ The total membership of those unions forming UCATT in 1955 was 384,010, which, compared with the December 1971 total of 262,610 shows a reduction in membership of 31% over 16 years
§§ AUBTW (61,097) joined UCATT (ASW)

Source: TUC Reports.

1969 and 1971. It altered its rules, in 1976, to make possible the recruitment of all grades of white-collar administrative workers. In these and other ways it sought to move from being a relatively 'closed' white-collar organization, concentrating on technical and supervisory staff, to a more or less completely open union for all grades of white-collar work in a wide variety of industries and trades.

The relatively exposed ASTMS was not alone in experiencing significant changes in size over the period 1960–75. Unions in our 'intermediate' zone of inter-union competition were similarly affected. These included UCATT, AEU (later the Engineering Section of the AEF and the AUEW), NUBE and the NUT. UCATT, in particular, underwent a quite radical reduction in size. Over the period 1955–71 the unions forming UCATT declined by 31 per cent overall (see Table 27).

However shortly after the 1971 merger the membership position began to recover. UCATT moved from its all-time low of 260,521 in 1973 to 293,521 by 1977. And the most notable recovery was among non-craft building workers – where the union gained some 21,000 members overall. In contrast to this there were much smaller increases among some craft groups and a further decline of 14,000 among the most craft-conscious group of all, the carpenters and joiners. Within this occupationally imbalanced recovery were considerable regional variations, as Table 28 demonstrates.

Also in the 'intermediate' area of union competition, the AEU (later the Engineering Section of the AEF and AUEW), experienced a growth of 19 per cent over the 1964–74 period. (This figure was nearly double that achieved by the GMWU in the same period.) In common with UCATT, the Engineers showed a

Table 28   *UCATT's membership by region, 1971–75*

Region	1971	1975	% change
Scottish	37,833	37,576	−0.7
Northern	24,559	25,749	+5
Yorkshire	20,235	20,627	+2
North Western	47,104	45,340	−4
Midlands	24,804	30,720	+24
Eastern	13,272	16,289	+23
London	35,467	39,975	+13
Southern	15,072	14,284	−5
South Western	12,689	13,765	+8
South Wales	11,901	11,504	−3
Northern Ireland	8,758	8,863	+1
Eire	10,229	10,094	−1
Totals	261,923	274,786*	+5

*This table excludes the non-manual section of membership as regional boundaries for manual and non-manual members do not coincide

decline in its most highly skilled section; membership of Section 1 of the AEU fell from 32 per cent of total membership in 1960 to 25 per cent in 1972. However, it was suggested in interviews that a large proportion of this decline was due to craftsmen opting to join or transfer to the lower paying, but traditionally non-craft Sections 5 and 5A of the union. Also the women's section grew, as a percentage of total membership, from 8 per cent in 1960 to 12 per cent in 1972.[18]

During the same period NUBE, the 'intermediate' white-collar bank union, did not expand as rapidly as the 'exposed' ASTMS. Yet it did increase by 95.7 per cent between 1960 and 1972. However NUBE's membership growth slowed somewhat after increasing very rapidly in 1967, when membership rose from 56,700 in June 1967 to 70,600 in November 1967. In 1975 NUBE had 104,225 members compared with 82,371 in 1968. Over the 1960–75 period NUBE also increased its female membership as a proportion of its total membership from 32.6 per cent in 1960 to 45.6 per cent in 1975.

The last union to be considered in the 'intermediate' area of membership competition is the National Union of Teachers (NUT). This grew in total membership from 225,181 in 1960 to 331,301 in 1970. It then decreased in size to 301,223 in 1971, only to rise to 315,691 in 1973. However, these global figures hide a downward shift in 'full' membership[19] from 214,432 in 1960 to 207,800 in 1973.

In the more 'sheltered' area of union competition the relatively closed ASB, NUM, POEU and NALGO all underwent membership changes in the period 1960–75. The ASB (Boilermakers) and the NUM (Miners) both suffered losses in membership as their traditional recruiting territories shrank. The NUM, for instance, declined from 638,988 in 1960 to 255,296 in 1975.

By contrast with the NUM, the POEU and NALGO experienced a far more favourable period of membership change. The POEU grew by 58 per cent from 1961 to 1971 while remaining within its expanding job territory. Similarly NALGO grew by 89 per cent between 1960 and 1973. This included a major leap of membership of 100,000 members between 1969 (397,036) and 1972 (498,170). There were, however, three minor mergers in NALGO's rapid expansion which marginally enlarged its territory by extending the union into universities and police authorities.

Having reviewed the major areas of membership change in all the unions in our sample, we can draw a number of conclusions about their relative growth experiences before turning to consider the question of change agents. The first point to make is that unions grouped as 'exposed', 'intermediate' or 'sheltered'[20] had a wide range of experiences, both positive and negative. Second, 'open' unions, such as the GMWU, did not always do better than 'closed' unions, such as NALGO, or the 'intermediate' AEU–AUEW(E). However, virtually all the unions that recruited predominantly or solely among white-collar workers experienced a higher growth rate than other unions – for example, ASTMS, NALGO and NUBE – although the NUT 'full' membership proved an exception to this generality. As far as women members were concerned the unions generally benefited from the movement of women towards unionization. But in the case of NALGO and the NUT, despite there being some scope for recruitment in this field, these unions proved exceptions to the general rule.

Geographically these 'other' unions also had quite different experiences. For instance, UCATT's growth varied quite markedly geographically, whereas NALGO's was quite general throughout the union.

It was thus only in the detail, and not in respect of general changes in membership growth, that the more 'open' and heterogeneous unions, operating in exposed and intermediate fields of recruitment, differed from more 'closed' and homogeneous unions, recruiting in more sheltered territories. Yet within the exposed and intermediate group there were interesting industrial and occupational membership shifts. Both UCATT and the AEU, for instance, experienced an increase in lesser skilled membership. ASTMS also revealed an upward and downward occupational shift, as well as a sideways industrial movement. Finally, some unions' areas of change, in terms of membership size, were subject to sudden vertical leaps in ways that cannot be directly explained by reference to mergers. This phenomenon occurred, for instance, in NALGO, NUBE and UCATT. The reasons for the above areas of change will be explored below by examining the relevant external and internal change agents.

Agents of change

External factors

The factors examined in analysing changes in the TGWU and GMWU also played some part in influencing growth rates in other unions. Employment trends obviously adversely affected the NUM and the ASB. Loss of jobs in two traditionally highly unionized sectors of industry, coal mining and shipbuilding, clearly reduced the membership of the industrially 'closed' NUM and the only marginally 'open' ASB. Similarly, but in the opposite direction, the 'closed' POEU expansion was partly accounted for by an expansion of employment in its sheltered territory.

White-collar unions recruiting primarily in banking (NUBE) and local government (NALGO), may also have benefited from an expansion in employment in their job territories. But even for these unions increases in employment did not directly and proportionately account for the increase in total membership. NUBE, for instance, grew by 96 per cent over the period 1960–72, while the banking workforce only expanded by 37 per cent. Similarly, NALGO expanded far more rapidly than the workforce in local government; between 1960 and 1973 total local government employment increased by 58 per cent while NALGO's membership rose by 125 per cent.

Moreover, changes in employment do not always correlate positively with movements in union membership. UCATT and its merging unions experienced membership changes that ran contrary to employment trends: these unions lost members in an expanding employment situation and gained members in a declining employment situation. In a highly fragmented and cyclical industry, UCATT found it harder to retain and attract members during high rather than low employment periods. Neither expanding nor contracting employment situations therefore necessarily lead to expanding or contracting unions.

White-collar unions also appear to have gained from the general trend of white-collar workers to join unions[21] Similarly, most of the unions examined had a faster rate of expansion among women members than men. Once again, we can assume that this was, at least in part, influenced by the general tendency for more women to join unions in this period – as noted by Price and Bain.[22] As a result the female proportion of total union membership increased from 18 per cent to 27 per cent between 1964 and 1974.

But there were again exceptions to this general rule. The NUT, for instance, experienced no radical change in its ratio of female to male membership of approximately 2 to 1. On the other hand, NUBE significantly increased its proportion of women membership, although it must be stated that it started from a relatively low level. In 1960 women only accounted for 33 per cent of NUBE's membership and the union organized some 27 per cent of women in banking. By 1968 women accounted for 45 per cent of NUBE's membership and the Union organized 37 per cent of women in banking. By 1972 60 per cent of NUBE's membership were women. As a result NUBE's density increased from 35 to 39 per cent between 1960 and 1970.

Variations in employment and national changes in attitude to trade unionism among white-collar workers and females therefore go some way towards offering an explanation for the decreases and increases in some unions' membership. However, it is clear that, as we found above in respect of the TGWU and the GMWU, external factors cannot provide comprehensive reasons for 'natural' membership changes in the unions examined. They do not satisfactorily explain, in the first place, why certain movements in an individual union's membership occur; for instance, UCATT's counter-cyclical movements, several unions' periodic leaps or falls in membership, certain regional imbalances in growth and the ability of some unions to reduce turnover. Second, external factors, as in the TGWU–GMWU comparison, do not offer a complete explanation as to why one union should grow faster than another in similar external circumstances. The causes of these so far unexplained areas of change are considered below.

Internal factors

So far as 'other' unions are concerned, the internal factors that need to be considered may be grouped under three headings: attitudes to growth, union images and governmental structures and procedures.

ASTMS was by far the most positive recruiting union encountered in the studies. Its attitude towards membership was described by an ASTMS NEC member in interview as 'if it moves, recruit it'. Lay officers in the union were told that 'The more members ASTMS recruits, the more credibility (and success) the Association has in the bargaining situation'.[23] Movements into new territories, either vertically or horizontally, were an intrinsic part of the union's overall expansionist national policy. No other union had a national policy of encouraging direct recruitment of white-collar workers in virtually *all* job territories.

However, many unions became more growth-conscious towards the end of the 1960s and it is easy to see why this should be so. The competitive impact of relatively expansionist organizations such as the TGWU or ASTMS, were beginning to make an effect. It is also reasonable to suppose that the merger movement, which we describe in detail in the next chapter, disturbed existing job territories and prospects and affected relative size. For all these reasons changing attitudes towards the importance of membership retention and expansion began to affect a range of other attitudes – most notably towards practices such as the closed shop and the deduction of union dues by arrangement with the employer (the so called 'check-off'). For instance, NALGO, which had only 30 per cent of its branches on check-off in 1966, raised this number to 90 per cent in 1973. It also began to actively pursue a closed shop policy after a 1965 Conference decision. As a result of these policies NALGO increased, for instance, its Lanarkshire branch membership from 500 to 1500 members and Glasgow Corporation from 3000 to 5000 members.[24]

The POEU also achieved 100 per cent membership of appropriate grades of post office employees in 1970, following the introduction of the check-off in 1965. The Engineers (AEU) also formally agreed to a check-off system at their Rules Revision Committee in 1970 and UCATT was reminded of the need for effective collections of subscriptions by an EEC member who pointed out that 'over 50,000 members in 1973 were excluded as a consequence of being over 26 weeks in arrears'.[25]

Changing attitudes to growth also affected the second factor listed above: comparative union images, or the view of union purposes and practices that a given leadership projects to members and potential members. ASTMS, for instance, cultivated an image of overall expansion and development coupled with effective national leadership and general militancy. At the same time ASTMS also adapted its image locally to suit more parochial needs and interests. Thus, despite its national affiliation to the Labour Party, ASTMS issued recruiting forms in the Legal and General Insurance Company which reassured insurance's presumed conservative employees by stating:

No Politics Please

If you join ASTMS there are no political obligations. We are a trade union not a political party. We don't care how you vote in an election. We don't even want to know, that's your business.

No other union appeared to be quite as determined as ASTMS to be seen to meet the needs of all kinds of political members. But both UCATT's and the AEU's (AUEW) expansions into semi- and unskilled occupations arose at least partly from their attempts to make themselves appear more attractive to nonskilled workers by seeking industrial rather than craft union status.

Moreover, a number of unions seemed through militant action itself to have some effect on membership growth. The previously moderate NALGO, for example, experienced a jump in membership in 1969–70 of 11 per cent when it took its first major industrial action.[26] NUBE, similarly, after a strike in 1963, increased its membership among Trustee Savings Bank employees by 16 per cent. Later, in 1967, NUBE again increased its membership from 50,000 to 70,000 in just three months, September–November, when it launched Britain's first clearing bank strike. UCATT also temporarily halted its long-term decline in membership in 1972–73 during and following 'The first real conflict with the building employers since the war'.[27] In the NUT's case, however, innovative industrial action helped to decrease its membership. The NUT's full (in-service) membership not only fell by 41,000 in 1970–71, following its strike, but a number of disenchanted members also left to found the Professional Association of Teachers dedicated to the principle of 'no-strike action'.

The third internal factor we need to discuss relates to union government and concerns the extent to which a given structure of government promotes the emergence of an effective and unified leadership. Once again it was the centralized[28] and concentrated ASTMS that was best able to operate a system of control conducive to membership growth. National officers (NOs) of the union can, for instance, check the weekly membership returns from divisional officers (DOs), both aggregate and by industry. Any loss or gain of over thirty members per week is itemized in ASTMS by group and branch. Moreover, with central direction of growth strategy, recruitment effort can be focused on specific targets mainly leading to 'concentrating recruitment efforts on the leading corporations in the belief that the larger concerns are the pace-makers'.[29] Thus, despite being very 'open' in its general recruitment approach, ASTMS is specific when it comes to organizing its publicity and recruitment machine.

But it is not simply that it helps, from a growth point of view, to have a governmental structure that is in its policy and administrative functions relatively centralized; it is also an aid to recruitment if a union is able to make special arrangements to provide new groups with administrative and decision-making structures that appear to fit their special needs. This clearly requires a certain flexibility of organization, and a readiness to innovate. The ASTMS provided for both the possibility of separate negotiating groups and specialist sections, for purposes of membership consultation and administration. These facilities now also exist in NALGO. But most of the other unions studied do not have such flexibility of purpose built into their structure of government.

We have now concluded our review of the natural growth developments in 'other' unions and it is time to summarize our findings. The first point to make is that, so far as external factors are concerned, similar influences can be seen at work to those noted in respect of the TGWU and the GMWU – most notably employment trends among white-collar workers and women. Second, not all the unions studied were able to take equal advantage of these trends and once again it may be said that favourable policies towards growth in particular unions enabled them to influence their own growth rates.

Finally, it would appear that in some cases the growth of particular unions was not at the expense of other unions but rather the result of making inroads into non-unionism. The study of 'other' unions thus added new evidence of how increases in membership were achieved through check-off and closed shops while raising further questions regarding the effects of changes in employment levels and the uses of militancy.

Natural membership change: summary and conclusions

We may now summarize what has been written about natural membership growth in this chapter as a whole in terms of our model of change outlined in Chapter 2. These can be reviewed by considering, first, areas of change: second, agents of change; and third, the conditions of natural growth.

Areas of change

In seeking to summarize what has been discovered under this heading it helps to distinguish between developments within and between unions. So far as *intra-union* change is concerned it is also useful to consider developments under four separate headings: composition, geographical location, chronology and turnover.

Composition

Most of the unions studied did not radically alter the basic composition of their membership as a result of non-merger membership growth. Most unions were content directly to recruit additional members within the various parameters set by existing job territories. Thus ASTMS's attempts to use direct recruiting methods to break into new industrial grounds was out of accord with normal union practice. New industrial and occupational job territories were, as will be shown later, normally penetrated by larger acquisitive unions merging with established and recognized smaller unions or associations already in the coveted job territory.

Within existing territories, however, the proportional composition of membership by sex, white-collar–blue-collar, occupational and industrial divisions were sometimes altered quite significantly by 'natural' membership growth. For instance, the proportion of women members in such disparate unions as NUBE and the GMWU grew quite noticeably; white-collar membership of the TGWU grew faster than any other trade group; the AEU and the unions forming UCATT became less craft-dominated, at least numerically; ASTMS also became more involved with clerks and managers on either side of its original supervisory grades. Thus, although unions' basic job territories were not normally greatly changed by 'natural' growth, the composition of unions' membership by sex and occupation were, in some instances, significantly altered by non-merger membership growth.

Geographical location

There were within the national growth figures of some unions several different geographical trends. In the GMWU, and UCATT, for example, some regions provided significantly different membership growth rates to those of the national average. Indeed, a small number of unions experienced a decline in membership in some regions and a rise in others.

Chronology

A number of unions experienced quite sudden and relatively large shifts in membership. It is not possible therefore to take, say, a five- or ten-year period of change in a union's membership and assume that membership consistently moved one way or another over that period. The TGWU,[30] for instance, experienced sharply contrasting rates of natural growth over consecutive five-year periods. NUBE, UCATT, NALGO and the NUT also underwent very sharp non-merger changes in membership following or during strike action which in UCATT's case went quite substantially against the longer-term trend. Therefore 'natural' membership growth or decline was not always the result of a continual long-term movement in membership.

Turnover

Beneath the industrial, occupational and/or sex facets of membership change, most of the unions examined experienced movements in and out of the union of quite significant dimensions. As cited above, the TGWU in 1966 lost over 400,000 lapsed members. There was, therefore, within the very membership of unions in the 1960s major scope for growth through more effective retention of existing members.

It can therefore be concluded that there was quite a number of different sub-areas of 'natural' membership change within the unions examined, and that it is not possible to develop a 'single-factor' view of the causes of intra-union 'natural' membership change. While membership growth owed proportionately more to women and white-collar workers than any other category of members, it was by no means dominated by changes in these groups. Other occupational, industrial or regional factors have to be recognized as influencing trade union growth, as do the causes of sharp leaps in membership. Moreover, in some unions such a change, or combinations of changes, were much more powerful in influencing growth than were the general white-collar and female trends towards unionization.

Furthermore, it was only in exceptional circumstances that a union's traditional tendency to be 'open' or 'closed' in its membership objectives determined its 'natural' membership growth. Apart from the particular circumstances of the 'closed', high-density and inexorably declining NUM, no other open or closed union behaved in a completely deterministic manner with regard to 'natural' membership change. For instance, the relatively 'open' AEU and UCATT, both in the intermediate zone of membership competition, experienced different growth rates. We may conclude from this that existing typologies, based on some single aspect of the nature of a union's existing membership and recruiting territory, do not serve to explain, as a general rule, the intra-union areas of natural membership change identified in the unions studied.

Turning to consider what may be concluded about areas of change *between unions*, we must begin by re-emphasizing that in broad terms industrial job territories were largely unaffected by this type of change – with the exception of ASTMS, and to some extent NALGO. Apart from these instances unions did not recruit aggressively in new industrial job territories. On the other hand, inter-union competition became far more intense within well established horizontal job territories – especially in respect of white-collar groups. Vertical expansion upwards by the TGWU, and the AEU's attempts to retain the membership of newly elevated white-collar craftsmen, brought both unions into conflict with ASTMS as it sought to move downwards into the same job territory.

As competition for members intensified, the number of inter-union disputes heard by the TUC noticeably increased, as shown by Table 29. This records certain unions' appearances before the TUC's disputes committees. The number of cases involving more fractious TUC affiliates, i.e. those that appeared ten or more times before disputes committees 1960–75 – rose quite sharply from 9 cases in 1960 to 19 in 1968 and 70 in 1970, as the competition for membership spiralled.

It can be seen from Table 29 that ASTMS stands out as the one union appearing at the Disputes Committee more times than its size would suggest was warranted. Between 1969 and 1975 ASTMS (301,000 members in 1974) made 60 appearances before the TUC's Disputes Committee, compared with the very much larger TGWU's (1,857,308 members in 1974) 51 appearances. It seems reasonable to suppose that it was ASTMS's attempt to extend recruiting vertically downwards into grades of workers coveted by other unions that placed it at the top of the TUC's Disputes Committee's list between 1969 and 1975.

But ASTMS was not the only union involved in increased inter-union competition. Changes in the membership composition of individual unions resulted in virtually all the unions we studied becoming similarly involved, either as aggressors or defenders of their traditional job territories – for example, NUBE versus the Bank Staff Associations in banking; NUBE versus ASTMS in banking and insurance; ASTMS, the TGWU, the AEU and others in engineering; NALGO and ASTMS in universities and health service; the TGWU and ASW (UCATT) in building; Boilermakers and the AEU (AUEW) in engineering; the NUT, NAS and PAT in education.

Thus we may conclude that, although 'natural' membership change did not often challenge industrial boundaries, it did lead, both with and without mergers,

Table 29 *Unions with ten or more cases before the TUC's disputes committees – no. of disputes per annum, 1960–75*

Name of Union	1960	1961	1962	1963	1964	1965	1966	1967	1968	1969	1970	1971	1972	1973	1974	1975	Totals
TGWU	2	2	4	2	1	3	2	2	4	4	14	11	10	4	3	4	72
ASTMS	—	—	—	—	—	—	—	1	1	9	8	9	12	6	8	8	61
GMWU	3	3	2	8	1	2	3	4	2	3	8	5	1	10	4	1	60
AUEW	—	—	—	—	—	—	—	—	—	—	—	7	15	6	8	15	51
EETPU	—	—	—	—	—	—	—	—	—	1	4	9	4	4	5	10	37
ISTC	0	0	1	0	0	2	2	0	1	2	4	4	8	4	4	2	34
APEX (CAWU)	0	0	0	1	0	2	1	0	0	0	4	2	6	5	6	6	33
ASBSBSW	1	1	2	1	0	2	3	4	4	0	1	1	1	4	1	3	29
NALGO	0	0	0	0	1	0	0	1	0	3	3	2	2	1	2	5	20
USDAW	1	2	0	1	1	1	1	0	0	2	4	2	0	2	0	2	19
AEU	0	1	6	2	1	3	1	1	2	—	—	—	—	—	—	—	17
AEF	—	—	—	—	—	—	—	—	—	4	8	2	—	—	—	—	14
ASSET	1	0	1	2	1	2	2	1	2	—	—	—	—	—	—	—	12
NUR	0	0	0	0	—	1	0	0	0	1	3	2	1	2	0	0	11
NUSMWCHDE	0	0	0	0	0	0	0	0	1	1	2	1	3	2	1	0	11
UCATT	—	—	—	—	—	—	—	—	—	—	—	—	3	3	3	2	11
URTU	0	0	0	0	0	0	0	0	1	3	3	1	2	1	0	0	11
NUB	0	0	2	2	0	0	0	1	0	0	1	1	2	0	1	0	11
ASW	1	0	0	0	0	0	1	3	0	2	2	0	1	—	—	—	10
NUPE	0	2	0	0	0	1	1	1	0	0	1	1	0	0	2	1	10
Totals	9	11	18	19	7	19	17	18	19	35	70	60	71	54	48	59	534

to a further blurring of vertical job territory boundaries within existing industrial boundaries. Hence the 'natural' vertical growth of unions made their occupational composition generally still more complex. Craft, industrial or general origins did not prevent unions from extending themselves vertically into new occupational territories.

Agents of change

Because we examined agents of change in the manner suggested by Chapter 2's model of change, the factors influencing growth in 'natural' membership were divided into external and internal factors. It will be remembered that external factors are those that, in terms of the model, act on an area of change bypassing the internal decision-making processes of the unions. Internal factors, by contrast, are those that pass through the internal decision-making processes before affecting an area of change.

Of course it could be argued that all membership change comes through the union, as all members have to be formally accepted and formally removed from membership. However, we would argue that as a heuristic device the external–internal division is useful as it allows those change agents that are largely outside the direct influence of the established leadership and existing membership to be considered separately from those that the established leadership and existing membership could be said to be influencing more directly.

The agents of change identified above will now be considered by reference to the kind of natural growth they induced. In this respect it helps to distinguish between two different types of membership change: *received* and *achieved*. The first of these is the result of external factors, but the second is primarily the result of internally induced change.

Received membership change

This involves workers more or less passively falling into, and sometimes even larger numbers falling out of, the membership of inactive recipient unions. The change agents that affect this aspect of 'natural' membership movement are by definition mostly *external*. They were, in the period studied, employment changes and favourable changes in white-collar and female attitudes towards unionization. External factors accounted for the major if not total change in union membership when 'closed', high-density unions or 'closed' sections of more 'open' unions organized in declining employment situations. It was in these circumstances that the NUM, the ASB and the TGWU's Docks and Road Passenger Transport trade groups lost membership.

On the other hand, many unions significantly benefited from expanding employment within their traditional job territories. These 'lucky' unions included those within the whole classified range, from the 'closed' and sheltered POEU to the 'open' and exposed TGWU. The POEU, for instance, gained from expansion in telecommunications employment, and in the TGWU the Public

Services and Civil Aviation trade group benefited from increased employment at Heathrow Airport. In these favourable circumstances new employees were brought within the job territories and hence recruiting orbits of high-density unions, which thus 'received' many of them into membership without any major recruiting initiative.

White-collar and female workers were also received into membership by some individual unions. The generally 'restrictive–passive' GMWU for instance, increased its national female membership by some 46 per cent, while its blue-collar male membership marginally declined. However, the GMWU's two growth regions showed what could be done through a more positive approach to female membership by gaining 80.4 per cent (Scottish) and 105.7 per cent (Northern) increases in women over the same 1963–73 period.

White-collar workers' tendency to join unions benefited nearly all the unions studied. White-collar unions expanded far more rapidly than predominantly blue-collar unions, and the white-collar section of the TGWU expanded at a greater rate than its blue-collar sections. Where the white-collar workforce became proportionately more female, as in banking, the membership of the relevant industrially 'closed' union, NUBE, rose and changed in its sex composition. Similarly, NALGO enjoyed the fruits of an enlarged employment area in local government and a favourable change in attitude among the white-collar workforce towards unionism.

It is not possible however to quantify the degree of individual union growth or decline owing to increases in received membership, apart from the limited circumstances where a closed and shrinking high-density union recruited solely in a declining-employment situation. But the GMWU's positive-regional and passive-national ratio, in terms of increases in female members, was around 2–1 in the positive-regions' favour. Also, ASTMS's positive–expansionist pursuit of white-collar membership placed it some distance in front of any of its competitor white-collar unions. Similarly, the TGWU's positive attitudes towards white-collar recruitment, as reflected in the formation of ACTSS, gave it a considerable advantage over the GMWU's white-collar section, MATSA. Thus some unions grew and some shrank without the union concerned consciously influencing either situation. On the other hand, some grew at a far faster rate than others, owing to their own efforts.

Achieved membership change

In the period studied unions positively oriented towards recruitment affected their growth rates by a variety of actions. The most important of these actions were those that enhanced the union's image, promoted effective recruitment campaigns, provided more local recruiting agents and increased security of membership. Through these means unions achieved increases in membership.

Unions that grew either nationally or regionally at relatively high rates were those that projected at these levels the image of 'delivering the goods'. ASTMS in particular worked hard at using the media to project a national image of responsiveness to white-collar needs. Moreover, with its highly devolved administrative groups organized around bargaining units, it also became all things to all members at the point of entry to the union. Somewhat less 'flexibly', the TGWU maintained a more consistent approach to unionization but departed from its traditionally centralized system of bargaining by encouraging the use of 'reference back' meetings (see Chapter 8) to give its members a more direct control over the bargaining process. It is worth noting that the main unions competing with both ASTMS and the TGWU did not actively encourage localized bargaining.

The most marked example of achieved growth through 'delivering the goods' was, however, the jump in membership over a very short time that certain unions experienced before, during and immediately after strike action. Thus NUBE, NALGO and UCATT all increased their membership by taking major strike action. UCATT managed, for instance, amidst rising unemployment in the building industry, to reverse its long-run decline by becoming more immediately relevant in the bargaining field. On the other hand, however, the NUT lost members through taking strike action. In this more professionally inclined and predominantly female union, the new-found militancy of 1969–70 resulted in a significant loss of members. But this was an exceptional case. Generally strike action influenced union membership positively.

Unions, notably the TGWU and ASTMS, also mounted successful recruiting campaigns. They penetrated non-unionized groups of workers in existing job territories – for instance the TGWU in garages and ASTMS in chemicals. The GMWU, through Cunningham in the Northern Region, also used the sole recognition agreement to good effect among new industries in the region. In the TGWU's pursuit of members the general devolution of bargaining and the accompanying growth in the numbers and influence of shop stewards further assisted the growth of the union. Devolution created many new recruiting agents at the point at which the union 'delivered the goods': the shop floor.

Finally, unions also boosted membership by increasing security of membership. Many of the unions examined sought to retain members more effectively by the use of the 'check-off'. This helped to reduce the immense losses suffered through high turnover. Further, a number of unions initiated and actively promoted 100 per cent membership or closed shop policies. In some instances, for instance NALGO, this produced quite rapid and significant increases in membership.

It can therefore be said that in our period there was ample evidence of the ability of unions to influence growth trends through their own actions. Unions as disparate as the TGWU and NUBE sought to do this by identifying themselves to potential members as organizations capable of 'delivering the goods' to specialist groups and occupations. In some cases actions of this kind resulted in chronological spurts in membership that cannot be explained in any other way. Then again, even in other organizations, such as the generally passive GMWU, aggressive policies in particular regions helped to reverse overall membership trends. Similarly, UCATT was able, through its more militant bargaining policy, to arrest and reverse a period of membership decline against a background of rising unemployment. It can also be argued that the more positive–expansionist unions fully exploited their bargaining advantages with effective nationally directed recruiting campaigns and an increase in local level recruiting agents – the shop stewards. Finally, unions acted, through the closed shop and the 'check-off', to retain more effectively the membership growth they both achieved and received.

The conditions of natural growth

It can be seen that individual union growth was clearly affected by both external and internal factors in the period studied. Some unions' patterns of growth were therefore influenced by whether or not they had an historical presence in industries and/or among occupations that became more inclined to join unions in the 1960s and 1970s.

However, it cannot be said that a union necessarily grew faster than any other union just because it had an historical presence in areas favourable to growth. Unions in such areas, such as the 'open' TGWU and the GMWU, had quite different growth rates. Moreover, even unions with a near monopoly in favourable areas, such as NALGO and the POEU, were not just receivers of new members. It was thus only the exceptional NUM that found its size largely, if not solely, determined by external factors.

Unions generally affected their growth, in both multi-union and single-union job territories, by engaging or not engaging in the activities identified above as producing growth. The fact that some unions in the early part of the period did not undertake these activities on a national scale gave other more consistently growth-oriented unions major advantages. Thus the restrictionist–passive GMWU's initial 'benefit-oriented' approach to membership provided their main competitor, the positive–expansionist TGWU, with the opportunity fully to exploit its organizational advantages.

One of the primary conditions for achieving relatively high union growth was thus a national leadership oriented and committed to growth as a priority. However, commitment alone was not a sufficient condition. Those committed to expansion had to have control of the means of acquiring a high rate of national growth if they were to realize their ambitions. The internal system of decision-making in the TGWU and ASTMS provided such opportunities.

Both the bifurcated TGWU and ASTMS provided their general secretaries with a concentrated and centralized (in the non-bargaining channel) government eminently suitable for the purpose of influencing growth. The general secretaries dominated the general policy-making channels and thus easily spread their growth ethic throughout the bureaucracy and into the lay ranks. They could virtually guarantee that the appointed full-time officers followed the national policy on expansion. Moreover, the national leadership in both unions was firmly in favour of using more militant and local bargaining policies to identify the union with the domestic needs of its actual and potential members. They believed in the service rather than the benefit-oriented approach to membership. The image projected by their unions was therefore in sharp contrast to that of some of their less demonstrative competitors.

It is not surprising therefore that the pattern of growth was uneven between unions recruiting in similar circumstances. Unions differed according to whether or not the national or regional leadership made growth a priority. They also differed in the degree to which their centralized–decentralized and concentrated–diffused systems of government allowed the leadership to achieve their goals – Jones in the GMWU, for example, would not have achieved the same growth effect as he did in the TGWU. Unions themselves therefore to a great degree shaped the conditions for growth between 1960 and 1975.

We turn now to the implications our findings have for aggregate union growth. The emphasis in recent theories has tended to be on external factors as the key, and only, variable influencing aggregate union growth.[31] For instance, in examining white-collar union growth it was concluded that 'No significant relationship was found between the growth of aggregate white-collar unionism and any of the following factors (including such aspects of trade unions as their public image, recruitment policies and structures)';[32] and similar conclusions were reached regarding total union growth when it was claimed that such 'indirect and secondary factors as union leadership are largely dependent upon and hence captured by the explanatory variables (that is, rate of change of prices, rate of change of wages, the level and/or rate of change of unemployment and the level of union density)'.[33]

There are, of course, some important differences in the method we used to assess the causes of disaggregated growth and those used by the above theorists to identify the causes of aggregated growth of unions. At the disaggregated level, we asked different questions. We did not, as can be clearly seen above, rely on the statistical methods employed in the aggregate studies. Further, we chose a different length and period of time and concentrated on the British situation to the exclusion of international comparisons. Nevertheless, despite these methodological and other differences, it would seem to us that there is *prima facie*, a conflict between the Bain *et al.* general theory of growth and our more limited findings regarding the factors that influence disaggregated growth. It would seem from our research, to put it no stronger, that unions' structure, government, policy and leadership significantly affect disaggregated and aggregated union growth.

Our analysis of disaggregated growth challenges the above aggregate theory in the following manner. If those individual unions that influenced their own growth rates did not do so at the expense of the 'received' expansion of their own or other unions, trade union variables can be said to have influenced aggregate growth. It is, moreover, highly unlikely that all or most of the achieved growth mentioned above occurred at the expense of received growth. Indeed, it was more often than not at the expense of continuing non-unionism. For instance, NALGO's recruitment of additional members in local government through the adoption of a closed shop policy was definitely not at their own or any other union's expense. There were no other unions in local government capable of recruiting these non-unionized workers. Similarly, the extension of the 100 per cent shop by the POEU directly affected its size. Furthermore, the general development by virtually all unions studied of the check-off system and consequent reduction in union turnover can be quite confidently claimed to have been largely at the expense of continuing non-unionism. Also, ASTMS's and the TGWU's selective recruitment efforts in areas of non-unionism, and the extension of the shop steward system in the TGWU and certain regions of the GMWU and UCATT, almost certainly positively affected their membership growth without depriving other unions of an immediate membership increase.

Growth associated with strike action was also generally at the expense of non-unionism. Moreover, the extension of the closed shop and the check-off meant that the sudden leap in membership often associated with strike action could be consolidated in many cases into a more long-term membership gain.

And, as explained above, underlying this aggressive recruitment activity was the advent of a new growth-conscious leadership. This leadership, for instance Jones of the TGWU and Jenkins of ASTMS, was also willing to accelerate local and shop steward involvement in the bargaining process. This resulted in the enhancement of the role of the most effective recruiting agent – the shop steward. Moreover, in the most flexible union, ASTMS, highly selective recruitment campaigns were used to attract into membership members who previously found it extremely difficult to associate themselves with trade unionism. It is difficult to believe that these combinations of activities did not help ASTMS to acquire members by more effectively penetrating parts of the non-unionized workforce normally adverse to unionism.

Thus, although our examination of various kinds of disaggregated growth in a limited number of unions cannot be used as conclusive evidence as to the factors affecting total union growth, it can be used to suggest that growth in the UK over the period examined was to some significant extent influenced by union leadership and other facets of union organization. This suggests that aggregate theories that discount internal factors may be oversimplifying the causes of union growth.

Finally, the above arguments regarding the influence of unions over aggregate growth are somewhat strengthened when the activities of the TGWU and ASTMS are placed within the wider context of unions' general attitudes and practices *vis-à-vis* membership in the 1970s. Because both the TGWU and ASTMS were relatively 'open' and recruited in exposed territories, they disturbed the inter-union *status quo*. This stimulated a competitive recruitment contest, similar and related to that in the merger movement (see Chapter 6) intended to restore the numerical balance. Furthermore, the advent of more growth-conscious leadership in the GMWU – both nationally and regionally –

also fed inter-union rivalries; and unions' needs for more representative (numerical) muscle in the TUC, for example, during discussions in the Social Contract, further heightened the membership contest. Also, inflation and other developments adversely affected some unions' financial standing and hence forced them to adopt a more effective means of retaining and acquiring members.

Thus individual unions' initial success in creating the conditions for their own growth caused others to emulate their self-help activities. Out of this concern for comparative numerical strength a growth spiral developed which, it can be very reasonably suggested, made a significant contribution to aggregate growth. It also, no doubt, brought home to a number of union leaders the advantages that their counterparts in the more concentrated and centralized (in the non-bargaining channel) unions enjoyed.

6 Change in job territory: mergers

The diversity of the merger movement of 1961–75 (see pages 67–74) did not produce any clearly identifiable industrial or occupational trends in union structure. It did, however, have certain size characteristics. Mergers normally involved a major and a minor, or a number of minor, unions. For example, of those TUC unions that merged by 'transfer of engagements', 65 per cent of transferring unions had less than 5000 members and 15 per cent fewer than 500 members. Only 9 per cent of transferring unions had over 25,000 members. By comparison, over 60 per cent of the unions to which they transferred had over 50,000 members in 1962. There was therefore a general absorption of minor unions by major TUC affiliates and hence the major unions became larger, more general or more open as a result of the merger movement.

So the unions involved in mergers can be most easily classified by reference to their relative size. Moreover, this characteristic is closely related to what we take to be the most important distinction between merging unions: their differences in motivation and strategy. Thus most minor partners in mergers share similar aims. They are usually motivated primarily by defensive considerations and are attempting to forestall extinction or some lesser, but still adverse, eventuality. But there are also cases where even the major partner to a merger is motivated by the search for greater security; this was the case in respect of the UCATT merger, where the major partner, the ASW, was also searching for the shelter of a larger amalgamation. This made the UCATT amalgamation a paradigm case of the *defensive merger* in action, and for this reason we have made a special study of it and analyse it in some detail below.

But although most unions became involved in mergers for primarily defensive reasons, we could discern two other important objectives that gave rise to merger activity. The first of these was the *consolidatory merger*, where the aim of those involved was to consolidate a shared position in a given industry or occupational area. This was the objective most clearly pursued by the AEU resulting in the AUEW, and we have made a detailed study of this merger.

Finally, unions such as ASTMS and the TGWU, who pursued active merger policies in our period, fall more readily into a third category, which we term *aggressive mergers*. The aim of the major partner here is to seek the basis for further expansion and development, sometimes into quite new job territories.

Because ASTMS and the TGWU are very different organizations, operating in contrasting job territories, we decided to study both of them in some detail.

Thus the bulk of this chapter is concerned with the contrasting and somewhat disparate merger activities of four major TUC unions, chosen to illustrate and exemplify the nature and processes of the merger movement in our period. Some reference is made to other unions and other mergers, but this is mainly in order to complement and support what has been concluded from the major case studies. Before turning to them, however, we shall end this introductory section with a few additional comments on the nature and process of the merger movement as such.

The first point to stress is that, as was mentioned in Chapter 5, the merger process can be concluded only by means of a *de jure* change. Whether a union chooses to move its members *en bloc* to another union by transfer of engagements or amalgamation, it has to go through a legal procedure. There is therefore in the merger process a point at which the joining together of the unions is clearly legitimized.

Changes in the law can, therefore, have a marked effect on mergers. Thus it is not a coincidence that most of the mergers studied followed the relaxation of the law on mergers in the Trade Union (Amalgamations etc.) Act of 1964. Prior to 1964 each union merging through an amalgamation needed to have a 50 per cent poll and a 20 per cent majority in favour of amalgamation before such a merger could take place. Voting in large unions rarely reaches the 50 per cent mark, even in important elections, hence the pre-1964 law on amalgamations mitigated against union mergers. From 1964 onwards the law was considerably relaxed. In the new legal environment a union could, through a transfer of engagements, transfer its members by a simple majority of those voting in the transferring union alone. Similarly, an amalgamation could be obtained if a simple majority of members voting in both merging unions was in favour of the amalgamation.

Furthermore, these legal arrangements have quite significant consequences for the internal process of change in unions leading up to a merger. Technical details require, in transfers and amalgamations, that the full-time leadership negotiate quite complex arrangements which are acceptable both under the law and to the membership of at least one of the merging unions. An examination of mergers must therefore focus on the reasons for, and means whereby, national *de jure* decisions are taken, and thus must be concerned primarily with a union's national decision-making processes. These may be activated as a result of membership initiatives and demands, working through the normal constitutional channels, or they may derive from national leadership priorities and strategies which are formulated and decided more or less independently of membership pressure. In either case the change agents to be examined are those that operate on the full-time national leadership.

If we consider first those change agents that have originated in the membership, it is clear that most of the larger unions examined had long-standing commitments to increase the size of their unions through mergers – for example, the Engineers' and the ASW's interest in industrial unionism stretched back into the nineteenth century. Similarly, the TGWU and the GMWU had vied for merger partners in the amalgamation boom of the 1920s;[1] and the Boiler-makers had been involved in the initial talks in forming the AEU held in 1914.[2] The larger of the merging unions, had, therefore, long-standing lay membership support for, or acquiescence in, mergers. They were all traditionally merger-oriented, even if, up to the 1960s, they did not show any urgency in their merger activities.

However, there is no sign that in the 1960s and 1970s lay membership in the major unions increased their support for mergers. Table 30 suggests that in 1970 there was no great interest in the AUEW amalgamation, even in those AEU branches that showed a marked enthusiasm for a politically important EC election in the same year. Indeed, three branches with relatively high turnouts in the EC elections failed to record any vote in the amalgamation poll, and only 8 per cent of the total membership participated in the poll. The type of rank and file interest in amalgamations that stimulated the merger movements in the

Table 30 *Branch voting in the AUEW(E) – amalgamation and EC5 ballots, 1970*

Branch	% of electorate voting on 2nd ballot for EC5	% of electorate voting in the amalgamation ballot
Carbrook 2	37	3
Chapeltown 2	23	12
Dromfield	50	2
Hillsborough	22	5
Intake	30	10
Parsons Cross	24	10
Rotherham 5	34	7
Rotherham 7	33	16
Sheffield 11	30	16
Sheffield 36	42	5
Sheffield 39	46	3
Colchester 3	28	3
Gainsborough 3	30	11
Leicester	17	4
Leicester 8	18	4
Leicester 14	18	4
Leicester 15	13	No vote returned
Luton Leagrave	23	2
Leicester East	23	No vote recorded
Stamford	30	3
Thurmaston	20	2
Towcester	30	No vote recorded

Engineers[3] and other unions in the 1920s was hence conspicuous by its absence in the later 1960s and 1970s.

But even the low figure of 8 per cent for AEU lay involvement was far in advance of formal lay participation in other major merging unions, such as the ASW, the TGWU and the GMWU, for these major unions all used the transfer of engagements methods. Hence their members were not constitutionally given any opportunity to express an opinion on the mergers negotiated on their behalf by their full-time officials. Indeed, in some major unions, such as ASTMS, the rules provided for the NEC to conclude transfers of engagements without any reference to the views of the existing membership – see for example Rule 15(a) of ASTMS.

In the 1960s, therefore, mergers affecting the major unions in our study did not receive their primary stimulus from the mass membership; they were faced with a series of *faits accomplis* arising out of the considerable discretion enjoyed by their national leaders.

Of course, minor merging unions were legally bound to bring their members into the merger process. Yet even here the full-time officials of the minor merging unions generally involved the wider membership in the decision only at the final stage – that is, in the ballot on the agreed terms and conditions of the merger. At this point the membership could only accept or reject the proposals as put before them. Usually they accepted by a significant majority in a relatively high poll. For instance, the AUFW recorded a 59 per cent poll and a 76 per cent majority in favour of its proposals to merge with the AEU. Similarly, the minor unions that joined ASTMS usually recorded a clear majority for the merger; for example, the Union of Insurance Staffs voted 10,921 for and only 1174 against the merger in a 70 per cent poll. An exception to the above examples was provided by the CWU's membership in 1965; they rejected a merger proposal negotiated by their officials with the GMWU and, five years later, joined the TGWU.

National full-time officials were therefore usually extremely influential and successful in promoting mergers in both major and minor unions. A consistent and traditional desire to grow, plus the post-1964 merger legislation, helped the national full-time leaders of major unions to launch initiatives without having to refer constantly to the wider membership for authority. In minor unions, on the other hand, there was normally some pressing need for an amalgamation which, under the right merger terms, could provide the national full-time leaders with sufficient discretion to conclude merger negotiations free of mass membership involvement. It is thus necessary to turn to the non-membership-inspired change agents influencing the national full-time leadership if we wish to identify those factors that actually produced the national merger movement of the 1960s and 1970s, in both major and minor merging unions.

The rest of this chapter therefore is centrally concerned to explain how change agents of this kind combined to precipitate action by national leaders in our four contrasting groups of unions: first in the case of the UCATT merger, next in respect of the AUEW, and finally by reference to the merger initiatives of the national leaders of ASTMS and the TGWU. In each case study we turn first to an analysis of the areas of change, before discussing change agents and the direction of change. In the final section of the chapter we seek to summarize and develop the results of the case studies, making some use of other relevant data drawn from the experience of other unions. We conclude with an analysis of the features that may be said to facilitate mergers in general.

UCATT: a defensive merger

Areas of change

Pre-UCATT
Prior to 1960 there had been no marked change in the structure of the largest unions in the building industry since the formation of the ASW (Woodworkers) in 1921. The pattern of building union mergers since that date tended to be horizontal – between similar geographically based craft groups. The only notable exception was the AUBTW's absorption of the National Builders Labourers and Constructional Workers Society in 1952.

The craft unions did, however, through 'natural' membership growth, tentatively open their ranks to semi-skilled workers. The decentralized ASW, for instance, agreed in 1952 to admit semi-skilled workers and women into membership; although it was clear from interviews that several ASW branches, in different regions of the UK, did not encourage the recruitment of any other than skilled workers right up to the late 1960s. This reluctance to recruit semi-skilled workers was placed at the door of the 'silver-arses' in the highly craft-conscious ASW.

Apart from the AUBTW the building unions remained overwhelmingly craft-oriented. Of the 383,010 members in the ASW, ASPD, AUBTW, ABT and Packing Case Makers in 1955 (the major unions in the later UCATT), by far the greater proportion were craftsmen. In a study of the composition of the largest of the craft unions, the ASW, by W.E.J. McCarthy and H.A. Clegg in 1959, 96 per cent of members sampled were identified as craftsmen. The ASW's membership was also found, Table 31 shows, to be concentrated in the construction industry. Thus, despite various rule changes to encourage the recruitment of non-craftsmen, the major unions in the UCATT merger were relatively unchanged in 1960 in terms of membership composition, compared with the 1940s. However, the unions in the building industry did closely associate with each other for bargaining and other purposes through the National Federation of Building Trades Operatives (NFBTO), which was formed in 1918. This originally grew out of industrial unionists' demands for the unions to unite 'building operatives in one revolutionary union'.[4] (At that time the industry contained '67 unions, local and national, and 13 local federations. . .'.[5] Partly as a counter to 'one union' demands, the ASCJ (ASW) successfully proposed the formation of the NFBTO. In 1954 the NFBTO was described, somewhat grandly, as 'The most highly

Table 31 *Industrial distribution of the membership of the Amalgamated Society of Woodworkers, 1959*

Industry	Proportion in sample	Estimated distribution of membership
	%	
Building and Civil Engineering	70	136,000
Shipbuilding and Ship Repair	8	15,000
Local Authorities and National Health Service	5	9,500
Engineering and Vehicle Building	4	7,500
Timber and Furniture	3	5,200
Government Establishments	2	3,800
All other industries	6	11,600
Sick and superannuated members and members in the Forces	2	4,000
Total	100	192,600

developed of all the industrial federations. . . . It handles all negotiations, both nationally and regionally, through its membership of the National Joint Council for the Building Industry, and can even call out any section of its affiliates in a local dispute without reference to the constituent unions'.[6] By the late 1960s it was described more accurately and graphically in interview, by one of its regional secretaries, as 'getting the rubbish the individual unions couldn't win' and as being 'relatively unknown on the [building] sites'.

We shall argue below that the failure of the NFBTO to achieve a significant degree of site bargaining, in a period when it was formally responsible for negotiations throughout the industry, was a factor of importance in producing the move towards merger in the 1960s.

Formation of UCATT

It was in these circumstances therefore that UCATT was formed by the minor ASPD, AUBTW and ABT transferring engagements to the major ASW. Guided, if not directed, by their respective national leaderships, the building unions changed the loose inter-union federated arrangements into a far more centralized system of government under the dominant influence of George Smith, general secretary of the ASW. The chronological sequence of events and the unions involved were described in Table 27 (page 149). This showed how the craft-conscious 'exclusive' ASW became part of a more widely based and 'open' union by joining with other smaller ex-craft unions. The result was an industry-based amalgamation – seeking to recruit virtually all workers in the construction industry irrespective of craft or skill. The factors that produced these changes will now be considered.

Agents of change

Four sets of factors interacted to make national leadership in all the UCATT unions aware of the difficulties involved in continuing to operate independently. By the end of the 1960s these factors had combined to constitute a more or less unanswerable case for a defensive merger of some kind. Most of the more important factors were associated with declining absolute levels of union membership, but there was also a secondary influence stemming from the TUC. We consider these developments in turn under four broad headings:

(1) Membership and finance;
(2) Membership, technological change and demarcation disputes;
(3) Membership and the influence of other unions;
(4) TUC policy.

Membership and finance

The ASW, ASPD and AUBTW all found themselves in acute financial difficulties in the mid and late 1960s. These arose out of the interaction between the rising costs of servicing members and an absolute reduction in numbers. Between 1955 and 1971 the unions that formed UCATT experienced a drop in membership of some 31 per cent. In 1955 they had 384,010 members and in 1971, 262,610 members. In the case of the AUBTW, this resulted in a loss of £28,476 in 1955, preceded by deficits in every year since 1952. In 1969 the AUBTW recorded that it 'probably faced the worst and most serious financial report . . . [with] an average deficit, over the last nine years of £14,000 per annum'.[7] Moreover, it was predicted that 'if there was a relative increase in 1969/70, 1970/71 and 1971/72, you [i.e. the AUBTW] would be insolvent at the end of 1972'.[8] Similarly the ASPD used up £139,000 of their reserves between 1960 and 1963.[9] Somewhat later the ASW reported in 1972 that 'there is a most serious deficit in our financial position, the most serious in fact, in the history of the Union'.[10] In 1971 the ASW had a deficit on receipts and payments of £386,245. It is therefore not surprising that Smith, the general secretary of the ASW, should write that 'the mergers . . . themselves mainly took place because of . . . [financial] difficulties in the building unions'.[11]

The unions tried to restore their financial positions by raising subscriptions and cutting services. But as the general secretary of the ASPD explained in 1969, 'whatever the increase in [individual] contributions . . . , the facts are that the [total] contribution income has not materially increased'.[12] This was partly because rising subscriptions led to even greater membership loss, and partly because those who remained in the union were often able to avoid the effect of increased subscriptions by transferring to 'cheaper sections' of the union. It therefore looked as if the unions in the building industry had reached a point of diminishing financial returns; the price elasticity of membership had become greater than unity.

But the unions involved in the UCATT merger also found it virtually impossible to economize on services and expenses during an inflationary period. Most important of all, they found it extremely difficult to reduce overall salary costs. UCATT, with a ratio of full-time officials to members of 1 to 1300 in 1971, had one of the highest, and therefore one of the most expensive, full-time official–member ratios in the UK. Similarly, on the benefits side, the combined ASW and ASPD spent over 50p per member of friendly benefits in 1970, a sum equalled or exceeded by only three other British unions.[13] Thus on a declining membership their financial positions were becoming untenable.

The reduction in absolute membership in all the merging unions could, *a priori*, have been caused by one of several developments in the building industry. These developments can be broadly divided into quantitative changes in overall numbers or particular occupations – say, a reduction in the number of craftsmen – and qualitative changes, which might lead to a reduction in union membership without an overall reduction in the labour force. For instance, under this latter heading it has been argued that an extremely important factor has been the growth of labour-only sub-contracting – for LOSC (or 'the lump', as it is called) has always defied union organization, for reasons we discuss further below.

But dealing first with quantitative changes, it has been estimated from Department of Health and Social Security and from Census returns that over the 1961–73 period the total of employers and self-employed in the construction industry increased from 169,000 to 435,000.[14] However, there was also a cyclical depression in the construction industry, starting in 1965–66, which reached its nadir in 1970–71. According to the Department of Environment's figures employment in registered firms totalled 1,161,100 in 1964 and 865,000 in 1970, a decline of 25½ per cent. Similarly, but far less dramatically, the employed plus employer and self-employed numbers fell from 1,821,000 in 1966 to 1,546,000 in 1971, a decline of only 15 per cent. But by 1973 the total number of people working in the industry, at 1,773,000, was nearly back to the mid-1960s peak employment level and exceeded the 1961 total by over 150,000. Thus on the latter definition the total workforce in the industry, while suffering short-term cyclical movements, did not shrink over the 1961–73 period as a whole. As a result, the total recruiting territory of the merging unions was no smaller in 1973 than in 1961.

On the other hand the number of craftsmen in the industry may have declined, even if the total number of operatives increased. As the merging unions tended to concentrate recruitment in craft areas in the construction industry, such movements were most likely to affect their levels of actual and potential membership. However, Table 32 suggests that there was little change in the percentage of carpenters and joiners working in the industry. Also, and more significantly, a comparison between ASW membership and carpenters and joiners employed in registered firms prior to the explosion of LOSC in 1966 suggests that changes in employment levels did not directly affect changes in ASW membership; in fact, Table 33 shows that as employment of carpenters and joiners increased the level of ASW membership marginally declined. Moreover,

Table 32 *Carpenters and joiners as a proportion of the total construction labour force including non-manual and self-employed*

Year	Carpenters and joiners as % of total construction labour force
1961	10.5%
1966	10.7%
1971	10.2%

Source: Census (1961, 1966 and 1971).

Table 33 *ASW membership compared with carpenters and joiners employed in registered firms*

Year	Carpenters and joiners employed in registered firms	ASW
1957	161,400	198,000
1958	157,500	199,613
1959	156,900	192,259
1960	161,300	191,726
1961	166,200	191,685
1962	171,600	193,851
1963	174,200	193,708
1964	174,500	191,587

in 1974 and 1975, during a slump in the construction industry, UCATT actually increased its membership against the movement in the business cycle – from 260,620 in 1973 to 261,492 in 1974 and 278,127 in 1975. There was therefore no direct positive relationship between levels of ASW membership and employment of craftsmen in the industry.

We now turn to qualitative changes and the reductions in membership. It has been estimated[15] that labour-only sub-contracting grew by 60 per cent from 1960 to 1966, to between 165,000 and 200,000. Moreover, after the introduction of Selective Employment Tax (SET) in 1966 LOSC doubled, according to figures commonly quoted in the press, to 25–30 per cent of the workforce or 400,000 lump workers by 1973.[16] Many of the ASW officials stressed, in interview, the inverse and causal relationship between LOSC and the degree of unionization. It was argued that, as demand for labour grew in the industry, so did LOSC. In turn, as LOSC grew, union membership declined.

The unions' leaders believed that LOSC had grown at the expense of union membership largely because the individual unions had failed to 'deliver the goods' to their members and potential members. As the president of the NFBTO stated in 1969,

> we have failed lamentably in some instances to grasp the really fundamental implications that have arisen out of a full employment economy. It is because of this that we can no longer claim to negotiate our members' earnings in large parts of the country, and we must, if we are to survive somehow retrieve that privilege and responsibility.[17]

The union leaders hence explicitly recognized that their existing bargaining practices had contributed to the decline in union membership. National collective bargaining via the NFBTO had not, first, kept pace with average earnings; second, maintained craft differentials; or, third, matched the immediate financial advantages of lump labour in periods of relative high taxation. In the first place, average earnings in the highly fragmented construction industry, under full employment conditions, consistently exceeded the nationally negotiated wage. By 1968, of the craftsmen's £22.72 average wage only £15.41 was negotiated nationally by the NFBTO. In 1976 the earnings average was £63 and the nationally negotiated basic rate £46.[18] Moreover 78 per cent of craftsmen and labourers in the largest firms[19] were working, in 1968, under some form of incentive scheme. There was therefore a growing opportunity for individuals or union representatives to negotiate wages at the site level in the 1950s and 1960s or for management unilaterally to initiate such schemes.

Unfortunately for the building craft unions, through their years of reliance on the NFBTO and national negotiations and the ASW's official opposition, since 1947, to bonus schemes, they were disadvantaged *vis-à-vis* the employer and the 'lump' worker once site incentives became the norm. The unions had few, if any, site negotiators. For instance, the Phelps Brown inquiry reported that only 11 per cent of company sites visited had shop stewards. At the AUBTW Conference in 1970[20] it was recorded that the union only had 1150 shop stewards in total. Yet there were over 80,000 firms and some 1300 local authorities that could employ bricklayers. Even in a major construction centre like the City of Birmingham, the ASW in 1969 had only two shop stewards on building sites: in the whole of the South West region the ASW had some 600 stewards in total in 1972, but only 97 were in the construction industry.[21] There were therefore in the 1960s large parts of the country where ASW and other craft unions had abdicated responsibility for site bargaining. In the unions' absence workers on the 'lump' negotiated individually, or accepted the employer's unilateral action, in setting the actual wage level which was consistently higher than that negotiated collectively by the union nationally.

Second, the near-exclusive craft unions had failed to maintain craft differentials. Crane drivers, steel fixers and steel benders and other plus-rated men, in particular, approached and sometimes exceeded craft earnings in the 1960s. For instance, in June 1968 the gross average weekly earnings of craftsmen were £22.49 and plus-rated men £24.20. Craft-conscious workers, such as the carpenters and joiners, cannot have found this to their liking.

Third, the unions could not, through national or local negotiations, match the

Table 34 *Approximate density figures by region for the ASW*

1965 (using 1961 Census and 1965 union membership)		1969 (using 1966 census and 1969 membership)*	
England & Wales	56	England & Wales	45
Midland	41	East Anglia	36
Eastern	42	Midland	29
Northern	77	Northern	73
North West	78	North West (incl. part of Wales)	65
South Wales	75	South Wales	59
Rest of Wales	36		
South West	42	South West	32
East & West Riding of Yorkshire	67	Yorks & Humberside	49
Southern	40		
London	65	London	51
London, South East & Southern	51	London & South East	39
		Scotland	64

* The figures for 1969 are likely to be more accurate than 1965 figures because of changes in the regional boundaries and the method used for assessing ASW membership.

Source: UCATT.

'lump' worker's ability to accrue a larger net wage than the directly employed worker. The 'lump' worker not only avoided union subscriptions; he also evaded other considerably higher imposts. In 1974, for example, a LOSC worker paid, on average, 32p[22] a week in deductions from wages; whereas, by contrast, a directly employed worker paid £2.73p a week, on average, in tax and insurance.

It is therefore not surprising that the Phelps Brown[23] inquiry should find that workers on LOSC were not usually unionized, nor that an ASW survey of its membership should highlight the fact that the areas known for lump working (Midlands, South Wales, South West, Southern Counties and London)[24] showed a marked decline in union density (Table 34). There were many quite substantial reasons for the ASW's and other craft unions' leaders' claims that LOSC and its growth were destroying the unions' membership base.

So the craft unions did not lose members in the building industry because of a major quantitative change; there was no long-term decline in the numbers of craftsmen working in the industry. There was instead a qualitative change in the standing of trade unions which led disaffected members to opt for non-unionism. This in turn produced pressures on the full-time leadership through, above all else, its impact on the unions' financial position. Extreme defensive action was needed in order for the unions to survive.

Membership, technological change and demarcation disputes
Members of the ASW consistently commented, in interviews, on the dilution of craft skills in the building industry. Off-site prefabrication, systems building, new

materials and other technological innovations were mentioned as developments that had reduced the content of the craftsman's job. There was implicit general agreement therefore with the tenor of the DOE's statement in 1967 that 'The main problem facing the Construction Industry . . . is the introduction of new techniques of building designed to build faster with less site labour'.[25] However, as shown above, it is difficult to substantiate claims that the numbers of craftsmen, particularly carpenters and joiners, working in the construction industry permanently declined between 1960 and 1973.

Moreover, even if there was some decline, the magnitude of the cyclical movements, and the growth of LOSC, made any changes in the composition of the construction workforce of little consequence in our period. But if the leaders of the unions believed that in the longer run they had not adapted their 'institutions to the quickening pace of change that has developed out of new technology',[26] this constituted a further reason for breaking away from their traditionally exclusive craft-recruiting territories. However, it was not as fundamental to the merger activity as the growth of 'lump' labour.

Technological change also produced some demarcation problems in the industry, although their extent is unclear. For instance, a NEDO survey in 1968 titled *Building Employers and Unions in Building* did not consider such disputes to be a major problem, apart from 'the long-standing disagreements between the wood-workers and the plasterers and between members of the plumbing trade and of the heating and domestic engineering unions'.

Unions with which the ASW, the ASPD and the AUBTW ultimately associated were not, however, those with which they had any major demarcation problems. Demarcation difficulties may therefore have stimulated merger talks, for instance, between the ASW and the Plasterers,[27] but they did not lead to mergers between such competing unions.

Membership and the influence of other unions

In the competitive membership situation facing the ASW, the AUBTW and the ASPD, a merger provided the opportunity for the major union, the ASW, to increase its relative size *vis-à-vis* other competing unions. In the building industry the most important of the 'other unions', outside the craft merger, was the TGWU. Reports of poaching by the TGWU appeared in several of the craft unions' publications in the mid- and late 1960s. For instance, in the *ASPD Journals* of 1968, Bristol Committee members 'were alarmed at the trend of members making application to join the TGWU. It was felt that unless some positive action was taken by the EC we risked losing a considerable number of members'.[28] By 1970 the general secretary of the AUBTW was also concerned that 'The necessity to merge has become more obvious since the Plasterers joined the TGWU . . . the TGWU in all parts of the country are now engaged in poaching members of all the building craft unions. . . . Construction workers have always been recruited on the basis of occupation . . . it is disturbing that a union like the TGWU should feel it necessary to recruit workers who, by occupation, should belong to another union'.[29]

'Other unions', particularly when they were general unions actually encroaching or threatening to encroach on craft unions' job territories, thus provided a push towards craft defensive mergers. They helped the craft unions' full-time leadership generate a 'something must be done' attitude. In this way they encouraged the conservative craft membership to cross traditional craft territories, if only to defend themselves against lesser skilled unions.

TUC policy

In 1924 and 1943 the TUC Conference proposed that reports be prepared on closer working between unions. In 1962 it was again agreed that 'the General Council report on the possibility of re-organising the structure of both the TUC and the British trade union movement with a view to making it better fitted to meet modern industrial conditions'.[30] But the notion of industrial unionism, the only clearly identifiable alternative to diversity, postulated at the TUC was rejected because, 'apart from its undesirability, [it would] be impractical for the British trade union movement'.[31] Hence, although the TUC was agreed, in principle, that there was a need for reform of the union structure, there was no consensus regarding the nature of the reform.

However, the TUC study of union structure, which covered some 70 per cent of affiliated unions, did effectively highlight the need for changes in the merger law. This, in turn, led the TUC to lobby successfully for such changes. Moreover, the inquiry exercise, and the consequent organization of meetings between unions with common recruiting interests, stimulated an aura of merger activity among TUC unions. Nevertheless, apart from these two important developments, the TUC did not play a major part in determining the form of actual merger negotiations.

The failure of the TUC positively to influence the formation of UCATT can be shown by noting and contrasting the composition of the committees that the TUC formed to encourage mergers and the final composition of UCATT. The TUC brought together in 1964 the woodworking trades for talks on closer working. These unions included the National Union of Furniture Trade Operatives (NUFTO), the Amalgamated Society of Woodcutting Machinists (ASWCM) and the ASW. In the Construction Trades group the TUC, under the auspices of the NFBTO, encouraged merger talks between construction unions. The ASW and the ASPD did not attend these talks in the mid-1960s. Ultimately, as mentioned above, the ASW, the ASPD and the AUBTW formed UCATT. The ASW and the AUBTW did not therefore merge with the unions that the TUC suggested were suitable bedfellows. Hence, although the TUC facilitated mergers by influencing a change in the law and by stimulating general merger activity, it did not have singular success in rationalizing the structure according to any pre-determined pattern.

Summary of change agents

All the change agents of any significance came directly, in terms of the model of change, to the full-time leadership. They usually adversely affected some aspect of membership. These change agents generally served to make a long-running commitment to mergers, generated previously through the constitutionally prescribed processes, of immediate and pressing concern to the executive officers of the three craft unions.

The change agents that had most effect on the merger were those that reduced the absolute membership and undermined the financial stability of the building unions. In brief, they threatened the very existence of individual unions and forced them into a defensive merger.

The most important of these agents for change originated in developments in the construction industry. But they were not primarily the result of reductions in employment or technological changes. Instead, the factors that provoked the executive officers to pursue mergers were those associated with the growth of labour-only sub-contracting, which in turn prevented the unions, as they were individually constituted, from 'delivering the goods' through the NFBTO's national negotiations. Thus, with ineffective national negotiations, and in the absence of site negotiations and site control through closed shops, members voted for individual negotiations under LOSC, and against collective bargains, by leaving the unions. In fact it was a diffusion of employers, caused by the growth of LOSC, that was the primary agent of change promoting merger activity among unions in the industry. The direction of their merger searches, and the factors influencing the actual UCATT mergers, will now be examined.

Direction of change

The ASW, ASPD, and AUBTW in forming UCATT did not immediately perceive its formation as the answer to their problems. Instead, there were four options under consideration in one or other of these three craft unions. First, the AUBTW considered joining a general union. Second, all three unions attempted to absorb the much smaller unions in the building industry with which they shared a common craft identity. Third, they sought merger deals with more substantial common craft, or close craft associates, within or without the industry. Fourth and lastly, they turned towards each other – towards dissimilar but industrially related crafts – for merger partners.

The first option, merge with a general union, was seriously considered only in the AUBTW. This was the only one of the three merging craft unions to have a significant labourers' section. It was therefore the one potential UCATT partner that had both membership and industrial affinity with the TGWU's predominantly unskilled building section. This was not, however, sufficient to outweigh the craft orientation of the AUBTW's leadership. Craft and trade objectives could not, it was considered, be pursued in a general union where the craft voice would not be given most weight in inter-union circles. The general secretary of the AUBTW was of the opinion that his unions should avoid the situation where, like the Plasterers, they would be 'lost, have no vote, inside the TGWU ... as far as the TUC is concerned'.[32] Thus, apart from temporarily attracting some support from the AUBTW's labouring section, the TGWU was not a serious merger option for the three premier building craft unions.

The second option, the absorption of smaller common craft unions, no longer offered a solution to the three unions' severe financial difficulties in the late 1960s because there were not many such unions left to be absorbed. By 1969 the number of unions in the Building, Woodworking and Furnishing group in the TUC had dropped to ten compared with eighteen in 1961. Of the missing eight, several had already, by 1969, been absorbed by the three major craft unions; for instance, the Street Masons, Paviours, etc. (1400) and the Amalgamated Slaters, Tilers etc. (2012) joined the AUBTW in that period. The ASPD had also absorbed the last of the small painters' unions, the Birkenhead Local Society of Painters and Decorators, in 1965. These minor mergers did not, however, noticeably help the three craft unions to escape from their financial difficulties. A position had therefore been reached by the mid- and late 1960s that pushed the three craft unions into activating option three: mergers with more substantial common craft unions.

The ASW and the AUBTW attempted vigorously to take this option. While the ASW sought to merge with the National Union of Furniture Trade Operatives (NUFTO) and the craft-exclusive ASWcM, the AUBTW courted the NAOP. NUFTO, as one of the larger unions in the TUC's Building, Woodworking and Furnishing group at, in 1970, 58,759 members, was crucial to the ASW's attempt to create a larger common craft–woodworking amalgamation.

NUFTO, however, would have added little to the ASW's strength in the construction industry: only some 6000 of NUFTO's membership were in that industry. On the other hand it was, for its size, a relatively wealthy union: it had a general fund of £1¾ million in 1972 and a surplus of £128,962 on that year's accounts.

The merger talks between NUFTO and the ASW faltered over the question of financial stability, common subscription rates and general structure and government of the proposed amalgamated union. In all these areas there were significant differences between the two unions which more than outweighed their common craft interests. Eventually the ASW's refusal to provide NUFTO with a trade group[33] arrangement was used by NUFTO to bring the merger talks to an end.[34]

During talks with NUFTO, the ASW had also been negotiating as the major building craft union under option four (mergers with dissimilar but industrially related crafts) with the ASPD, the AUBTW and the much smaller white-collar ABT. Failure to gain mergers with fellow woodworking unions under option two therefore did no more than intensify the ASW's search for mergers with these building craft unions; for it was only by making itself a force to be reckoned with in the building industry that the ASW could hope to restore its relevance and thus increase its membership within its traditional job territory.

The ASW, and particularly Smith, the general secretary, was determined to use such a merger to carry through a centralization process that would give UCATT a more influential role in national negotiations with employers and the government. It was, for instance, the ASW's declared intention to make national negotiations meaningful by narrowing 'the gap between real earnings and [nationally determined] basic rates'.[35] UCATT further hoped to use its new combined weight at the TUC to make the newly formed Construction Committee an effective lobby in government circles. Centralization out of rationalization was the ASW's objective.

The broad direction of merger change under option four, was therefore generally conditioned by the industrial affinity and status of the membership of the three craft unions and the ASW's perceptions of the unions' bargaining needs. But it was the detailed merger negotiations, involving NUFTO, the ASWcM, the NAOP, the ABT, the AUBTW, the ASPD and the ASW, that ultimately determined the final merger partners. The actual direction of change was influenced in these detailed negotiations by the interaction between the degree of pressure stimulating the merger activity and the nature of a union's internal organization. Thus, unions' systems of government, the political affinities between potential merger partners and the personalities of the officials involved in the merger negotiations were of prime importance in determining the outcome of the ASW's search for a merger. The kind and degree of pressure stimulating the UCATT merger and the factors setting the parameters of the merger search have already been explored; the influential features that determined the actual direction of change within the wider potential merger area will now be further examined.

All three craft unions forming UCATT were relatively diffused, compared with, for instance, the TGWU around 1960. Despite the *de jure* centralization of bargaining, the same three unions were also *de facto* and *de jure* at the more decentralized end of the vertical plane of non-bargaining government. There was, however, in the ASW a long-running and controversial scheme to regionalize the union. The intention was to replace the entrenched and influential district management committee system of local government with regional committees. Hence the ASW's national leadership could be expected to use the merger to move towards a less decentralized system of government.

Merger by transfer of engagements of the ASPD and the AUBTW to the ASW did not, therefore, on the face of it, imply for the two lesser merging unions a major change in their types of government. For the ASW it had even less implication for government, at least in the short run, because the transfer of the ASPD and the AUBTW meant they would accept the ASW's rules. The details of government within the existing ASW rules were, however, questions of importance in the merger negotiations.

Questions regarding the structure, procedure of decision-making, numbers, status and method of choosing leaders all played some part in the merger negotiations. NUFTO, as mentioned above, rejected a merger with the ASW over the issue of trade groups, and both the ASPD and the AUBTW were also attracted to the idea of a trade group structure. Indeed, a motion against transferring to the structurally unified ASW was carried at the AUBTW's 1970 Conference by 35 to 26.[36] However, during this Conference's proceedings, the chairman pointed out that the final decision lay with the EC and membership. Furthermore the Conference was also reminded that the merger was 'essential in order to survive in this very competitive world of ours'.[37]

Questions regarding the efficacy of existing structures were therefore, in the view of the national officials, concerned more with a defensive strategy for survival than with safeguarding the separate craft's autonomy. For, prior to the mergers, the unions had already tried, unsuccessfully, structural adjustments as a means of salvation. The AUBTW, for instance, attempted to rationalize its structure and save money in 1967 and 1968 by encouraging costly district committees to disband and regroup around less expensive branch conferences; in this situation the ASW's much more extreme proposal was seen to offer possibly the last chance of saving the unions from collapse.

In the light of severe financial difficulties, therefore, the AUBTW and the ASPD did not baulk at accepting, largely unchanged, the internal structure of the ASW, despite the ASW's refusal to concede the lesser merging unions' requests for a vertically bifurcated trade group structure of government. So UCATT inherited the ASW's *de jure* single vertical channel of decision-making; although the ASW's structure was later changed when, following the ASPD–ASW merger, 'The Joint Committee [of the ASW/ASPD] decided in the circumstances to set aside the [1969] vote which had been taken [on regionalization] and [put] the whole of the voting propositions to the whole of the merged membership';[38] on this second occasion the controversial proposals were agreed.

The ASW's established leadership therefore managed generally to centralize decision-making by carrying through, concurrent with the merger, a number of rule changes. Regionalization, appointment and not election of regional secretaries, biennial as against annual conferences, centralized branch accounting, etc., were all part of the changes developed out of the merger package. The ASW and particularly its general secretary thus took advantage of the mergers to increase the centre's power *vis-à-vis* the localities, whose district management committees were disbanded. Later the NFBTO was also disbanded and direct responsibility for national bargaining returned to the union's national full-time officials. Changes in both the levels of government and location of decisions were thus executed during the mergers and were used to centralize decision-making in UCATT.

But in adhering to its single-channel system of decision-making the ASW ensured that its merger would not embrace all woodworking or building unions. Both the NUFTO and the NAOP made structural recognition of their specialist craft position, in a separate trade group, a condition of merging. This may have been because, unlike the ASPD and the AUBTW, the NAOP felt threatened by the ASW's encroachment on its traditional job territory. It was stated, for instance, at the NAOP's Conference in 1967 during the amalgamation debate that 'The ASW have done more damage to the plastering industry by taking over their work by numerical strength than anybody'[39] (this was a reference to the ASW's claims to work on plasterboard). Thus, even though forced by financial difficulties into seeking a defensive merger, the Plasterers' delegates, wary of the ASW's territorial incursions, sought structural means of retaining 'our identity, if not as a union then as a trade'.[40] The vertically differentiated TGWU was therefore seen as structurally more acceptable because it provided the NAOP with the opportunity for going 'into the TGWU as a craft group' and gave the NAOP 'the possibility of creating a set of circumstances within . . . [the TGWU] where we would be left almost to ourselves'.[41] Hence a minor craft union could be attracted into a merger with a general union if the alternative was absorption into a major craft union with which it competed for a dwindling amount of work, particularly when, as will be shown below, there was also a clash of personalities.

Inter-union differences regarding both existing and proposed procedures for decision-making did not, on the other hand, markedly affect the direction of the merger. The established national full-time officials of the actual and potential merging unions had a common political interest in reaching an accommodation on this aspect of the merger negotiations. Moreover, opposition factions, which obviously had a vested interest in the forms of decision-making adopted in the merger, tended to be muted in their criticisms of the mergers largely because they had an ideological commitment to 'one union'[42] for the industry. It was thus difficult for such groups, divorced from the actual merger negotiations, both to support the merger in principle and yet to oppose it in detail. Furthermore, in the ASW, where the left faction was grouped around the Building Workers Charter group (founded in 1968), the left opposition were further restricted by the mechanism of transfer of engagements. Under the transfer of engagements the wider ASW membership were not required or asked to express an opinion on the mergers. The opposition's influence inside the ASW was therefore, apart from its activities in the National Conferences of 1967 and 1968, severely limited by the processes employed in both mergers and the ASW's own government system.

Despite the failure of National Conferences, and hence the lay opposition to influence directly the outcome of merger negotiations, much concern was expressed by some lay delegates about the status of the new merged unions' National Conference. Members in the ASPD,[43] for instance, did not want to lose the decision-making powers of their Conference. They had achieved decision-making status for this body only in 1967. It was, however, generally agreed in the merger that there would be a gradual harmonization of the procedure of decision-making at all levels in line with the ASW's existing practice. This meant acceptance, for the ASPD and the AUBTW, of the ASW's procedure. This in turn gave the full-time officer-dominated Joint Committee of the EC and GC the opportunity to nullify National Delegate Conference decisions by putting them to a vote of the whole membership.

There was thus no concerted opposition to the merger from those who wanted a less centralized union. The left did not offer an alternative merger strategy. Procedures for decision-making in the new union were thus determined by national full-time officials. They, naturally, did not want to diminish their own influence in government by altering existing procedures to their own disadvantage. The result was that inter-union procedural differences were not a noticeable barrier to the formation of UCATT.

Most of the merging unions' negotiators were far more interested in the numbers, status and method of choosing the immediate leadership of the new union than with the details of the decision-making procedure. As the general secretary of the ASPD stated, 'full-time officials should have their service agreements honoured above all'.[44] Lay delegates expressed somewhat similar thoughts in the NAOP merger to the extent that, 'Where we get the greatest representation, this is the Union we have to go with'.[45] If autonomy and all it entailed could not be guaranteed by a structural trade group arrangement, the focus was switched to guarantees for some kind of proportional representation on national bodies for the merging unions and on continuity of service for full-time officials. It was another, if lesser, means of both satisfying vested individual interest and preserving a vestige of the smaller merging unions' identity within the larger organization. It represented the last stage in the paradoxical fight of the minor defensive merging unions to retain a separate identity through a merger.

In forming UCATT, the ASPD in 1969 and the AUBTW in 1971 were allocated a specific number of seats on the new Executive and their full-time officials guaranteed at least five years' employment. After the first five years the officials, apart from the appointed regional secretaries,[46] were all eligible for re-election.[47] The incumbent general secretaries of the smaller unions were also allocated specific positions in the larger union,[48] while the full-time executives of the ASW and the ASPD were joined on a full-time UCATT executive by members of the AUBTW. This latter union previously had a lay EC. Thus UCATT had five ASW, five ASPD and five AUBTW members on the executive. This body was to be reduced, by retirement, resignation or death, to five ASW, three ASPD and three AUBTW. Ultimately the craft composition of the EC was to be proportionately representative.[49] In the meantime each craft was divided into electoral divisions matching the number of EC seats. The lay, and far less influential, General Council (GC) was also divided between crafts, but on the basis of nine ASW, three ASPD and three AUBTW.

Leading members of the merging unions, both full-time and lay, were thus assured of key positions in UCATT. While gradually moving towards proportionate representation on the EC and GC, the existing leadership was guaranteed security of tenure on condition that they carried in elections the confidence of their traditional craft electorates. Hence even in the extremely difficult financial circumstances surrounding the UCATT merger, existing full-time officials sought and gained acceptable terms of continued employment.

Other secondary factors influencing the direction of change were the political allegiances of the potential merger partners and the personalities of the leading officials. All three unions tended to be on the 'right', or of 'moderate' political persuasion, although the AUBTW was, if anything, to the left of the ASW. NUFTO, which rejected the merger with the ASW, was, in contrast, influenced in its decision by a number of left-wing officials who considered the ASW to be rather too right-wing. The ASW itself, however, did not appear to be very concerned with the political leanings of potential or actual merger partners. As the largest and leading union in the industry's merger movement the ASW assured itself, and its moderate majority, of a dominant position in the new union by its proposed constitutional amendments. The regionalization programme, for instance, favoured the moderate centre against some of the leftist districts. Similarly, the distribution of seats on the EC and GC, while admittedly further diffusing, somewhat, the national decision-making process, did not significantly undermine the moderates' hold on the union, at least in the medium term. The ASW's leadership was not therefore deterred from proposing mergers to smaller unions with oppositional elements. The ASW could count on its own *de jure* control of the constitutional arrangements and its moderates' *de facto* influence over the electoral process to maintain the moderates' dominance. There was thus for the ASW little to fear from mergers, on its own terms, with politically differentiated minor organizations; but for such organizations, for example NUFTO, moderate ASW dominance was unattractive and a factor helping to prevent a merger.

Individual personalities and differences of opinion, particularly whether or not the general secretaries of the unions involved were friendly towards each other, played a significant part in some of the mergers. Smith, the general secretary of the ASW and later UCATT, dominated much of the union merger activity in the construction industry. He achieved this position partly through force of character, partly because of his position as leader of the largest union, but also because his centralization proposals comprised the only clearly spelt-out scheme of rationalization broadly acceptable to the leadership of the two other predominantly craft unions.

Smith's individual dominance of the merger movement in the building trades did however also contribute to a number of clashes which slowed down and hindered the formation of UCATT. For instance, the ASPD–ASW merger was affected by personality differences; the merger could be completed only when the general secretary of the ASPD neared retirement. Also in another proposed merger, the ASW–NAOP arrangement, differences between the leadership of the ASW and the NAOP actually played a major part in preventing the ASW–NAOP merger from taking place. The ill feeling between the two leaderships showed, for instance, in the NAOP's 1967 debate on amalgamation: 'I think it is insufferable for the ASW to have the temerity to come along [and ask for a merger], after the dirty trick they played on the General Secretary when he was turfed off the NFBTO Executive Council'.[50] It would appear that this comment was provoked by the fact that the ASW's leadership had preferred an alternative candidate to the NAOP's general secretary in an election to the NFBTO's Executive. Because mergers are very much in the control of the full-time leadership, a perceived slight of this nature helped guide the NAOP to the TGWU rather than the ASW (UCATT).

Summary of direction of change

The primary parameters of the building craft unions' merger searches were set by the change agents that stimulated the merger activity, the craft consciousness of the unions and the perceived solutions to the unions' common problems, as suggested by the ASW. Once the ASW had decided rationalization and centralization of decision-making in the bargaining and non-bargaining fields was necessary to 'deliver the goods' and hence restore the union's membership and financial standing, the primary area for the ASW's merger search was reasonably clearly defined.

Once the merger search began, all the unions involved in the merger movement sought to protect their identity within the new union. They would, preferably, have stayed completely autonomous. This was why they had previously supported the NFBTO and shunned amalgamation, despite their traditional commitment to one union for construction. But in the 1960s a basically defensive, 'something must be done in order to survive' hypothesis, generated by financial difficulties, circulated throughout all the craft-based unions. Also running parallel to the above hypothesis was the acceptance of a supporting thesis, which was that the building unions had to achieve a certain minimum size if they were to become efficient and influential. The general secretary of the AUBTW stated, for instance, that 300,000 membership was needed to be influential,[51] and the general secretary of the ASW raised the estimate to 350,000.[52]

Faced by these problems and a limited number of solutions, the unions agreed to merge in order to retain some vestige of their craft identities. The merger negotiations normally focused, therefore, on the degree of independence to be given by the major to the minor merging union. Claims for trade group representation, positions on the EC and GC, guarantees of employment, etc., dominated most of the merger negotiations. All were concerned with protecting the individual officers' positions and the identity of the minor merging unions. The form of union government was thus of major importance in merger negotiations once the primary parameters, in which the merger search took place, had been set. The primacy of governmental considerations were, however, sometimes overcome in the UCATT merger by personal differences between leading merger negotiators. But in the absence of highly organized factionalism or parties, the established leadership of the major union (ASW) generally determined the actual direction of change according to the degree to which the primary pressures for change reduced the minor merging unions' leaderships' insistence on remaining virtually autonomous.

AUEW: a consolidatory merger

Areas of change

Pre-AUEW

From time to time the AEU has sought further mergers of unions in the engineering industry. However, until the amalgamation of the AUFW and the AEU in 1967 to form the AEF there had been no significant mergers affecting the AEU since 1920, although, as noted in the study of 'natural' membership change, the AEU admitted women to membership in 1943[53] and also became more active in recruiting semi- and unskilled workers after opening two new sections, V and Va, for this purpose in 1926.[54] Hence the AEU, unlike the ASW, was moving towards becoming a general union for the engineering industry before its amalgamations in the late 1960s and early 1970s.

Nevertheless, the full-time officials of the AEU who dealt with merger negotiations were not diluted to anything like the same extent as the rest of the membership. Virtually all elected full-time officials of the AEU were and are skilled members of the union. Thus, although the composition of the Engineers changed, its national government functions remained firmly in the control of skilled full-time officials who also controlled the merger negotiations.

Formation of the AUEW

The AUEW was formed by amalgamation in January 1971. This merger brought together the AEU (1,194,530) and AUFW (65,000) which merged in 1967, with the newcomers to the amalgamation, DATA (105,418) and the much smaller CEU (27,435). Three of the unions (the AEU, the AUFW and DATA) were hence very strongly engineering craft-based, although DATA (later TASS), the draughtsmen's union, was a white-collar organization. The CEU, on the other hand, was less of a craft union and also somewhat on the fringe of mainstream engineering because of its construction industry bias.

The amalgamation was dominated numerically by the AEU, which had a million more members than any other merging union. (The CEU was even smaller than some AEU districts.) The AEU was attempting to consolidate its dominant position in the engineering industry through the formation of the AUEW. This merger can therefore be seen in the same light as the 1920 AEU amalgamation, which was 'a further step in the unification of the Engineers first begun by Allan and Newton in 1851'.[55] The change agents influencing the formation of the AUEW will now be considered.

Agents of change

The main change agents influencing mergers with the AEU sprang, as they did in the ASW, from movements in membership. However the general aura of the merger movement, at least partly generated by the TUC's call for rationalization

Table 35 *AEU membership, 1940–72*

Year	Total membership*	Section 1		Section 5	Section 5a	Women
			%			
1940	454,126	169,849	(37.4)	123,035	56,947	Nil
1950	715,946	266,319	(37.1)	204,947	122,867	34,341
1955	853,557	290,593	(34.0)	259,388	150,523	61,868
1960	972,587	310,865	(31.9)	340,283	149,723	76,665
1965	1,048,955	294,884	(28.1)	384,564	181,473	98,851
1966	1,054,571	294,684	(27.9)	388,886	184,548	99,134
1967	1,044,150	293,373	(28.0)	385,270	184,749	97,356
1968	1,073,119	290,667	(27.0)	395,020	196,303	111,868
1969	1,130,926	293,558	(26.4)	418,668	212,825	125,003
1970	1,202,218	299,270	(24.5)	444,073	234,500	140,860
1971	1,194,530	296,838	(24.8)	444,527	233,354	139,364
1972	1,145,826	290,566	(25.3)	424,351	221,946	134,250

*The discrepancy between the total and the combined figures, given in other sections, is made up of Sections 2, 3 and 4 and other small groups of membership in the union. Sections 2 and 3 were closed before 1960 and Section 4 was, and is, for apprentices and junior workers

of the national inter-union structure, also helped to provoke thoughts of mergers. But, other than bringing together engineering unions in group conferences for 'engineering trades' and 'metal-using trades' between 1964 and 1968, the TUC's guidance did not noticeably affect the actual AUEW merger. There is therefore little point in rehearsing the comments made above on the TUC's direct influence, or lack of it, on the ASW merger, apart from re-emphasizing the importance of the legal changes the TUC promoted, without which, it can be reasonably suggested, the AUEW would not have been formed. The following analysis of change agents therefore covers:

(1) Membership;
(2) Membership and technological change;
(3) Membership and the influence of competing unions.

Membership

Under this heading we will consider the effect of absolute, as against potential and relative membership change on the unions of the AUEW. Tables 35–38 show the extent to which the membership of the four unions changed in the period under consideration. It can be seen from these tables that the AEU, DATA and the CEU grew over the 1960–70 period: the AEU increased its membership by 24 per cent, DATA by 36 per cent and the CEU by 19 per cent between 1960 and 1970. But the AUFW, between 1960 and its amalgamation with the AEU in 1967, dropped in membership by 11 per cent.

Table 36   *DATA membership, 1960–71*

Year	Membership
1960	63,888
1962	70,396
1965	65,893
1968	73,024
1970	86,789
1971	105,418

Table 37   *AUFW membership, 1960–7*

Year	Membership
1960	71,376
1961	73,966
1962	72,900
1963	70,514
1964	69,280
1965	70,822
1966	66,481
1967	63,265

Table 38 *CEU membership, 1960–72*

Year	Membership
1960	22,693
1964	20,936
1968	27,007
1970	26,959
1972	27,435

The AUFW, therefore, was the only merging union in the AUEW that suffered an absolute loss of membership prior to amalgamation. Moreover if the 2240 membership that the AUFW gained in 1966 and 1967 from mergers with the Associated Society of Moulders, etc., and the Amalgamated Moulders and Kindred Industries, etc. is deducted from the AUFW's membership in 1967, the AUFW is shown to have declined by 15 per cent over the 1960–67 period. Moreover, this total figure hides a much more marked decline in craft membership. The skilled membership of the AUFW, in Section A, stood at 30,456 in 1960 and 21,117 in 1967. By 1972 it was further reduced to 15,050. Thus over the 1960–67 period the skilled membership dropped by 31 per cent. Over the longer 1960–72 period the decline was 51 per cent. At the same time as the craft membership declined, in total, the semi- and unskilled workers marginally increased. As the AUFW was a highly craft-conscious union, dominated in all its major national offices by time-served apprenticed members, such a change cannot have been welcomed.

Thus, despite official and formal protestations that the AUFW was not seeking a merger because of (a) Dwindling membership, or (b) Problems with finances. . .',[56] shifts in membership were undermining both the absolute size of the union and its composition, both of which developments had implications for the AUFW's financial position, as shown below. During interviews it became clear that this was recognized by the union leaders as a problem even if it was not, quite understandably, publicly acknowledged as such while actively seeking a merger with the AEU.

Unlike the merging UCATT unions, however, the AUFW did not wait until extreme financial difficulties developed out of membership decline before undertaking a serious merger search. Throughout the 1960s the AUFW was aware of the consequences for finance of the diminishing and changing composition of its membership. Despite increases in subscriptions, the union's income from contributions declined from £250,308 in 1960 to £248,842 in 1967. As early as 1959, 'contribution income was more than £8,000 less than in 1958, despite the increased rate of contributions due in the last quarter of the year'.[57] There was a commonly expressed view in the AUFW that 'the stability of our funds . . . depends upon maintaining a high proportion of our members in Schedule 1'.[58] This was the craft, high-subscription and high-benefit section of the AUFW. It was also the section that, as noted above, declined by 31 per cent in membership between 1960 and 1967. Administrative changes in 1962 and 1964, intended to make more effective use of contribution income and to change contributions and benefits, improved but did not eradicate the financial problems. It was felt that the union 'need[ed] a membership of not less than 70,000 to maintain our administrative machine'.[59] By the mid-1960s it was looking as if the AUFW could not reach 70,000 membership in the Foundry industry, and hence it can be assumed that financial, as well as absolute, membership considerations stimulated the Foundry Union to search for mergers.

Membership and technological change

It was stated in a number of interviews with full-time officials of the AEU, AUFW and DATA that technological developments in the 1960s in the engineering industry had limited their opportunities for growth within their existing job territories. In the words of an AEU executive councillor, the 'honeymoon growth period' experienced by the AEU after the Second World War had come to an end: an average growth rate of 25,664 a year between 1950 and 1960 had fallen to 13,664 per year between 1960 and 1966. The traditional blue-collar job territory of the Engineers only marginally increased by 0.5 per cent from 2,406,060 in 1961 to 2,417,300 in 1971.[60] Thus, although the AEU's membership had increased, the remaining growth area was static and the growth rate of the union had hence suffered a relative decline.

A much more dramatic but similarly adverse change was faced by the AUFW in its traditional recruiting area. Potential membership for the AUFW in 1961[61] was 140,990, giving a density of 52 per cent. By 1971, the AUFW's potential traditional membership was down to 95,700 and its density up to 68 per cent. The number of moulders' and coremakers' jobs, the most highly skilled in the union, slumped from 69,280 to 44,000, a 37 per cent decline, in the same period. Technological change was responsible, according to the AUFW's general secretary, for closing one foundry a week in the early 1960s – a development that mainly accounts for the decline in absolute membership and the diminishing financial status of the AUFW in the period leading up to its merger search.

Technological developments in engineering also adversely affected DATA's recruiting potential. DATA's potential and traditional job territory, draughtsmen, stood at 168,550 in 1961 and 149,500 in 1971,[62] a reduction of 11 per cent. Furthermore, while draughtsmen were in decline in nearly all industries between 1962 and 1968, other white-collar jobs in engineering and related industries were expanding. The editor of the *DATA Journal* acknowledged, in the June 1969 edition, that, 'while technical and technological occupations proliferate and expand our traditional base contracts'. Thus DATA appeared to be missing an opportunity, because of its restrictive recruiting area, to join the competitive scramble for members in the expanding white-collar field of engineering employment.

Membership and the influence of other unions

The recruiting activities of other unions, particularly of the TGWU and ASTMS, served to highlight the relative failure of the AEU and DATA to exploit fully recruitment opportunities in the industry. These competitor unions, through their higher growth rates, further limited the engineering unions' potential for recruitment. Similarly, the CEU was feeling the competitive pressures of the Boilermakers and the TGWU in their section of the engineering industry. Only the AUFW, which faced, in contrast to the AEU and the DATA, an absolute decline in membership, was largely aloof from and undisturbed by competitive inter-union pressures for membership.

Furthermore, some members in the AEU considered that part of the TGWU's expansion came at the expense of their own union. In 1973, following the yet more rapid growth of the TGWU in the late 1960s, this feeling was strong enough for the Engineers' NC to call for an end to the Tripartite Agreement on spheres of influence signed with the TGWU and the GMWU in October 1966. The NC claimed that this had become 'a hindrance used by the TGWU to obstruct the pursuance of claims of blatant [TGWU] poaching of AUEW members being referred to the TUC Disputes Committee'.[63]

The AEU's national full-time officials were thus well aware of the highly competitive inter-union bargaining and recruiting situation that existed in engineering. The TGWU was seen by some officials of the AEU as the usurpers of their union's natural rights in the engineering industry. Craft- and differentials-conscious members of the AEU resented the TGWU's 'second to none' wage parity claims made on behalf of the TGWU's semi-skilled workers.

Moreover, outside the engineering industry the AEU's and the TGWU's differing growth rates had implications for their relative positions on various other bodies. An expansion of the TGWU at the expense of the AEU not only prevented the AEU from fulfilling its historic goal of making itself the 'one union' for engineering, but it also placed the AEU at a more immediate disadvantage in more elevated circles. The AEU and the TGWU were, for instance, competitively pre-eminent in representing, respectively, the craft and semi-skilled workers' views at the TUC and in government circles. In a period of growing government involvement in industrial relations, a union's relative size and hence, to some large degree, its relative influence assumed a new importance.

Like the AEU, DATA also found itself facing a recruitment challenge. But for DATA the challenge came mainly from ASSET and the AScW (later merged into ASTMS), and not the TGWU. Although DATA grew by nearly 20 per cent between 1955 and 1964 it did not come anywhere near its competitor unions' expansion rates. Over the same period, for instance, the AScW grew by 75 per cent, ASSET by 103 per cent and the CAWU (later APEX) by 42 per cent.[64] Moreover, as DATA drew approximately 50 per cent[65] of its recruits from members of the AEU newly promoted to the drawing office, it was open to further recruitment pressures should the AEU decide to extend its own job territory vertically upwards through 'natural' recruitment. The AEU could, for instance, have used its supervisory branches as the base from which to penetrate the general white-collar employment field in the industry. Thus DATA was faced in the 1960s by actual developments in other unions and possible developments in the AEU which could further radically narrow its potential membership base; a base already threatened by technological changes.

Summary of change agents

Developments in membership, absolute, potential and relative, therefore created an atmosphere among the above four unions in the 1960s that something had to be done; as one member put it, 'we had to go somewhere'.[66] This general search for members led in turn to a reactivation of the unions' traditional commitment to one union for engineering. The membership changes emanating from technological and competitive union pressures pushed the national leadership into actively searching for merger partners. Thus once the major engineering union (the AEU) signified its interest in amalgamations and revived 'one union' ideals, minor engineering unions sought terms favourable to their own membership in much the same way as the minor unions did in the UCATT merger. However, no minor union within the AEU's merger sweep was in immediate and dire financial straits. The alternative to a merger with the AEU was not, at least in the short term, extinction, for any of the minor unions involved or for the AEU itself. The AEU, unlike the ASW, was thus more concerned with consolidating than defending its position.

Direction of change

All the unions directly involved in forming the AUEW were stimulated to undertake a merger search by a desire to mitigate the effect of restrictions on their recruitment activities. If mergers were to be entered into they had, therefore, to offer some potentially advantageous alteration in a union's existing job territory. Changes in job territory were seen as means of avoiding the unpleasant side-effects of developments in the engineering industry. This much, at least, was determined by the primary change agents examined above.

Within the parameters of the merger activity set by the primary change agents, there were many options. The three, not mutually exclusive, that exercised the main interest of the unions were similar to those that attracted the main attentions of the UCATT unions: first, absorbing smaller common craft unions; second, joining with other craft-related occupationally based unions recruiting in the same industry; and, third, joining other similar occupationally based unions which were not generally confined to the same industry. Like the building trade unions, none of the unions ultimately forming the AUEW gave more than a passing nod to the existence of interested general unions. For instance, the AUFW did no more than acknowledge the GMWU's tentative approaches for a merger. However, one of the unions, the NUVB, which was involved initially with the AUFW and the AEU in merger talks, did opt for transferring to the

TGWU rather than amalgamating with the AEU. This preference of the NUVB for the TGWU, and the NUVB's previous talks with the AEU, were both of some considerable importance for the later formation of the AUEW, as will be shown below.

The chronological order of events leading to the formation of the AUEW played, as it did in UCATT, an important part in determining the actual direction of the merger movement. As preferred options were unsuccessfully pursued, particularly by the AUFW and DATA, second-order preferences became of more importance.

Option one, the absorption of smaller common craft unions, attracted the AUFW. The Foundry Union had a long-standing commitment to form one union for all foundry workers. But this first preference was not seen as excluding option two. In 1962, for instance, when it was recognized that 'changing techniques were making it more than ever apparent that the [trade union] movement was in great need of this [structural change]',[67] a motion was carried urging both 'amalgamation with other trade unions of the foundry industry'[68] and the formation of 'a metal workers' union',[69] a policy that had previously been established in 1956.[70] Thus when the AUFW found its merger overtures rejected by the foundry-based Stove and Grate Union (5000), the General Iron Fitters (2000) and the Dressers' Union (6000), it turned its attention more definitely towards its second option.

Option two was, throughout the 1960s, the preferred option of the AEU. There were no minor common craft unions left in engineering that were both of any significance and were willing to be absorbed into an otherwise unchanged AEU. Even the very small unions, such as the Military and Orchestral Music Instrument Makers (156 members in 1960), generally refused to be absorbed into the AEU in the late 1950s, largely, it would appear, because they wondered 'what would happen to our identity in the event of amalgamating with the very big societies'.[71] Hence, once the AEU became seriously interested in amalgamations it had to offer changes in its own structure as an inducement to the smaller unions in the industry to join with, rather than be absorbed by, the giant AEU.

Within DATA options two and three were supported by different groups. The interplay of these two groups, together with the activities and attitudes of the other potential merger partners, eventually determined the outcome. Option three, a merger with similarly occupationally based unions not necessarily confined to the engineering industry, had been a possibility since the early 1940s when DATA (AESD), ASSET and the AScW began recruiting adjacent groups of technical staff in engineering.

In 1958 the AESD Conference carried a motion in favour of trade union cooperation and eventual amalgamation in the engineering industry, thus combining options two and three. Following this, preliminary discussions took place with ASSET, the AScW and the AEU and in each case the initiative was sympathetically received. In 1961 the executive reported that there was no immediate prospect of amalgamation with any of the other parties but that bilateral agreements on joint co-operation had been made between the AESD and each of the three unions.

In 1962 the AScW conference carried a motion to approach other technical unions regarding the possibility of forming a federation to cover the industries in which they all had membership, but not at that point to seek amalgamation. No federation was formed, but in 1963 a jurisdictional agreement was reached between the AScW, ASSET and DATA (AESD) clarifying their spheres of interest in the technical field.

In 1966 the DATA conference swung towards option three by declaring itself in favour of 'one organisation as the union for all technical staff in engineering, shipbuilding and related industries, including services to industries like steel, chemicals, plastics etc.' Merger talks with the AScW began in 1966 but the objectives of the two organizations differed substantially. The AScW regarded the merger as a first step in the formation of a broadly based technical union throughout the public and private sector. DATA's major purpose, on the other hand, was to secure its base in the engineering industry where the vast proportion of its membership was concentrated.

In these fundamental differences of approach lay the seeds of the specific differences which ensured the failure of the merger negotiations. Moreover, those who were in favour of an amalgamation of DATA with the AEU were strongly influential in the negotiations and ensured that a hard bargain was struck. For instance, DATA insisted that the AScW raise its subscriptions from 2s 6d to 3s 9d to come into line with its own subscriptions. In 1967 the talks came unsuccessfully to an end. The AScW subsequently merged with ASSET to form ASTMS. In words reminiscent of those used by the much smaller Military and Orchestral Music Instrument Makers in rejecting a merger with the AEU, the general secretary of the AScW rejected DATA in 1967 by declaring that 'It was a question of the AScW disappearing and becoming an enlarged DATA. . . . We are not prepared to abandon 50 years of existence overnight'.[72]

In the meantime the AEU had become more interested in a merger with DATA, and DATA's reservations about merging with a 'right-wing' AEU had been removed by the replacement of Carron with Scanlon. Thus, DATA turned to option two, a merger with the AEF, which was itself formed out of the AEU–AUFW amalgamation of 1967.

So when the AUEW was finally formed in 1971 it was not the first option chosen by any of its minor component unions. Both the AUFW and the DATA had tried and failed to complete merger negotiations with other unions before joining with the AEU to create the AUEW. Moreover, the AEU itself did not specifically set out in the early 1960s to form the AUEW out of the AUFW, DATA and the CEU, although it should be stated that the AEU was not, in its attempt to consolidate its position in engineering, very discriminatory in its search for merger partners. But within the AEU's merger sweep, which took in all members of the Confederation of Shipbuilding and Engineering Unions (CSEU), the union did have preferences. In its drive both to diversify its membership and beat off the encroachments of the TGWU, the AEU particularly sought mergers with the Boilermakers, the Foundry Workers and the Vehicle Builders, while also approaching the Sheetmetal Workers. The focus of this craft-oriented sweep was, however, the NUVB. The AEU was of the opinion that an amalgamation between the AUFW, NUVB and AEU could 'build a ring of steel around the engineering industry'.[73]

A merger with the NUVB (some 80,000 members) offered the AEU and the AUFW several advantages. It would have primarily extended the AEU's membership in the motor industry, a part of the wider engineering industry which, compared to foundries, had rapidly expanded since the Second World War. Moreover, it would have provided the AUFW with an opportunity to link itself to the foundries associated with the motorcar industry; and would have strengthened the AEU's position *vis-à-vis* the TGWU in vehicles. An NUVB merger thus offered the AEU a greater return, both relative and absolute, than did the AUFW.

It is thus not surprising that the AEU placed at least as much stress on merging with the NUVB as it did on merging with the AUFW. It was in order to attract both the NUVB and the AUFW into a merger that the AEU made the crucial offer of some degree of autonomy to interested unions. Instead of insisting on merging unions' accepting the AEU's rules virtually unchanged (the AEU's policy in the 1940s and 1950s), the AEU in January 1966 suggested in its *Journal* that

aspirations [for autonomy] can be accommodated through amalgamation or a federation which has as its basis trade groups or sections. . . . In this way major interests would not be disturbed and unions would retain their identities as catering for a specific industry. This is important to the NUVB as most of its members are engaged in the production of motor cars.

With this statement the AEU publicly declared that it was creating the circumstances in which merger talks with interested unions could be progressed.

Thus within the broad directions of merger activity, determined largely by the primary change agents and the occupational and craft composition of the union's leadership, the engineering unions undertook a fairly widespread merger search. But the factors that determined the more limited area of actual merger activity were, as in the UCATT, largely internal to the unions themselves. They involved several important features of union organization, including systems of government and administrative details, political affinities and the personalities of the officials directly involved in the merger negotiations. These secondary factors, which shaped the actual mergers, will now be examined in the above order.

Certain aspects of government and administration played an important part in the preclusion from the amalgamation of at least two potential merger partners. Structural and administrative aspects of government very much influenced, for instance, the NUVB's decision to join the TGWU in preference to the AEU, and the AScW's preference for ASSET as against DATA.

The AScW argued for trade groups in its merger talks with the large and more viable DATA. It did this in order to safeguard its non-engineering interests. Each trade group, under the AScW's proposals, was to have a substantial degree of autonomy. By contrast, DATA saw the engineering industry providing the major focus of attention with the AScW's public services' membership, such as the universities and the health service, being only peripheral to the merged union's main activities. Also, under DATA's proposals the full-time officials of the AScW were to be placed in a subordinate position within the merged union. For instance, the AScW's general secretary was to be only one of the joint assistant general secretaries, instead of, as the AScW proposed, deputy general secretary. Similarly, the AScW's deputy general secretary was to be demoted in the new organization to only one of several national officers; and only those AScW officials with a background in engineering were to be given divisional officer status.

It was in the face of these differences that the talks between the AScW and DATA collapsed in 1967. The AScW's EC recommended to the union's Annual Council in 1967 that negotiations with DATA be terminated and that informal discussions with ASSET continue.

The NUVB also wanted, and finally insisted on, in its abortive merger negotiations with the AEU in 1966, the equivalent of a vehicle trade group. Moreover, the NUVB wanted the AEU to transfer its 90,000-plus vehicle building membership into this trade group. Thus the NUVB's leadership would have had responsibility for, in the new union, some 170,000 members in the vehicle building sector of the new union. In exchange the AEU, under the aegis of the wider joint unions system of government, would have had general control of the total combined memberships' non-trade affairs. Following the AEU's refusal to grant such a trade group arrangement, the NUVB accepted a trade group offer from the structurally vertically bifurcated TGWU in April 1972, following long-running negotiations with the TGWU, which for a time ran parallel with those involving the AEU.

The merger negotiations involving the AEU and the NUVB, and, off-stage, the NUVB and the TGWU, illustrate the importance of different systems of government in the merger movement and its role in shaping the structure of trade unionism in the vehicle building industry. The AEU's refusal, or rather inability, to offer the NUVB merger terms comparable with those proffered by the TGWU ultimately resulted in the TGWU, and hence the industry's semi- and unskilled workers, exercising a greater influence, if not hegemony, in the industry. The TGWU's and the AEU's bid for the NUVB was thus a 'fight for supremacy in the industry'.[74]

The merger negotiations between the AEU and the NUVB reached a climax in June 1966. There was, it would appear,[75] some confusion at this meeting as to what the AEU had actually previously offered the NUVB. This confusion possibly arose from the fact that the AEU switched negotiators at a critical point in the proceedings. Prior to the 2 June 1966 meeting the president of the AEU,

Carron, and to a lesser extent the general secretary, Conway, had dictated the AEU's negotiating position. At the crucial meeting on 2 June 1966, the AEU instead sent EC members Lewis and Scanlon to continue the negotiations. It would appear that Carron and Conway were engaged elsewhere at that particular time, and that Scanlon as the EC member representing the division with the biggest vehicle membership was considered most suited to deal with the NUVB.

There are somewhat conflicting stories regarding this meeting. Some NUVB members considered that the AEU withdrew a previous offer to give the NUVB control of a separate trade group, including in its membership the AEU's members in the vehicle industry.[76] On the other hand, some AEU members tend to consider that the above offer was never made and that the NUVB used the AEU's refusal to give such a promise at the June meeting as a cause, or excuse, for withdrawing from negotiations. What is clear, however, is that failure to agree to a transfer of the AEU's vehicle membership to the NUVB was the sticking point for both unions that, at least formally, ended the negotiations.

The AEU's ability to actually carry through a transfer of membership on the lines suggested by the NUVB must be doubted. For, the union's internal process of decision-making would have made such a move highly problematical. At one level, for instance, the craft-conscious toolmakers in the AEU and the vehicle industry would not have warmed to the suggestion of a transfer to the predominantly semi-skilled NUVB. They may even have successfully resisted it. Further, the AEU's full-time officials themselves would not have appreciated either the loss of membership involved in the transfer to the trade group or the prospect of playing second fiddle to NUVB negotiators in the car factories. Indeed, Scanlon himself and the influential divisional organizers in Birmingham and Coventry would have found their power bases in the AEU's highly competitive electoral situation disturbed by the NUVB's proposals.

Ultimately, therefore, the NUVB's demands for trade group status could not be met by the AEU's full-time negotiating officials. The EC of the AEU could not guarantee to change the traditionally geographically divided AEU into a trade group structure without placing the question of rule changes before the heavily factionalized NC or Rules Revision meeting. The NUVB's demands thus raised in an extreme form the kind of problems the AEU would have faced in any radical restructuring of the union along industrial lines. There were too many officials with a vested political interest (see Chapter 4) in maintaining the AEU's geographical divisions for the merger negotiators to promise to deliver a radical overhaul of the union's system of government as a condition for a merger.

It was therefore necessary for the AEU to conclude merger negotiations with the NUVB, or any other union, without offering radically to change its own system of government. Only if the proposed rule changes needed to facilitate the merger were neutral in their impact on the AEU's own vested and well organized political interests could the national negotiators promise to deliver the constitutional goods to the minor merging union. Thus, in the absence of any internal and fundamental unifying force, such as financial survival, the AEU's merger negotiators were bound to preserve the identity and autonomy of the AEU in much the same way as the leaders of the AUFW, DATA and NUVB, etc., strove to safeguard the identity of their own (by comparison) smaller organizations.

The NUVB could not therefore realistically hope for the same or similar trade group arrangements from the AEU as it could expect to derive from the already vertically bifurcated and concentrated TGWU. Also, the greater general flexibility of the TGWU in government matters further enhanced the TGWU's competitive position in the bidding for the NUVB *vis-à-vis* the AEU. For instance, when the TGWU's leadership finally completed the merger in April 1972 they had already made provision for a separate trade group for all their vehicle membership. Furthermore, they had transferred the TGWU's full-time official most adversely affected by the NUVB's transfer, Evans, to a new and more senior position in the union's hierarchy. The TGWU also created two extra positions for NUVB members on the GEC, in addition to the regular trade group representation, and appointed NUVB officials to non-elected positions within the TGWU. The AEU's negotiators could neither match these inducements to merge, within the union's existing system of government, nor guarantee to change the constitution to provide them sometime in the future.

Thus differences in government systems, particularly whether or not the major merging union was willing and able to offer the minor unions a trade group structure and accommodate leading officials with secure[77] and high-status jobs, played an important part in determining the composition of the AUEW. Two unions, the NUVB and the AScW, that could have altered the recruiting territory of the AUEW quite substantially went elsewhere, primarily because other unions offered them better terms during parallel merger negotiations.

In these circumstances, none of the unions that actually joined the AEU were finally called upon to completely submerge their own systems of government within that of the wider organization. The AEU instead agreed to a federated form of government for the newly formed AUEW. All four merging unions retained their own diverse systems of government largely unchanged inside the umbrella of the wider AUEW rule book (see page 101). It was only after the initial merger, when the growth and growing importance of the political and industrial/political decision-making of the joint bodies was more clearly recognized, that questions of procedures and numerical representation became major sticking points, preventing the rationalization of what was, and is, a loose federation, rather than an amalgamation, of unions.

Thus with merger talks taking place on several fronts at the same time (the AEU and the NUVB, the TGWU and the NUVB, the AEU and the AUFW, the AUFW and minor foundry unions, the AEU and DATA, the AScW and DATA, the AScW and ASSET, etc.), the minor merging unions' full-time leadership were in a position to assess the comparative worth of the offers being made. In this situation the ability of the major unions' merger negotiators to meet the minor unions' demands was largely pre-determined by the major unions' existing systems of government. Those major unions that had flexible systems of government clearly had a distinct edge in the search for merger partners.

The personalities of the merger negotiators were, in the formation of the AUEW, secondary influences compared with governmental factors. There was, in the general merger search in the engineering industry, no dominant personality playing a role comparable to that adopted by Smith (general secretary of the ASW) in the UCATT merger.

In the absence of a common threat of extinction, the engineering unions did not generate the need for an 'ideas man' to assume a leadership role. Moreover, the highly diffused government system of the AEU, in the absence of a unifying threat to its very survival, did not provide the opportunity for national leaders to embrace a Smith-style role in merger negotiations. Thus, although the reputed friendship between Roberts, NUVB general secretary, and Carron, AEU president, was said to be influential in initiating the merger talks between the two unions, it was not strong enough to bring it to a successful conclusion.

Political affinities, on the other hand, were more important for the diffused engineering unions than for any of the other merging unions studied. In a union riven with political divisions, the negotiators leading for the AEU were naturally drawn towards mergers with political allies. When the political allegiance of the AEU's leading merger negotiators changed, usually following elections, the direction of the merger search was, within pre-set parameters, rearranged. It was not therefore entirely fortuitous that, under Carron, the AEU's merger negotia- tions were successfully concluded with the politically amenable and moderate AUFW, or that later, in Scanlon's period, the more left-inclined, and Communist-led, DATA and CEU joined the AEU. At a period when political and industrial/political matters were becoming more important elements in union decision-making generally (see Chapter 4), the political leanings of the AEU's merger negotiators were obviously not divorced from the proceedings at hand. However, the importance of political affinities – left/right persuasion – in the AEU's merger search must not be overstressed.

Political considerations of this kind did not set the major industrial and craft parameters of the search. But they did help facilitate positive conclusions between political allies. Under the all-pervading influence of governmental factors, bargaining considerations played only a minor part in shaping the detailed direction of the unions' new merger search. The AEU, unlike UCATT, had no grand scheme to centralize the bargaining process. Bargaining was decentralized in all the merging unions, except for the CEU, which operated a national agreement on actual terms and conditions.[78] The unions were generally content to continue with this bargaining arrangement in the amalgamation. In fact, the federated structure, with its guarantees of a high degree of sectional autonomy, was specifically intended to leave the four merging unions independent agents in the national and local bargaining fields. DATA's original demands, for instance, that their section should have 'authority to deal with its own industrial policy, including the right to call strikes of its members',[79] deterred formal institutionalized co-operation across sections in the bargaining field. Nationally the four sections also continued to affiliate separately to the CSEU, Labour Party and TUC. Locally joint shop steward committees remained unofficial bodies. Actions, such as DATA's use of the full amalgamated union to press for improvements in its national procedure agreement[80] with the EEF, were therefore more of an exception than a general bargaining rule. There was therefore little change in the merging unions' bargaining activities after the amalgamation; nor was any great change expected. Although 'one union' beliefs acted as a powerful motivating force in determining the direction of the mergers, the bargaining rationale that underpinned it in the 1920s[81] was noticeable for its absence in the 1960s. By then an extension of job territory and not job regulation was the immediate goal of the merging unions in the engineering industry.

Summary of direction of change

In common with the UCATT merger, the parameters to the AEU's merger search were set mainly by the change agents stimulating the AEU's merger activity. In contrast with the ASW, however, the AEU did not have some grand scheme of centralization and rationalization to put into operation. There was, in the AEU, no fundamental failure to 'deliver the goods' to its existing and past membership which demanded a major restructuring of its organization. The AEU, in contrast to the ASW, was not attempting through the mergers either to restore the relevance of its set-piece national negotiations or to readjust, beyond the margin, its own system of government. On the contrary, the AEU was merely seeking to secure or consolidate its position within its traditional, but increasingly competitive and limited, job territories. There was no mandate for the AEU's merger negotiators either to step outside the union's original base or alter its basic system of government. The AEU's negotiators were therefore somewhat restricted in their merger search. It was thus within two constraints, affecting first the area of merger search and second the form of amalgamation, that the AEU directed its merger activities.

Some other smaller unions searching for mergers in engineering were, on the other hand, primarily seeking defensive means of protecting their actual or relative membership positions. There was among these unions a general feeling that in the scramble for mergers they had to go somewhere to defend their interests and to continue to exist in a highly competitive world. Economies of scale, needed for the efficient servicing of members, appeared to demand that several unions with diminishing job territories and higher costs should merge with larger organizations. But these minor merging unions were not as constrained as the AEU in their search for mergers. The NUVB, for instance, did not feel compelled to limit its merger search to unions with a majority of members in the engineering industry.

Competitive inter-union bargaining therefore developed in the engineering industry. The terms offered by the TGWU to the NUVB were, for instance, compared by the latter union with those proposed by the AEU. It was in this highly competitive situation that the different major unions' systems of government played an important part in determining the outcome of inter-union merger negotiations.

ASTMS and the TGWU: aggressive mergers

Areas of change

ASTMS was formed in 1968 from ASSET (50,435), the major merging union and the AScW (21,523), the minor merging union. This late 1960s merger was however the result of a long line of merger talks. In 1943, 1951 and 1952 merger talks took place between these white-collar unions. Further, in 1963 the AScW and ASSET, in conjunction with DATA (later TASS), reached a jurisdictional agreement clarifying their spheres of interest in the technical field. This agreement was the forerunner of the abortive merger talks, referred to above, between the AScW and DATA in 1966 and 1967. It was thus following these unsatisfactory discussions that the AScW and ASSET finally merged into

Table 39 *Mergers* involving ASTMS, 1969–76*

Year of merger	Union	Membership
1969	National Association of Footwear Supervisory Staffs	very small
1970	Carreras Supervisors Organisation	600
1970	Medical Practitioners Union	5,000†
1970	Prudential Male & other Staff Associations	5,000–6,000
1970	Union of Insurance Staffs	17,000
1970	Royal Insurance Group Staff	6,000
1973	Forward Trust Staff Association	750
1973	Assurance Representatives Organisation (Eire)	1,250
1974	Midland Bank Staff Association	10,100
1974	Clydesdale Bank Staff Association	1,351
1974	Pearl Agents	5,000
1974	Guild of Hospital Pharmacists	1,607
1974	ICI Staff Association	N.A.
1975	Kodak Senior Staff Association	2,032
1975	Engineers Surveyors Association	2,250
1975	Union of Speech Therapists	484
1976	United Commercial Travellers Association	14,000

*Other staff associations joined ASTMS in this period (for instance, the 'National Farmers Union Insurance Society' in 1970) by winding themselves up and joining ASTMS *en bloc* rather than going through the transfer of engagements process

†It is likely that this was a gross exaggeration by the MPU and that the actual membership transferred was nearer to 1000

Table 40   *Mergers involving the TGWU, 1968–74*

Year of merger	Union	Membership
1968	Scottish Slaters, Tilers, Roofers and Cement Workers	under 2,000
1968	National Association of Operative Plasterers	12,839
1969	Process and General Workers Union	2,180
1969	Amalgamated Society of Foremen, Lightermen of River Thames	under 2,000
1969	Irish Union of Hairdressers and Allied Workers	under 2,000
1969	Port of Liverpool Staff Association	under 2,000
1970	Sheffield Amalgamated Union of File Trades	under 2,000
1971	Scottish Commercial Motormen's Union	21,000
1971	Watermen, Lightermen, Tugmen and Bargemen's Union	under 2,000
1971	Chemical Workers' Union	15,100
1972	National Union of Vehicle Builders	79,687
1972	Scottish Transport & General Workers' Union (Docks)	2,000
1973	Iron, Steel & Wood Barge Builders and Helpers Association	under 2,000
1974	Union of Bookmaker Employees	2,100
1974	Union of Kodak Workers	4,500

ASTMS without the inclusion of DATA. After the formation of ASTMS the mergers listed in Table 39 helped to expand still further the fastest growing union in the TUC.

The TGWU, itself formed in 1922 from eighteen merging unions, was also highly involved in the inter-union scramble for mergers that developed in the late 1960s. This represented an about-face for the TGWU. For between 1951 and 1961 no unions merged with the TGWU and between 1961 and 1965 only 3000 members were added to the TGWU through mergers. Yet, following the rise to power within the union of Jones, the TGWU completed fifteen mergers between 1968 and 1975. The unions absorbed through transfers of engagements by the TGWU in this latter period are listed in Table 40.

As can be seen from the tables, both ASTMS and the TGWU were highly successful in bringing new unions within their respective white-collar and blue-collar spheres of influence between 1968 and 1974. The manner in which these two expanding unions approached and used the merger movement to their advantage had much in common. ASTMS activities will provide the main material for analysis of 'aggressive' mergers, while the TGWU will be used to provide supporting evidence of 'aggressive' merger activity.

Agents of change

In the numerous mergers undertaken by ASTMS and the TGWU, there were obviously a wide variety of change agents. These mergers were again affected by

the merger aura stimulated by the TUC's sponsorship of inter-union merger talks and by the more favourable legislative climate of the post-1964 period. More clearly than in the 'defensive' or 'consolidatory' mergers studied, however, the concentrated ASTMS and the TGWU were led and directed in their merger searches by a national leadership intent on membership growth through acquisition. On the other hand, the minor merging unions joining ASTMS and the TGWU were affected, to a greater or lesser degree, primarily by defensive considerations arising from membership decline or stagnation or, in some cases, failure to grow at the desired rate. This, as in other unions already examined, often produced financial difficulties. The primary change agents will hence be discussed first by reference to the minor unions' membership problems and, second, by examining the major unions' growth orientation under the headings:
(1) Membership decline/stagnation (minor merging unions);
(2) Membership growth opportunities (major merging unions).

Membership decline/stagnation (minor merging unions)
The initial merger founding ASTMS was at least partly, if not largely, stimulated by the AScW's membership position between 1964 and 1966, when it increased its membership only marginally from 20,061 to 21,523 at a time when other white-collar unions were showing more significant membership gains. With such a small and stagnating membership the AScW considered itself incapable of effectively servicing its existing membership, or exploiting the membership opportunities that helped ASSET to grow over the same period from 35,038 in 1964 to 49,835 in 1966. Moreover the AScW's membership in 1966 was spread thinly over a wide range of industries. This made it extremely difficult and expensive to service, and the possibility of effective industrial action was considered remote by the AScW's national leadership. In fact, the AScW was heavily dependent on DATA in engineering for taking the lead in negotiations and, if any, in the consequent industrial action in pursuit of wage increases, and hence tended to rely on other unions for any advances it made. Thus the AScW hoped to break out of the vicious circle of stagnant membership and declining financial assets by merging into a more effective bargaining and servicing union.

Other more minor unions, which later joined ASTMS, found themselves in a similar position to that of the original minor founder union, the AScW. The MPU (merged 1970), for instance, affiliated to the TUC on a nominal membership of 5000 in the Health Service for several years when, in fact, its membership was around the 1000 mark. A union of this size was incapable of providing the back-up legal and research facilities its membership desired in a changing and inflationary industrial relations world. But the drive for a merger was finally precipitated by expensive litigation which made its financial position precarious. There was thus the added threat that, if the MPU did not merge, it would cease to exist. Similarly, the Guild of Hospital Pharmacists (merged 1974), with some 1500 members, was finding it difficult to exist in the early 1970s in the face of reorganization of the Health Service. Confronted by mounting financial difficulties, the Guild sought a defensive merger.

Associations or unions merging with ASTMS in insurance, banking and finance, for instance Prudential Male and Other Staff Associations, also approached mergers from a predominantly defensive position. By and large, these associations and unions were motivated to seek mergers by their need for more specialized professional negotiators in an increasingly complex industrial relations world of new techniques and legislation. In short, they did not have the expertise to cope with the new world or the finances to hire the necessary expertise. In the words of one senior official of a staff association,

we had a nice cosy affair with management and no one got very irate for many years. But we were playing second division standards while the management moved into the first division with consultants, job evaluation, and organisation and method study. At that stage as part-time amateurs we could no longer cope. The paternalism of decades was going and as staff we realised our short-comings and needed full-time experts.[82]

Even the largest insurance union, the Union of Insurance Staffs, also experienced financial problems which limited its ability to meet the growing complexity of new techniques, and it too sought defensive mergers to preserve and, if possible, improve its position in the insurance industry.

Amongst other unions joining ASTMS with similar survival problems was the Midland Bank Staff Association. The MBSA faced a decline in membership from 14,000 in 1968 to 10,000 in 1974. In the same period its policy of relying wholly on domestic negotiations was undermined by NUBE's successful pursuit of national negotiations for all the major banks, including the Midland. The establishment of professionalized national negotiating machinery thus spelt the end of the MBSA, structured, as it was, in its amateur fashion around local bargaining. Hence the Association sought a merger as an escape from its growing difficulties.

A defensive merger search was also precipitated among some staff associations by the repeal of the Industrial Relations Act (IRA). The ICI Staff Association and the Kodak Senior Staff Association (KSSA) were products and victims of the IRA's birth and death. Both associations were, to some extent, founded by management and staff to keep out orthodox trade unions entitled to seek recognition under the IRA. The KSSA, like most internal senior staff associations, was in these founding circumstances non-political and company-oriented. It thus, not surprisingly, found it difficult to be an effective bargaining agent, particularly with its limited size and resources. Hence once the IRA was repealed, and the KSSA's membership became much more open to poaching by other unions, considerable doubt was raised regarding the ability of the KSSA either to retain its existing membership, or gain recognition as a union through acquiring a Certificate of Independence under the proposed Employment Protection Act (EPA). With these difficulties in mind the leadership of the KSSA sought a defensive merger.

A number of the minor unions which eventually joined the TGWU were similarly affected by adverse developments that threatened their viability as independent unions. Faced by growing financial difficulties, the declining NAOP, for instance, sought a defensive merger (see pages 180–7). The smaller of the minor unions were also exposed to changes in servicing needs (examined above), which could not be met from the resources available in their very limited job territories. Unions affected by these considerations included the Union of Kodak Workers and the Sheffield Amalgamated Union of File Trades.

Thus the majority of the minor unions merging with ASTMS and the TGWU were faced with questions of survival. They were generally concerned to find some way of continuing to service a declining or stagnating membership in a deteriorating financial situation. Moreover, a number of them were faced with changing and more complex bargaining and/or legal environments which were outside of their normal experiences and abilities. Hence their leaders were driven by the desire to continue some kind of organizational existence to search for mergers.

Membership growth opportunities (major merging unions)

In the period leading up to the formation of ASTMS, and the later mergers pursued by ASTMS, the leadership of ASSET played a driving role in maintaining ASSET's and then ASTMS's growth momentum in the 'natural' recruiting and merger fields. Indeed, the AScW–ASSET merger was specifically intended to strengthen the unions' abilities to penetrate those areas that were 'substantially under-organized'.[83] The two unions together would 'accomplish much that has hitherto been just beyond the powers of the two organisations acting as separate entities',[84] by giving them the 'persuasiveness of numbers.'[85]

ASSET was therefore, as were the minor unions, merging to increase its 'numbers'. But it was not pressing for mergers because its own membership or financial position was becoming untenable or less secure. Indeed, as shown above, ASSET was expanding quite rapidly at the time of its merger with the AScW. ASSET's and later ASTMS's approach to mergers was therefore not defensive. Equally, apart from certain aspects of the initial AScW–ASSET merger, ASTMS mergers were not consolidatory. ASSET was just as intent on using the AScW merger to expand itself horizontally into new areas, such as health service and universities, as it was to exploit the AScW's national engineering procedure agreement to secure its own position in its traditional engineering territory.

ASSET's approach to mergers was therefore, compared with the AScW and other more minor unions, conditioned by a desire more for faster growth, than for slower death. More 'numbers' meant more power and not just survival to ASSET and later ASTMS. The 'persuasiveness of numbers' was for ASSET and ASTMS an aggressive and not a defensive guiding principle.

Thus it was not an accident that ASTMS was structured internally to facilitate growth by acquisition. Its vertical industrial divisions (see Chapters 3 and 4), virtual 'group' autonomy within the highly devolved branch organization and extreme flexibility of structure were all intended to make it easier for minor unions to enter the fold. The union's growth purpose was thus translated into its structure, much as the TGWU's organization had been designed for this purpose in the 1920s.[86] Just as the TGWU was formed to become the general manual workers' union, so ASTMS was given the potential to develop into the white-collar counterpart of the TGWU.

In the late 1960s the TGWU itself also turned, or returned, to mergers to enhance its growth rate, and its influence relative to other unions, through increased numbers. This renewed zeal for growth by merger owed much, as in ASTMS, to the general secretary's commitment to expansion. Two changes initiated by the general secretary-elect, Jones, signalled the start of the TGWU's drive for growth through mergers. First, the new general secretary overturned his predecessor's policy of refusing mergers to unions in financial difficulties, which, in the light of the above comments on minor merger unions' motives for seeking mergers, was a crucially important change in TGWU policy. Second, Jones positively used and amended the union's structure to encourage unions to merge with the TGWU. Under Jones's initiative, for instance, the union's delegates at the 1967 BDC passed a motion calling on the GEC to give consideration to 'removing any constitutional obstacles to attracting other unions to amalgamate with the TGWU'.[87]

Following this decision rule changes were made in 1968, again under Jones's guidance, which, among other things, established a new trade group structure, including the formation of the Vehicle Building and Automotive trade group, and made provision for the creation of autonomous craft sections within the various trade groups. Each of these changes assisted the TGWU in its merger talks. The trade group additions and autonomous craft sections were, for instance, formed to provide the NUVB and the NAOP, respectively, with a high degree of bargaining and organizational autonomy. In a highly competitive inter-union scramble for merger partners, the TGWU's concern to satisfy minor merging unions' demands for special recognition of industrial and craft identities did not pass unrewarded.

Hence both ASTMS and the TGWU deliberately structured themselves internally in a manner calculated to boost their opportunities in the merger movement. Moreover, neither shunned the minor unions in financial difficulties. Thus, not being primarily motivated by their concern to defend or consolidate an existing industrial position, ASTMS in the white-collar, and the TGWU in the blue-collar, field entered the competition for mergers aggressively intent on gaining the advantages that accrued to those unions that had the 'persuasiveness of numbers'.

Summary of change agents
The minor merging unions were generally led into seeking mergers because their existing leadership could find no other way of meeting the pressures that the changing industrial relations environment demanded of their limited resources.

In many cases these pressures threatened the very financial viability of the minor unions. Most such unions thus sought to defend some vestige of their existence by preferring a merger now to extinction later. On the other hand ASSET (later ASTMS) and the TGWU joined and stimulated the merger movement by their much more positive approach to the developing numbers game. These two unions aggressively sought mergers and structured their internal system of government to compete more effectively in the merger process.

Direction of change

Neither ASTMS nor the TGWU were noticeably constrained in their merger searches by traditional merger goals and parameters. These two general unions did not, therefore, within their respective white-collar and predominantly blue-collar occupational spheres of interest, have the clearly graded preferences identified above in the craft-dominated ASW and AEU mergers. Unlike the ASW and the AEU, the two aggressive merger unions did not move through a series of clearly identifiable options, occupational or industrial, in their merger searches. But ASTMS and the TGWU pursued, in particular, mergers that offered access to potential growth areas and/or promised a numerical advantage *vis-à-vis* some competitor union. Hence there was for ASTMS and the TGWU no clear direction of merger change other than in ASTMS's case to grow bigger in the white-collar field and for the TGWU to increase its size in virtually any area of employment.

The factors that influenced the major aggressive unions' pursuit of mergers were therefore mainly those that attracted or repelled the minor merging unions they courted. And it was the minor merging unions' perceptions of the advantages and disadvantages of joining ASTMS or the TGWU, rather than some other interested union, that mainly determined whether or not ASTMS or the TGWU successfully completed a merger. The features of ASTMS and the TGWU that affected the merger decisions of potential minor merging unions were similar to those examined in the UCATT and AUEW mergers; that is, the potential minor merging unions' leaders were concerned with the larger unions' existing job territories, their systems of government, their administrative details, their political tendencies and the personalities of unions' leaders.

Territorial similarities, of an industrial and occupational nature, helped shape the initial ASSET–AScW amalgamation that formed ASTMS. First, the minor union, the AScW, was drawn towards a merger with either ASSET or DATA, by its industrial (engineering) and occupational affinity with both unions. Second, and more negatively, the AScW finally refused the merger with DATA and hence accepted ASSET's terms. By contrast with DATA, ASSET was more than willing fully to accommodate and use the AScW's non-engineering membership as the launching pad for its later merger drive in the Health Service which consequently brought the comparatively small numbers in the MPU and the Guild of Hospital Pharmacists into ASTMS (some 3000 in total).

Outside the Health Service, however, ASTMS did not rely on industrial similarities for its initial merger contacts. Once the union had agreed to extend vertically upwards and downwards in its 'natural' recruitment of white-collar workers and thus deepen its white-collar occupational base, it attracted to it potential merger partners that had no industrial associations with ASTMS. Among these unions and staff associations were those in banking and insurance which brought the largest mergers – for instance the UIS 17,000 members – into ASTMS. In these industries, therefore, ASTMS used mergers to open up new industrial territories.

In contrast, the TGWU's largest mergers were all with unions with which it had a previous close industrial association. The four largest unions joining the TGWU, that is, NAOP, SCMU, CWU and NUVB, for instance, each recruited members in industries with significant numbers of TGWU membership. In a highly competitive merger climate, in which, for instance, UCATT wanted to merge with the NAOP, the GMWU with the CWU and the AEU with the NUVB, the industrial affinity of the highly diversified TGWU was no doubt instrumental in bringing the TGWU into the minor unions' merger reckoning in the first place. Thus the TGWU's main mergers did not noticeably widen its already extremely diverse industrial base but they did improve its competitive position in a number of multi-union industries.

It was, however, above all other factors, the systems of government employed by ASTMS and the TGWU that gave their two merger-conscious general secretaries, Jenkins and Jones, respectively, the opportunity to offer minor unions merger terms that brought them flooding into membership. In the defensive search by the minor merging unions for agreements that guaranteed them some large degree of autonomy and financial and service advantages, the highly decentralized but concentrated ASTMS and TGWU were, other things being equal, best placed to negotiate acceptable mergers. Thus, when ASTMS found itself in competition, for instance, in the Health Service with CoHSE and NUPE for the MPU and with the Association of Professional Scientists and Technologists (APST) for the GHP, and in insurance, finance and banking in competition with APEX for the MBSA and so on, it used its flexible system of government to good effect.

The overall effectiveness of ASTMS's approach to mergers can be well illustrated by examining further the MBSA's transfer of engagements to ASTMS in 1974. In this merger, as will be shown below, the rather left-wing and militant ASTMS was at its most flexible and accommodating in its search for a satisfactory outcome to its negotiations with a most right-wing and anti-union staff association.

The MBSA, as noted above, primarily sought a merger because of its shrinking membership and bargaining difficulties. In spite of reluctantly joining the newly created national negotiating machinery, the MBSA still found itself domestically in difficulties with NUBE which refused to sit with the MBSA in local negotiations. Moreover, NUBE and the other staff associations were holding discussions on forming a single national trade union for bank staff. At the same time management was taking a much tougher line in negotiations and industrial relations were becoming more professionalized. Furthermore, the MBSA could also foresee difficulties arising with the repeal of the 1971 IRA, when the 'independence' of the MBSA might not be so readily accepted and hence its bargaining role in a multi-union environment might be seriously questioned if not denied. In the words of the MBSA's general secretary, 'we saw the need to retain our individual autonomy and our domestic negotiations and yet we needed the ability to have a strong national voice and sufficient resources to cope with the complexities which must arise in the coming years'.

The MBSA therefore sought a merger in order to escape from its difficulties. It rejected however the idea of a merger with other staff associations or NUBE because they would not accommodate the MBSA in an autonomous manner or continue its policy of local bargaining. The MBSA might have found APEX politically more palatable than ASTMS, but at that time APEX did not provide the autonomy that ASTMS could offer. After an informal approach by letter from Jenkins in 1971 the MBSA executive committee unanimously decided that in all the circumstances ASTMS came closest to the MBSA's own philosophy and behaviour in their provision for autonomy and their commitment to company bargaining. They already had the examples of the Prudential and other staff associations that had merged with ASTMS, which demonstrated their ability to retain a high degree of autonomy within ASTMS in conducting their own affairs.

In negotiations the MBSA managed to achieve most of their terms, except that they failed to get a seat on the ASTMS NEC as of right. The satisfaction felt by MBSA with the new arrangements are revealed in the following speech by Claude Smith, general secretary MBSA, who himself became initially the secretary of the Midland Bank Staff section after the merger and later consultant adviser to the ASTMS Finance sector:

It is not my job to 'do a commercial' about ASTMS, but, as I believe it is a trade union with which more and more of you may have to deal with, perhaps I may say one or two things about it. First of all, I would assure you that it is quite unlike the ordinary trade union to which some people take exception. One of the interesting things is that, unlike the engineers or the miners or the railwaymen, ASTMS elect a lay Executive Committee, and it is then the lay Executive Committee which appoints the permanent officers who work on contract; and therefore there is no question that a small militant left-wing can elect a general secretary who is all-powerful and once he gets that position that he is elected there for life. ASTMS has no strike clause in its constitution, it never has unofficial strikes, it has no shop-stewards, it has as most of you know a very good track-record of achievement with the minimum difficulties, and it is hard to find any evidence of employers criticizing the way it acts. With its belief in company house bargaining it is organized in a rather unusual way in that most of the sections are autonomous; and as an example the Midland Bank Staff section, of which I am now secretary, is the second largest section in the union, and within our Instrument of Transfer we conduct our own affairs exactly as we did before, but we do now have the advantage of a very large and efficient back-up organization which can give us considerable assistance. On many occasions in the past we have endeavoured to set up or to assist the setting up of white-collar organizations so that we can have a public voice and a lobby in Parliament, but that has never been achieved because the Government say that they wish to deal directly with the TUC. I will not repeat my criticisms of the TUC but I wonder perhaps if the time has not now arrived when some of us with experience with industrial relations should be prepared to play a part in it and to inject a more moderate outlook and more temperate voice. I believe with the present climate that now is the right time, and I hope that we may be successful in this way because as we all know one of the things that have bedevilled this country for a number of years is the attitude of the unions. There is undoubtedly a need for a more responsible outlook on the part of trade unions and I think we must play our part in this, but that is not to abrogate our duty of looking after the people whom we represent. . . . We may have had special problems in banking, we probably have, but I commend to you the thought that perhaps the best of both worlds can be achieved by belonging to a large white-collar organization such as ASTMS, which is a member of the TUC that speaks with a strong voice at national level and yet believes firmly in domestic negotiations.[88]

It is clear from the above quotation that ASTMS used its highly flexible system of government to guarantee the minor merging unions a very high degree of autonomy. Such action was common in ASTMS's bid for mergers. For instance, the UIS's reluctance to associate with a union affiliated to the Labour Party was overcome by ASTMS's agreeing to UIS's membership contracting 'in' rather than 'out' of the political levy. In this merger the reasonably large minor union (the UIS) was also guaranteed one seat on ASTMS NEC for five years. These adjustments were made possible by ASTMS rule 15(a), which allows the NEC, and therefore in practice the general secretary, to establish any machinery required to facilitate mergers – a position which an opponent of ASTMS's bid for competitive merger advantage claimed enabled ASTMS to 'offer the union in an opportunist search for mergers'.[89] It was this extreme flexibility that enabled ASTMS to overcome difficulties associated with political incompatibilities and/or personality differences which prevented minor unions merging with less flexible organizations.

The TGWU was also flexible in its bid to accommodate minor merging unions, following the rule changes of 1968 (see Chapters 3 and 4), although it did not carry its flexibility to the extremes adopted by ASTMS. For instance, during its merger negotiations with the NUVB, in competition with the AEU, the TGWU adjusted its internal structure to encourage the formation of district committees and create a Vehicle Building and Automotive trade group at least partly in order to meet the NUVB's merger aims. Similarly, structural changes that offered the CWU a degree of autonomy in a new Chemical, Oil and Rubber trade group, not matched by the competitor GMWU, were also instrumental in attracting that union into the TGWU (see Chapter 4). The TGWU also paralleled ASTMS by making special provision for membership of the union's GEC and BDC for particularly large or attractive merger candidates. Thus the NUVB secured two representatives on the GEC in addition to the regular trade group representatives provided for under rule 6.2b. This was achieved by deeming the NUVB section of the Vehicle Building and Automotive trade group National Committee to be a separate 'trade group' within a trade group, and therefore entitled to elect an additional representative to the GEC. The other additional delegate was declared to be non-voting and hence was not required to be sanctioned by the rules. The TGWU also made special provision for the delegates to the former NUVB's Conference to become delegates to the TGWU's BDC as representatives from the Automotive trade group. How this was achieved within the TGWU's rules is not clear.

Thus the TGWU used, as did ASTMS, various discretionary elements within rules to meet minor merging unions' individual requirements. ASTMS in particular did not reject mergers just because the minor merging unions had dissimilar systems of government, or dissimilar political goals, or dissimilar bargaining arrangements. Even though the TGWU did not go to ASTMS's extraordinary lengths to conclude a merger satisfactorily, it tended to be far more flexible in its arrangements than were the AUEW or UCATT.

Summary of direction of change
The merger search parameters of ASTMS and the TGWU were not set by any consistently defensive or consolidatory considerations. In the absence of such considerations the two major merging unions were not noticeably discerning in their merger searches. ASTMS and the TGWU were instead concerned with mergers that would significantly increase their actual or potential membership. Moreover, if such mergers also offered to increase significantly the aggressive unions' relative standing *vis-à-vis* some competitor union, the search for a satisfactory conclusion to a merger was intensified, as in the case of the NUVB.

The minor merging unions were, on the other hand, generally motivated to seek mergers for defensive reasons. They also tended, with few exceptions, to want to join larger unions with which they had an occupational and/or industrial identity. In many cases there were, within this narrower search area, several options. For example, in the Health Service the MPU had ASTMS, CoHSE and NUPE interested in a merger. ASTMS and the TGWU had, within this competitive environment, merger advantages, particularly if the occupational or industrial identities of the minor and major unions competing for mergers were generally similar. For it was in these situations that ASTMS, and to a somewhat lesser extent the TGWU, offered the minor unions degrees of autonomy and special provisions that other major merging unions could not match. Hence with the minor merging unions stressing autonomy more than any other objective, the government systems of ASTMS and the TGWU gave them a major advantage in the scramble for territory.

Thus the direction of change of ASTMS and the TGWU was much less predictable than that of UCATT and the AUEW. Neither ASTMS nor the TGWU was historically committed to 'one-union' goals, and few of the minor merging unions had fixed ideas regarding the desirability or otherwise of moving towards industrial unionism when faced by questions of their own survival. Therefore the direction of change of ASTMS was towards establishing itself as the 'TGWU of the white-collar world', while the TGWU, in many ways its unconscious inventor, continued to add more members and improve its relative position in the union hierarchy.

Summary and conclusions: features that facilitate mergers

All the unions examined, regardless of their systems of government, were led into mergers by their national full-time officials. No union experienced anything that could be described as a general membership drive for amalgamations. The 1960s and 1970s mergers were thus distinctly different from those, like the AEU, that received their impetus in the 1920s from local level, rank-and-file, amalgamation committees. Agents for change that promoted mergers hence made themselves felt at the national level mainly through those processes that bypassed the constitutionally prescribed policy-making channels. The existence of constitutionally processed policy decisions urging the formation of an industrial union did, however, play a part in some unions in shaping the direction of this merger activity.

The *change agents* that promoted mergers were themselves largely the product of previous developments in the areas of change. All the merging unions examined tended to react initially in the merger field in response to changes that affected some aspect of size, which produced in turn *defensive, consolidatory* and *aggressive* approaches to mergers.

Size change agents were of two, not mutually exclusive, kinds. First, there were absolute changes in size and, second, relative size developments. Significant and adverse absolute changes in size provoked the most marked *defensive merger* activity. All the unions forming UCATT and the minor AUFW in the AUEW merger were primarily stimulated in their merger search by a decline in their absolute membership, as were a number of the minor unions joining ASTMS and the TGWU. A significant and continuous decline in membership in an inflationary period threatened the financial viability of many of the above unions, unions that had already attempted within the confines of their existing and traditional job territories to mitigate or reverse their numerical and financial decline. Their common problem was that they could not independently maintain or improve their existing levels of services and benefits over the short or medium term. In extreme cases even the unions' survival was brought into question. Such defensive unions thus, as a member of the AUEW commented, paradoxically 'amalgamate in order to remain independent'.

A similar kind of adverse absolute change created a defensive posture among some of the white-collar unions and associations which merged with ASTMS. Several small white-collar organizations maintained a bargaining presence, such as the Engineer Surveyors' Association, on a membership of 1000 to 2000 members. In their case the absolute change came from the increased demands on the organization and not from the decline in membership. Industrial relations legislation, innovations in bargaining, such as job evaluation and incomes policy, and the general increased demands on the organization exposed sucn unions' and associations' inability to service membership effectively from a narrow base. A belief developed in this situation that such a union could survive only with a much higher level of membership if it was to continue to provide the services needed by its membership in the 1970s. The small white-collar unions and associations found themselves, as one official remarked, needing 'full-time experts'.[90] Unable to afford such experts from their own limited resources, the very minor white-collar unions opted as a defensive measure to merge with ASTMS. They needed a larger absolute membership in order to survive as a viable organization.

Secondly, relative size developments produced, in some unions, *consolidatory* and *aggressive* mergers. Major and minor merging unions in the AUEW merger came into an amalgamation primarily intended to *consolidate* the AEU's position as the premier union in the engineering industry. Through this amalgamation the AEU and the more minor merging unions expected to preserve the craftsmen's hegemony in the industry. The relative size changes that brought about such a consolidatory merger were those that challenged the individual union's growth expectations and/or adversely influenced its position in some sphere of inter-union competition. The AUEW's component unions were affected in both these ways. DATA, the AUFW and the AEU itself all experienced lower growth rates than past experience had led them to expect. Moreover, in DATA's and the AEU's cases competitor unions also had relatively and significantly higher growth rates than either union.

In ASTMS and the TGWU mergers were pursued more *aggressively* than in the other major merging unions. In the numerous mergers entered into by these unions minor merging unions driven by defensive motives joined major unions seeking to enhance their relative positions *vis-à-vis* other competitor unions. Led from the top, ASTMS and the TGWU generally outbid their competitors for the privilege of rescuing minor unions from extinction. This was not, however, an altogether altruistic act. Both major unions expected to make effective inroads into the minor merging unions' new and relatively unorganized job territories – or, on the other hand, to prevent the better organized areas of job territory falling to some other competitor organization.

The *direction of change* given by the above changes in some aspect of size did nothing to produce a more logical or planned inter-union structure in Britain. The TUC's efforts to create certain patterns of unionism through its industrial committees were not successful, although its promotion of legislative changes, which made mergers considerably easier, opened the way for the merger movement. Inter-union structures were therefore primarily affected in an *ad hoc* manner by the mergers encouraged by the legislative changes.

The mergers, however, gathered considerable momentum of their own as the past absolute and relative size changes, mentioned above, interacted with the existing structure of UK unions to produce a scramble for mergers that developed its own dynamic. The individual merger was turned by this combination of circumstances into a merger movement. In the first instance, a merger stimulated by absolute size reasons disturbed other unions' relative size considerations. These disturbed unions, in turn, sought mergers in order to restore the *status quo* in respect of their relative size or to reduce the competitor unions' recently gained relative size advantage.

The mergers were encouraged to develop in this way by the existing structure of UK unions. There were in the engineering and building industries, for instance, no clear boundaries, in the 1960s, to the various unions' recruiting territories. Prior to the merger movement, several formerly exclusive craft unions had extended vertically within their original industrial and craft bases while the general unions had spread themselves horizontally across several blue-collar occupations in a number of industries. ASSET also achieved, mainly through mergers, a similar multi-industrial base in white-collar employment. A minor union seeking a merger was thus faced by a number of options, even if it narrowed its search to its industrial base or related occupations. Only the highly craft-conscious minor unions, in practice, rejected outright the option of joining a general union, such as the TGWU. Minor merging unions such as the NAOP, the NUVB and the AScW were thus all in a position to assess competitive bids for their membership and job territories, from more than one union.

In this environment the merger proposals made, for instance, by the ASW to the ASPD and AUBTW threatened to weaken the relative strength of the TGWU in the building industry. Similarly, the AEU's merger talks with the AUFW, NUVB and the other minor engineering unions could, if successful, have undermined the TGWU's relative position in engineering in general and in the highly competitive vehicle industry in particular. Outside these industries the TGWU's relative position in the TUC and its committees was also likely to be adversely influenced if the ASW and/or the AEU were successful in creating two new craft-dominated industrial unions. Also, ASSET faced an intense inter-union recruiting contest with DATA if that union, and not itself, was successful in merging with the AScW.

Competition for merger partners in the industries examined, and in the ASSET's, and later the ASTMS's, bid for rapid growth, was thus intense. Jones's and Jenkins's ascendancy in their respective and highly concentrated unions, the TGWU and ASTMS, and their own commitments to an aggressive merger policy, made their unions 'the predators' of the merger movement. Any misunderstanding or difficulty between the AEU or the ASW and its potential merger partners was fully exploited by the TGWU. Similarly, ASSET took advantage of DATA's inability to complete a merger with the AScW. Through this kind of competitive merger action and the widespread belief that a minimum size of union was necessary to remain efficient and effective, a feeling of 'we must go somewhere' developed among the minor unions and heightened their awareness of the costs of remaining fully independent.

In the competitive merger searches parameters were set by a combination of factors. Normally the causes of the size changes, the perceived solutions to the adverse effects of such changes, the historical growth objectives and existing membership affinities between merging unions interacted to set the parameters of the search. If the causes of the adverse absolute or relative size changes were perceived to be irreversible, largely because they arose from exogenous factors, the affected unions reacted by seeking mergers that could, in a quantitative manner, immediately compensate for the previous perceived adverse size changes. The parameters of many of the unions joining the AEU, TGWU and ASTMS were influenced by such ideas.

On the other hand, if the merger search was stimulated by adverse size developments arising largely from endogenous factors, the merger search parameters were influenced by different considerations. If, for instance, adverse size changes were perceived as the product of shifts in actual or potential members' attitudes to unionization, as in the ASW's, ASPD's and AUBTW's situation, the search parameters were influenced by the unions' attempt to change those attitudes. In the ASW's case, the mergers were not intended primarily to provide an instant change in job territory; the ASW merged with the other unions in the same predicament in order to change the qualitative nature of union activity in the building industry. There was an assumption that the separate unions' original members could be retained and potential members recruited through a restructuring of unions in the building industry. It was thought, in the ASW, that the combined merged unions could 'deliver the goods' which independently they had failed to provide. A number of small white-collar unions that later joined the ASTMS appeared to be influenced by similar reasons. The perceived causes of the adverse size changes thus influenced the parameters of unions' merger searches.

However, for unions led by highly craft-conscious national officials, historical growth objectives and membership affinities were the most important factors determining the merger search parameters. Even though the conditions that originally spawned ideas of industrial unionism had changed somewhat by the 1960s, it still remained a powerful influence on the parameters of the ASW's and AEU's merger searches.

By contrast, the leaders of the TGWU and the ASTMS faced no such historical and internal constraints on their merger activities. The TGWU's and ASTMS's existing members had affinities across many industries in, respectively, blue-collar and white-collar occupations. But even if they, the existing membership, had objected to their leaders' merger activities breaking into new job territories, the concentrated and highly flexible systems of government safeguarded the national full-time leadership's discretion in this field of activity. The TGWU and ASTMS were therefore operating within a wider merger area than were the more craft-oriented unions.

Generally, a union seeking a merger remained clearly within the above search parameters until its originally identified options had been exhausted. It was normally only as a last resort that a minor merging union sought a merger outside its immediate job territory. On the odd occasion that minor unions broke prematurely out of their natural territories the personal preferences and antagonisms of the leading merger negotiators played an important part in the decision.

Several minor merging unions, however, had membership affinities of more or less common value with more than one union. The NUVB, for example, with its mixed skilled and semi-skilled membership could have opted for either the AEU or the TGWU. Both these unions co-operated with, while competing for, NUVB membership in the vehicle industry. Similarly, the AScW had much in common with ASSET and DATA: the MBSA could have opted for ASTMS or APEX, the CWU was open to approaches from the GMWU and the TGWU, and so on. It was during the often parallel and complex negotiations that unions' internal structures and systems of government influenced, if not determined, mergers and hence the external structures of British unionism.

The TGWU and ASTMS therefore had in certain situations *features that facilitated mergers.* They both had wider parameters of merger searches than any other unions. If a blue-collar or white-collar union was moved by either absolute or relative size changes to increase its membership, *per se*, by a merger, the TGWU and ASTMS respectively were the most pro-merger unions likely to have an affinity with the minor union's existing membership. And, unlike the other interested unions, the TGWU and ASTMS provided minor merging unions with the trade group structures that guaranteed a high degree of industrial autonomy within the larger organization. Unions merging in order to retain at least a vestige of independence were allocated a degree of autonomy by the TGWU and ASTMS which could not be matched by most other unions.

In the actual detail of merger negotiations, the TGWU and ASTMS also provided the merger negotiators with more discretion than any other major merging union. *De jure* and *de facto* decision-making procedures, as they affected mergers, were at the national level within the broad control of the two aggressive unions' general secretaries. For instance, staffing levels and the allocation of jobs within the national hierarchy were largely at the two general secretaries' disposal. Furthermore, and in some competitive merger cases crucially, such positions were appointed placements for life. National leaders of minor unions taking their members into the TGWU and ASTMS were not, therefore, faced with an unknown and politically divided electorate, such as they could find in the AEU.

Moreover, if a minor merging union was seeking advantages associated with relative size considerations, the TGWU and ASTMS were both extremely influential in, respectively, the blue-collar and white-collar inter-union fields. The TGWU's position as the largest union in the TUC, for instance, made it an attractive merger proposition for minor unions seeking a voice of some consequence in the higher levels of inter-union policy-making. However, if the merging unions sought growth through mergers as a means of competing with the TGWU or ASTMS, they were likely to reject out-of-hand merger overtures from the two predators of the merger movement.

Major merging unions' systems of government were thus of considerable importance in shaping the direction of a minor merging union's search for merger partners. If a major union could not accommodate a minor union's desire for autonomy, the minor union moved on to consider other offers. In competitive parallel merger negotiations, involving differently structured major unions, the highly diffused and inflexible AEU found itself at a distinct disadvantage. It was in this situation that competitive inter-union pressures and the AEU's own inability to restructure itself internally caused the AEU to form a federation around the four merging unions. Thus the AEU's four parts were given a high degree of autonomy. But this arrangement also significantly lessened the value of the relative size advantages originally sought from the merger. It, in effect, maintained four separate voices in fields where one larger and more homogeneous voice would have been, and was expected to be, superior.

By comparison with the federated AUEW and the vertically bifurcated TGWU and ASTMS, UCATT produced a third kind of merger. The UCATT merger, unlike the others, involved both major and minor unions intent on reaping more than just the benefits associated with an immediate size increase. The leaders of UCATT aimed at a radical restructuring of the union's organization through mergers. Their intention was to use the merger to centralize and rationalize the organization and the bargaining function. Under intense pressures the merging unions agreed to subsume their identities within a new union. Hence UCATT, formed by transfers of engagements, was much more integrated than the Amalgamated Engineers.

Thus mergers were not only shaped by existing systems of government; but they also, in turn, influenced the form of government adopted by major merging unions. In the scramble for new job territories the major merging unions sought to make themselves more attractive to the minor merging unions. Hence there was a move, for instance in the AEU, to sectionalization (a policy also previously followed by the Boilermakers in their amalgamation), and an adjustment to acknowledge industrial interests in the GMWU, while ASTMS had a proliferation of industrial groups.

Finally, it can be concluded that, given existing membership affinities, systems of government and the factors promoting change, the merger movement of the 1960s and 1970s appears as a somewhat random process. Certainly it appears to lack direction, or movement in any preordained conscious form. The only observable 'trend' or 'pattern' is towards fewer and larger unions; there are no 'models' or overall policies designed to 'rationalize' or 'improve' the structure and/or government of British trade unionism. Indeed, it is difficult to see how attempts by the TUC or others to shape British unions according to some overall plan, even if concerned with 'relating union structures to changing patterns of industrial organization',[91] could have produced a movement towards industrial unionism or some other theoretically orderly construct. For, in the competitive and internally directed merger movement of the 1960s and 1970s the pursuit of numbers, however defined, came to overshadow all other objectives.

7   Changes in the character of job regulation

As we said in our brief description of them in Chapter 3, the areas of change in job regulation with which we are concerned can be divided into two dimensions: changes in *character* refer to the strategies and tactics used in the process of job regulation; changes in the *structure* of decision-making refer to the level at which decision-making in job regulation takes place and the degree of participation in the decision-making processes at each level. This is the bargaining as opposed to the non-bargaining aspect of internal government as described in Chapters 3 and 4.

Empirically, 'character' and 'structure' as we have defined them are closely intertwined. They can, however, vary independently, and the causal relationship between them can differ. In the case of the NUT and NALGO, changes in the area of both character and the structure of bargaining took place; but the most fundamental change was in the former area, and the changes or demands for changes in structure, although they followed from the changing character, were not a necessary concomitant. In both cases the demand for greater militancy was associated with a demand for greater participation in the existing decision-making process rather than a demand for a change in the level at which collective bargaining was conducted.

On the other hand, in the case of the AUEW, TGWU, NUM and UCATT, who form the focus of our discussion on changes in the decision-making structure, the causal relationship was either reversed or, in the case of the NUM, evenly balanced. In all these cases, although the degree of militancy may have increased in quantity over the period, the change in the pattern that that militancy took, which was the major change, was closely dependent on and part of changes in the decision-making structure.

The strategy and tactics or means used in the process of job regulation will be analysed along two dimensions – the type of action used and the intensity with which that action is pursued. As far as the type of action is concerned, we distinguish between political and industrial action. 'Political' is used in its broadest sense to include all types of action involving the state and its associated institutions. 'Industrial' covers the two types of job regulation often referred to as 'unilateral' or 'autonomous' job regulation, which involves the union alone, and bilateral job regulation or 'collective bargaining', which involves the employer, whether a private or public corporation or the state. The intensity with which the action is pursued is defined in terms of the readiness to contemplate all forms of industrial or political action. This will be referred to by the shorthand term 'militancy', and can be used to define both political and industrial activity, although for the most part it will refer primarily to the latter.

The period since 1960 has been marked by an increased involvement by all unions in the political arena, associated with the state's increased intervention in the field of collective bargaining both through incomes policies and through attempts to change the industrial relations framework and the internal power structure of trade unions through legislation. The increased involvement in the political arena was most marked in the public sector because the state is the direct or indirect employer there and hence could directly affect the implementation of its more general policies in that sphere. The public sector was in the forefront of the 'serious explosions of strike activity' between 1968 and 1974.[1] While the explosion affected most trade unions, the previously quiescent public services accounted for a major part of it.

The general upsurge in public sector militancy in the 1960s and early 1970s was largely attributable to the degree of discrimination against the public sector as a whole that was exercised not only during periods of informal incomes policy but also during the statutory incomes policy of 1965–69 which was intended to apply equally to public and private sectors alike. As with incomes policy in general, policy towards the public sector has alternated between 'hard' and 'soft' phases, but the 'hard' phases have tended to be more prolonged and more frequent in the public sector. There have been three phases of 'hard' policy towards public sector claims since 1960 in which the government has concentrated on them without attempting to enforce the same degree of pay restraint in the private sector: viz. 1961–2, 1968–9 and 1971–2. As can be seen in Table 4 (page 35), these attempts were accompanied by peaks of public service and public sector militancy.

The available statistical evidence on incomes supports the view that there was an increasing degree of discrimination against the public sector during the 1960s. The effects of this on pay levels have been an important cause of industrial unrest. The DE does not publish separate wage and salary indices for the public sector, but trends in public and private sector incomes can be compared by calculating the respective increases in employment income per head from the national income statistics.[2] The results of this calculation over the period 1958–71 are given in Table 41. This shows there was no evidence of sustained deterioration of relative pay in the public sector up until 1967, variations in favour of one section generally being followed by a reaction in the other direction. In 1968, however, private sector incomes rose twice as fast as incomes in the public sector, while the retail price index rose by 5.6 per cent. In 1969 and 1970 public sector incomes continued to lag behind the private sector although they did manage to keep up with the rate of price increases. The trend was reversed in 1971 when the increases in public sector incomes exceeded that in the private sector, but not all the ground was recovered; if the period of Labour Government incomes policy as a whole (1964–70) is taken, the rises in the public sector were 48.5 per cent compared with 57.8 per cent in the private sector.

Table 41   *Increases in income per head, 1958–71*

	Public	Private
	%	%
1958	3.3	4.8
1959	4.1	4.6
1960	7.3	5.1
1961	5.6	6.8
1962	5.7	3.9
1963	5.3	4.6
1964	6.2	7.0
1965	8.4	6.7
1966	5.0	6.6
1967	6.5	5.8
1968	3.9	9.1
1969	6.1	6.9
1970	11.2	12.5
1971	13.6	12.0

Source: National Income Blue Book.

The reasons for the rapid deterioration in the public sector relative wage position in 1968 are related to the differential impact of an incomes policy which, unlike the 'hard' phases mentioned earlier, was intended to apply equally to the public and private sectors. There were two reasons for this differential impact. The government was able to ensure that the policy was applied more strictly to public employees, simply because it had greater control over that sector as an employer. Moreover, as Liddle and McCarthy have argued,[3] a much greater proportion of the public than of the private sector came under the scrutiny of the NBPI.

Moreover, even if the policy had been uniformly applied throughout the public and private sectors there would still be some tendency for private sector wages to move ahead because of the criteria used and the policy's emphasis on productivity, particularly in 1968 and 1969. Thus those for whom productivity bargaining was either not practicable, such as teachers, nurses and civil servants, or could not be introduced quickly, as in the public services in general, were left behind in the earnings race. In our own sample the POEU were the only public sector union making early and continuous use of the productivity criterion in wage bargaining. It is perhaps significant that it was also the only union to remain largely untouched by the tide of militancy in 1960 and 1970, although it did successfully use a one-day token stoppage in 1969 to progress current negotiations more quickly. It was not until 1970–71 that large numbers of public service manual workers began to benefit from productivity payments, but this was too late to prevent the growth of strong pressure, at first from rank-and-file employees and later reflected by the official union leadership, for sizeable increases in basic rates of pay to compensate for the ground lost both in real pay terms and in relation to the private sector in 1968. All the unions in our sample with membership in the public services changed character in response to the above discrimination that arose from growing state intervention. But NALGO and the NUT have been selected as the major focus of the study of change in character for several reasons. First, they operate exclusively in the public sector. Second, they are white-collar unions and illustrate the changes in character taking place generally within that sector since 1960.[4] Third, they manifested much greater changes in character, partly because they had much further to move, than other unions in the sample. For example, in 1960 neither NALGO nor the NUT were affiliated to the TUC, whereas the rest of the sample were, and NALGO had never and the NUT had rarely undertaken industrial actions of any kind.

In the rest of the chapter, therefore, we shall be concentrating on the areas, processes and agents of change as they applied to NALGO and the NUT. The wider relevance of the variables will also be demonstrated by a brief reference to the other unions studied before moving to the summary and conclusions.

NALGO's changing character

Areas of change

Political action

NALGO has always eschewed party political involvement, and still does. Since achieving recognition in 1942 it has been able, by and large, to rely on normal collective bargaining arrangements in its job regulation activities, although it mounted specific political campaigns on occasion. After 1960, however, NALGO found it increasingly difficult to continue as an effective organization without action on the political front, and specifically without affiliation to the TUC.

NALGO affiliated to the TUC in 1964 but that was not the first time that the issue had been raised. It had been debated as early as the 1920 delegate conference, and proposals for affiliation were defeated in conferences in 1920 and 1921. In the 1930s and 1940s the question again came up. In 1942, on a card vote of 48,179 to 32,705 a referendum of the membership was agreed.[5] The subsequent ballot showed 58.7 per cent in favour of affiliation on a poll of just over half of the membership. However, affiliation was not proceeded with as a majority of the *members* (rather than of those who voted) had not positively indicated their support for affiliation. The matter was not debated again until the end of the Second World War, when the 1945 conference rejected it by a clear majority of 71,000 to 39,000. At the next three conferences the question of affiliation to the TUC on a non-political basis was raised, but this was rejected by the 1948 conference when the normally influential lay National Executive Council, a directly elected body, reported that, while 'there might be no organic link between the TUC and the Labour Party, there was undoubtedly a spiritual one'. In the ballot that followed, 64.4 per cent of the membership rejected affiliation, and the issue faded until the mid-1950s. In 1955 NALGO secured what many members felt to be a disappointing salary increase, and that year's conference was asked to support affiliation on the basis that 'the bargaining power of the NEC can only be strengthened by the affiliation of NALGO to the TUC'.[6] However, affiliation was again rejected, by 51.5 per cent of the membership, on the lowest turn-out apart from the wartime vote.

At the 1962 annual conference the issue was raised again. But this time the NEC was supporting the recommendation that NALGO should affiliate to the TUC, having already as an NEC voted 37–21 in favour.[7] In the May prior to the conference, the NEC had published a White Paper which laid out the factual background to the TUC and the pros and cons of NALGO affiliation. The paper stressed that: 'The National Executive Council has considered the question of affiliation to the TUC mainly in the light of current events related to economic policy and future prospects . . . which may have a possible impact upon present day machinery for collective bargaining'.

At conference, the NEC's motion to hold a ballot of membership on a simple majority basis was carried, although in the face of some opposition which concentrated on the fear of mass membership resignation should NALGO affiliate. Great pains were taken by the NEC to stress that, should NALGO affiliate, it would do so solely on an industrial and not on a political basis. However, when the ballot was held the membership rejected affiliation by the narrow margin of 5823 votes. Despite this rebuff, the NEC continued with its pro-TUC campaign. In the November 1963 issue of *Public Service*, it published a statement that included the following: 'so long as NALGO remains outside the TUC it must become a powerless spectator on the sidelines. Only inside the TUC has it any hope of influencing national economic and wages policy and adequately protecting its members'.

The council also resolved to put the following motion to the 1963 conference:

That despite the result of the ballot on affiliation to the Trades Union Congress, in the light of current events related particularly to salaries and service conditions and the future prospects affecting the membership of NALGO, the National Executive Council adheres to its view that it is imperative for NALGO to become affiliated to the Trades Union Congress and recommends council to take appropriate action accordingly.

The 1963 conference saw something of a reversal of the previous year's decision, the NEC's stance being approved by 139,200 to 94,353 on a card vote, and approval being given to its policy of seeking to change the membership's attitude to affiliation. This mandate was carried out by the full-time officers, and by pro-TUC education and propagandizing in *Public Service*. The NEC decided, in the light of an independent motion in favour of affiliation, not to put forward a motion of its own at the 1964 conference. At conference the motion was carried on a card vote by 199,949 to 67,444, and a ballot of the membership was authorized for the following September, when affiliation on a non-political basis was finally approved, by a majority of 53.8 per cent of those voting.

It is difficult to define precisely the impact that affiliation to the TUC has had on NALGO policy and strategy. It is fair to say that it has been an important influence in breaking down NALGO's previously parochial and isolationist policies, and in leading it to take a greater interest in broader social and economic problems. These broad changes were institutionalized when the 1972 conference approved the NEC's recommendation that the Service and Conditions Committee of the NEC should be renamed the Economic Committee and its role as 'a forum for the discussion of broad economic and social policy and the dissemination of information' be recognized.[8]

Industrial action
After 1960 NALGO laid the foundations for taking militant action by making several constitutional changes. In 1961 it adopted a strike clause in its constitution. Before, *ad hoc* extra-constitutional procedures existed for the withdrawal of labour, but these were extremely complex and were not backed up by provisions for a strike fund. In practice, however, all attempts to take strike action had been discouraged, although at the 1951 conference the establishment of a 'fighting fund' had been authorized. (The object of the fund was to raise a special reserve of £500,000 by 1960, with £50,000 being paid in per annum from general reserves.[9])

The debate at the 1961 conference was sparked off by a request for permission to take strike action over recognition by the Rhondda Transport Company branch. The NEC had been unable to act because of the lack of constitutional power either to authorize a strike or pay strike pay. Albert Nortrop, chairman of the NEC, spoke in favour of the adoption of a strike procedure, assuring the delegates that 'We still adhere to the principles of collective bargaining. We have not weakened our faith in that method. But when we are deprived of the machinery, we must fail unless our constitution gives us the weapon for final action'.[10] By a majority of 30 to 1 the motion authorizing the calling of a strike and the payment of strike pay was carried. However, by way of qualifying their motion Albert Nortrop for the NEC added, 'we are not envisaging for a moment a commitment to wholesale strikes. . . . The Council [NEC] is convinced that the need for withdrawal of labour on a large scale will never arise'.[11] Conference did not approve any additional levy to the 'fighting fund', which in 1961 had reached the £500,000 originally envisaged ten years earlier. Following the ratification by conference, the NEC agreed on a strike policy, based on the principle that no industrial action would be undertaken without a ballot of the membership section concerned, authorized by the Emergency Committee of the NEC.

Since 1961, three major examinations have been made of strike policy in NALGO – in 1967, 1970 and 1974. At the 1966 conference a motion was presented by the Hull and Leeds branches in conjunction with the North Western and Yorkshire district councils requesting the NEC to prepare a report on sanctions. In May 1967 the NEC produced a White Paper on the subject which reached some rather pessimistic conclusions. Strikes, it argued, must be judged by their results, and the danger of 'an expensive waste of time' had always to be guarded against. Strikes against single national employers (the National Health Service and the electricity and gas industries) stood little chance of success, while those in local government stood only a slightly better chance. If strikes had to be called, selective rather than total action was to be preferred; while token strikes, work-to-rules and overtime bans were rejected as ineffective. At conference that year the document was accepted, but it was criticized for being a 'timid document', and tagged as 'NALGO's gift to the employers'.[12] The general fear was expressed, however, that incomes policy and challenges to it might bring NALGO into direct confrontation with the government, and conference concurred with the opinion of the Metropolitan branch that the report 'was unpleasant but honest'.[13]

In 1970 a more militant line in strike action was proposed by the NEC. This consisted of a three-stage approach consisting of a short demonstration stoppage without pay in the service concerned to demonstrate solidarity, selective stoppages with pay of total authorities or units within authorities, and selective stoppages with pay of particular departments or occupations. At the same time, the NEC proposed that the contributions to the 'fighting fund' should be raised from the £100,000 per annum agreed in 1966 to £250,000 per annum. It was further emphasized that the NEC did not intend that the strike ballot should be dropped.

In May 1974 the NEC agreed a new strike procedure which it recommended to conference. A branch wishing to undertake industrial action would report the matter to the district organization officer, who if unable to resolve it would in turn report the issue to the general secretary. After consultation with the chairman of the NEC the general secretary could then authorize a ballot, thus obviating the need for the full Emergency Committee to consider the matter. Action at district level was to be sponsored by the appropriate service and conditions committee after consultation with the district representatives and the district officer. The Emergency Committee, not as previously the full NEC, would then have the power to authorize a ballot. Further, the operation of the Emergency Committee was simplified by the authorization of panels of the committee under the chairmanship of the chairman or vice-chairman of the NEC to act in the name of the full committee. While the Emergency Committee actually took the decision on whether service and conditions groups could take industrial action, the final authorization was to be given by the NEC. The NEC's right to authorize action without a ballot in an emergency was to be retained.

It was not until 1965 that the first real possibility of a major strike emerged.[14] This development took place not in local government but in the electricity industry, where traditional staff–manual differentials had been upset by a 1964 agreement which allowed the upgrading of manual workers to staff status and provided for productivity payments. In response staff workers opened negotiations for a new grading structure in December 1964. In May 1965, following a ballot in which some 75 per cent of the electricity group voted for some form of strike action, the NEC agreed to authorize a policy of selective strikes. Faced with this threat, the Electricity Council (the employers) referred the matter to the Ministry of Labour, who in turn stemmed the action by referring it to the NBPI.

In February 1966 action was authorized for NALGO staff in the Rochdale Transport department. The staff demanded their upgrading by two grades after platform staff had been granted a 10s. per week attendance bonus in 1962 and a further 10s. in 1965. The local authority, however, reached a satisfactory decision before the action could get under way. In 1967 a much more important threat of strike action took place. Local government officers in Scotland whose settlement date followed that of their English colleagues found their 7 per cent award (paid to their English counterparts a few days earlier) vetoed by a government-imposed pay freeze. On 28 March 1967 the Scottish District Council backed a call for strike action by 83 votes to 33, and on 1 April the NEC authorized the holding of a strike ballot in Scotland by 42 votes to 19. Action was, however, averted on 4 April when the Department of Economic Affairs allowed the payment of the award by 1 July. The principal effect of the incident was to bring home to NALGO the irrationality of maintaining separate negotiating machines in England and Scotland. The problem was eventually resolved in 1969 when the employers' sides of the joint council agreed to their merger.

More dissatisfaction developed in September 1969, when a local government group meeting rejected a two-year agreement reached earlier on 9 July 1969. The crux of the matter rested on the impending relaxation of incomes policy and the apparent ability of other white-collar groups to secure better deals. The question of strike action was raised, but the general mood of the meeting was summarized by Glyn Philips (chairman-elect of the Local Government Service and Conditions Committee) as 'the members are not prepared on this issue of pay to come out on strike at the moment'.[15] By November the employers' side of the NJC agreed to reopen negotiations, and by January satisfactory interim awards were secured. The situation culminated in a 15 per cent pay claim for 1970, backed by mumblings of militancy and threats to boycott the general election work, and achieved relative success when a $12\frac{1}{2}$ per cent award was gained in June 1970.

The second issue over which NALGO passions were aroused in 1969 centred on Richard Crossman's proposals for an earnings-related state pension scheme. It was felt that the provisions of this scheme might threaten the position of those (like local government employees) already benefiting from adequate private schemes. Potential interference in these rights produced an almost atavistic response among the membership, particularly the senior groups most immediately affected. In January 1970, a successful call was made by Plymouth branch for a special meeting to be held on 9 January, which called for, among other motions, 'the NEC to initiate an immediate referendum to ascertain the support for strike action'.[16] This motion was, however, countered by the NEC, and on a card vote their stance requesting more state financial support for the new scheme and negotiations with the local authority employers to secure the best possible arrangements for NALGO members was carried.

The year 1970 can be seen as a turning point in regard to NALGO's attitude to militancy. Although by no means a major dispute, the authorization in February of NALGO's first official strike established a significant precedent. On 9 February 1970 twenty-one members of the Leeds Cleansing department (eighteen NALGO, two NUPE and one non-unionist) took unofficial strike action over their non-involvement in a 25s. per week bonus scheme enjoyed by the manual members of the department. In December 1969, representation had been made to management requesting their inclusion in the scheme, but this had met with little response. At the 11 February meeting of the Emergency Committee, it was agreed unanimously to make the strike official, and by 20 February a satisfactory settlement was reached.

However, the Leeds strike is by no means the only reason for singling out 1970 as a turning point. Some of these have already been mentioned; for example, the 12½ per cent settlement for local government staff was essentially a pay-off for threatened militancy. Similarly, 1970 marked the adoption of a new strike policy and the raising of the annual contribution to the reserve fund by 150 per cent. That year also saw an unprecedented number of applications to the Emergency Committee – twelve, although of these two were not approved, one failed to secure a majority in ballot, and six were settled without action. Further, 1970 saw the establishment of precedents that could be used to build up more militant action in the future. The Leeds decision led to the possibility of large-scale official actions such as the 1974 London weighting dispute, and opened the door for the integration of militancy into salaries policy; while a walkout by thirty-one copy typists at the Scottish Gas Board led the Emergency Committee to concede the principle of retrospectively making up strike pay. Similarly, the type of action pursued in London would not have been possible had not the reserve fund been built up to more realistic proportions. Perhaps most important, however, was the change in attitude that appears to have taken place in that year. Members became willing to discuss the possibility of strike action seriously, as can be seen from the disputes over pensions and the local government settlement, which alone represents a major change in attitude from the type of statement made at the adoption of the strike clause in 1961.

Since 1970, reported cases of militancy in NALGO have become apparently more common. Certainly the district officials interviewed felt that militancy was becoming more common in NALGO and that this could be seen particularly at local level, where direct action has been found to be both speedy and effective in solving minor disputes.

Despite the apparent growth in militancy at local level over specific issues, it could not be assumed that all calls for militant action would be supported. For example, in October 1973 it was suggested by Geoffrey Drain, the newly appointed general secretary, that industrial action might be necessary in the National Health Service over some of the problems created by reorganization. Following the secretary of state's failure to overrule the Pay Board veto on negotiated reorganization payments, the request was made to the NEC for a ballot on industrial action. This was authorized in December 1973 but the result was negative,[17] and therefore suggestions for action were dropped. Nevertheless, industrial action was undertaken over a 30 per cent wage claim by certain para-medical staff in the Health Service; again, however, this action was essentially sectional.

In the London weighting campaign, undertaken in May/June 1974 in the face of TUC opposition, NALGO showed that it had learned some lessons from the failure of the ballot in the NHS. The London weighting issue first came into the open in October 1973, when a mass rally was held to protest against the Pay Board's intended usage of the 1967 NBPI criteria for its investigation into London allowances. In November the Metropolitan District Council agreed on a programme of action, although no action was taken at the time. Similarly, at a special conference called to consider the matter, a NALGO Action Group amendment calling for a one-day strike by 7 December and demanding a £500 allowance for all London staff was effectively defeated. In December, a ballot was conducted of staff in the Metropolitan district which, although generally more supportive than the one conducted in the NHS, was still patchy in its response.[18]

The result of the ballot was referred back to the 'London Weighting Panel' to recommend a course of action. At the same time a ballot was conducted of electricity staff in the London area in support of a similar claim for a £400 increase in the London allowance. After considering the results, the London Weighting Panel prepared the following programme – an initial ban on overtime and work with agency staff followed by branch and departmental strikes. It was further agreed that these strikes should be on full pay. The action was thus to be taken selectively where the support was greatest.

Industrial action began on 25 February with a ban on overtime and working with agency staff in some six London boroughs and the London Borough Joint Computer Committee. This action was escalated on 7 March to include more boroughs, and a further escalation was planned from 25 March. But this latter action was stemmed by the employers' side offer of interim payments of an extra £216 per annum for inner London and £186 per annum for outer London backdated to 1 November and free negotiation on the rest of the £400.

At this point, however, the issue was complicated by the intervention of the Pay Board. The London action had commenced before the general election and was aimed at the Conservative Phase III policy. However, despite the return of a Labour government with a claimed 'Social Contract' with the TUC that unions would moderate their wage claims, NALGO felt that its circumstances had not changed and continued to press ahead with the action. The offer was still subject to Pay Board approval, which obviously could not be granted except at the discretion of the secretary of state, who, at a meeting with the general secretary on 1 April, insisted that NALGO wait for the Pay Board's report in July and hinted broadly that its results would be generous. Faced with this impasse NALGO continued with its escalation planned for 25 March by bringing out the whole of the Islington branch. Following NALGO's meeting with the secretary of state a curtly worded request was sent by the TUC Economic Committee to NALGO asking it to respect the 'Social Contract' and drop its action. This request was refused by NALGO, who countered by arguing that the Social Contract was not particularly relevant to a claim that had been outstanding for more than a year.

The action on the London weighting dispute was significant in that it represented NALGO's first use of industrial action in support of a major wage claim; it showed the possibility of effective action on a selective basis; and it marked a major change in NALGO's use of strike pay. There was some concern over the depletion of strike funds in what was, after all, a comparatively small-scale action, and although there was some talk of using militant action to support the 1974 20 per cent local government wage claim, the cost of such action and the fact that NALGO would again be flouting the Social Contract were probably weighty factors in NALGO's decision to settle for 14 per cent without industrial action and within the terms of the Social Contract.

NALGO therefore showed quite significant changes in character over the period studied. It revoked its isolationist policies by joining the TUC; it also discarded its traditionally non-militant image and adopted a strike clause and raised funds so that it could have the 'weapon for final action'. Moreover, NALGO shortened its procedure for calling strikes and authorized its first official strike action. The next section will examine why all these changes occurred.

The processes and agents of change

We shall deal first with major external factors producing discontent and hence a need for change in NALGO's strategy and tactics. Next we consider the external constraints facing the union's leadership in its response to the need for change. Finally, we shall examine the internal constraints that determine the strategy actually chosen by considering the articulation of membership discontent and the response of the leadership.

The causes of discontent
The causes of discontent can be broadly divided into those of a general nature and those that specifically affected NALGO (or, as will be shown later, the NUT). Both NALGO and the NUT were influenced by those general factors that influenced the character of public sector and white-collar unions. As mentioned

in the introduction (pages 221–3), NALGO and the NUT were, as public sector unions, subject to discrimination in wage bargaining arising from the state's incomes policies.

Associated with these policies was the *absolute and relative deprivation* experience by low-paid workers in the public services. Their position actually worsened during the 1960s incomes policies, partly because of the unintended consequences[19] of an incomes policy that had been sold in terms of its ability to aid the lower paid, and also because of the increasing impact of taxes.

Relative deprivation, as opposed to the absolute deprivation of the low paid, was also a major factor in the growth of militancy – specifically in the case of the miners,[20] but more generally in the case of the white-collar workers, particularly those in the public services.

The impact of the erosion of differentials felt by white-collar workers on the growth and militancy of trade unions in that sector has been documented in detail elsewhere[21] and has been specifically mentioned by many white-collar trade union leaders.

Certainly our own studies of NALGO, the NUT and NUBE indicate that the growth of militancy was closely associated with the perceived erosion of differentials. The important reference groups for this feeling of relative deprivation were manual workers in general and other white-collar workers in similar occupations elsewhere. This perceived erosion of differentials was exacerbated by incomes policies in the 1960s because of the NBPI's strategy of breaking the accepted conventions for pay determination, such as comparability, on which the public services in general and white-collar workers in particular were heavily dependent, and of substituting other considerations, such as productivity.[22] Not until 1969 did the NBPI begin to relax its policy on comparability, specifically in its second reference on the pay of the industrial civil service.[23]

NALGO was directly affected by the emphasis on productivity by the NBPI and its consequences for differentials *vis-à-vis* manual workers in the public sector. In particular, militancy at local level seemed to be centred on those groups closely associated with manual workers, and it often rested on the theme of the non-involvement of non-manual staff in manual bonus schemes which could function only with their co-operation. District officials interviewed singled out such groups as having a greater propensity to be militant. Thus, for example, the demand for strike action in the 1965 electricity dispute had stemmed from the disruptive effects on differentials of a productivity deal negotiated for manual workers in the electricity industry in 1964.

The effect of productivity deals which began to develop in the public services only in 1969, after the end of the Labour Government's incomes policy, continued to reverberate among NALGO members. For instance, in April 1971 a further request by electricity staff to withdraw co-operation from a manual workers' bonus scheme was deferred while a possibly acceptable solution was put forward by the employers, and in December Tyneside Gas members asked the Emergency Committee for permission to withdraw co-operation in a manual workers' bonus scheme for which they were not receiving the promised additional payment. In April 1973 *Public Service* reported industrial action in Aberdeen, Leeds and Sheffield over the question of the non-recognition of the co-operation in manual workers' bonus schemes.

NALGO's militant upsurge of 1969–70 can be closely related to changing relativities with other white-collar groups. In 1968 and 1969 NALGO members lagged behind other public sector white-collar workers with whom they compared themselves, and the rejection of the 1969 local government settlement in September of that year was strongly influenced by the levels of settlement reached by other white-collar groups.

The proposed 1969 agreement allowed for increases of $3\frac{1}{2}$ per cent per annum in 1969 and 1970. Such an agreement might have been acceptable in earlier years, but in 1969, marked as it was by the pre-election relaxation of incomes policy and the increasing frustration of public sector and white-collar employees at not benefiting from the productivity elements in incomes policy, it was not. NALGO's negotiators were sent back to the table with instructions to secure better terms. In January 1970 an interim agreement for special grades allowing roughly a 2 per cent increase overall was reached with the employers to stave off discontent until the negotiation of the annual agreement in July 1970. After a threatened boycott of general election duties a settlement of $12\frac{1}{2}$ per cent was announced at the local government group meeting at the annual conference in 1970. It was against this background of the apparent success of militancy that the debate on strike policy took place in 1970 and was carried more or less uncritically. Indeed, few spoke against the raising of subscription that the adoption of the new strike policy entailed.

The compression of differentials continued, however, after 1970, exacerbated by Phase II and III of the Conservatives' incomes policy which favoured the low paid. Members in London, experiencing the explosion in house prices and the rise in transport costs, were particularly discontented by those parts of the incomes policy that insisted that any increase in London weighting should be offset against general pay settlements.

Indirectly, the other arm of the Conservatives' intervention in industrial relations, the Industrial Relations Act, also influenced NALGO. It unintentionally helped produce a concrete alteration in rule which facilitated strike action. This change occurred in 1973, when NALGO sacrificed the principle of no strike action without a ballot to allow the NEC to initiate strikes in emergency circumstances. The change took place in the light of the TUC's call for one-day protest strikes in the summer of 1972 against the imprisonment of dockers under the Industrial Relations Act and against incomes policy. NALGO could not participate in these actions as insufficient notice was given for a strike ballot. The above rule change helped the NEC overcome such problems. In 1974 this rule was further relaxed when areas with particular local difficulties, for instance the Edinburgh Gas branch, pressed for streamlining the strike procedure in situations where action had to be immediate to be effective.

Government intervention in bargaining therefore led NALGO to review its bargaining strategy and tactics. Relative deprivation associated with the compression of differentials caused a sense of grievance which NALGO's traditional methods of job regulation could not express or assuage. Moreover, affiliation to the TUC and the consequent acceptance of a wider trade union commitment also caused, again in connection with government intervention in industrial relations, a review of the union's procedures for calling strike action.

External constraints on the choice of strategy

The availability of alternative strategies ultimately led both NALGO and the NUT towards industrial action and affiliation to the TUC. At the beginning of the period the essentially co-operative philosophy of Whitleyism rendered the use of militant action unlikely; but the intervention of the state in collective bargaining, starting with the 'Pay Pause' of July 1961–March 1962, started to undermine the co-operative tradition. In this round of settlements the government refused to implement any awards made to civil servants by the Civil Service Arbitration Tribunal. NALGO was in a similar position, and continued to be similarly, if not so drastically, affected through the rest of the period studied as different governments 'took on' a succession of public sector unions.

Unions outside the TUC found themselves at a particular disadvantage. In this period the government allocated the TUC six seats on the National Economic Development Council as the sole representatives of the trade union movement. The TUC was also invited to and involved in discussions with the government on incomes policy. Furthermore, the $2\frac{1}{2}$ per cent guiding light that followed the pay pause was rejected by the TUC and was not enforced in the private sector.[24]

NALGO and the NUT therefore faced something of a dilemma. They were finding it increasingly difficult to influence the behaviour of the government, their employer, in its legislating role. The solution was to find some third party through which they could influence government. Although the TUC was a natural candidate, in the past a large proportion of NALGO's members had opposed affiliation. An alternative was to create an institution free from partisan political commitments but at the same time powerful enough to influence government policy.

The NUT took the initiative in 1961 by calling a conference of central and local government employees. This was the forerunner of the Conference of Professional and Public Service Organizations (COPPSO). NALGO and another eight white-collar organizations responded to the NUT's invitation and there were six observers.[25] COPPSO lasted for three and a half years. It was clearly intended to represent white-collar and professional views to the government. Its tone in its short existence was set by its first public statement in August 1961 when it expressed 'its strongest opposition' to the Pay Pause and described its impact on the public sector as being 'unjust, unreasonable and seriously damaging to good staff relations'.[26] However, the development of the machinery of incomes policy led to a growth in COPPSO's ambition. It placed itself on a more formal footing and sought recognition on the NEDC. This latter position was denied to COPPSO by the chancellor, who argued that the NEDC had not been constituted as a representative body and must be limited in numbers. COPPSO therefore failed to achieve its objectives: it failed to prevent the implementation of the Pay Pause, and it failed to gain direct access to government decision-making, the government preferring to deal only with the TUC as the representative of organized labour.

The lack of any other effective body left the unions in COPPSO with the stark choice of the TUC or nothing. The NALGO NEC, recognizing that the pragmatic case for affiliation to the TUC now outweighed the ideological arguments against, decided in 1962 to support affiliation, although it took them a further two years to convince the membership.

NALGO's militancy was further influenced by the bargaining behaviour of unions in related job territories and by the TUC. Most of those interviewed felt that these factors had an important impact on NALGO. For instance, joint committees involving NALGO branches and manual unions were cited as influencing NALGO. Para-medical staff took unofficial action at Leeds in 1974 as a result of a joint ASTMS–NALGO committee decision. Moreover, NALGO's entry into the TUC brought with it a package of general attitudes that would have appeared alien to NALGO in the past. These influenced the development of unionate concepts such as showing solidarity and refusing to black-leg during other unions' disputes.

Thus NALGO, limited in its options when faced by a major qualitative change in its employer's policy, was pushed towards accepting affiliations and adopting new forms of bargaining behaviour.

Articulation of membership discontent and the response of the leadership
So far we have been discussing the external stimuli or change agents that affected the character of NALGO. These factors influenced the attitude of the membership and limited the choices available to the leadership. We now turn to the internal mechanisms that articulated the discontents and influenced the strategies pursued by the leadership. We also examine an important change in NALGO's leadership which these factors helped produce.

As far as affiliation to the TUC is concerned, NALGO had debated the question of affiliation several times and on occasion had achieved a majority of those casting votes, but not of the whole membership, in favour. Until 1962 the NEC had been either opposed to or certainly not sufficiently convinced of the justice of the cause to campaign in its favour. After 1962, however, the NEC became convinced, for the largely pragmatic reasons already outlined, that affiliation to the TUC would be advantageous to NALGO, and proceeded to campaign vigorously and ultimately successfully for affiliation.

NALGO's stance on industrial action, we will argue, was affected by three separate internal changes which interacted to make it more militant: the first was the extensive use of the provisions in the constitution for changing existing policy where it interfered with militant objectives; the second was the change in the composition of the NEC and change of general secretary; and the third was the NALGO Action Group.

Up to 1969 the leadership had been pressured to adopt a more militant policy, and to make specific changes in the rules relating to strikes, by individual groups or branches who wished to take sectional industrial action in relation to specific grievances. The growing militancy, however, was also reflected in an upsurge in the use of special conferences. NALGO provides these special conferences either at the direction of the NEC or at the request of at least fifty branches. There were only three such conferences between 1920 and 1954. After 1954 no further conference was called until 1965, when, worried at the effect of cost of living rises on the current three-year agreement negotiated in 1963, the Eastbourne branch initiated one. The real upsurge in the use of the special conference came however in 1969, with the rejection of the local government two-year agreement. This was at the instigation of the Northumberland County branch. The outcome of this meeting was the resignation of the then National Local Government Committee chairman, and the eventual reopening of negotiations with the local government employers. This was followed by further special group meetings to vet the progress of the reopened negotiations. Similar such meetings were held in the gas and water services in 1970 to scrutinize the agreements reached for these services. They resulted in a membership rejection of the gas settlement.

Since 1970 there has been something of a decline in the use of special conferences to vet proposed agreements. It also seems that more typically these conferences are now being used by the negotiators to provide a means of consultation with the membership rather than as previously by the membership to censure the negotiators. Thus, in March 1972 the National Electricity Committee called a group meeting on the question of whether staff were prepared to accept the principle of redundancy in order to achieve parity with manual productivity schemes. Similarly, a special group meeting was called by the NEC in 1972 to consider the impact of reorganization on local government staff. However, the NEC rejected an application in early 1971 to hold a special conference to consider the question of NALGO's stance on the Industrial Relations Act.

The growing tendency for national service and conditions committees to call their own special group conferences and for such conferences to take radical decisions appeared to threaten the power of the NEC. The autonomy hitherto granted to the committees to determine their own policies and conduct their own negotiations came into conflict with the 'complete executive powers' that, according to the rules, rested with the NEC. Therefore the NEC presented to the 1972 conference proposals for integrating the special conferences within the normal decision-making procedure. One part of the proposals stated that:

It should be made clear to the special group meeting that any recourse to militant action and the authorization of expenditure in relation to such action must be subject to the final decision of the Council upon considering the result of the ballot which would have to be held to determine such action.[27]

Although the proposals did not change the degree of lay participation, they did ensure that the various service and conditions committees, which had been granted considerable decision-making autonomy, involved the executive at an early stage if a dispute seemed likely to arise. In doing so, and getting the proposal through Conference, the NEC succeeded in demonstrating that it was still the ultimate authority within the union.

The second internal change was the demise of chief officer influence, which removed a powerful bastion of traditionalism and non-militancy and thus facilitated, and reflected, the change in bargaining behaviour.[28] A rough count of the numbers of chief officers on the NEC shows that in 1930 they formed 39 per cent, in 1950 19 per cent and in 1973 5 per cent of the NEC.[29]

Although these figures should not be interpreted too literally,[30] they are indicative of developments. They are also backed up by the opinions of those interviewed. For it is now widely held within NALGO that it causes considerable role conflict for management beyond a certain level to play an active part in union affairs, even though such members retain membership as an 'insurance policy' and the union negotiates their salaries.

Not only was the changing mood of the membership reflected in and facilitated by the changing composition of the NEC; it also affected the position of the non-elected general secretary. Walter Anderson, who was becoming increasingly out of tune with the membership, was replaced in October 1973 by Geoffrey Drain, who supported and encouraged the changes that were taking place in NALGO's character. In a sense Anderson represented the traditional NALGO, advocating caution and if possible avoidance of controversy; whereas Drain is a much more overtly political character, and since his appointment has on many occasions made his personal support for a more aggressive strategy known.

Given the importance of this change in leadership, it is perhaps worth examining the background to Anderson's resignation. Principally the issue centred on the question of NALGO's involvement in the machinery established under Phase II of the Conservative incomes policy – the Pay Board and the Prices Commission. What precisely happened, however, is ambiguous. Initially the Economic Committee (the inner cabinet of the NEC established to deal with national issues and relations with the TUC) recommended NALGO's co-operation with these organs, but the February 1973 meeting of the NEC rejected the Committee's recommendations by 40 votes to 19. In part this reversal stemmed from a procedural muddle in the Economic Committee's report, which, while recommending co-operation with the Pay Board, rejected the Phase II package as a whole as inadequate, particularly on the question of food prices, housing and land policy, and its lack of a socially progressive taxation policy. But, as Anderson pointed out at the meeting, the motion had to be accepted or rejected as a whole.

Apparently Anderson personally considered inflation to be the major danger to the national economy and was prepared to support drastic action to contain it. Thus, 'NALGO Action Group News' of November–December 1972 reported: 'The sight of the General Secretary, Walter Anderson, pontificating on TV during the recent TUC/CBI/Government talks over prices and incomes policy, has made his support for incomes policy clear in the face of opposition from other General Council [of the TUC] members.' Evidently, Anderson felt that the reversal by the full NEC of the Economic Committee's proposals represented a personal slight on the views he had been publicly espousing, and regarded it as a vote of no confidence in his leadership. Thus he explained the reasons for his resignation:

I am not prepared to be a cipher on the TUC General Council and I no longer feel confident that I can express a NALGO point of view on that Council and be supported. . . . I am not resigning because the TUC has taken a line, I am resigning because the NALGO Executive has cut the ground from under my feet in what I have been saying. . . . I've said in the TUC and in the NALGO Executive let's express opposition to the Government, and then say that although we are so much opposed to the Government, we are prepared to do our best to cure the inflationary situation and we will, therefore, accept representation on the Pay and Prices Board to find a solution in the interests of our country and our members.[31]

This issue was, however, only the precipitating factor, and it was hinted by those interviewed during the study that relations between the NEC and Anderson had been deteriorating for some time. In particular, he did not like the new-style radicalism that was developing in NALGO, and this was illustrated by his attacks on the activities of the left-wing 'Action Group'. A more general problem lying behind it, however, was the potential tension arising from the development, since NALGO had affiliated to the TUC, of the virtual independence of the general secretary in his TUC role, which highlighted the differences of view. The general secretary was placed in the position of making policy for the union, a role traditionally the prerogative of the lay membership; finding himself increasingly looked upon by the media as the spokesman of NALGO, again traditionally a lay prerogative; while the views he was expounding were out of sympathy with the NEC.

Finally, we consider the role of the NALGO Action Group (NAG). It was not a completely new type of phenomenon in NALGO – there had been 'ginger groups' before;[32] nor did it encompass all those who wanted NALGO to adopt a more militant line. However, it has enjoyed an influence far beyond its actual numerical support, not least because it has been able to reflect and stimulate the growing mood of militancy among the NALGO membership, and has been concentrated in certain areas, such as the Metropolitan District, which has enabled it to initiate local militant action, as for example in the 1974 London weighting campaign.

The origins of NAG lay, as did many of the new developments in NALGO, in the 1969 rejection of the two-year settlement. It was established by a group of young activists as a means of canvassing support for the special conference which led to the rejection of the settlement. The immediate objectives of the group were, therefore, short-term, but the changing political milieu – the election of a Conservative government and the introduction of the Industrial Relations Act – led to its continuance as a left-wing group defending trade unionism. In its early days NAG emphasized such policies as a more radical and egalitarian wages policy and support for trade unionists' action at Upper Clyde Shipbuilders, and attacked such policies as the hiving-off of certain sections of the nationalized industries. Within NALGO it pressed its own objectives in relation to salaries, union democracy and general political issues.

As in the case of other rank-and-file groups in white-collar unions (as we shall see later with the NUT), NAG's success has lain mainly with younger workers, particularly among the graduate and new professional groups, although no precise details on membership breakdown are available. Thus, Anderson described the group as 'a lot of youngsters who think they can put NALGO to rights overnight'. However, he added, 'but unfortunately it's attracted some older people who ought to know better'.[33] Almost certainly its membership represents a small minority of the total NALGO membership, and although it has members scattered throughout most of the country, it is generally agreed to be concentrated in certain urban areas, particularly the Metropolitan District. One explanation put forward for this by those interviewed was that the district had been run in the past by the most traditional type of leadership, and that this leadership seemed to constitute a remote clique. The strong organization of NAG could have been a reaction to such leadership. However, it is also true that many of the rank-and-file organizations in the other white-collar unions, particularly in the NUT, have also been strong in the London area and this may also have been a factor.

NAG has had some success in gaining branch office, especially in certain London boroughs. In 1974 it had three members on the NEC, two from the Metropolitan District and one from a National Services and Conditions Committee – hardly enough to determine the course of NEC policy. At Conference NAG's success has also been limited, although given the growing atmosphere of militancy within the union it is difficult to distinguish a specifically NAG stance.

Expressions of discontent within NALGO therefore affected the leadership towards a more active use of those procedures in the rule book that could facilitate sectional strike action, such as the special conferences. But, second, militancy also threatened the nature of NALGO's traditional leadership, to some extent undermining its authority. Moreover, it provided the 'new' left with a cause, and ultimately provoked change in the type of officer taking national office and in the position of general secretary itself.

The NUT's changing character

Areas of change

Political action[34]

The NUT, like the traditional craft unions on the one hand and 'professional' groups such as the British Medical Association on the other, has combined the pursuit of better terms and conditions of employment through collective bargaining with the aims of autonomous regulation of the occupation.[35]

In pursuing these twin and closely related objectives the NUT has relied heavily on political pressure group tactics used in relation to both national governments and their immediate employers – the local authorities. During the period under study, however, these traditional methods have been supplemented by much more vigorous and aggressive collective bargaining strategies including more frequent use of direct action. Despite the reservation of certain members, the NUT retains its dual 'professional' and 'trade union' aims, believing that the two can be combined: 'Militant action and toughness in salary negotiations are not incompatible with the establishment of a measure of professional self-government, as the doctors have surely shown.'[36] Like NALGO, however, it found that after 1960 it had little impact on government decisions affecting pay and conditions, and increasingly felt the need for concerted pressure through inter-union bodies.

In the NUT, as in NALGO, the issue of TUC affiliation[37] had formerly divided the union along ideological lines broadly between those who saw the NUT as primarily a professional organization and those who regarded it as a trade union. After 1960, however, the issue was seen increasingly in pragmatic rather than ideological terms. But in spite of this stance the executive of the union was opposed to affiliation as late as 1966. It based its opposition on a number of points, both openly expressed and implied.[38] Perhaps most importantly there was a fear that affiliation would result in a loss of membership. This was an issue that had concerned NALGO, and although its affiliation had not resulted in a major outflow of members, the NUT had more to fear given the availability of alternative organizations. It was also felt that affiliation could have proved a barrier to trade union unity or amalgamation in the profession, given that some organizations might oppose close relations with a TUC-affiliated union.

Another major consideration that closely parallelled the debate within NALGO was that of political neutrality. While the NUT executive felt that NALGO's membership of the TUC indicated the possibility of an affiliated union remaining non-political, it was feared that the majority of the membership would fail to appreciate this. The final two factors expressed against affiliation were that joining the TUC could lead to the adoption of practices perhaps appropriate to manual trade unions, such as strikes and the closed shop, but certainly not appropriate to a professional organization like the NUT, and that, rather surprisingly, the union would achieve little in the way of influence on economic planning through affiliation.

By 1967 the NUT NEC had moved to a position of support for affiliation, and at the 1968 conference a motion to ballot the membership on the issue was moved and carried. This resulted in a poll of approximately 30 per cent of the membership who rejected affiliation by a ratio of 4 to 3. At the 1970 conference, however, the issue was again raised, and this time the Executive was mandated to seek affiliation without recourse to a ballot of the membership. The NUT affiliated on 1 May 1970.

Industrial action

Before the 1960s teachers were extremely reluctant to take strike action, although it was not unknown.[39] During the 1950s the teachers were becoming more aggressive in their demands, and the 1958 conference rejected a salary award already approved by the Executive; it was after 1960, however, that the pressure for more militant action showed a marked increase.

The year 1961 is a significant 'base' year in an examination of the NUT's willingness to support militant action. It was a year in which initially there appeared to be considerable support for action on an unprecedented scale, although the action itself was very limited and was finally rejected. This volte-face was to echo throughout subsequent years, becoming to those who opposed militant action demonstrable proof that it could never be maintained; and even to those who supported such action it counselled caution.

The confrontation of 1961 began when the NUT Executive divided 26 votes to 15 in favour of rejecting the provisional agreement reached in the Burnham Committee in May and decided to hold a special conference. The special conference confirmed that negotiation should continue on the 'widest front', but that in the event of a breakdown there should be selective strike action supported by a levy of the whole membership.

By the time the Burnham Committee next met in July the Pay Pause had been announced, and the minister of education advised the teachers' panel of the Burnham Committee that there were insufficient funds to meet the revised claim. The Executive abandoned its plans for militant action and decided, along with other unions on the teachers' panel, to press their case by political action.

However, the Executive continued to be divided on the issue. Changes in policy occurred during the summer, eventually culminating in September in a further recommendation for strike action. (By this time the union had tried selective strikes and, alternatively, staying at work but resigning *en bloc* from the LEAs.) Various proposals for action were put to members in fifty-nine areas in referenda in September. Only 43 per cent of the membership (51.4 per cent of those voting) voted for full strike action while a further 6.1 per cent voted in favour of the 'strike and work' option. Sixty per cent of teachers in those areas selected for strike action voted in favour, but this fell short of the 75 per cent majority required. Only 37 per cent (50 per cent of those voting) were willing to support a levy of 5 per cent to finance a strike in selected areas. A further special conference called in October voted for a one-day national strike and for a ban on school meal duties. However, in the light of the referendum result the Executive decided against any strike action. At the close of 1961 the teachers were faced with a salary award with which they did not agree but which remained operative until April 1963. There was widespread criticism of the Executive's handling of the affair, and membership dropped from 237,964 in 1961 to 213,344 in 1962.

In January 1963 a further salary award, which did not fall significantly below the target adopted by the NUT conference in 1962,[40] was tentatively agreed in the Burnham machinery. The award exceeded the 'guiding light' of the prevailing incomes policy, and was verified at a special conference. The Executive's satisfaction with the award was soon dispelled, however, by the minister of education, Sir Edward Boyle's, decision to redistribute the award in favour of senior and long-serving teachers, and to include ministerial representatives on the management side of the Burnham Committee by order of Parliament. There were two lobbies of Parliament, and MPs were thoroughly briefed on the union's case. The action failed to revoke the decision but may have had some effect on the ultimate ratio of DES to LEA representatives on the management panel, which was reduced to 15 to 26 by the time Michael Stewart became minister in 1964, Boyle having recommended parity.

Given the direct representation of the DES on Burnham and the increasingly aggressive stance of the NUT conference, it was likely that there could be a series of deadlocks within Burnham and that arbitration would be the rule rather than the exception. Consequently the Executive sought and conference accepted in 1964 the relaxation of the rule introduced in 1962 by which the Executive was prevented from suspending or modifying conference policy without ratification of such changes by a special conference. This did not prevent deadlock, however, and in 1965 a pay claim went to arbitration. The award was considered unsatisfactory, but was put into effect by ministerial order and lasted until 1967.

Faced with militant resolutions from the 1966 conference and the unsatisfactory outcome of arbitration in 1965, the Executive did not ask for arbitration when the Management Panel rejected their 1967 claim.[41] Instead, they examined alternative courses of action. An Action Committee was established, primarily in order to avoid the prevarication and muddle of 1961.

Following a special conference in May 1967 a 'phased series of sanctions' was begun with the primary objective of winning a salary settlement in line with the 1966 conference decision. This was intended to give a better basic scale, end the primary–secondary differential, and safeguard the salaries of young teachers affected by secondary reorganization. Unlike 1961, there was no shortage of support. Of 627 local associations of the union, 543 were willing to withdraw from the school meals service, and 514 were willing to refuse to teach alongside the unqualified. The action began in September after the arbitration award had conceded only their point on a secondary reorganization.

The action continued until the end of November and was a substantial success. Compulsory school meal duties were abolished in 1968; it was agreed that unqualified staff would not be employed after 1970; and the primary–secondary pay differential was reduced. In return the NUT agreed that negotiations for the next salary settlement would not begin until the autumn of 1968, to be implemented in early 1969. The editor of *The Teacher* argued that 'Teachers everywhere may justifiably claim that, had it not been for the NUT's determination to end compulsion – provided by deeds as well as words – it would never have happened'.[42]

When Burnham met in 1969 the Management Panel rejected the teachers' claim on the grounds that they exceeded the prevailing $3\frac{1}{2}$ per cent norm of the government's incomes policy. The executive retreated from a potential display of militancy and announced that: 'this is the best settlement that can be obtained by negotiation. The Executive has no confidence that arbitration would yield a better settlement and is convinced that a reference to the Prices and Incomes Board would be damaging to the teachers' interests'.[43] The special conference called in February 1969 endorsed this line, but certain groups within the union were not satisfied with this approach. Indeed, '100 rebels' ousted the Executive from its chamber in Hamilton House, the union's headquarters, in an attempt to gain membership support for an overthrow of the Executive.[44]

The annual conference in 1969 reversed the decision of the Executive and the special conference: the Executive was instructed to pursue the pay claim. At its conference, two days after the NUT's the National Association of Schoolmasters (NAS) voted in favour of pursuing an interim award. This common objective was to lead to a shortlived unity between the two organizations.

The months following the call for an interim increase saw a number of demonstrations not only within the ranks of existing teachers but also among student teachers. In May the University of London Institute of Education students organized a one-day boycott of lectures involving 23,000 students. The Inner London Teachers' Association held half-day strikes of London teachers in July, in which 7000 teachers took part. Rank and File, the main left-wing group within the union, welcomed such action and argued its necessity in the light of Executive inactivity.[45]

The initiative at national level eventually came from the NUT Action Committee. In a rather caustic note to the Executive, it requested that 'it be recorded that the Action Committee was of unanimous opinion that the NUT must take action in the event of a breakdown in negotiations for an interim salary increase'.[46] As a result, an intensive publicity campaign was conducted in August.[47] The scene was set for unprecedented action. The Action Committee had drawn up plans for a series of half-day strikes in selected areas. Although these would not come into effect until there was a breakdown in negotiations, it was decided that the crucial date would be 10 November, after which the Executive would approve strike action unless Burnham met their demands. Arrangements were also made to boost the sustentation fund by means of a levy.

In the period up to 10 November the Executive sponsored mass rallies and local associations held protest marches. When the Management Panel's offer of £50 per annum was rejected on 10 November, the Executive immediately mounted strike action in selected schools.[48] By 25 November, the height of the action, some 26,000 teachers in fifty-five areas were involved in strike action of one day or longer.

The real test was to come with the second wave of strike action planned for 1 December. These strikes in selected areas were to last for a fortnight. There was no shortage of support. 'More than 50,000 teachers in 5,000 schools have volunteered to take part in an unprecedented strike'.[49] Of these, 250 schools were chosen in eighty-one local authority areas, involving 3500 teachers. This action was complemented by a strike of some 500 NAS members (the NAS having established a £40,000 strike fund). This co-ordinated action was followed by a formal agreement between the NUT and NAS which provided that there should be no unnecessary duplication of action within schools and areas and that no teacher would undertake work for a colleague on strike. This expression of unity, significant as it was, remained subject to a clause that neither organization would 'poach' the other's members during the strikes.

The campaign continued, and in January 1970 the government, in view of the impending general election,[50] recalled its minister for urgent talks at the Treasury. In January the Management Panel made a firm offer of £50 per annum, emphasizing that 'they did not at present have power to negotiate independently with the teachers. It was stated explicitly for the first time that the important decisions about teachers' pay were being taken by the Government and not in the Burnham Committee'.[51] The Teachers' Panel, having got wind of a 15 per cent offer to the nurses, rejected the offer.

Within six days of the offer the NUT initiated further action, 'the largest in the history of British education. 4783 members in 355 schools in 74 authorities will strike for a fortnight . . . the total cost of the strikes, together with those of last term, will be about £500,000'.[52] The|teachers' slogan, 'Forward into the seventies with the fighting union', was a far cry from the events of 1961.

The Management Panel offered teachers a complete and immediate review of salary scales if action was terminated. Whether intentional or not, the effect of this offer was to produce a split in the teachers' organizations. The NAS, having already called for an increase in the interim demand and acceptance of arbitration on specified conditions, was prepared to accept the review if it was undertaken by an independent body.

On 8 February the NUT put into effect strikes in key urban areas which resulted in the virtual paralysis of education in those areas.[53] Recognizing that it would soon reach the limits of strike action, the union canvassed possible examination boycotts.[54] Also, realizing some members had not yet had the opportunity to participate in the action taken to date, a national day of protest was planned to coincide with the next Burnham meeting.

On 2 March the news broke that a settlement had been reached under which teachers would obtain an interim award of £120 per annum, only £15 short of the full claim. *The Teacher* announced: 'The Government gives in'. The Executive regarded it as 'a substantial victory for the Union and a complete vindication of its policy of militant action over the past four months'.[55]

Despite victory on the interim salary award, the union was still committed by conference to pursue the 1971 salary claim 'unremittingly using all the resources of the Union'. The union's claim emphasized the necessity of increases in the basic scale, particularly at the lower end, and argued for an increase of the order of 37 per cent. It also argued for a reduction in the number of increments from fourteen to ten.[56]

In October the Management Panel rejected the basic scale in favour of a complicated pattern of five overlapping scales comprising incremental points within each. In rejecting the offer, the NUT general secretary argued: 'the real reason for the management side preferring separate scales is that they would remove from the teachers the opportunity of arguing their salary claim upon the inadequacy of the basic scale',[57] an argument particularly relevant to the NUT with a high percentage of its members on the basic scale. The NUT also opposed arbitration[58] because it feared that an arbitrated award would fall foul of the government's intention to limit public sector wage increases to 9 per cent. However, the April 1971 Special Salaries Conference decided against militant action and to seek arbitration on better terms. They secured only a 10 per cent award.

The Executive called a special conference in November to prepare a salary policy for 1972. However, the passage of the claim was effectively blocked by the imposition of a wages standstill in November 1972 and Phase II in the year from January 1973. But the salary claim of 1972 had also asked for an increase in London allowance from £118 to £220 per annum. In October 1972 the Management Panel notified the Teachers' Panel that the government had requested delay in making an offer. A joint delegation of LEAs and teachers' organizations sought the opinion of the education secretary, who advised them that if they could reach agreement before midnight that day she was authorized to approve it. At a hastily convened meeting of the Burnham Committee, the Management Panel offered an increase of £12, later changed to £18, which the teachers rejected. The London teachers were prepared for strike action, and the Action Committee and Executive approved a half-day strike of all London teachers on 23 November.

The half-day strike resulted in a march and lobby of Parliament involving 10,000–15,000 teachers out of a total of 35,000 NUT members in London. Three further phases of strike action were overwhelmingly supported, but some London associations were determined to extend it by unofficial action.[59]

In July 1973 the teachers' associations sought unsuccessfully to gain Pay Board recognition of the London allowance claim as an anomaly within the intended report on anomalies arising from Phase II of the incomes policy. But in October 1973 the government requested the Pay Board to inquire into all aspects of London allowances, to be completed by June 1974. The union, in common with other organizations, sought to emphasize the problems of labour shortages in London by directing its members not to cover for staff who were absent through illness for more than three days and for staff shortages. By the end of the year several London schools were operating on a part-time basis. In February 1974 the NUT Executive increased the claim from £300 to £350 per annum (rejecting Rank and File demands for £500).

At the NUT 1974 conference the Executive announced plans for further strike action over the London allowance and the Action Committee announced a mass lobby of teachers for 29 April and a referendum of London teachers on strike action. The referendum failed to indicate 66⅔ per cent support, although 75 per cent of the London membership of 37,000 voted.[60] However, some 200 teachers began unofficial strike action and the Inner London Teachers' Association passed a motion condemning the Executive's failure to lead members in all-out strike action. The Executive stood firm and condemned unofficial action as 'contrary to the decision of the Action Committee on this issue at this time. It will serve no useful purpose'.[61]

The Pay Board report on London weighting issued in July 1974,[62] failed to satisfy the NUT and encouraged further unofficial action by the teachers. With the growth in unofficial action the Executive announced its intention to hold a further referendum of London teachers with a view to mounting strike action unless a Burnham meeting planned for September reached a satisfactory settlement. However in September agreement was reached in excess of the figures contained in the Pay Board report.

In the meantime the NUT submitted evidence to the Pay Board inquiry into relativities, claiming on the basis of research done by Ruskin Trade Union Research Unit that teachers had fallen seriously behind other groups, both manual and non-manual. The Relativities Board in January 1974 mentioned the problem of teachers' pay, and in settling for an increase within Phase III the teachers' panel agreed with the management panel, a 'reopener' clause providing for re-negotiation in the event of changed circumstances or success in an application under the relativities procedure. The question of strike action was raised at the 1974 conference, but many Executive members supported the sentiments of Laurie Green (EC) that 'there was hope for the future – and if this was not realised within the next few months then the profession would have to recognise that it was back in the 1969 position and act accordingly'.[63] However, the president argued that strike action was not necessarily a cure. He stated that, while there was no dichotomy between being a profession and demanding adequate salaries, 'there has grown up a dangerous tradition, which has not lacked support from successive Governments, that every claim for improved conditions, if it is to have any chance of success, has to be preceded, or accompanied by, some show of industrial power. . .'.[64] However, the question of strike action was not put to the test, for in May 1974 an independent inquiry, chaired by Lord Houghton, into teachers' pay was announced. The NUT were not enthusiastic about an independent inquiry which bypassed Burnham, in which they were the dominant teachers' organization. They nevertheless submitted evidence, and the outcome of the inquiry was highly satisfactory.

Thus the NUT's industrial action reached an unprecedented scale in 1969 and 1970. The relative success of this action clearly set the pattern for later conflicts. However, the NUT's somewhat hesitant approach to strikes was still conditioned by its 'professional' outlook. The action was often limited in its scope and duration. Its form, for example staying at work but resigning from the LEAs, was also sometimes different from that normally practised by more traditional unions. But regardless of these limitations, it did represent a marked increase in militancy. The reasons for this change will now be examined.

The processes and agents of change

The general external factors[65] affecting the bargaining behaviour of public sector and white-collar unions were largely common to both the NUT and NALGO. The general effect will not therefore be covered in this section. But we will briefly establish the particular effects of these general factors on the NUT, as we examine the causes of discontent, before turning to the external constraints influencing the leadership activities. Finally, the internal articulation of discontent and the leadership's response will be considered.

The causes of discontent

The NUT in common with NALGO experienced relative deprivation. A study carried out in the autumn of 1968, six months before their first national militant action, recorded that: 'It would seem . . . that the teachers feel that there is a growing differential between themselves and those other professions they would regard as their peers, and a narrowing of the differential between themselves and those skilled and unskilled groups whom they would rate lower in status.'[66]

Evidence that this feeling of relative deprivation had considerable basis in fact was made clear later in the Houghton Report on Teachers' Pay.[67] The comparison of average teachers' earnings with the general movement of salaries and wages in the period 1965–66 to April 1974,[68] the date of the last increase before the Houghton inquiry, showed that, while the salaries of primary and secondary schoolteachers had only increased by 78.1 per cent over the period, the salaries index had increased by 108.8 per cent and the wages index by 135.0 per cent.

The crucial conference decision in 1969 to reject the management offer of 6 per cent and to pursue a militant policy to achieve a better offer was clearly affected by external comparisons with other groups of workers who were breaking through incomes policy, and particularly by the recent award to pilots of 15 per cent. Moreover, the 6 per cent award also affected internal differentials. It favoured those at the top end of the scale at the expense of those lower down – particularly young teachers, active in the Young Teachers' Movement and Rank and File, whose pay was low in absolute terms and who had increased in numbers rapidly in the previous few years. It was these pressures that produced an interim flat rate claim for £135 and the related militant action.

External constraints on the choice of strategy
In the Pay Pause period of July 1961–March 1962 the government interfered with awards to teachers made by the Burnham Committee and made unilateral changes in the machinery for setting teachers' pay. Faced with this major and continuing intervention by government, the NUT's leadership considered, as did NALGO, its options: acquiescence, political pressure or direct action.

The NUT's leadership initially responded by attempting to combine political pressure and direct action. It was not particularly successful in either. As shown above, its strike action in 1961 was abortive. Similarly, the NUT's attempt to organize a political pressure group through COPPSO, while initially showing some promise, failed to achieve its objective (see pages 233–4).

Following the failure of COPPSO, the NUT prevaricated. The clear alternative to COPPSO was the TUC. But the NUT was preoccupied with the effect of affiliation to the TUC on the union's policy of political neutrality. Moreover, it still believed that it could further exploit the traditional NUT method of influencing events by direct political pressure on the government.

The union therefore reverted to isolated political action as its major tactic and its Executive claimed, following the intervention of Boyle in the Burnham award of 1962, that 'since the Minister's decision was one involving ministerial responsibility . . . that the Union's action had to be Parliamentary, and would involve political action'.[69] Criticism within the union that it should not engage in politics was countered by the Executive's statement that the government was 'choosing to make education the plaything of party politics and by doing so they will pay the price . . . the teachers will be involved through their professional associations, in party politics'.[70] The subsequent lobbying and similar activities, including meeting with the secretary of state, although possibly mitigating the effects of the minister's intervention, did not achieve its objectives.

The union was not, for example, consulted in the negotiations between unions and employers leading to the 'Declaration of Intent' that heralded Labour's incomes policy of 1965. But the NUT did manage, subsequently, to discuss incomes policy with the secretary of education, Michael Stewart. However, when the union again asked to discuss the impact of incomes policy on Burnham negotiations after 'the period of severe restraint' (July 1966–June 1967) with Michael Stewart, by that time secretary of state in the Department of Economic Affairs, they were told that he discussed such matters only with the TUC and CBI, and were referred back to the DES. Thus, the NUT was then faced with the choice:

between restricting their activities to pressure on the DES within constraints set by Government expenditure priorities and by national economic policy established elsewhere, or supplementing this pressure by joining the TUC, as the only means of access to decision-making outside the education sector. . . . For on the NEDC, in the drawing up of the Declaration of Intent, on the National Plan, on the formulation of incomes policy after the 'freeze' of July 1966, and in the cuts in Government expenditure after devaluation, the TUC was consulted and the teachers' association were not.[71]

In 1967 the Executive put this dilemma to the members and advised affiliation to the TUC. Their advice was not finally accepted until 1970.

The NUT's leadership were influenced in their decision to join the TUC and their choice of action in the industrial field by the activities of the NAS and other unions recruiting in the teaching profession. As we have pointed out before, the NUT is an all-grade teaching union surrounded, in contrast to NALGO, by other unions competing for sections of its membership on sex, grade or more general professional and political grounds. In this exposed job territory the NUT feared that affiliation to the TUC and direct industrial action would drive some of its more conservative members into the ranks of the competing unions. There was also the possibility, however, that failure to act positively would drive the more discontented members into more militant unions.

At the beginning of the 1960s the NUT was particularly concerned with the actions of the NAS. Indeed, in 1961, when the NUT failed to take industrial action against the Pay Pause, there is good reason to believe that some of the 20,000 who left the NUT in that year joined the more militant NAS. Also, the acceptance of NAS into membership of the Burnham Committees, against the wishes of the NUT, undermined the position of the NUT's Executive. For the NUT had relied upon the exclusion of the NAS from Burnham as a demonstration that militancy was irresponsible. Now it appeared that the NAS had secured representation via its militancy.[72] Throughout the period up to 1968 those who supported militancy in the NUT could point to the seemingly effective example of the NAS. Evidence that the NUT Executive was fully aware of the influence of the NAS example was demonstrated at the union's 1968 conference when they claimed, following the union's own successful action over school meals supervision,

Our actions of the last year have exploded this myth of theirs (referring to the NAS), their claim to be the men's militant union. Our increased recruitment at this time was from the ranks of the NAS as well as from teachers who did not belong to any organisation.[73]

However, the NUT's support for militant action from 1968 onwards was also partly responsible for the formation of the anti-strike Professional Association of Teachers (PAT). PAT attracted into membership some of those in the NUT who felt that militant action conflicted with the teachers' claims to professional status. This new union also constantly criticized the NUT on these grounds. For example, during the campaign on London weighting in 1974 the PAT criticized industrial action on the grounds that it had the effect of 'encouraging truancy, worrying parents and exacerbating the situation'.[74]

The NUT also feared a backlash from some members, similar to those attracted to PAT, if they affiliated in isolation to the TUC. In addition, the union felt that if it affiliated it might 'entail the abandonment of [the union's] policy of professional unity based on negotiations'.[75] The NEC, however, having weighed these factors against other pragmatic reasons in favour of affiliation, decided to support affiliation. (It may not have been entirely coincidental that, by the time the members voted in favour, the inter-union problem had been largely solved because the NAS and the ATTI had already affiliated to the TUC.[76])

Thus, the NUT's leadership was clearly constrained in its choice of options by its inability to create an alternative pressure group to that of the TUC. In the face of the government's refusal to deal with COPPSO, and also its refusal to deal with the NUT, other than through the DES, the NUT's leadership turned rather reluctantly to the TUC. Also, in its use of industrial action the NUT found its options limited by the more 'unionate' NAS and the 'professional' PAT. Whatever the leadership of the NUT decided to do in terms of industrial action, they seemed doomed to lose members to one or other of these unions.

Articulation of membership discontent and the response of the leadership
In the NUT the question of TUC affiliation had been less often aired than in NALGO. It was not debated at all between 1939 and 1965. The leadership assumed, with some justification, that the membership at large opposed affiliation to what appeared to be a predominantly manual, unprofessional and politically motivated body. It therefore needed the failure of the traditional political means of influence and the collapse of COPPSO to persuade the leadership that affiliation was the only real option. Even then, when the Executive moved for affiliation in 1967 it failed to get a favourable ballot. It was not until the conference itself committed the Executive to campaign for 'understanding and acceptance' of affiliation to the TUC in 1969 that the proposal was successfully carried in 1970. Hence in common with NALGO, affiliation to the TUC required a vigorous campaign by the leadership to get it accepted.

In contrast, in both the NUT and NALGO the development of a more militant industrial policy was initiated by the membership, often in the face of national leadership opposition or at least inaction.

The reactions of the NUT's leadership to membership pressure did not take the form of a dramatic change of leadership as it did in NALGO. However, there were internal developments which transformed the situation between 1961, when the union failed to take industrial action against the Pay Pause, and the 1958–69 period, when they did undertake successful industrial action. In the paragraphs that follow we discuss some of the reasons for the failure of militancy in 1961, the build-up of militancy after 1961 and, finally, the role played by internal pressure groups such as Rank and File.

Militancy among the membership at union conferences began to build up in the 1950s. In 1954 delegates to annual conference determined the figures within which their representatives on Burnham were to negotiate; in 1955 conference censured the Executive for its inadequate handling of salaries and instructed it to 'develop immediately a more militant salaries campaign'; and in 1958 conference rejected a salary award already approved by the Executive.

It was this build-up, together with the increased frustration evidenced in letters to *The Teacher*, that persuaded the Executive by a narrow majority to call a special conference in June 1961 to ratify the proposals for a token one-day strike.

The special conference committed the union to its first-ever national strike and to its first systematic area strikes for over thirty years. However, this was passed by a majority of only 16,000 out of a total of over 200,000 votes. Subsequently the strike proposals were rejected by the members in referenda.

The Executive had been deeply divided on the issue, and those who opposed militant action continued to use the failure of the referendum as an argument against further militant action well into the 1960s. The rejection of the proposals in the referenda helped to foster the view that the majority of teachers were unwilling to take militant action and that the problem lay in the 'distortion effect'[77] of the minority of activists determining a policy at a special conference which was out of tune with the majority.

However, looking at the situation more closely, it would seem that events overtook the 1961 special conference's militant policy. The subsequent culmination of events within a short period of time during the summer probably demonstrated to the membership that strike action against the government was not a viable proposition and persuaded them to reject the proposals. For example, it was clear to the members that 'no teachers' organisation is financially geared to a strike'.[78] Since the only realistic method of supporting national strike action was to raise a levy, and the referendum asked whether members would be prepared to support a levy of 5 per cent of gross salary to finance a strike, it is not surprising that the vote in favour did not reach the required 75 per cent majority.

Moreover, the questions used in the referendum were far from straightforward; there were, for instance, separate national and section questions. Also, the referenda referred to 'technical' and 'industrial' strike action.[79] In this case the question was whether members supported one form of strike action or the other. In the national referendum, therefore, members were asked three questions: Will you give financial support (i) for strike action? and (ii) for a technical strike? or (iii) for an industrial strike? In the sectional referenda there were two questions: Will you support and participate in (i) a technical strike? or (ii) an industrial strike? Such dual questioning produced confused responses. Again, it is not surprising that the union did not get the 75 per cent support required for action.

The complexity of the referenda, together with the equivocation of the Executive, succeeded in giving the impression that the union's policy was unclear and that the Executive was giving no clear lead. In the circumstances the simple proposition that teachers were unwilling to strike in 1961 may be something of a 'myth'. However, it was a 'myth' that affected the deliberations on the question of militancy for the next few years. The difficulties of 1961 also highlighted the problems the Executive was encountering with the conference. As a result of the unpopular 1961 settlement the 1962 annual conference was determined to restrict the Executive's discretion in handling salaries. Among the motions passed at the conference were the simple declarations that conference is 'the supreme authority of the union'[80] and that the Executive was bound by conference decisions and any diversion from them required ratification by a special conference. At the same conference a call for strike action was made and one strike supporter argued that 'A show of strength now, however small, would rally many, including a lot from the NAS and those who left the union a year ago'.[81] However, the Executive rejected calls for a strike and a delegate declared that 'In view of the painful experience of 1961, a strike would only cause a lot of heated arguments and discussions in staff rooms and at local meetings'.[82] *The Teacher*, supporting the Executive, also stated that 'political action offers a better way of putting the case than does militancy in the form of strikes or other sanctions'.[83] The sharp reminders of 1961 were enough to re-emphasize the use of more traditional forms of pressure.

At the 1964 conference the NEC managed to wrest some of its power back from the 1962 conference. They argued that the job of NUT representatives within the Burnham Committee was made almost impossible by the conference's rigid mandate. The Executive therefore sought, and was granted, relaxation of the rule on ratification of salaries introduced in 1962.

In 1966 the NUT conference directed the Executive to 'conduct an unremitting public campaign with all the means at its disposal' to achieve their salary demands. Conference also instructed the Executive, 'failing satisfactory settlement . . . to call a special conference in order to receive further instructions'.[84] Further, it asked the Executive to set up a working party to consider (a) bringing up the sustentation fund to a 'realistic level for action';[85] (b) a review of the referendum procedure for withdrawal of members; and (c) a reduction in the 75 per cent rule for action to 66⅔ per cent.

A special conference was called in May 1967 which outlined proposals for action if that year's negotiations failed. The Executive, however, intended to keep a tight grip on the situation and remained unwilling to extend the concept of direct action to include strikes.[86] To this extent the experience of 1961 remained a powerful constraint. However, the Executive did establish an Action Committee, 'with full powers to act, to organise and control union action in connection with sanctions arising from the Special Conference'; it also appointed an action officer. As noted above (pages 241–2), the sanctions organized more effectively by the Executive in 1967 proved successful.

The success of the 1967 action produced some change in the attitude of the Executive towards strike action. Indeed, it recommended to the 1969 conference that selected area strikes, financed by a levy with a target of £500,000, be considered. The Executive was however at the same time coming under considerable pressure to undertake yet more militant action. The views of the discontented membership were being vociferously articulated by the 'left-wing' Rank and File movement, whose strength and support was becoming increasingly apparent. The Rank and File group within the union were particularly instrumental in highlighting deficiencies in the Executive's handling of salary negotiations. They also repeatedly criticized the Executive's retreat from more militant action.

In 1969 the annual conference reflected the build-up of opposition to the Executive. Certain groups expressed their dissatisfaction not only with the outcome of negotiations but with the secrecy that surrounded the Burnham Committee and its deliberations. This was taken up by one Executive member, who argued 'why do we go on like King Canute opposing the wave of demand for publicity which exists among our own members?'[87]

Several motions at the annual conference censured the Executive. The Inner London Teachers' Association called for a 'substantial interim increase on the basic scale to come into effect as from April 1st 1970'. Such motions received widespread support from local associations throughout the country. Max Morris, a member of the Executive, led the call for an increase in basic salary, envisaging a figure of £1000 rising by ten annual increments to £2000 per annum. The Executive's amendment, intended to tone down these demands, provided for an Executive review of salary structure which would be presented to annual conference in 1970. This amendment was 'heavily defeated' and the original motion, with a mandate that the Executive call a special conference in the event of deadlock in negotiations 'to decide what further action should be taken', was passed.[88]

But the union still lacked sufficient funds to support such action. The conference accepted a report by the Executive which provided for a 'short sharp boost' to the sustentation fund by increased subscriptions and a levy. As Rank and File pointed out, the chairman of the Management Panel of Burnham noted that 'the NUT strike would not hold out longer than 36 hours'. They continued, 'Conference has since made the magnificent gesture of pushing up subscriptions still higher and increasing our staying power by an extra nine hours. On our own we are almost powerless.'

Despite the pressure, however, the Executive continued to prevaricate over the 1969 negotiations, and the initiative for direct action in the absence of a favourable response from the management finally came from the NUT Action Committee. The subsequent campaign of militant action led by the Executive proved successful, even according to the Rank and File organization, which reluctantly accorded the Executive some praise by claiming:

we have won a substantial success . . . it is not, of course, a complete victory but is very far from a defeat and it is quite wrong to describe it as a 'sellout'. Whilst the scale of militant action undertaken by the Executive was inadequate, militancy had paid. The policies advocated by this journal over the past two years have been vindicated. . . .[89]

The Executive was able to carry conference along with it in 1971 and 1972 when it decided it would be unable to sustain further militant action in the face of the government policy so soon after the previous action.

The lack of support among the membership for further militant action was indicated in a survey of local association opinion, and the reasons why the circumstances were not as propitious for militant action as they had been during the previous action were outlined by the general secretary:

last winter we had certain advantages. We had a Government within a short time of a general election; we had a united teaching profession and a clear-cut issue, what is more important we had a Union which was prepared to act . . . the most disastrous thing a union could do is to lead its members into militant action that cannot be won. Conference must decide how much difference a Government with four and a half years to go instead of a few months will make. . . . [It] . . . must decide whether there is an issue here round which the teaching profession can be united. . . . [It] . . . must decide what chances there are of getting the Government to change its mind and recall Burnham and make a better offer, for I would remind you that it has been the Government rather than the local authorities that had been the restrictive influence. . . . [It] . . . must also have regard to what is going on in the world around us, not least what has happened to the Post Office workers . . . it may be that in the next few months the determination of last winter could emerge again. . . . A union that is afraid to take industrial action does not deserve to be called a union. But there are times to attack and times to dig in and fight a rearguard action.[90]

While the Executive rejected widespread national militant action, it was nevertheless prepared to support the London weighting claim. However, the half-day strikes suggested and carried out under the Action Committee's authority did not satisfy some of the London members. At a meeting called by the Action Committee the official policy of the union and that of Rank and File collided. *The Teacher* reported the meeting as being taken over by 'a disruptive minority' who 'followed a pre-arranged plan . . . had their own portable microphone and knew how to silence the public address system, which they did in order to prevent the President from continuing the meeting'.[91] Attempts were made to introduce a motion calling on London teachers to support extended strike action in co-operation with all other unions, both manual and white-collar, against the government's incomes policy. This clearly went far beyond the policy of the Executive. Whether influenced by these events or not, the Action Committee announced that there would be a further one-day strike of all London teachers on 21 March. Some 11,000 teachers took part.

Apart from some unofficial action in London in 1974 the rest of the union continued to support or acquiesce in the more cautious policy. The 1974 conference also supported the Executive when it tried to regain some of the initiative in formulating salary policy. It argued for change on the grounds that the whole process of negotiations had become too complex and had moved at too rapid a pace to be determined by resolutions at conference. The Executive therefore issued its own salary memorandum seeking flexibility in the next round of negotiations, and this was, with one or two amendments, adopted by the 1974 conference in preference to the prioritized motion framed in terms of specific demands.[92]

Some members of the Executive believed that the growth of militant demands within the union was largely attributable to a 'militant minority' largely composed of younger teachers. Thus, one member of the NUT Executive 'attributed the militant mood to the growth of the size of the "hard core of permanent militants" especially among young teachers'. He explained that the 'great influx into the union of young teachers has had a decisive effect on union decisions, largely due to the impatience of youth not so steeped in the respect-ability of the teachers.'[93]

Among the 'militant minority' two factions stand out – the Young Teachers' Movement and the Rank and File organization. The division between career teachers and those already established in the profession, and the young teachers at the base of the pyramid, is a fundamental one in the NUT. The Executive largely consists of the former.[94]

The young class teachers have been mobilized in various ways within the NUT. As early as 1928 an 'official' Young Teachers' Movement began, and in the 1930s a Young Teachers' Advisory Committee was established. In 1960, on the Executive's initiative, the first National Young Teachers' conference was held, and was continued annually thereafter. During the 1960s the conference began taking decisions that went far beyond the main NUT conference, particularly in advocating affiliation to the TUC and taking militant action. The limits of tolerance were reached in 1972, however, when decisions of the Young Teachers' conference included the abolition of the multi-scale salary structure and the creation of a single scale; the establishment of a statutory body within schools, curtailing the head's power by giving assistant teachers more control; and a more militant campaign by the Executive on class sizes.[95]

Although the two organizations were distinct, the Young Teachers' Movement having been established much earlier than the Rank and File, they tended to coalesce in their youthful composition and their policies. The link was explicit in 1972: the motions on salaries, control and class size (mentioned above), which were passed at the Young Teachers' conference, had been sponsored by the Rank and File faction. As a consequence, the Executive attempted on grounds of expense and organizational need to curb the influence of the Young Teachers' organization. It ended the Young Teachers' Advisory Committee and the Young Teachers' conference but accepted the continuance of Young Teachers' sections by local or county associations if they wished, and subject to the understanding that the relevant association would take full responsibility for the operation of such sections.

Following these Executive decisions many letters to *The Teacher* argued the superficiality of the reasons given and claimed that they were constructed to disguise the real reason – the militant stand of young teachers.[96] Such was the mood of local associations throughout the country that the Executive was moved to 'think again'.

Some Executive members were concerned about going back on their original decision, and felt that the Young Teachers' section was becoming a 'union within a union'.[97] Nevertheless, the Executive decided by a majority of one to reinstate the Young Teachers' Advisory Committee. At the 1973 annual conference an attempt to refer back the paragraph of the Executive's report discontinuing the Young Teachers' conference was unsuccessful.

In addition to moving against the Young Teachers' Movement, the Executive also attacked the Rank and File. The Rank and File organization describes itself in its journal 'Rank and File' as a left-wing group within the NUT. Its broad objectives are 'to increase democracy both in the NUT and [in] schools, to turn the NUT into a militant union capable of fighting for the demands of the rank and file, and to examine the role and priority of education in society'.[98]

The origins of the organization can be traced back to the NUT conference of 1967 when the results of arbitration in that year had led to discussions in London among union members and the creation of a left-wing journal with the aim of organizing rank-and-file opinion in the union. Several motions backed by the Rank and File were submitted to the union's annual conference and gained popular support. By 1971 the Rank and File had an executive committee in London and was becoming a voice to be reckoned with. In the spring of 1972 the union's president threatened to sue the group over allegedly defamatory articles in the organization's journal, and more recently another president, Max Morris, himself a Communist, attacked the Rank and File in *The Teacher*, which resulted in a stream of letters both for and against the Rank and File. The organization appears to have had an influence much greater than its actual membership, and its strength tends to be concentrated in London, where it succeeded in gaining two National Executive seats.[99]

Although the Rank and File and the Young Teachers' Movement attracted considerable publicity for their policies and activities, it is clear that they were articulating a view that was shared by a large number of teachers in the late 1960s – they reflected a growing mood of militancy among the membership at large. Nor could the young teachers with their demands for bigger increases in the basic scale and militancy in its pursuit be dismissed as an unrepresentative minority. For as the Executive themselves claimed, they did represent 66 per cent of the total membership. The view that they were largely articulators and mobilizers, rather than instigators, of the militant mood and dissatisfaction with the leadership in the NUT is supported by the fact that, once the National Executive established its credibility with the action in 1969, the unofficial movements were less successful in gaining support for their additional policies for reform. Its influence continued, however, to shape events in London, where its major membership lay.

It can be concluded therefore that the leadership of the NUT was under substantial internal pressure from a discontented membership and a quite vocal, if relatively small, left-wing faction formally to adopt a more militant industrial policy. This pressure did not lead, as it did in NALGO, to a significant change in leadership; but it did move the balance of power on some important issues, and at certain points in time, in favour of the conference. However, the Executive of this traditionally 'professional' union was generally able to ride the tide of militancy and maintain control of the union.

The changing character of other unions

In this section a brief supporting reference will be made to certain character changes among other unions in the sample. All the unions who had membership in the previously quiescent areas of the public services, whether white-collar or manual, experienced an upsurge in militancy primarily because of the tendency for government to apply their general incomes policies more harshly in the public sector, and to single out the public sector for special treatment on several occasions. For NUPE, the TGWU, GMWU and AUEW, however, the rise in militancy is discussed as part of the analysis of the changes in the structure of job regulation and therefore will not be analysed further at this juncture.

ASTMS and NUBE, as white-collar unions, experienced many of the changes in character in relation to militancy that were experienced by NALGO and the NUT. Both ASTMS and NUBE were, of course, already affiliated to the TUC, although NUBE experienced a brief period of expulsion arising from the TUC's policy of opposition to the Industrial Relations Act. ASTMS differs from NUBE, NALGO and the NUT in that it had been prepared to take, and had taken, industrial action prior to the period under study, although the extent to which it resorted to such action increased during that period. It too, however, experienced a qualitative change in the two previously quiescent areas of the public services (primarily the NHS) and in the new area into which it had extended its organization in the period under study, the finance and insurance sector. In that sense, therefore, developments in those sectors of ASTMS membership closely parallelled developments in NALGO and the NUT on the one hand and NUBE on the other.

Both NUBE and the bank staff associations adopted a much more aggressive stance than in the past. At NUBE's annual delegate meeting in 1960 the original strike clause formulated in 1922 was replaced by one that made strikes against particular banks a realistic possibility.[100] The first use of the new strike clause occurred later in the same year in a dispute with the Derby Trustee Savings Bank (TSB) over managers' salaries. The industrial action began with a ban on overtime after an inadequate offer had been rejected. The employer then issued threats of dismissal, and after a secret ballot the union called a strike, but at the last moment the employer agreed to negotiate and a substantial salary increase resulted. In 1963, in a dispute over salaries and a demand for arbitration machinery in the TSB, protest meetings were held throughout the country and a strike ballot was taken in a number of TSBs. The support was strong, and in four branches where the union was particularly well organized NUBE held strikes on three successive Saturday mornings. This was the first time NUBE had called a full strike, and it led to the first national arbitration procedure in banking. Earlier in 1963 NUBE held a strike in the Habib Bank of Pakistan. The bank dismissed some NUBE members during a dispute over pay and the union called a strike which lasted a fortnight and ended in partial success for the union.

The strikes in the TSB and Habib Bank could take place only because of the change in the strike clause, but they also represented strike action in areas where the union was not competing with internal staff associations and where it had a high degree of organization. The situation was far different in the major clearing banks, and militant action in that area took place only some years later as part of the struggle for recognition. It was the recognition issue that enabled NUBE to mobilize its membership on a national basis for industrial action. It embarked on a highly organized national campaign, 'Action 67'. Even so, NUBE focused on those banks and areas where the union was most highly organized. On 24 and 25 November 1967, 2800 members at some 300 bank branches were called out in South Wales.[101] On 5 December 3000 NUBE members attended a rally in the Central Hall, Westminster. This was followed by a mass lobby of MPs. On 29 and 30 December 1967 and 1 January 1968, a further 6000 members were to join the strike in selected towns in Yorkshire, but at that juncture the action was suspended because recognition had been agreed by the employers.

Ironically enough, the first pay agreement reached by the newly formed joint National Council, which was also the first major pay award since 1965, was referred to the NBPI.[102] The Department of Employment and Productivity (DEP) agreed only to a $3\frac{1}{2}$ per cent rise from July 1969 pending the outcome of the NBPI report. The general secretary of NUBE warned that the reactions of the staff to the interference with their first settlement under new machinery were likely to be angry.

NUBE organized a protest meeting at Central Hall in November 1968 followed by a mass lobby of MPs and held a half-day strike on 10 January 1969 accompanied by a further lobby of MPs. Agreement was reached to pay the $3\frac{1}{2}$ per cent from July 1968.

Successful strikes in Edinburgh, Nottingham, Liverpool and Sheffield TSBs were held on 7 and 8 February 1969 following the refusal of the TSB Employers' Council to negotiate on NUBE's pay claim. Agreement was reached in April 1969 and increases backdated to May 1968. The next major militant action undertaken by NUBE was in relation to a dispute with the Co-operative Bank over pensions. After several months of talks the union decided to ballot its members on strike action, and in a ballot of the 1360 Co-operative Bank staff in December 1973, 86 per cent voted in favour. The strike, which was the first to be taken by any trade union over a pension issue, failed to secure any improved offer, and the action was discontinued. At the NUBE conference in April the Executive was criticized in a resolution passed by a large majority for not paying full strike pay to those taking part in selective strikes, and the delegates voted for a voluntary levy of 10p per month per member. The president replied that the union could not afford full strike pay: 'An all-out strike would cost £10,000–£15,000 per week. Look at the balance sheet and be realistic. If you think we can afford full pay, then instruct us to pay it. But when you come back in four weeks' time you will be coming at your own expense, not the union's.'

ASTMS has experienced growth of militancy in its traditionally quiescent areas such as the public services and insurance, banking and finance in the private sector. For instance, in the insurance area there was a long-running and highly expensive strike action by 2500 members in the Co-operative Insurance Society, initially over pay, which gathered momentum when the employers threatened to lock-out. The strike was a costly failure, although, the NEC argued, the publicity given to the CIS members' grievances contributed to achieving a much more satisfactory settlement the following year. A specific campaign directed against low pay in the insurance industry was begun in 1974 and three sets of industrial action, authorized by the NEC, were initiated at Scottish Legal, the Refuge and the Royal Liver, involving considerable numbers of women. In 1975 ASTMS members at the Prudential Assurance Company conducted a three-week campaign of sanctions including one-day token strikes, aimed at securing the full £6 increase for all rather than the tapered increase with a maximum £6 offered by the employer. In the public sector, ASTMS took part in the wave of militant action within the NHS in 1974 in which the majority of ASTMS members were involved at some point. Previously in 1966 and 1969 token stoppages had been used in ASTMS's (and previously the AScW's) campaign to secure an improved salary and grading structure for university technicians.

Again in common with NALGO and the NUT, the ASTMS and NUBE were adversely affected by government intervention in wage bargaining. NUBE, although organizing predominantly in the private sector, was in 1965 concerned by its deteriorating position *vis-à-vis* manual workers. They were also concerned that their general status in the community had declined. This feeling was exacerbated by the impact of incomes policy. Bank salaries and conditions were referred three times to the NBPI, and a fourth reference on bank charges had indirect implications for pay.[103] In the first reference the NBPI rejected all the arguments put forward for an increase above the norm and recommended that 'in future the cost of living should be given less weight than has been in the past customary in the settlement of bank salaries'. The second reference concerned the first pay agreement reached after recognition, which sparked off greater discontent in NUBE and, as we saw above, resulted in strike action and other forms of protest. In its report the NBPI conceded that earnings in banking had declined in comparison with those for similar staff in national and local government and the nationalized industries but saw no need for it to be rectified in the national interest. In the final direct reference on pay in 1969, which referred to an arbitration award on hours reduction, the report was not implemented because incomes policy was by this time dead.

Apart from overall dissatisfaction with the general erosion of differentials, NUBE specifically experienced a number of other external causes of discontent. The recognition issue, and employers' decision to retain Saturday working and pensions, were particular sources of concern for NUBE. In the face of these problems NUBE followed the NUT's lead and showed an interest in the formation of COPPSO by attending the inaugural meeting as an observer.

The failure of third-party intervention in general and of political pressure as a means of achieving recognition was important to NUBE's decision to opt for militant industrial action. As early as 1919 the Bank Officers Guild (BOG) had applied to the Minister of Labour and the banks for a Whitley Council for the banking industry. The employees had refused. Again in the Second World War further attempts had been made to secure recognition by approach to the minister of labour: this, again, had been unsuccessful.[104] The 1960s saw the final push by NUBE for sole recognition and a change in strategy from third-party pressure to the use of direct action. Complaints were made by the union that the employers were preventing NUBE 'from exercising its proper and normal function as a trade union', by supporting and using the staff associations. The ILO requested the British government to hold a full inquiry, and in April 1963 Lord Cameron was appointed by the minister of labour to chair one. The inquiry found against NUBE's specific complaint that four named staff associations were employer-dominated, but the main objective of giving a public airing for NUBE's recognition claim was achieved and Lord Cameron recognized NUBE's wider intentions by making a series of suggestions for improving the state of industrial relations in banking.[105]

A joint working party of employers, staff associations and NUBE met between 1965 and 1967, but the proposals for national machinery were rejected by the Westminster and National Provincial staff associations and talks broke down. NUBE then turned to industrial action to achieve its objective.

Summary and conclusions

All the unions in the sample, blue- and white-collar, experienced some change in the character of job regulation over the period studied in at least two respects: a growth of political action and a growth in militancy, largely in response to increased government intervention in collective bargaining arrangements. Whereas for the majority of unions this was simply a further development along well established lines, for white-collar unions in general, and particularly for those in the public services, it involved a major qualitative change. For NALGO and the NUT it involved a change from a position of eschewing militant action and participation in the wider trade union movement prior to 1960, to one that involved affiliation to the TUC and the willingness to take militant action in pursuit of bargaining aims.

After 1960 the NUT gradually adopted a strategy that involved the use of militant action on a national scale. NALGO, which represents a much wider range of occupations in a variety of public services, did not need to take actions that involved the whole membership. Nevertheless, it undertook a series of more limited actions in pursuit of sectional claims, which would have been unthinkable prior to 1960. NUBE similarly moved to more aggressive industrial action on a sectional basis. This union also adopted direct action in respect of recognition following the failure of political pressure and third-party intervention in this area.

The major change agent was the developing discontent among the membership at their declining economic position as both public sector and white-collar employees. In particular, they expressed feelings of relative deprivation *vis-à-vis* comparable groups. Various phases of incomes policy fuelled this discontent in respect of inter-industry comparisons by discriminating against the public sector. Moreover, incomes policy also reduced white-collar–blue-collar differentials by promoting productivity bargains more suited to manual than to white-collar employees.

In meeting this discontent the alternative strategies available to the leadership were rapidly narrowed by the interventions of successive governments in pay bargaining. Moreover, other competing unions, particularly in the NUT's case, further limited the leadership's options by appearing to benefit from actions that departed from the traditional means of remedying grievances. For example, the NUT's use of industrial action helped establish PAT. It is therefore not surprising that the national leaders of unions with 'professional' attitudes towards bargaining behaviour should approach strike action in a rather hesitant manner. Also, the NUT's and NALGO's initial reluctance to sponsor affiliation to the TUC, and their preference for COPPSO, sprang from the same traditions. But faith in the existing methods of solving wage and, in NUBE's case, recognition problems, through political pressure, traditional bargaining machinery and arbitration, was finally undermined by repeated government intervention both in the structure of existing machinery and in its output.

In both NALGO and the NUT the decision to seek affiliation to the TUC was a response by the leadership to the largely external developments that limited both the usefulness of individual political action and collective representation through COPPSO. In NALGO the Executive, once committed to the decision, pursued it with vigour and campaigned to secure an affirmative response from the membership. The NUT's leadership was rather less decisive. It feared the repercussions of affiliation on its 'professional' image and, hence, on its competitive position *vis-à-vis* non-affiliated teacher unions. A resolution from the normally more militant NUT conference was therefore needed before the leaders launched an active and successful campaign for affiliation.

In a sense, however, affiliation to the TUC was largely an extension of the traditional political pressure group methods of seeking to influence the state as the employer, although it must be recognized that, especially in the case of NALGO, it brought other character changes in its wake. In comparison, the demand for direct industrial action to achieve policy objectives was a much more fundamental character change for the NUT, NALGO and to some extent NUBE. In this change external factors and constraints combined with internal pressures to produce a new policy of direct industrial action in the field of job regulation. In all three unions the procedures for calling strikes were overhauled and attempts made to raise the funds needed to sustain strike action. Ballots were extensively used to test membership opinion. After initial difficulties, particularly in the NUT, the leadership proved itself capable of organizing an effective strike.

The leadership did not itself, however, escape unscathed from these changes. Pressure from within the NUT and NALGO affected the balance of power between conference and the Executive. Generally the Executive's authority was challenged by the more militant conference delegates. Indeed, in NALGO this challenge from below led to changes in the leadership and the resignation of the general secretary.

Although some members of the leadership in both unions blamed the un-official left-wing movements for the above events, their role was probably a minor one. The militant mood pre-dated the existence of the NALGO Action Group in NALGO and of the Rank and File movement in the NUT. These movements did, however, publicize, articulate and mobilize membership dis-content, particularly during the events of 1969 and 1970. Both unofficial move-ments were strongest where discontent was greatest – among those in the basic grades living in London – a factor brought particularly heavily to bear in the direct action taken over the London weighting dispute. Government inter-vention in wage bargaining thus had the indirect and unintentional effect of providing the nascent opposition group with a cause around which they could mobilize support for radical changes in leadership and methods of job regulation.

8 The structure of decision-making in job regulation

As we noted in Chapter 3 most unions have decentralized collective bargaining functions within the union to some extent over the period under study. Unions have differed, however, in the degree of external and internal pressure to devolve that has been exerted upon them and in the leadership's response to that pressure. The two unions that form the focus of this chapter, the TGWU and UCATT, have been chosen because they represent the two opposite poles in leadership response. The TGWU, under the leadership of Jones, grasped enthusiastically at the opportunities offered for both decentralization and diffusion and accelerated the process. The leadership of UCATT, on the other hand, while faced with a bargaining environment that encouraged site bargaining and strong membership pressure for bargaining at this level in some areas, attempted to resist the process and took steps to centralize collective bargaining within the union.

In most unions, except for those operating in closely defined spheres, it is difficult to be precise about the changes that have occurred. Most of the unions in our sample who organize in the private sector cover a multiplicity of companies. Moreover, the more decentralized and diffused the bargaining arrangements, the less likely that central records will be kept of the procedures in each case. As the TGWU itself stated in its evidence to the Donovan Commission in 1966, 'It is not possible to say what proportion of agreements are settled on a national, district or local basis'. The union also estimated in 1966 that it concluded some 2000 settlements a year in addition to the major national negotiations listed in the annual report. Few unions keep records of the numbers of shop stewards or other lay representatives who take part in negotiations, so the comments that follow are based largely on such relevant aggregate information as does exist but primarily on interviews with key officials.

In examining the TGWU, UCATT and other unions we will again use the model form adopted in other chapters by considering the areas of change before examining the processes and agents of change.

The TGWU: the decentralization of collective bargaining

Areas of change

The TGWU developed its job regulation strategy after the mid-1960s in several ways. It marginally moved formal bargaining levels downwards; it radically extended the scope and relevance of lower level bargaining; it sought to increase lay participation in bargaining by directly involving shop stewards in negotiations; and it encouraged the use of reference-back procedures.[1]

In 1966 the union claimed, in evidence to the Royal Commission, that 'The pattern is often for agreement to be reached nationally or centrally on broad principles and for its application to be worked out locally in the light of individual circumstances. Nor is it possible to express a general view of the advantages and disadvantages of each method'.[2] In contrast, in 1969 the general secretary elect stated that 'the union has turned increasingly to local agreements, local negotiations, because of . . . the possibility of involving a much greater number of shop stewards, elected representatives, in the actual negotiations'.[3]

In some circumstances the TGWU was able, unilaterally, to shift bargaining away from the national level. For instance, in 1967[4] the TGWU temporarily withdrew from the municipal busmen's NJIC. The union at first attempted to pursue at national level the claim outlined in the 'Busmen's Charter',[5] but when the Employers' Federation refused to negotiate on this basis, the union side, dominated by the TGWU, claimed that this refusal to negotiate, *de facto*, dissolved the NJIC. Once the NJIC was dissolved, the TGWU then proceeded to pursue the claim at local level.

There were also other developments which permanently fragmented industry-level negotiations into national company or regional/district and local negotiations. These included the Liverpool Dockers' secession from national negotiations following the Scamp Report in 1967[6] which, according to a national secretary in interview, started the decline in importance of national negotiations in the docks. The union[7] was also party to the CSEU's withdrawal from the Engineering industry's national agreement in 1971 (see below) which unilaterally shifted the final stage in engineering procedure in federated firms from the national to the local level.

There were, therefore, some significant movements away from national bargains towards lower-level negotiations. However, a clear majority of the TGWU's twelve national secretaries commented, in interviews, on their continued involvement in numerous national negotiations. Changes in the number of NJICs listed in the union's annual reports also revealed, at least quantitatively, that NJICs only marginally declined between 1956 and 1974, from 136 to 124.

In contrast, changes in the scope and relevance of existing bargaining levels were repeatedly cited in interviews as a key factor affecting and enlarging the TGWU's lay membership involvement in bargaining in the 1960s. The TGWU was thus part of the growing trend towards 'two systems' of bargaining identified by the Donovan Report.

Exact details of the extent to which the importance of workplace wage determination has increased in the TGWU are difficult to produce, largely because the

TGWU covers so many industries. However, an appreciation of the movement can be gained by considering how far national agreements account for wage rates and earnings in those industrial groupings that have high TGWU membership concentration. It can be seen, using this method, that in 1967 substantial parts of the TGWU's membership were affected by the growth in the scope and importance of workplace agreements. For instance, large parts of the Metal and Engineering group, Building, Docks, Food Drink and Tobacco (formed in 1969 mainly out of the General Worker and Flour Milling groups), all relied in 1967 on other than industry-wide negotiations for determining their average earnings. These four groups together accounted in 1967 for some 48 per cent of the union's membership.

It is possible to gain an impression of the comparable position in 1974 and 1975 by contrasting the nationally negotiated rates reported in the annual reports of the TGWU with figures from the New Earnings Survey (NES) which analyse earnings of adult males by agreement.[8] A comparison, using material from these sources, is made in Table 42. As the table shows, up to 79.2 per cent of employees benefited from PBR systems of some sort. The NES does not distinguish between PBR and productivity deals.

The difference between 'other' and NJIC in Table 42 also suggests that there was quite a substantial amount of local bargaining over basic rates, in addition to localized PBR and overtime negotiations, at least in Engineering, Garages, Docks and Chemicals. Of these groups, the shift in local bargaining scope and importance was more pronounced in the docks than anywhere else. Fringe benefits continued to be negotiated at the centre, as is the case in most industry-wide negotiations; but between 1960 and 1975 the local docks' level had officially replaced national negotiations as the most significant bargaining level for determining the membership's actual wage. This change, which coincided with Devlin Stage II and the National Modernization Committee in February 1969,[9] provided a framework for local agreements. By the time of the 1970 annual report, local agreements had been reached and were in operation in at least nine ports.

Many national industrial and company-wide negotiations retained the appearance of substance but, in fact, were reduced to little more than determinators of national or company minima, hours and fall-back or guaranteed payment, although they also drafted guidelines for local interpretation. There were, of course, as always in very large unions, significant exceptions (for example at the company-level ICI and Fords), but generally the movement towards local determination of actual wages noted in Donovan continued in the post-1967 period.

In the TGWU the growing importance of workplace bargaining increased the role and numbers of shop stewards, and their ratio in relation to members.[10] The ratio of stewards to members changed from 1:157 in 1955 to 1:114 in 1965 and 1:53 in 1975. In 1965 there were 637 members to each senior shop steward or convenor and in 1975 the figure was 433:1. At the same time the ratio of full-time officials to members changed – the number of members per full-time official

Table 42 *Composition of earnings by industry*

Industry	(1) NJIC	(2) Other	(3) Gross	(4) PBR	(5) OT	(6) % on PBR	(7) % on OT
Engineering (1975)	£32 (craft); £25.50 (unskilled)	£39.90	£56.50	£7.50	£7.20	49.9	58.8
MVRRT (Garages) (1975)	£30.40 (craft); £27.20 (semi-skilled); £25.40 (unskilled)	£37.20	£45.30	£2.80	£5.10	25.0	56.9
Chemical and Allied Industries (1975)	£24.52 (lowest rate)	£43.90	£55.50	£1.50	£5.50	24.5	35.9
Rubber (1974)	£22.50 (min. earnings level)	£26.50	£46.10	£10.00	£6.50	60.4	60.0
Docks (1975)	—	£27.70	—	—	—	55.6	55.6
Municipal Bus (1974)	£26.86 OMO (double decker driver) to £21.48 (conductor)	£27.70	£46.50	£4.40	£11.70	79.2	87.8
Local Authorities England and Wales 1975	£30 (grade A) to £33.25 (grade C)	£34.80	£47.50	£6.10	£5.70	68.6	54.1
Building and Civil Engineering Joint Board 1975	£40 (craft); £34 (labourer)	£39.30	£53.50	£7.70	£6.40	59.2	62.6

1 Figures in this column refer to NJIC rate or equivalent. They were taken from the TGWU reports of either 1974 or 1975
2 Figures in this column are taken from the New Earnings Survey (NES) for full-time men for the relevant year and are the same as NES's 'All other pay', which includes not only basic pay but any items other than overtime payments, PBR etc. payments and shift etc. premium payments. It is therefore likely that for the period examined it also includes some threshold payments
3 Figures in this column are the same as 'Total' average gross weekly earnings in NES
4 Figures in this column are the same as PBR etc. payment in the NES Table 43 (April 1975) or Table 43 (April 1974), depending on the date of the agreement used for the NJIC column
5 As in (4) OT is taken from NES Table 43
6 As in (4) percentage on PBR is taken from NES Table 43. It refers to the percentage of those workers in the sample who received PBR etc. payments
7 As in (6) except percentage receiving overtime payments

Table 43 Ratio of members to full-time officials, TGWU

Region	Full-time officials			Members			Ratios		
	1968	1970	1974	1968	1970	1974	1968	1970	1974
1	132	123	122	352,623	390,285	450,608	2671:1	3173:1	3694:1
2	20	20	19	69,961	81,935	90,237	3498:1	4096:1	4749:1
3	35	34	33	112,243	129,005	137,085	3207:1	3794:1	4154:1
4*	35	28	27	111,618	111,438	110,666	3189:1	3980:1	4098:1
5	45	43	47	246,209	270,610	334,701	5471:1	6293:1	7121:1
6†	78	73	60	177,544	208,391	236,713	2276:1	2855:1	3945:1
7	54	48	60	118,011	129,369	166,559	2185:1	2695:1	2776:1
8	21	21	20	68,112	75,411	82,041	3243:1	3591:1	4102:1
9	27	25	25	71,678	82,464	87,564	2655:1	3299:1	3503:1
10	21	20	15	43,712	52,740	52,851	2082:1	2637:1	3512:1
11	36	35	38	96,220	101,709	99,738	2673:1	2906:1	2625:1
Head Office	26	24	19						
Total	530	494	485	1,473,505‡	1,638,686‡	1,857,308 ‡	2780:1	3317:1	3829:1

*Region 4 in 1968 is the previous Regions 4 and 13 added together
†Region 6 in 1968 is the previous Regions 6 and 12 added together
‡Includes some numbers not allocated to regions.

increased. Table 43 shows a clear reduction in the number of full-time officials and a very marked increase in the ratio of members to officials. Region 5 is clearly outstanding as the region with consistently the highest ratio of members to full-time officials between 1968 and 1974.

It is possible to explain at least part of these regional variations in ratios of members to full-time officials by reference to the composition by trade group of the membership in the regions. Region 5 (Midlands), with, in 1974, one full-time official to 7121 members, had 49.75 per cent of its membership concentrated in just two trade groups, Power and Engineering and Vehicle Building and Automotive. Two features of these trade groups in the Midlands help to explain this difference: first, the long-standing reliance by the TGWU and other unions on lay representatives in the engineering and car factories and, second, the concentration of membership in the car industry in that region. No other region has such a high degree of trade group concentration. The more even spread of membership across trade groups in other regions can therefore be put forward as a major factor contributing to the lower ratios of members to full-time officials found in this region.

Another factor influencing the variation in ratios is the geographical spread. For example, in Region 3, the South West, which stretches from Bristol to Land's End, the union need more full-time officials just to cover the geographical area, even though the density of the members per square mile is far lower than in the Midlands.

It is not however possible to explain the changes over time in the FTO to member ratio in all regions solely or mainly by reference to geographical or industrial factors. The minor adjustments in regional boundaries in 1968, for instance, helped to rationalize the officer position in four regions but they were not drastic enough to account for the overall change in the ratio. Also, the major industrial change in membership, which arose from the merger with the National Union of Vehicle Builders (NUVB), did not directly account for the changes in the FTO to member ratio, noted above, even though it made a major contribution (some 57,000) to the increase in the Vehicle Trade Group, from 78,509 in 1969 to 163,601 in 1975; for the TGWU also increased its officials by guaranteeing jobs to NUVB full-time officials as part of the merger agreement. And, apart from Vehicles and ACTSS (ACTSS is an occupational unit and therefore cannot be related to any particular industry's development), the trade groups showed little change in proportions of total membership between 1969 and 1975. Thus, the TGWU did nothing in the face of an expanding membership and rapidly growing shop floor negotiations to maintain its ratio of FTO to members. Indeed, the total number of full-time officials was reduced at a time of rapid membership growth.

The relatively high growth in shop stewards suggests that lay representation on local level negotiating bodies may also have increased. Such shop steward growth, it can reasonably be assumed, would result in an increase in both the number of local negotiating bodies and the bargaining scope of existing local committees. However, there was also an extension of lay involvement in negotiating bodies above the local level. In a number of interviews and in union publications, reference was made to the introduction of lay members to national negotiating bodies. Thus increased lay participation on negotiating bodies can be considered by commenting, first, on the local scene and, second, on the composition of more elevated bodies.

An attempt was made in a questionnaire to ascertain whether lay involvement on local negotiating bodies had increased, decreased or remained the same between 1965 and 1975. The district officials were also asked to describe the composition in 1975 of such bodies, for instance whether they had all lay members, no lay members or some full-time officials (that is, mixed lay and full-time officials). Finally, the officials were asked to break their answer down by trade group. This last question was posed because it appeared from interviews that useful distinctions could perhaps be made between the degree of lay involvement, and the rate of increase of lay involvement, by trade group. A summary of the answers received is given in Table 25 (page 147).

The replies from the districts tended to confirm the comments made in interviews at regional and national level. There was clearly a significant increase in lay involvement in local negotiations affecting most of the union's membership between 1965 and 1975. The only major deviation from this general change was in passenger services.

The bargaining differences between passenger services and other trade groups revealed in Table 25 stem mostly from the continued importance for busmen of centralized union–management negotiating committees above the garage level. These negotiation committees determine the actual wages of a considerable proportion of busmen in the four main sectors: London, National Bus Company, Municipal and Passenger Transport Executives. But the bargaining structures, at least during the period under examination, provided the membership affected by the four major bus negotiations with an effective reference-back procedure. It is likely, therefore, that the busmen had not pressed for, nor the union seen it necessary to make, radical changes in the composition of busmen's bargaining groups in order to increase lay participation.

A number of district officials also made a distinction in the questionnaire between the shop steward's and branch official's role in negotiations in passenger services which they did not make for other trade groups. They identified, in passenger services, the branch official or delegate and not the shop steward as the main negotiator. The shop steward's role in the garage, it was stated, was generally limited to individual grievance-processing and schedule negotiations, and did not involve dealing with direct money issues. Furthermore, unlike other industries, where productivity bargaining increased the shop steward's bargaining scope, the one-man operations (or OMO) productivity deals did not appear to have a similar effect on the shop steward in passenger transport. Thus the 40 per cent of passenger services' replies that reported 'no change' in terms of increased lay involvement can be largely explained as an exception to the general rule by reference to specific industrial factors.

The relatively low percentage for the Docks and Waterways under the 'more' column is somewhat misleading. If replies from London Docks alone had been included in the Docks and Waterways column, it would have shown a marked shift to more lay involvement in local negotiations. However, this increase would have been due in part to the union's recognition of the unofficial shop stewards' existing role pre-Devlin[11] rather than because of any recent growth in the shop stewards' bargaining activities. Prior to Devlin the union had not welcomed the stewards' activities in the docks, and it had successfully opposed at the 1951 BDC[12] a motion seeking to establish the right of dock workers to have shop stewards. This led, at least officially, to a position where the full-time docks official was expected to 'deal directly with every grievance in the docks'.[13] In practice, according to Jack Dash, a leading member of the Unofficial Docks Liaison Committee, the unofficial shop steward processed many issues, except those directly concerned with money, and the full-time official 'mediated between members and employers'. Official recognition of shop stewards in these circumstances therefore acknowledged and regularized an existing situation as well as increasing the shop stewards' new-found official involvement in the bargaining process, particularly in official wage negotiations.

The other three trade groups that showed a relatively less marked shift to lay involvement in negotiations between 1965 and 1975 – the Engineering part of Power and Engineering, Building, and Commercial Transport – were all groups with comparatively well established patterns of local bargaining with lay involvement prior to 1965. This is partly reflected in the relatively high 'same' percentage they respectively recorded: 17, 29 and 14 per cent. (The high 22 per cent 'same' for Docks came mainly from the non-London Docks and Waterways replies.) Building, Engineering and Commercial Transport were, and are, all highly fragmented industries with a multiplicity of small employers. In this type of industrial organization it is virtually impossible for employer–union negotiations at a national level to determine actual wages at the plant level, be it shop floor or building site. It is, therefore, not unexpected that these three groups recorded some of the highest level of 'all lay' involvement in negotiations locally as well as high 'same' percentages and, hence, a less noticeable extension of lay involvement.

There is no comprehensive guide to the extent of the change in the composition of bargaining bodies above the workplace, whether at national, trade group or regional levels. Stress was however laid on this facet of devolvement in interviews, and the general secretary, Jones, wrote that 'We should be ready to introduce the active lay member and the local officer much more into national negotiations, training boards, etc., than has been our past practice.'[14] According to a long-serving officer, this represented a significant change in policy: the previous general secretaries had prevented even local full-time officials from sitting on training boards.

Most trade groups[15] were affected by this shift in policy. Thus, for example, the docks, during the Phase II (Devlin) negotiations in 1969, introduced a majority of lay members into their negotiating team. Commercial Transport re-shaped their negotiating teams with the oil companies from the mid-1960s and eventually provided for about four senior shop stewards and ten or eleven full-time officials to be present at major negotiations. Passenger Services (buses) over the three years up to 1975 replaced five or so regional officials with lay representatives on the municipal negotiations. In Civil Air Transport, where the TGWU is the sole or dominant union, bargaining arrangements were changed to include lay members on all JICs. In general, therefore, the TGWU since 1965 has sought to increase lay representation on its negotiating committees at the expense of the full-time officials.

Even if none of the above changes had taken place in the TGWU, the introduction of reference-back procedures, which devolved responsibility for acceptance or rejection of an offer to the membership immediately concerned, would have significantly altered the nature of bargaining in the union. The TGWU's centrally appointed full-time officials' virtual independence of the members or shop stewards in negotiations was curtailed by an Executive and BDC acting under the influence of a general secretary who, unlike his predecessors, approved of lay participation in bargaining. Jones, for instance, referred approvingly to the practice in the West Coast of the USA where 'negotiations took place with an audience of 200 working dockers who were thus kept in touch all the way with the negotiations'.[16]

Prior to 1969, with a number of exceptions, it had only been the docks and bus sections that had regularly and traditionally operated a reference-back procedure. By 1975, however, one of the national trade group secretaries could claim that there was 'no way' in which he would sign an agreement without reference back to either a delegate conference, shop stewards or the membership.[17] Although not all the national secretaries subscribed to this extreme view of their obligations to refer agreements to the membership, most of them considered they had a duty, wherever possible, to consult the membership prior to signing an agreement.

Not all the union's full-time officials, however, welcomed the new emphasis on reference-back procedures. Keeley, the union's negotiator with Fords in 1969, found it difficult to reconcile his perception of the full-time official's role, conditioned by some twenty-one years of negotiation for the TGWU, with this change in the union's attitude. He resigned, under pressure, in 1969[18] after failing to comply fully with a delegate conference decision. In 1970 at Fords, following Keeley's departure, the TGWU 'insisted on reporting back to the members at every stage . . . and the final £4 [was] accepted by a majority vote'.

These changes had a major impact on the role of full-time officials within the TGWU. Some full-time district officials reported that in 1965 there were no convenors or senior shop stewards in their districts. Thus, although the situation varied between industries and districts, with some areas characterized by strong workplace and shop steward independence, such as vehicles and the docks, the predominant relationships within the TGWU both between local FTOs and lay shop stewards and between higher and lower FTOs within the TGWU had been hierarchical.

These traditional relationships between FTOs and shop stewards began to change during Cousins's period as general secretary. Cousins started to change the status of national secretaries by involving himself more directly, on odd occasions, in some national secretaries' bargaining activities, for instance in docks and buses. Cousins's involvement in the London bus strike of 1958 turned the national secretary into no more than a cipher. Cousins, for reasons that remain obscure, also started to bypass national secretaries and use regional secretaries as his intermediaries with the mass membership.

Later, under Jones's leadership, changes in bargaining policy further undermined the national and district full-time officials' influence over the membership and limited their discretion in negotiations. Encouragement of shop stewards ran parallel with a decline in the numbers and bargaining discretion of district full-time officials.

The processes and agents of change

As shown above, the level at which collective bargaining takes place and the degree of participation by union lay and full-time officials is not fixed, although traditions once established are often difficult to change. The procedures, as well as the substantive content of collective bargaining, are a reflection of the inter-plays of power relationships between the parties involved at different points in time.

It is rarely within the power of a single union to determine the level at which negotiations should take place because of the role of the employer and because of the multi-union character of many collective bargaining situations. Only in bargaining units where a union is the dominant partner both *vis-à-vis* other unions and the employer will it be able unilaterally to determine effectively the level at which it will collectively bargain. Even where, as in the case of the CSEU, unions have unilaterally abrogated a procedure agreement and consciously attempted to shift the level of bargaining either permanently or as a bargaining ploy, it has depended on the co-operation of employers either individually or collectively to conduct negotiations at another level. Indeed, by definition, it could not be otherwise as far as 'collective bargaining' or 'joint job regulation' is concerned. One might expect therefore that external factors are predominant in explaining changes in the structure of bargaining.

We will find, however, that although for the most part the external factors including the activities of the employer set the basic parameters, they did not fully determine the course of action of the TGWU or the other unions studied. The main external factors influencing the structure of decision-making in job regulation can be divided into two basic dimensions: the context in which the union's bargaining strategy is determined, and the content of collective bargaining. In each case the factors identified act as both change agents and external constraints on the union in formulating policy. We shall deal with the context and the content in turn. Finally, we will consider the strategy adopted by the TGWU when it was faced by these external developments.

The collective bargaining context

The context of bargaining was primarily affected by employers, the state, other unions and the nature of the TGWU's membership. Many employers, in areas organized by the TGWU, unilaterally initiated action that devolved bargaining. This was usually accomplished by employers leaving an employers' association and/or withdrawing from industry-wide negotiations.

Metal Box, for instance, withdrew from the Tin Box JIC and moved to individual factory bargaining in 1969 and 1970, but back up to company–union bargaining in 1971.[19] Cadbury-Schweppes ended their association with the Cocoa, Chocolate and Confectionery JIC in June 1968 and subsequently divided their negotiations between national Confectionery and Food Groups, and introduced plant bargaining.[20] Oil companies disbanded their negotiating machinery for transport drivers in 1965–66 when they individually withdrew from the Oil Companies' Conciliation Committee.[21] Mergers and takeovers on the employers' side, which produced 'fewer large industrial corporations like Courtaulds',[22] also made NIJCs redundant and led to them being replaced by 'company and plant bargaining'.[23]

Employers can also effectively prevent unions from introducing greater lay participation on national, company or plant-level negotiating bodies. Thus, for example, in 1975 and 1976 the Ford Motor Company refused to accommodate the TGWU's request for more convenors on the company-wide negotiating committee. Employers also play a vital role in determining how effective lay officials within the plant will be by the facilities they provide. These include time off with pay, physical facilities for conducting their duties, and provisions for consulting members. The state now lays down minimum standards of facilities, but there is still a wide variation in practice between different employers.

The state and its agencies sought to influence the structure of bargaining in several other ways during the period studied. The Donovan Commission and its brainchild the Commission on Industrial Relations were specifically concerned with procedural issues. In particular, Donovan proposed that the informal relationship that had developed at the shop floor should be formalized, that the number of full-time officials operating at the local level should be increased, and that shop stewards should be more closely integrated with the full-time officials. The TGWU generally took the opposite course, increasing the ratio of shop stewards to members but reducing that of FTOs to members. It also tended to informalize and loosen, if not reverse, the traditional subordinate relationship between shop steward and full-time official that existed in the TGWU in the 1950s.

On the other hand, individual inquiries into specific industries and companies did affect bargaining in the TGWU. For example, the inquiries into the dock organization[24] helped considerably the devolution of bargaining in this industry. Moreover, the NBPI reports on Road Haulage, Local Authorities Workers, Engineering Workers, Bus Industry, Civil Engineering, Building, Car Delivery and ICI[25] all encouraged the TGWU to examine its organization and preferred payments systems.

Incomes policies also had a major impact on the level of and responsibility for collective bargaining in the TGWU and other unions. The nature of the impact has been complex and varied. For example, the incomes policy pursued between 1966 and 1969, particularly in the latter stages, encouraged productivity bargaining and hence, as we argue below, decentralization and diffusion. But the early phases of the 'social contract' severely circumscribed the activities of the shop floor negotiators and put the bargaining onus on to the national leadership of the TGWU. It was, however, as will be shown in the section on the content of bargaining, the growth of productivity deals, often encouraged by the state's incomes policies, that had the greatest impact on the dispersal of bargaining decisions in the TGWU.

Operating in an exposed job territory, the TGWU was also affected in its bargaining behaviour by its multi-union environment. It was stated in interviews that the major obstacle to further extension of lay participation in the TGWU's national negotiations was the attitude of other unions on these bodies. The opposition of craft unions to further changes was particularly stressed. It was claimed that these unions specifically objected to shop stewards participating in negotiations that were presently staffed solely by full-time officials.

Finally, in respect of the bargaining context, the nature of membership is also an important factor in the degree of lay participation in job regulation. In general, the conditions under which lay participation is likely to be high are those where the membership is stable, where there are coherent and articulate occupational or industrial interest groups with a tradition of solidarity, and where there is a degree of employer recognition that enables lay officials to perform their union activities free from the fear of victimization. A number of the TGWU's trade groups clearly has pockets of members with these features. Also, the mergers with the NUVB and the CWU brought into the TGWU groups of workers with traditions of shop floor organization which must have reinforced the union's devolutionary trends.

The content of collective bargaining
A major factor in the determination of the level at which collective bargaining takes place and the degree of lay participation is the content of the collective

bargain. The more complex and company-specific the payments and grading systems, the more likely that they cannot be fully regulated at national or even company level and that the lay officials will have the greater competence to conduct them. This applies to Payment by Results (PBR) in general, to productivity bargaining in particular, and to job evaluation schemes. Conversely, the greater the influence of local lay officials, the more likely they are to attempt to retain the type of payment system amenable to shop floor control.

The development of productivity agreements had a very significant effect on bargaining in the TGWU. Productivity bargaining was first introduced in industries not previously associated with PBR systems, predominantly process industries.[26] The TGWU had a major presence in these industries. Later this kind of bargaining was given impetus by the NBPI and their incorporation into the 1966–69 phase of incomes policies.

The productivity criterion first laid down in the 1965 White Paper on Prices and Incomes and repeated in the White Paper on Prices and Incomes Policy after 30 June 1967 allowed increases in pay above the norm 'where the employees concerned, for example by accepting more exacting work or a major change in working practices, make a direct contribution towards increasing productivity in the particular firm or industry'.

By the time the NBPI produced its second comprehensive report on productivity agreements in 1969, the register of productivity cases kept by the Department of Employment and Productivity recorded some 3000 agreements covering approximately 6 million workers or 25 per cent of all employed workers. The number of cases averaged about 60 per month in 1967, 75 per month in the first half of 1968, 200 per month in the last half and then fell to a lower level of 150 per month in 1969.[27]

The TGWU fully participated in this boom. In the union's reports for 1968 and 1969 references were made, among others, to productivity bargains in Oil Delivery, Courtaulds, Paint Industry, NJIC for Rubber Manufacturing (where rewards for skill, responsibility, effort and productivity were to be negotiated locally), Soap, Candle and Edible Fats, Chemical Industry and in the government's Industrial Service, where the 'most significant development was in the field of productivity bargaining where a great deal has been and is still being done locally'.[28] These agreements, and many others, although made mainly at national, industry or company level, were applied locally.

The NBPI reports also made it clear that productivity agreements had implications for the level at which bargaining took place, and the influence of those levels. Thus Report no. 36 stated: 'It is evident that an agreement tailored to suit the individual needs of an undertaking, as a productivity agreement must be, is liable to be at odds with the common policies of an employers' association.'[29] It also noted that many of the pioneer companies in productivity bargaining had had to leave their respective employers' associations to be able to negotiate their productivity agreements at company or plant level. Other employers' associations, as indicated in Report no. 123, had adopted a lesser role in wage determination by providing only for the negotiation of minimum earnings levels at industry level. Also, the report noted, the growth of productivity agreements involved a devolution from company to plant level. In addition, as explained in a research paper of the period, productivity bargaining makes heavy demands on trade union officials:

Productivity bargaining tends to commit unions heavily in terms of the time and effort of its officials. . . . Insofar as productivity bargains at the level of plants or undertakings become more common, the greater the strain this will put on trade union resources. This is a most important point. There is no doubt that if productivity bargaining is to become more general it will be essential for trade unions to increase the numbers of their officials.[30]

It is thus not surprising, bearing in mind the above comment and the reduction in the level of officering in the TGWU, that those groups in the TGWU that showed the highest percentage for 'more' shop steward involvement (see Table 25, page 147) in negotiations came from trade groups where there was a marked tendency to adopt productivity bargaining. The TGWU's deputy general secretary was therefore on strong ground when he stated that productivity bargaining allowed the union to 'substantially raise the level of joint consultation and participation of shop stewards in negotiation and operation of comprehensive plant agreements'.[31]

The alternative strategies

In the TGWU as well as other unions, there were alternative strategies that could be pursued within the parameters dictated by the environment. To explain why the TGWU's leadership took the particular course they did requires an examination of the internal factors involved.

The demand for decentralization and diffusion of collective bargaining among TGWU members pre-dated the growth of productivity bargaining and had been repeatedly expressed in the 1950s and 1960s. At least as early as 1949 a motion for wider use of the 'reference-back' procedure was defeated. In 1957 the BDC debated a motion 'That no agreements shall be concluded between negotiating officers and employers without the general consent of the membership affected by such agreements',[32] but it was lost. In later years motions seeking to include consultative stages as a matter of policy in established negotiation procedures were generally either defeated, withdrawn, replaced by Executive Statements or accepted subject to qualification by the GEC.

In addition to motions coming before the BDC, there were more direct pressures on the leadership to change its policy. Strikes, particularly at Fords or in the docks, brought to the immediate notice of the GEC and particularly Jones, as the executive officer most intimately involved, the membership's desire for more say in the signing of their own agreements. Moreover, the unofficial organizations within the union, such as the unofficial Docks Liaison Committee, were able to capitalize on the union's failure to accommodate the membership's desire for direct control over their own wage agreements at the local level.

Before 1960 the union's Executive was overwhelmingly condemnatory of unofficial strikes; for instance, the TGWU held inquiries in 1949 into an unofficial London docks strike; in 1950 into the work of a group arising from that strike and calling itself the Committee for Trade Union Democracy; again in 1950 into a strike at Smithfield meat market; and in 1952 into unofficial action at Salford docks. These led to the expulsion of some members and the debarring from office of others, but in general those involved were given 'final warnings' or charged not to engage in unofficial activity in the future. The inquiries did not look to the TGWU itself to see if the reasons for the unofficial action lay within, but rather they were content to use the old bogey of communism as the explanation. One report concluded:

Finally we desire to record that in our considered opinion the agitation leading to the unofficial London docks strike of June and July [1949] and the attempt to extend the strike on a national basis was part of a wider plan, inspired from Communist sources, the object of which was to dislocate the trade of the country and so add to our economic difficulties.

The general condemnation of unofficial strikes was reinforced by the BDC in 1951, when a motion supporting the executive's action was carried. There was only minor criticism from the 'floor' of conference. Deakin wound up the debate by saying that he preferred negotiations to strike action and that 'I have never said and never believed . . . that the communists are responsible for every dispute . . . but they have been responsible for most of them'.

The union's attitude to unofficial action changed course significantly when Frank Cousins became acting general secretary in 1956. Referring to an unofficial dispute at Standard Motors in his second quarterly report, Cousins notes that 'we deemed it advisable to move away from the previously accepted policy in relation to unofficial disputes and take control'. Furthermore, the union began to look to its own structure for an explanation of these strikes, and to see the reorganization of branches as a more appropriate response to the problems in the northern ports than simply laying the blame on communist agitators. By the mid-1960s the TGWU's concern with unofficial action was much reduced despite the Donovan Report's well-known conclusion that at that time 95 per cent of strikes were unofficial. The unofficial strikes that still occurred did not generally find their way into GEC minutes except in simply being recorded. In many cases, like other unions, the TGWU used them as an informal bargaining lever.

But whatever the shop floor reality in the early 1960s, the TGWU did not officially encourage the devolution of bargaining or the growth of shop steward power in this period. The union's 'Members' Handbook' was not fundamentally changed between 1947 and 1966. There is in this handbook virtually no mention of the shop steward's bargaining role. Indeed, it was implied that anything less than NJIC bargaining was purely a passing phase on the path to the national level. 'In addition [to NJICs or similar bodies] . . . the union has *concluded many agreements with individual firms. As settled machinery for collective bargaining extends this type of negotiation tends to decrease in importance.*'[33]

Similarly, in the educational documents before 1969 the union rarely considered the role of the shop steward or of shop floor bargaining. The contrast between these documents and the post-1969 'Union in Action' pamphlets that replaced them is remarkable.[34] Perhaps a statement by the union in 1962 sums up the union's policy prior to 1968 fairly accurately: 'generally speaking, the policy [is] that negotiations are a matter for permanent officers of the union with lay representation as required in particular cases conditioned by prevailing circumstances'.[35]

It is quite probable that the union could, by giving ground on specific issues and to external criticisms, for example the Devlin recommendation on shop stewards, have retained its existing overall bargaining policy relatively intact. Bevin, Deakin and Cousins had each, prior to 1968, successfully resisted constitutional and other pressures both for decision dispersal and major restructuring of trade groups. Moreover, as far as can be assessed from interviews and statistics, there was no mass 'voting with their feet' by members who wanted more say.[36] The move by the GEC in 1969 to wholeheartedly welcome 'the progressive outlook' that would lead to agreement 'conforming as closely as possible to wishes of the membership concerned'[37] therefore marked a very radical change in the TGWU's leadership attitude towards the devolution of bargaining.

One of the most influential internal factors bringing about this change was the philosophy of the new general secretary Jones, who, given the power wielded by the general secretary within the TGWU in the decision-making process, was able to stamp his own philosophy on the union. That philosophy was summed up by his statement in 1969 that 'Our success [i.e. TGWU's] . . . is going to be determined by the extent to which we can decentralize – spread – decision-making among the work people, and above all get industrial agreements settled where they are going to be operated. That is the key'.[38]

It was this kind of thinking that led the TGWU to use productivity bargaining as a means of decentralizing bargaining. The union sought to define productivity bargaining as a continuous process which would extend bargaining into areas previously reserved for the exercise of managerial preogatives by the 'extension of the range of mutual agreement'.[39] This was in direct contrast, as the union noted, to those employers who 'took the view that what they wanted was not productivity *bargaining* but a productivity *bargain* – a bargain where the employer hopes to obtain sole control in return for one substantial change in the wages structure'.[40]

Jones's[41] commitment to the decentralization of bargaining was based on both ideological and pragmatic grounds. Decentralization and diffusion of bargaining was part of a grand design to democratize the union and industry. As Jones, who chaired the Labour Party's working party on Industrial Democracy set up in May 1966, later stated, 'If we can bring *most* workers into making decisions about many things previously regarded as being the sole prerogative of management then a major step will have been taken towards industrial democracy', and 'the key to the expansion of industrial democracy remains in the process of negotiation itself. This fact is the key to the whole question of localised productivity bargaining.'[42] Furthermore, in his policy-shaping speech on bargaining at the 1969 BDC, Jones stated, with regard to membership involvement in determining the outcome of negotiation, that 'There is no aspect of the union to which I am more personally committed than to this principle, and what we are talking about here is practical democracy and that is what the trade union should be about.'[43]

Because of the powerful position of the general secretary within the TGWU (described in Chapter 4), particularly his ability to ensure that lower-level full-time officials who are appointed carry out known policy, the strategy once determined could be implemented. The resignation of Keeley was an extreme example of the pressures that can be applied to create conformity among full-time officials.

However, the policy change Jones carried through did not represent an overnight switch from centralized to decentralized and concentrated to diffused bargaining. As shown above, multi-national companies and governments had already, through productivity bargaining, increased lay involvement in some industries. The policy switch was therefore at least partly a recognition of previous changes which had bypassed the formal policy-making structure as well as a declaration of the new leadership's intentions. It was thus in the area of image building that it was most significant, inasmuch as it announced a turning point in the leadership's position. This ensured that devolution was adopted with enthusiasm and was promoted throughout the union, instead of, as would have been the case with the pre-1960 leadership, being accepted reluctantly only in those areas where such developments were too strong to resist.

The UCATT: the centralization of bargaining

Areas of change

Since the establishment of the National Wages and Conditions Council in 1920 the ASW (later the dominant union forming UCATT) relied on central negotiations with the employers, via the NFBTO, to determine the standard craftsmen's rate for the job. These negotiations also standardized conditions throughout the building industry by an elaborate collection of National Working Rules. In 1974, however, the employers pressed the unions to accept incentive schemes. This was opposed by the ASW but accepted by the NFBTO. Having been outvoted on what for the ASW was a matter of principle, the union did not play a particularly active or dominant role in the NFBTO for some fifteen years.

By 1968 78 per cent of all craftsmen and labourers working for the largest firms were covered by site-based payments of some kind. Moreover, out of the average gross weekly earnings for craftsmen in 1968 of £22.72p, only £15.41p were negotiated centrally by the union.[44] In 1938 the standard rate formed 110 per cent of the craftsman's earnings, whereas in 1974, just after the peak of site level earnings was reached, the corresponding figure was 67 per cent.[45] The proportion of total earnings accounted for by payment by results increased considerably between 1968 and 1976, while the reverse trend was developing in manufacturing industry.

The ambivalent attitude of the ASW to incentive bonus payments and their lack of strong site organization in many areas meant that many employers unilaterally determined wages on site according to the needs of the local labour market. In 1967 the general secretary of the NFBTO complained that

the principal contract employers in this country . . . are dead against one agreement for the building industry. . . . The reason I have told you before. They prefer a low basic rate and then add bribes to that – their incentives, plus rates and so on – in order to attract labour to the large scale contracts in this country.

Similar statements were made at other conferences, and the officials interviewed in the Midlands, South West and Southern regions, in particular, agreed that in these low union density regions the craft unions had little, if any, part in negotiating incentive schemes.

The 'wage drift' engendered by incentive and bonus schemes, which resembled the situation in engineering and some other manufacturing industries, was however in the building industry exacerbated by the growth of Labour Only Sub-contracting (LOSC), which replaced rather than simply supplemented the collectively negotiated industry-wide agreements.

Thus by 1970 the ASW virtually fit the example described in the Donovan Report:[46] national level negotiations, conducted largely by FTOs, bore little or no relation to earnings on the shop floor, which, if they were negotiated, were often settled by shop stewards, sometimes with little reference to FTOs. To understand why this was so involves some explanation of the distribution of bargaining roles in UCATT (ASW) over the period until 1970.

Historically UCATT, and particularly its major constituent, the ASW, stands out among the unions studied as the one whose leadership most consistently opposed the devolvement of collective bargaining authority – despite the fact that, like the AUEW, it began as a locally controlled craft union. District management committees, similar to the AUEW's district committees, were formed in 1872 to co-ordinate branch activities. They also supported their own full-time officials. By 1914 there were forty-one management committees enjoying considerable autonomy. As Connelly notes, 'their negotiating and protective functions made them extremely important parts of the organisation. From district levies, some of them were able to build up considerable financial strength from which they derived a certain power and independence from the Executive Council at the centre.'[47]

Management committees retained their financial independence until 1956. It was only after the membership voted for central financial responsibility following the 1954 conference's support for central control that district officials' salaries and conditions were standardized nationally. Up to 1921 the local officials also bargained for wages in their particular districts, but with the formation of the NFBTO and the national agreement of 1921 the district management committees were deprived of some of their control over wage negotiations. In practice the extent of the deprivation was determined by the strength of union organization at the district level. However district management committees were themselves abolished in the late 1960s.

Until 1970 the basic characteristic of the official bargaining structure was that the national negotiations were conducted at one remove through the NFBTO, which structurally resembled a single union. There were arrangements for recognizing 'federation stewards' on building sites and a system of 'federation branches' consisting of delegates from branches of the affiliated unions in each area. Each region had a regional council, consisting of representatives of the individual unions together with delegates from the 'federation branches'. The regional secretaries of the federation were full-time servants of the NFBTO itself and were appointed by the General Council, the national governing body of the federation, which comprised delegations from all the affiliated unions.

While the NFBTO structure had a regional organization, the ASW did not. Site organization both on the part of the NFBTO and its constituent unions was patchy. Thus the NBPI[48] in 1968 found that organization at site level varied regionally but was generally at a low level. Out of twenty-six sites visited, twelve were without any shop stewards and only two had federation stewards. The Phelps Brown inquiry found that only 11 per cent of company sites visited had shop stewards but that trade union representation was greater on the larger sites. At the 41st Conference of the AUBTW it was reported that

regarding the active stewards . . . the total nationally is only 1,500 . . . there are over 80,000 firms . . . about 1,300 local authorities . . . there seems to be a need for an even greater improvement of activity by shop stewards . . . Divisional Councils can organise from time to time meetings of shop stewards only in two divisions, in the No 1 (London) and No 8 (Manchester, Mersey, N.E. Lancashire, Mid-Cheshire, North Wales and Shropshire) divisions.

In the *ASPD Journal* from 1964 to 1970 the only regular notices of shop steward meetings were issued by London, Liverpool and the North East; the same areas complained when in 1967 shop steward council meetings were reduced from twelve to four per year.[49] The ASW[50] had only two shop stewards active on building sites in the City of Birmingham in 1969; in the South West Region (covering Herefordshire, Gloucestershire, Somerset, Devon, Cornwall,

Wiltshire and Dorset) in 1972 UCATT had 600 shop stewards recorded, of whom only 97 were in the construction industry.

Generally speaking, the areas of high-density membership (over 50 per cent density) were those that had the highest degree of site organization, although there were pockets of highly organized sites, for example in Leicester, within low-density regions. In the high-density areas such as the Northern, North West and South Wales regions, and also in Leicester, there was a history of site negotiations over bonus incentives and plus rates by the shop stewards extending back at least to 1947. These negotiations normally took place with the prior knowledge and sometimes the assistance of the local full-time officials. On some large sites there were both bonus stewards and site stewards, for example in the Liverpool district, and it was claimed in the Northern region that as many as 250 UCATT shop stewards would attend their quarterly meeting. Even in these strongly organized areas, however, the strength of site organization was slipping back towards the end of the 1960s with the growth of LOSC.

Because of the patchy nature of organization, the instability of the labour force and frequent changes of site which militated against the formation of a stable shop steward cadre, members of UCATT and its constituent unions are highly full-time officer-dependent. This is reflected in the high ratio of FTOs to members, which in 1970 was 1:1500 and in 1975 1:2000.

Thus over the period to 1970 UCATT (ASW) experienced changes in job regulation that threatened to undermine its historical commitment to centralized bargaining. Wage drift was diminishing the value of the national agreement, made through the NFBTO. Moreover, the union also had reason for thinking, in the light of its relatively poor shop steward organization, that neither it nor the NFBTO was playing a major role in determining the level of earnings on site.

The processes and agents of change

In examining the processes and agents of change in UCATT we will follow the presentation used in respect of the TGWU without, we hope, repeating some of the general comments made in that study. We therefore examine the external factors before turning to consider the strategy adopted by UCATT's leadership.

The collective bargaining context
UCATT traditionally had the support of the employers' association in maintaining formal negotiations on an industry-wide basis for the construction industry, despite the high degree of 'wage drift'. The advantage of a standard rate for the employers in the construction industry was 'the benefit of known labour costs for tendering purposes, and the importance of labour costs as an element of total costs, although the employers also chose to introduce incentives in 1947'.[51]

Attempting to enforce national agreements, even with the employers' association's support, is not however particularly easy in a highly fragmented industry such as building. Moreover, there is also in the industry considerable employers' hostility to unionization and a policy in some areas of blacklisting union militants. Such actions are particularly effective barriers to unionization in an industry where the place of employment changes repeatedly as jobs are completed. In this kind of anti-union environment it is obviously difficult for the union to establish a strong shop steward system.

Variations in the levels of demand for labour – cyclical, seasonal and geographic – also make it difficult to enforce a standard of national agreement in the building industry. This was very noticeable in the period studied, when, as shown in the study of the UCATT merger, the growth of LOSC was closely associated with a high demand for labour. LOSC and the high demand for labour then in turn influenced the level of earnings as employers competed with each other for labour and particularly craftsmen. In these circumstances the competitive instinct overrode the employers' commitment to the national agreement.

The state also inadvertently and indirectly undermined the agreed standard wage by its restrictive incomes policies and taxation policies. As in other industries, the externally imposed constraint on wage increases tended to have a much greater impact on national agreements than on actual earnings. In an industry as fragmented as building, it was much easier for the craftsmen working on the 'lump' (LOSC) and the individual employer to avoid the policy than it was for the national employers' association and the NFBTO. Furthermore, the introduction of the Selective Employment Tax (SET) (see Chapter 6) and high levels of direct taxation and insurance encouraged both employer and worker to enter into individual contracts as a means of evading and/or avoiding the state's imposts. This clearly ran contrary to the attempts made by the union to maintain the collective, national and/or site agreements.

In its job regulation policy UCATT was further influenced by the presence of other unions in the industry. The TGWU more than any other union was seen as competing for members. As the TGWU grew in militancy, UCATT could not afford, by comparison with the TGWU, to be failing in its efforts to service its actual and potential membership.

Finally it should be said that UCATT's membership showed several of the features associated with a high level of membership participation in bargaining. They had a long tradition of union organization and solidarity built around a coherent occupational and industrial interest. They did not, however, have a high degree of employer support for site level bargaining. But neither, as will be shown later, was the union strongly committed to increasing low-level negotiations.

The content of collective bargaining

When incentives were introduced in 1947 the ASW opposed them because:

in post-war years new methods of construction have been introduced which have reduced the emphasis on skill and increased the value of higher levels of production. Moreover, the volume of production of individual and groups of workers is capable of measurement; a factor which has contributed to the growth of the practice of labour-only subcontracting.[52]

The earnings from the two elements, incentives and LOSC, were the factors that helped produce the wage drift noted above in the areas of change. For instance, in 1973 the NEDC Council Report stated that average earnings were in the area of £40 per week when the basic wage was about £26 per week. Moreover, during the same period earnings for workers on the 'lump' were quoted at £20 per day in London.[53]

By officially opposing incentives the ASW's leadership encouraged both employers and, where they existed, shop stewards to determine earnings free of union involvement. This policy weakened the union's relevance to members on building sites. And when LOSC grew in the 1960s the union's problems were compounded both by a further reduction in the contribution of the national agreement to actual earnings and by a consequent reduction in membership (see Chapter 6). In this very difficult environment the leadership sought for a strategy for job regulation that would restore the national standing of the union in the building industry.

Alternative strategies

Both the leadership of UCATT and the main opposition, the left-wing 'Charter' Group, were agreed on the need to combat the problem of LOSC and to de-casualize the industry. They both also wanted to make the union more immediately relevant to its actual and potential membership. The two, however, differed quite significantly on how this should be achieved.

The strategy of the general secretary, after he took office in 1959, was to pursue a policy of strengthening centralized bargaining and to resist diffusion of bargaining power by regaining the bargaining initiative from the workplace negotiators. On the other hand, the Charter Group's preferred strategy was to focus all aspects of job regulation at site level and to maximize local site organization. Their method of removing the 'lump' was grass-roots militancy and the blacking and picketing of sites where such labour is employed. Allied to this approach would be the extension of the closed shop and the enforcement of no-'lump' clauses in contracts with site employers.

Local bargaining appears, at least initially, to be a feasible strategy for UCATT to pursue. Indeed, the highly fragmented construction industry fulfils few of the conditions thought essential for the development of centralized collective bargaining and a standard industry rate. Controlling labour supply at the local level is a prerequisite of controlling the wage paid at the local level in a highly fragmented, competitive industry with a localized product market and no effective national employers' association (effective in the sense that it can control the activities of all the employers in the industry). As Cole wrote in 1913,

Working for a local market and for the most part on discontinuous jobs, labour in the building trade must be organised to some extent on a local basis. The locality is the unit which has to be paralysed; and as jobs are discontinuous, action has to be taken rapidly . . . success depends, in the building industry, on the complete paralysing of the job, or the locality; all the sections must act together and there must be some means of controlling all possible blacklegs.[54]

An examination in 1956 of the success of the building unions in the USA supports Cole's view:

over 80% of all workers in the industry in 1945 were covered by collective bargaining arrangements; of these, approximately 95% worked under closed shop provisions . . . the closed shop device is particularly fitted to the building industry because of the relatively short duration of jobs, the high rate of labour turnover, and the small size of firms. Under these conditions it becomes imperative for the union to exercise close control over the hiring practices of employers in order to prevent the continuing employment of non-union workers.[55]

The experience of the US construction unions is also borne out by the areas of strong UCATT organization in Britain. For instance, the Leicester district followed this pattern. In Leicester the ASW responded to the introduction of incentive schemes in 1947 by jointly determining bonus and plus rates, enforcing a closed shop policy and using the district office as an employment exchange for the local building industry. Other areas with a relatively high density of membership also pursued similar policies; in the Northern, North West and South Wales regions there is a long history of site negotiations over bonus incentives and plus rates. These areas tended, understandably, to be opposed to UCATT's official policy of centralization. Instead they tended to favour strong local control over job regulation, the extension of the closed shop principle, and measures to make FTOs more directly accountable to the membership.

There are, however, practical difficulties in adopting the localized approach as a universal response to the declining relevance and influence of the building unions. Because of previous difficulties UCATT was weakly organized in large parts of the country. It did not have the capability in many regions to exert the strong localized control typical of the stronger areas. Thus, a further decline in the importance of national negotiations would have placed the less strong areas in an even more difficult position. Indeed, in the absence of a fully fledged shop steward organization the end of national negotiations would have made the union less relevant than it already was by encouraging more employers to determine pay unilaterally according to their own needs.

The leadership also had political reasons for resisting pressure for devolution. In the construction industry site organizations tended to be 'left' in orientation. It was also unofficial and inter-union in character and hence largely outside the control of the official union hierarchy. This may be partly due, as Lord Cameron remarked in his 1967 Report on the Barbican and Horseferry Road sites, to the fact that

In a labour force the composition of which is variable and where it is obviously impracticable to have an elaborate code of procedure for intimation of candidatures, meetings for elections and election procedures themselves, it becomes easy for elections on what is an almost haphazard and casual basis to be controlled by persons determined to have themselves, their associates or nominees appointed or elected, always assuming that these persons are possessed of the necessary union qualifications and membership.[56]

It is more probable, however, in an industry in which the environment is often hostile to unionism, that those willing to 'stick their neck out' and organize sometimes need a strong ideological commitment to the 'struggle' to sustain them. In these circumstances inter-union and inter-site co-operation is often a necessary prerequisite to establishing a strong local union organization. The leadership's preferred strategy of strengthening centralized bargaining and regaining the initiative from the local level can therefore also be seen as an attempt if not to reduce at least to counter the growth of 'unofficial' movements and the 'left' at site level within the union.

In pursuing its own strategy the ASW's leadership attempted between 1970 and 1975 to restore credibility to their long-standing centralization policy through a variety of channels. In addition to the merger that formed UCATT (see Chapter 6), they tried political pressure to outlaw the 'lump' and they adopted a more militant industrial policy as well as accepting direct responsibility for national bargaining when they disbanded NFBTO. These actions were intended to improve the effectiveness of national wage negotiations.

UCATT received some support from the state and its agencies in its campaign against LOSC, primarily because the lack of control over 'lump' rates was a threat to incomes policies. For example, a Pay Board working party established during the period of Conservative incomes policy in the early 1970s found that there was 'sufficient evidence to show that some forms of labour-only sub-contracting by groups of self-employed operatives act against the aims of the [pay] code sufficiently to cause concern'. LOSC also involved a loss of revenue to the Exchequer.[57]

In 1970 the Labour government under some pressure from the building unions drafted the Construction Industry Contracts Bill, which broadly followed the recommendations of an inquiry headed by Phelps-Brown in 1968, the principal element of which had been the establishment of registers for the employers and the self-employed. The Bill died with the defeat at the polls of the Labour government. However, the new Conservative administration was also concerned about lost revenue through LOSC and introduced measures in the 1971 Finance Act. Evasion was commonplace, and the measures (being designed primarily to benefit the Exchequer rather than the union) were not in line with UCATT's own campaign. UCATT felt the legislation merely legitimized the 'lump' without impeding its growth, and the Conservatives eventually established an inquiry, the Misslebrook Committee, into the matter. George Smith commented that 'unfortunately this body failed to reach the kind of fundamental conclusions needed to resolve the problems of the industry and so, at the instigation of the unions, has been wound up on the basis of a generalised report'.[58]

In 1973 Eric Heffer, a UCATT-sponsored MP, attempted to steer through

Parliament a Private Member's Bill to 'prohibit labour-only sub-contracting (self-employment) in the building and construction industry'. Mr Heffer appeared to have instigated the Bill on his own initiative, although UCATT did give him assistance once it knew he was preparing it. The measures proposed were far more stringent than any previous ones and would have made it illegal for anyone to enter a contract involving the supply of labour to work as self-employed for most construction operations. When the Bill was presented the union actively supported it, and the Building Workers Charter Group was prominent in demonstrations in support of the Bill. On 18 May 1973 the Bill failed to get a second reading in the House of Commons. At this point UCATT was forced to return to bilateral arrangements of a voluntary nature with the employers. A register was established of forms that would, in strictly limited fashion, agree to control 'lump' labour.[59] The register was generally ineffective.

UCATT therefore continued to exert political pressure, primarily through the TUC's Construction Industry Committee. At its 1974 Conference the union received a commitment from the new Labour secretary of state for the environment who said that, although he believed it 'impractical to adopt the extreme solution of making work on the lump illegal',[60] the government intended to introduce measures that went beyond its own 1970 Bill. The tax exemption certificate scheme was tightened up and a Construction Industry Manpower Board was established, but without any legislative teeth. In the face of employers' opposition this was the best the unions could achieve through political action.

In parallel with its efforts to persuade the state to control LOSC, UCATT also attempted to make the practice less attractive and to reduce wage drift by forcing up the national wage rates beyond those available to 'lump' workers at the site level. George Smith, UCATT's general secretary, made this point in respect of the 1972 pay claim, which precipitated that year's dispute, when he said that 'We are by no means making an extravagant claim but merely asking for payments that are being negotiated at site level to be incorporated in the national agreement'.[61]

The building strike of 1972 was the industry's first national strike action since 1924. Agreement was reached after a three-month strike for a £6 per week rise. The deal was described by the unions as 'without doubt . . . the best that has ever been negotiated by any union at national level' in the construction industry.[62] The deal was due to last two and a half years and it included cost of living threshold payments.[63] During the strike the union's EC had taken the novel step of allowing individual company agreements. At the 1974 conference, however, the general secretary, adhering to the centralization strategy, reported that this step 'was not particularly successful' and UCATT made no attempt to extend the application of such agreements.

It was also no coincidence that the first national strike should follow both the formation and restructuring of UCATT (see Chapter 6) and UCATT's subsequent direct intervention in national bargaining as the dominant building industry union. As mentioned in Chapter 6, the merger that formed UCATT was intended to put greater 'muscle' behind national negotiations and to further centralize power in the ASW and other merging unions by replacing the district organization with a regional system of government. Moreover, the new union needed to prove itself in the industry almost immediately to halt its decline and match the wage demands that its chief competitor, the TGWU, was making. Furthermore, UCATT's withdrawal from the NFBTO, and then from its successor the National Federation of Construction Unions (a withdrawal that caused the disbandment of both federations), made the new union the dominant negotiator in its direct dealings with the employers. In this new role there was no hiding behind the NFBTO or other unions should the national negotiations fail to 'deliver the goods'. Militancy in UCATT was therefore, as in the TGWU, associated with restructuring, but in this case it was intended to confirm the value of centralized rather than decentralized bargaining.

The success of the 1972 strike did, however, depend to a considerable extent on the role played by local activists. This, together with the increased representation of Communist and other 'left-wing' elements at conference and on the General Council and EC, ensured that rule changes made in 1975 gave more recognition to shop stewards. The changes included measures to increase and institutionalize the position of shop stewards, strengthen local branch organization through the provision of full-time branch secretaries, and increase the liaison between branch and site organizations by establishing joint branch/steward committees.

The union still attempts, however, to exert a high degree of control over shop steward activities. Thus, in the rules shop stewards are responsible to the regional secretary. On the other hand, the control of lay members over the activities of FTOs has been increased by the extension of elections to include the five-yearly election of regional officials who were previously appointed. Moreover the lay regional councils have been strengthened and meet more frequently than they did initially. Fundamentally, however, the characteristic of FTO dependence or hierarchical control in the collective bargaining process continues as the official mode of organization. In practice the highly organized areas exert considerable local autonomy.

Thus, as a result of internal pressures, made more effective by the creation of a more unified decision-making structure following the UCATT merger, and the fact that in many cases the leadership's policy of centralization of bargaining was undermined at site level, the union has in practice proceeded by a mixture of both the unofficial and official strategies. Moreover, there has been a general 'leftward' shift in the composition of the national level leadership as a result of recent elections. These changes, combined with a growth in activity at site level, also produced a change in character in the period under study from a traditionally moderate, craft-conscious stance to a more broadly based militant policy. This development is now, after the 1975 rule changes, associated with a greater degree of formal diffusion of power at the site level, which may, over time, further weaken the union's traditional and present commitment to centralized job regulation.

Other unions

Of the other unions studied it is worth commenting on the decentralizing tendencies in the AEU–AUEW(E), the GMWU and NUPE and the centralizing movements in the POEU, the NUM and NUBE. We will examine the decentralizers before turning to the centralizing unions. In each section the areas of change will again be described before the processes and agents of change.

The decentralizers

Areas of change

Many other unions experienced decentralization of bargaining in some respect, including NALGO and the NUT, but in none was the change so comprehensive or so purposefully executed as the TGWU. The *AEU* for instance, was already highly decentralized and diffused in 1960; this tendency was however developed further after 1960. In federated companies the proportion of total earnings excluding overtime accounted for by the nationally negotiated minimum remained low over the period under study. As a percentage of union members' average earnings[64] (excluding overtime) the national minimum was 61 per cent in 1961, 56 per cent in 1965 and 59 per cent in 1972. Only 10–15 per cent of the membership in federated firms are on the minimum.[65] Non-federated private companies already used a combination of company-wide and workplace negotiations. The importance of workplace bargaining was, as in the case of the TGWU, increased by the growth of productivity agreements and more sophisticated PBR schemes.

The AEU also had a long history of shop steward involvement in negotiations at the district and domestic level. There were already 23,500 shop stewards in 1960 giving a ratio of stewards to members of 1:41. By 1973 there were 37,369 shop stewards, reducing the ratio of stewards to members to 1:30. The existing degree of decentralization and diffusion of power was reinforced by the abandonment of the final (national-level) stage of the Engineering Disputes Procedure in 1971 and the temporary disbandment of national level pay negotiations in 1972. These two developments constituted the major change in the AUEW during the period under study and reflected the new leadership's preference for shop floor power.

The *GMWU*'s major response to the growth of workplace bargaining and the need for adequate servicing at that level was different to the TGWU. Instead of relying more heavily on shop stewards, the GMWU followed the Donovan recommendation of an increase in the number of FTOs dealing directly with the shop floor. At the 1974 Congress a new FTO, to be known as district officer, was introduced. This followed a study by Professor Hugh Clegg and the Warwick University Industrial Relations Research Unit into the workload of the union's regional officials, which was commissioned following a decision of the 1971 Congress. The report concluded that there were insufficient FTOs in first-line contact with the membership at the local level. In the report, however, it was envisaged that the new district FTOs would encourage a certain degree of 'independence' on the part of the shop stewards: 'District Officers would have a special responsibility towards shop stewards. One means of coping with the rising volume of business from the plant is to develop the potentiality of shop stewards to handle business for themselves, by training them and improving the plant procedures through which they operate. . . .'[66]

Whereas the ratio of FTOs to members in the TGWU has decreased, in the GMWU it has increased, although compared with the TGWU the GMWU had had a rather low level of officering in 1960. In 1963 the GMWU's ratio of FTOs to members was 1:4974; in 1968, 1:4789; in 1973, 1:4807; and in 1976, after the introduction of district officers, it was 1:3809.[67] The figures slightly understate the full complement of FTOs since there were some full-time branch secretaries, and the introduction of branch administration officers in 1965 produced an additional seventy-seven FTOs at local level by 1973. Taking such FTOs into account for the 1976 figure the ratio would be 1:3164. Such an increase has not, however, necessarily implied an increase in FTO dominance. In general, the increase in FTO coverage has accompanied increasing lay participation and lay independence in collective bargaining processes. In fact, the union generally started to follow, at local level, the pattern set by the Scottish and Northern regional secretaries, who on taking office in 1959 and 1964 respectively were the first to begin to involve shop stewards in negotiations. Until their appointment, nowhere in the union (except in rare circumstances) would shop stewards conduct negotiating themselves.

In 1969 the GMWU introduced a system of national and regional industrial conferences, but these were not incorporated into the union's rule book and had no formal status in the decision-making structure. The 'purpose of industrial conferences will be to act as forums for discussion on industrial policy and as sounding boards for lay reaction to industrial development'.[68]

As we noted in Chapter 3, *NUPE* was initially the most centralized and concentrated union in our sample as far as job regulation was concerned. Towards the end of the period under study an attempt was made with a similar purposefulness to that in the TGWU to diffuse power within the union, particularly at local level.

Until the mid-1960s, the amount of local bargaining within NUPE was negligible. Even at the height of productivity bargaining, basic pay determined centrally accounted for 72 per cent of total manual pay in 1973, 70 per cent in 1974 and 68 per cent in 1975. Moreover, if account is taken of service supplements, London allowances, shift premiums and overtime pay, the rates of all of which are determined on an industry-wide basis, then an even higher proportion of total earnings is determined nationally: 87.6 per cent in 1963, 86.2 per cent in 1974 and 78 per cent in 1975.[69]

Prior to 1960 the relationship between NUPE's FTOs and lay members was, as in the TGWU and GMWU in the public sector, one of FTO dominance, but in

NUPE more uniformly so.[70] The channels for securing the leadership's accountability to the membership were largely ineffective. In 1974 the Warwick study reported that in their survey 51 per cent of branches had neither a direct nor an indirect delegate at the last National Conference held in May 1973.

Membership participation increased during the period under study, however. At the 1967 Conference the EC introduced a rule amendment to allow for the establishment of three national rank-and-file policy-making committees (Local Government, Health Service and Water Works), which 'would consider in detail the affairs of members covered by that committee'.[71]

By 1974 there were four national committees in rule (the Craftsmen's National Committee having been established), five in name (including an additional Committee for Universities) and six in practice (including the Ambulance Advisory Committee). These national committees were, like the EC, also highly dependent on the national FTOs who serviced them.

The most dramatic change in NUPE, however, was the rapid growth in shop steward organization. Thus, in 1974 only 12 per cent of branches in the Warwick study claimed to have had stewards for more than ten years; in 1970 39 per cent of branches had no union stewards at all and another 26 per cent had three or less, whereas by the middle of 1974 only 11 per cent of branches had no stewards and 56 per cent had four or more stewards. NUPE's EC Statement on Provision for Union Stewards dates only from mid-1970, and formal employer recognition of stewards and the provision of facilities dates from January 1969 in local government and 1971 in the NHS.[72]

The inexperience of such a rapidly created cadre of shop stewards,[73] however, ensured that the relationship of members and lay officials to the FTOs was still largely one of dependence. Many lay officials, according to the Warwick survey, still acted only as channels of communication between the FTO and the membership rather than as participants in the resolution of members' grievances and local mobilizers of membership action. For example, over a third of branches in their survey said that neither the branch secretary nor stewards met management on a day-to-day basis to deal with members' grievances or problems.[74] Further change was therefore required to facilitate further devolution of collective bargaining functions, to increase lay participation, and to reduce the dependence of the membership and lay officials on FTOs.

The 1973 NUPE National Conference decided to hold a Special National Conference on union reorganization and the EC commissioned a research team from the University of Warwick to examine the whole problem of reorganization.

The proposals suggested by the Warwick report for integrating the new national committees and the new shop steward organization more closely with the rest of the union's decision-making structure were accepted by the EC, and rule changes to effect them were submitted to a special National Conference on Union Reorganization in January 1975 and adopted by the conference. At the same time it was decided to increase the number of FTOs.

The processes and agents of change
The context in which the AEU–AUEW(E) and the GMWU bargained in the private sector underwent many of the changes described in the study of the TGWU. Both the AEU and the GMWU faced employers who took action, either by leaving an employers' association or withdrawing from industry-wide negotiations which unilaterally devolved the level of negotiations.

In common with all the other union studies, the three decentralizing unions were also affected by the state and its agencies' intervention in industrial relations. Incomes policies in particular promoted decentralizing trends. The GMWU was influenced by the Donovan Report and one of its authors, H. A. Clegg, in its decision to increase the numbers of FTOs (noted above) employed at the local level of union organization, although it should be mentioned that the new district officer was also probably at least partially modelled on the TGWU's officer structure.

The Donovan Report, together with the Industrial Relations Act of 1971, had an indirect impact on the course of the negotiations for a new procedure agreement in the engineering industry between the employees (EEF) and the CSEU. (In these negotiations the AUEW(E) was the dominant union voice.) The parties to the engineering procedure made only sporadic attempts to revise the procedure until 1969 when the EEF took the initiative. It is likely that the EEF was at least partly prompted to open talks on a revision of the procedure by adverse criticisms from, among others,[75] the Donovan Commission.

Subsequently the 1971 Industrial Relations Act played a role in determining the stance of both parties in the breakdown of negotiations and the withdrawal of the CSEU from the procedure in 1971. On the other hand, the unions' obduracy on the issue of a new procedure was reinforced by the Industrial Relations Act 1971. For, as the 1970 CSEU annual report stated, the threat of 'possible Government legislation for industrial agreements to be legally binding' was a major reason for not wishing to agree to a new procedure which the unions regarded as being unsatisfactory in a major respect: the absence of a *status quo* clause.

The employers, on the other hand, were anxious to achieve new agreements, either individually while the impasse at national level remained, or if possible collectively, through the achievement of a new national agreement. This was because of the effect of the Industrial Relations Act on employers, in particular the emphasis put on the need for clearly established written procedures in the 1971 Industrial Relations Code of Practice.

The bargaining context of the AEU, the GMWU and NUPE was also influenced by the presence of competing unions. In particular, the TGWU had a presence in all three unions' job territories. However, in the public sector the GMWU's greatest rival was NUPE. In the GMWU's case it tended to resist but later reluctantly followed the practices of its competitors. Thus, for example, it is very clear that the GMWU's introduction of industrial conferences was heavily influenced by the TGWU's trade groups and their attractiveness to potential members in the job territory shared by both unions. The introduction of district officers (as mentioned above) was similarly influenced by the TGWU. In the public sector NUPE and the GMWU tended to have similar policies regarding both commitment to centralized bargaining and FTO dominance prior to 1960, although they may have differed in other respects. NUPE, however, made the running in the switch to greater lay participation in bargaining, and it is unlikely that this has not also rubbed off on GMWU members.

The AUEW(E), although a major force within the Confederation of Shipbuilding and Engineering unions (CSEU), found its autonomy in relation to its strategy of decentralization in 1972 being undermined from without by some of the smaller craft unions in the CSEU. In particular the Foundry Workers,[76] the Pattern Makers and the Boilermakers continued to defend national agreements. For instance, even when the AUEW(E) were successful in devolving bargaining in engineering in 1972 the executive of the CSEU upheld the national negotiations in the shipyards, a move welcomed by the Boilermakers' president, who said: 'It would have been tragic if we had gone – in a shipbuilding industry which has received so much Government assistance – to the chaotic stage we have reached in the engineering industry. We could have brought the whole house down around our heads.'

In respect of the GMWU and NUPE the nature of their predominantly blue-collar membership suggested that they would be more favourably inclined towards centralization than decentralization of bargaining. The conditions for dependence on full-time officials in NUPE

owed much to the widely dispersed and fragmentary nature of NUPE membership, for whom close contact on the job, always an advantage for factory-based unionism, was the exception rather than the rule. This was not helped by the lack of trade union background among NUPE members (particularly women) many of whom had become trade unionists for the first time upon joining NUPE. . . . Understandably, all of these new trade unionists looked first to the full-time officials for guidance, support and judgment as well as representation before anti-union employers.[77]

To some extent the same could be said of the GMWU's membership, particularly in the public sector. In contrast, the AUEW(E)'s membership had all the contrary features associated normally with membership independence of full-time officials.

The leadership of all three unions therefore experienced a number of sometimes contrasting factors affecting the context in which they bargained. But in this context the content of bargaining also influenced the unions. For instance, the AUEW(E) had for many years in the engineering industry encountered various forms of PBR systems. This obviously helped to limit the impact of national agreements, which were sometimes seen as 'meaningless' in prosperous areas. Moreover, the national negotiations were further limited in their importance by the agreements of 1964 and 1968 which gave another impetus to workplace negotiations by encouraging productivity bargaining. The 1964 deal produced a 'general framework for local productivity bargaining',[78] while in

1968 'The parties agree[d] that improvements in pay and conditions could be negotiated at the domestic level provided . . . there is a measured increase in labour productivity or efficiency'.[79]

NUPE's and the GMWU's membership in the public sector were late in jumping on the productivity bargaining bandwagon. In their case the impact of productivity agreements on the relative importance of various bargaining levels lasted well into the second half of the period under study.

In 1967, following Report no. 29 of the NBPI on local authorities, the NHS and Gas and Water Supply,[80] locally agreed bonus and productivity schemes were introduced in both the NHS and local government. In 1966 the NBPI estimated that 16 per cent of males employed by local authorities in England and Wales were covered by incentive bonus schemes.[81] By 1974 the local authority employers claimed that among full-time manual employees 49 per cent were receiving work study payments, 7.5 per cent were receiving other productivity payments and 8.2 per cent were receiving lead-in payments. Similar proportions were involved in the NHS. In 1973 the general secretary of NUPE claimed that 60 per cent of the membership were on bonus schemes of some kind and it was estimated that they were worth an average of £5 per week.[82] In that year, however, conference voted against embarking on any new schemes.

Thus in NUPE, as in the TGWU and the GMWU, a major contributory factor to the greater participation of lay members in the bargaining process was the introduction of productivity bargaining:

The development of local bargaining and locally negotiated bonus schemes, largely resulting from National Board for Prices and Incomes Report 29, called for decisions by those groups of members affected by the proposals and for the monitoring of such schemes by lay members once they had been put into practice. In providing them with the opportunity to accept, reject or modify such schemes, rank and file members gained an importance in the bargaining process that was unknown to the mass of NUPE membership in the past.[83]

The introduction of productivity bargaining also increased the work load of local FTOs, who previously had little direct part in the national level bargaining process.

Alternative strategies

In the face of the above external factors affecting the context and content of bargaining, the leaders chose their strategies. The leadership of the *AUEW(E)* underwent a noticeable change in attitude towards devolution and shop floor militancy in the late 1960s and early 1970s. This change was greatly influenced by the political changes at the top of the union's hierarchy, including Scanlon's rise to the Presidency (see Chapter 4). Whereas Carron was prepared to allow shop floor bargaining – indeed, in the face of the dispersed nature of the union's power structure he could do little else – Scanlon and the left 'progressives' who elected him to power in 1968 positively encouraged it.

One manifestation of the change in leadership attitude was that the reaction to shop floor strikes changed from Carron's 'Get them back to work' instructions to Scanlon's positive encouragement of such actions. This change is illustrated by the marked increase in dispute benefit between the Carron and Scanlon periods: payments rose from £114,709 in 1967 to £605,094 in 1970.[84]

However, the most spectacular indication of the difference in leadership attitude was shown by Scanlon's attempt to shift bargaining more towards the local level by withdrawing from the 1922 Procedure. Before the presidential election in 1967 the union's official view of the much maligned National Procedure was expressed by Lord Carron in February 1966 in the union's evidence to the Donovan Commission.

It has been said in the past that the Procedure for the Avoidance of Disputes is an unnecessarily slow process and is, in many cases, used by the employers as part of a general process of delay rather than as a genuine attempt to settle any particular dispute. *This is a view that the AEU would not agree with as a general rule today. . . .*

And the evidence continued:

one of the brighter aspects . . . has been the change of attitude on the part of the employers at national level towards the Disputes Procedure. . . . Negotiations are now taking place in a more cordial and co-operative atmosphere and given goodwill on both sides many of the criticisms of the past may no longer be relevant in the very near future.

However, the unions did

feel the Agreement itself could well be modified to rid it of one outstanding anomaly, and to meet the union's position on one or two other points. . . .
. . . . Thus over the years – the last time in 1961 – we have approached the EEF with a view to the *maintenance of the status quo* . . . the whole procedure has been exhausted – but with no success.[85]

The official view during Lord Carron's period of office was therefore that, although the union preferred some amendments to the Procedure, it was far more sympathetic to it than the various outside critics.[86]

Indeed, this view was shared by many of the divisional organizers and EC members during the Scanlon period, many of whom did not take a consistently adverse view of the old agreement largely because most of them felt that the union and the members could safely ignore it, or as one EC member put it, 'the Procedure was OK because it was obsolete'.

Even within the 'progressive' camp outright opposition to the 1922 National Procedure was not universal. For instance, Reg Birch (on the extreme left of EC) had with John Boyd (a moderate) reached agreement with the employers on amendments to the procedure including a *status quo* clause.[87] However, Scanlon and the majority of the progressives were determined to secure an end to the 1922 procedure. They were determined not to agree to a 'patched up' agreement which might become enforceable under the Industrial Relations Act. They were not, therefore, willing to enter into new talks for a national procedure unless their demands were met in full by the EEF. In March 1976[88] these demands were met and a new agreement was signed.

The new leadership's determination to achieve a major revision of the national procedure was important in seeing it through to its radical conclusion. Scanlon's own ideological satisfaction in the achievement of the new procedural agreement was manifest in his presidential address at the 1976 National Committee:

The Executive Council are in the happy position this year of being able to place before you the new Procedure Agreement recently concluded between the CSEU and the EEF. It brings to an end a period in our history when, following the 1922 lockout, we were subjected to a Procedure Agreement which was repugnant to us in its conception and imposition. So distasteful was it that, as our strength grew, so more and more members treated it with contempt until, in 1971, we withdrew from it completely.... We now have a procedure agreement which, in a true sense, has been mutually agreed.

Scanlon and the progressives' commitment to shop floor bargaining similarly influenced the union's withdrawal in 1972 from attempts to secure a substantive national agreement. The president looked for domestic negotiators to achieve the bargaining objectives which the union could not deliver at national level. On this occasion, however, the leadership of the AUEW(E) and the membership were not wholly united. Indeed, a motion on the agenda for the NC that year called for a renewal of national talks. Moreover, it went on to argue that the decision to refer the national claim to plant level would do 'untold damage to the dignity, status and prestige' of the union and place shop stewards in an intolerable position.[89]

In the highly diffused AUEW(E) the rank and file were in a position not only to put hostile motions but also to refuse to implement the national policy. The thirteen points contained in the original claim[90] were arbitrarily trimmed down in some districts to suit the members' local requirements. For instance, in the Tyne District the stress was laid on an increase in the minimum and actual wage rates and on two extra days' holiday. Moreover, it was claimed by observers at the time that less than 50 per cent of EEF members actually had the claim put to them.[91] The Sheffield and Manchester Districts were most active in pursuit of the claim. By June 1972, in contrast to other districts, they had presented 90 per cent of their EEF members with the claim.[92] These two districts featured regularly between 1960 and 1973 as the areas with some of the lowest average earnings (less overtime) in the union. They thus had most to gain from new arrangements incorporating the 'thirteen points'. Moreover, in 1971 these two districts were dominated by the left or progressives.

The evident lack of response at local level, with the exception of the Manchester and Sheffield areas, brought criticism from Scanlon at the 1972 NC. Scanlon complained that, while the EC was continually receiving resolutions accusing it of abrogating leadership by abandoning national negotiations, some stewards, able to negotiate high earnings within their own establishments, had done 'nothing to challenge the miserable basic rates and holiday entitlements' in the engineering industry as a whole. He also went on to admonish the NC members for 'some surprising contradictions' between their votes for the local bargaining strategy and their 'criticism and inactivity in its application'.[93] In the face of these difficulties national negotiations were resumed in 1973.

It can therefore be concluded that the AUEW's leadership was not entirely successful in its chosen strategy of devolution. Although the new leadership of Scanlon and the left-wing progressives created the pre-conditions for formal domestic substantive and procedural agreements by withdrawing from the existing national negotiations and procedures, they could not ensure compliance with their strategy. The AUEW(E) was, in fact, already so decentralized and diffused that the leadership had little chance of actually enforcing their strategy at the local level.

Unlike the TGWU, the *GMWU* did not actively seize upon the favourable external circumstances to decentralize enthusiastically their collective bargaining functions to the shop floor. The response varied between regional secretaries and NIOs; some encouraged the devolution of bargaining and the development of shop steward organization but others were much less enthusiastic. One official claimed, for example, that he did not think he was paid a salary simply to be a postman. In the early 1960s the NIO responsible for the electricity industry was heavily committed to centralized control of negotiations, as were, for example, the regional secretary for Lancashire and the regional secretary for Liverpool, in whose region Pilkington's was situated. In contrast, as mentioned above, the Scottish regional secretary, Alex Donnet, and the Northern regional secretary, Andrew Cunningham, pursued policies that encouraged shop steward activity and helped devolve bargaining responsibilities. The reasoning behind their policies was similar to the pragmatic factors influencing the TGWU, namely as an aid to growth and as an economy measure. During the 1960s a number of other regional secretaries retired and were replaced by officials who, it was clear from interviews with them, took a similar view to Donnet and Cunningham. Thus Jim Mason was appointed regional secretary in Birmingham and West Midlands and Cyril Unwin in Midlands and East Coast regions in 1965 and 1970; Harry Robertson was appointed regional secretary in London; Derek Gladwin in the Southern and Walter Aldritt in the Liverpool, North Wales and Irish region after 1970.

The autonomy of regional secretaries was strengthened in the collective bargaining sphere by the established general secretary's lack of interest in this area of the union's activities. But after Donovan he marginally changed his attitude towards the decentralization and diffusion of bargaining, from one that had been almost wholly unsympathetic. However, he still did very little positively to encourage it. He simply made adaptations when change of some kind became unavoidable. Thus, all the changes that occurred during Lord Cooper's ten years in office, while providing a potential for fundamental change in the future, were largely cosmetic.

The introduction of industrial conferences provides an example of this attitude. At the union's congress in 1968 a motion was carried unanimously and was supported by Lord Cooper, but the structure that eventually emerged was markedly less ambitious than the movers of the motion had envisaged. The objective of the leadership was to 'construct a way of improving our industrial communications which preserves our system of overall central control and regional flexibility while encouraging greater membership participation and identification'.[94]

However, the provisions for operating industrial conferences were rather unclear. Regional secretaries and NIOs were largely free to interpret them as they saw fit. Thus, as in the case of other attempts at decentralization and diffusion of bargaining, the actual effect was largely dependent on the power and attitudes of the regional secretaries and NIOs. The result was that those new regional secretaries who were favourable to devolution and had supported the creation of industrial conferences operated the new system in a positive manner, whereas the 'old guard' were determined that the industrial conferences should not usurp their own power.

Given Lord Cooper's general approach to collective bargaining, which left regional secretaries and NIOs free to deal with problems in an *ad hoc* manner if and when they saw fit, the explosion of mass membership (some 9000 members) discontent at Pilkington's[95] in 1970 came as a traumatic shock.

The strike at Pilkington's began as a substantive wage dispute, the first strike since 1870, but soon turned into a strike against the GMWU when the latter refused to declare it official. It brought to the surface a mounting discontent against the GMWU which was articulated by the unofficial Rank and File Strike Committee (RFSC). In the fifth, sixth and seventh weeks of the strike the GMWU tried to regain the initiative from the RFSC but failed to do so. The strike was finally ended after seven weeks by the mediation of the TUC. During the strike the NEC set up a sub-committee to inquire into the branch organization at St Helens (91 Branch) and 'its appropriateness to the needs of our members in the Pilkington factories in St Helens'. The sub-committee heard evidence from officials and staff at Liverpool regional office and from shop stewards and members of Branch 91. They were also provided with copies of the GMWU evidence to and the report of the Court of Inquiry into the dispute.[96]

The internal report[97] concluded that the constitutional provisions for lay involvement in collective bargaining and other issues already existed but had been allowed to atrophy. The sub-committee recommended the reorganization of the branch on a plant rather than geographical basis and steps needed to rejuvenate the democratic branch procedures.

Although the deterioration of the Pilkington branch could have happened in many other unions, there have rarely been such explosive results. For the GMWU, however, the significance of the Pilkington's dispute went much wider. Nine thousand members could not be shrugged off or possibly encouraged to leave the union, as had happened in some similar cases in the past.[98] The

Pilkington explosion was a clear warning of what could happen if members became alienated from the decision-making processes within the union. Hence, although reforms emerging from the inquiry were largely concerned with the 91 Branch, the trauma at Pilkington's acted as a catalyst for other changes not immediately related to it. It called into question the adequacy of officer coverage at the local level; it also strengthened the case for industrial conferences.

The disaffected Pilkington members, in forming a breakaway union – the Glass and General Workers' Union (hoping ultimately to transfer to the TGWU), also highlighted the importance of inter-union competition to the GMWU. As the internal inquiry states,

We must remember that in many of the plants and industries in which we are involved, we will not be able to come to terms with our failures in isolation from the activities of other unions. In manufacturing and the process industries, in the service industries and even in the once 'safe' public sector we are often the weak link in a chain of inter-union tension. In multi-union situations internal crises of the kind we have faced at Pilkington would provide a field day for the other unions. Our ability to retain our membership ultimately depends on our broader credibility as an organisation.

While Pilkington's was indicative of discontent among the rank and file, the younger officials and the 'new wave' of regional secretaries were equally keen for change in the union. David Basnett was elected general secretary in 1973 on a 'platform of change', and he influenced two developments that are of particular importance in the collective bargaining context: the strengthening of industrial conferences, and the introduction in 1974 of a new type of FTO – the district officer.

The new general secretary moved cautiously in relation to industrial conferences – not surprisingly, since many of the regional secretaries and some NIOs were still opposed to their being given any real power; indeed, he opposed a motion at the 1973 Conference to strengthen their powers and increase lay involvement in them. However in a report accepted by Conference in 1975 the structure of industrial conferences was formalized and improved to make them more effective and representative of lay opinion.

The introduction of full-time district officers also followed the new leadership's concern to make the union more responsive at local level. Although the new officials were still subject to the authority of the regional secretaries (rule 19, new clause 5a), 'A District officer shall at all times be under the control of and work under the direction of the Regional Secretary'. The introduction of a new officer, rather than simply extending the number of branch administration officers, enabled a fresh approach to be made in the definition of their responsibilities. First, by introducing a new officer, the task of shifting the emphasis of the union's local officials away from administration towards servicing the local membership was made much easier. Such a shift in emphasis was the key change required by Basnett. Second, Basnett was trying to ensure that far more money was available to develop a network of local officials with the aim of creating a network of district officers, similar to the district secretaries in the TGWU. The latter, the leadership believed, had been an important factor in the TGWU's ability to service and recruit their local membership.

Thus a combination of internal pressures was crucial to changes in job regulation in the GMWU. The lay membership pressure, exploding most dramatically at Pilkington's, and the gradual emergence of more progressive regional secretaries and a general secretary committed to changing the image of the GMWU, together prompted changes in the organization of collective bargaining. These have involved an attempt to strengthen lay participation and an expansion in local level FTOs. None of these changes have, however, much reduced the power of the regional secretaries, and the success of such measures is still largely dependent on the willingness of regional secretaries to operate them in the spirit in which they were conceived.

In contrast to the AUEW(E) but in common with the TGWU, *NUPE* had no tradition of decentralization and diffusion.[99] While the development of productivity bargaining in the late 1960s provided the external impetus for decentralization and diffusion, it was the leadership and FTOs of the union who sponsored the radical change from high dependence of lay members on FTOs to a position of greater independence, and the growth of shop stewards.

The centralized and concentrated NUPE was facing a growing workload from rapid membership growth, productivity bargaining and the reorganization of local government and health service. If they continued with the same system of decision-making and did not considerably increase the number of FTOs, there would be a reduction in the level of service to the members. This course would not have helped NUPE in its attempts to remain economically and industrially viable in a highly competitive union environment in which the trade-off between subscriptions and services is a crucial factor in joining one union rather than another, particularly in the lower paid areas covered by NUPE. Thus, as in the case of the TGWU, an ideological commitment to greater democracy combined with issues of economy and effectiveness to persuade the leadership and the FTOs to choose the other strategy, which was increasing lay involvement and participation in the bargaining process.

The transition to a greater role for lay officers began by using persuasion and encouragement as the main instrument of change. As Fryer *et al.* commented,

a number of full time officers, sometimes aided by active lay officials, have coaxed, encouraged and even bullied in order to foster the growth of union stewards and the development of greater membership involvement and self-reliance. Certainly, it must be said that full time officers, both national and local, formally and informally, have played an important part in thus 'sponsoring' democracy and greater involvement in the union.[100]

However, as the Warwick authors stressed, there were limitations to such an approach while the basic structure of the union remained untouched: 'If an expansion of democratic involvement and self-reliance is desired, then it should follow naturally from the operation of the Union's overall structure. . . . This is certainly not to deny the value of the initiatives and dedication of many individuals, but simply to emphasise the importance of a *structural framework* for such efforts.'[101]

It was presumably with such considerations in mind that the leadership of NUPE took the step in 1973 of asking the academics at Warwick to undertake a study of all aspects of NUPE's work with a view to improving its organization to achieve both greater efficiency and greater democracy.

The Warwick team found several weaknesses in the existing organization of NUPE as far as collective bargaining functions were concerned. The coverage and size of constituencies of shop stewards varied widely, and they were not clearly integrated into the existing union structure, particularly at branch level. Thus, in 1970 a statement on Provisions for Union Stewards issued by the EC declared that 'To support Stewards in their activities at the work place and to maximise co-operation between the Branch and the Stewards the Branch should: establish a Branch Committee which includes the Stewards; or establish a Stewards' Committee within the Branch'.[102] But the Warwick study found that only 32 per cent of branches had a functioning branch committee and only 22 per cent of branches said that they held branch committee meetings which were in effect meetings of the stewards in the branch; 52 per cent of the branches did not hold special meetings for union stewards, and 65 per cent of stewards said that they were not involved in any committee of the branch or section or at their place of work.

The team also found some ambiguity in the role of the national committees, established in 1967, and agreed that they should be more closely associated with the formulation and progress of national negotiations in their area.

It is therefore not clear how successful NUPE's leadership will be in weaning its members away from their traditional dependence on FTOs, especially given the nature of their membership. The changes recommended by the EC clearly represent, however, a serious attempt to create attitudes more conducive to lay participation. This and the structural changes should, in the longer run, lead to the implementation of the leadership's devolutionary strategy.

The centralizers

Areas of change

The POEU, NUM and NUBE had rather more success in achieving or retaining centralized bargaining than UCATT, although by the end of the period under study there were signs that the NUM might be unable to sustain it.[103]

Although throughout the period under study the *POEU* was engaged in productivity bargaining,[104] it negotiated nationally on all elements of pay. It considered that a centralized policy was essential if it was to ensure that gains from productivity were to be spread evenly among the membership. There was also the long-standing view, supported by the vast majority of the membership, that national rates should be retained, and that many more sections of the membership would lose than would gain from decentralization to local or regional bargaining. Maintaining such a policy, however, was not without its difficulties.

Members tended to resist productivity agreements as a whole and to attempt to reduce the pace of their introduction to allow time for them to be absorbed. At the same time local branch officials demanded additional FTOs and more lay representatives to ease the workload arising from the increased volume of changes in work practices. The leadership resisted the demands[105] on the grounds that the major negotiations on pay and conditions were still conducted at national level. They did however concede that developments in the Post Office involved more on-the-spot negotiations at regional and area levels and that these might necessitate the full-time secondment of area secretaries.

The need at local level for additional support for branch officials was expressed in a motion to the 1968 Conference asking for the establishment of local branch representatives in each workplace. At the 1970 Conference the constitutional position of branch representatives within the POEU was agreed. By 1973 approximately 2000 branch representatives had been appointed.

In the case of the NUM the transformation from local to national negotiations was achieved by three major agreements. The National Day Wage Agreement of 1955 placed every existing day wage job (of which there were over 6500 local titles) within thirteen separate grades. But while this established the principles of a national day wage rate, piecework rates continued to be a source of inequities both between various piecerate jobs and between the latter and day rates. The 1966 National Power Loading Agreement (NPLA) was intended to place all power-loading workers on to a day wage rate. From 6 June 1966 area and pit agreements that were based largely on piecework were to be gradually replaced by 'standard shift payments' (based on measured day work) to men working on power-loaded coal faces (90 per cent total coal production at that time came from such work). Differences between areas were such that a uniform national rate was not in operation until the introduction of the national day wage structure in June 1971.

The NPLA produced a rapid change in the contribution of the industry-wide basic rate to the total earnings of miners. For example, over the short period September 1968–April 1970 the proportion of total earnings accounted for by basic pay increased from 69.0 to 79.2 per cent while the element accounted for by payment by results decreased from 11.5 to 2.3 per cent.[106] An attempt to reverse this process by introducing pit-based productivity deals put to the NUM executive in September 1974[107] was rejected by the membership in November in a decisive 3:2 ballot.

As the amount of piecework and associated local bargaining declined, so the number of local disputes declined. At the same time the NUM's willingness to take action nationally increased and there were prolonged national strikes in favour of a much higher basic national rate in both 1971–72 and 1974.

The shift to national-level pay negotiations transferred the centre of influence to national level and those area officials who sit on the NEC. Branch power was also reduced *vis-à-vis* the areas as well as the national level. Whereas before 1966 delegates to the Area Council were privy to the precise course of bargaining at their individual pits, after 1966 they were dependent on the area officials, not only for communicating and interpreting the results of national negotiations, but also for carrying branch views to the national level.

NUBE achieved recognition from the clearing banks after a fifty-year struggle, culminating in strike action in 1967. The Joint Negotiating Council for Banking in English Clearing Banks was officially ratified in May 1968. The new agreement provided for joint negotiations by NUBE and the internal staff associations with the Federation of London Clearing Bank Employers at national level to cover a wide range of issues. After that date NUBE attempted, against the opposition of its partner in negotiations, the staff associations, to shift the maximum number of issues to the national level. For example, they tried without success to transfer the issues of pensions and holidays from the company to industry-wide level.

Full domestic recognition in all the clearing banks was not achieved until 1969. Now domestic (company) negotiations cover all negotiable issues not negotiated at industry level. The scope of issues negotiated at domestic level has widened, especially with the introduction of sophisticated job evaluation schemes.

The high degree of centralization and FTO dominance that was suited to the pre-1968 non-recognition situation came under increasing strain with the development of collective bargaining as the primary union activity. The increasing scope and complexity of negotiations in the banks led to demands for greater institutional autonomy ('internalism'), and this, combined with the transition from being a union providing 'individual services' to one heavily involved in collective bargaining, led to demands for greater lay participation for reference-back procedures and for more effective officer coverage and utilization.

The demand for greater autonomy was recognized by the incorporation of national advisory councils into the union rules in 1975, following a rule amendment by the EC. Moreover, a major step towards giving certain sections of the membership even greater autonomy and separate identity was made at the 1976 Conference when a rule amendment which allowed the EC to establish a separate section of the union if appropriate, with its own national committees for each employer, section council, section conference and its own geographically based and exclusive branches, was passed.

The large amount of work arising at the institutional level as a result of the increasing scope and complexity of bargaining and the inability of NUBE to afford extra FTOs resulted in the negotiation of secondment of union representatives[108] along the lines developed earlier by the staff associations. Another development following a well established practice in the internal staff associations, and of course in many 'bona fide' unions, was the introduction in 1972 of office representatives.

The processes and agents of change

The context in which the POEU bargained was changed when the Post Office became a public corporation and in consequence altered its management structure. The Post Office management had made it clear to the Select Committee on Nationalized Industries in 1967[109] that it preferred a system of regional or local bargaining to the civil service system of national-level negotiations. Although the POEU resisted this pressure, the devolution of many other management functions to regional level was a major factor in the development of area co-ordinating committees in the POEU whose function is to co-ordinate branch representation to management.

Although all the unions were influenced to some degree by the state's and its agencies' intervention in industrial relations, NUBE in particular was affected by the CIR. For instance, the introduction of a comprehensive office representative system in Williams & Glyns Bank was largely precipitated by a CIR report on the Bank which stated that NUBE's contact with the membership left much to be desired. In comparison with NUBE the competing union – the Staff Association – was found by the CIR to have more effective internal consultative machinery and an extensive system of office representatives. The CIR suggested that NUBE could usefully adopt the best aspects of the WGSA's organization; this the union duly did.

Although in this case the staff associations indirectly helped NUBE establish a 'shop steward' system, it is probable that the existence of competing staff associations generally had a negative influence in relation to NUBE's development of shop stewards. The staff associations had for a long time had 'office representatives' and 'seconded representatives' supported with facilities from the banks. This was seen by NUBE as part of the general lack of independence from the employers that characterized internal staff associations. NUBE was hypersensitive to the introduction of such systems within their own structure because of their historical association with employer domination, and this may have been one reason for the slow introduction of such lay officers following recognition.

NUBE's centralization policy was also to some extent influenced by the nature of its membership. The 'green' nature of the membership and hostility of the major employers to NUBE prior to 1968 were factors leading to membership dependence on FTOs. During the pre-1968 period NUBE members could suffer victimization for participation in union duties. This put a premium on having FTOs to take up cases and to organize the membership, secure in their position of independence of the employer. This, of course, placed NUBE's bargaining in a very different context to that enjoyed by the POEU and the NUM.

NUBE's bargaining context was therefore, among the centralizing unions, the one most exposed and most sensitive to pressure from other unions. Whereas NUBE was committed to centralized bargaining in the clearing banks, both ASTMS and the internal staff associations were committed to company-level bargaining. Indeed, the question of which level of bargaining is most suited to the banking sector proved to be a major point of controversy between NUBE and the staff associations.

In contrast the POEU increased its independence *vis-à-vis* other unions during the period under study. The POEU has always attempted to achieve maximum independence to pursue its own collective bargaining strategy, when appropriate, as typified by its decision in 1919 to have a separate Whitley Council for engineering staffs in the Post Office.

Although the Post Office management has always tried to impose similar arrangements to those in the rest of the civil service on the POEU, the POEU succeeded in staying outside the civil service Central Pay Settlements arrangements[110] except when it suited them not to. Attempts were made by conference delegates at various times to move away completely from the civil service system, rejecting the notion of 'fair comparisons' and depending completely on normal commercial criteria.[111]

Moreover, the change of the Post Office to corporation status mentioned above strengthened the independence of the POEU to pursue its own collective bargaining objectives and strategy. The Post Office was no longer bound by the Priestley pay formula for the civil service. Within the new corporation they have been able to make agreements covering the whole of their membership and have had more flexibility in negotiating productivity agreements. Although the POEU is a member of the Council of Post Office Unions (COPOU) which replaced the Whitley staff side organization of the civil service period, it has resisted any move towards the degree of joint union negotiations which prevailed when the Post Office was part of the civil service.

The content of NUBE's bargaining changed over the period studied through the introduction of job evaluation schemes and job restructuring exercises. It was these developments, rather than the productivity bargaining experienced by the POEU, that brought devolutionary pressure to bear on NUBE. The introduction of job evaluation schemes that could only be negotiated and monitored at local level increased the pressure from members for greater decentralization and diffusion of collective bargaining responsibility. The growth of job evaluation and clerical work measurement also had a similar impact on the level of bargaining in other white-collar unions, including NALGO.

For the NUM, however, the changing content of collective bargaining had a centralizing and concentrating impact. In the NUM the gradual elimination of piecework since 1966 in favour of a day wage structure reduced the amount of collective bargaining and the participation of officials at pit level and increased the power of the centre.

Alternative strategies

The *POEU* maintained its commitment to a centralized collective bargaining strategy despite the growth of productivity agreements. This strategy was carried without substantial opposition from membership. It was also well suited to the bargaining environment in which the POEU operated.

Productivity deals were enthusiastically grasped by the leadership of the

POEU, not only as a means of benefiting under the incomes policy but also as a means of establishing greater recognition for the technical expertise of their membership. The NEC and Charles Smith (general secretary) in particular supported the Labour government's incomes policy on political grounds, as did the majority of orthodox Labour Party activists in the union. Charles Smith was then sufficiently influential as a result of his reputation for 'delivering the goods' to carry the rest of the indifferent membership with him, at least in the early stages. The NEC would have been unable to retain the support of the membership, however, had the POEU not been able to manipulate incomes policy and productivity bargaining to their advantage. The POEU did rather better than many other unions during the period of incomes policy, particularly those in the public sector and the civil service.[112]

The leadership's enthusiasm for productivity-based agreements was based on several factors. They broadly argued that technical changes would happen in any case and they therefore ought to profit by them in wage terms and secure a greater degree of joint regulation in their introduction. Moreover, the POEU was on record as having favoured the expansion and development of telecommunications and had taken considerable political action to encourage such a policy. The union was also aware that increased efficiency in the context of an expanding industry would not carry the threat of redudancy.[113]

The POEU leadership waged a considerable campaign to secure the membership's acceptance of productivity bargaining. The *Journal*, the education programme and, in 1968, a 'teach-in', which was also attended by management, were used to popularize the policy.

Although on the whole beneficial to POEU members, productivity deals could have easily caused splits in the union. The POEU in 1960 had but recently succeeded in welding the organization together following a series of secessions of particular occupational groups.[114] General restraint on incomes combined with productivity agreements threatened to create similar conditions to those that had caused 'breakaways' in the past. It was imperative therefore that all should benefit from the productivity schemes.

The leadership's original strategy was to negotiate long-term productivity agreements centrally, which, although affecting particular groups of members, would lead to across-the-board increases for all groups. But the tightly drawn criteria for productivity increases laid down in incomes policy White Papers and the attitude of the Post Office initially prevented such an approach. Therefore the leadership evolved the strategy of 'caterpillar tactics' whereby it varied the grade with which bargaining was opened and for whom it gained the largest proportionate increase from year to year to ensure that all were eventually treated equally. For such a strategy to work it was essential that the agreements should be determined centrally.

Despite attempts to ensure that grades were treated equally, however, there were still forceful complaints in letters to the *Journal*, at Conference and at the 1968 'teach-in'. From 1968 onwards, therefore, claims were submitted for across-the-board productivity increases, and following the end of the Labour government's incomes policy and the transfer of the Post Office to corporation status, the employers had the flexibility to meet such demands.[115]

There was little opposition to the centralized nature of negotiations over productivity. Opposition focused on the issue of productivity bargaining as such and on the need for additional union manpower to cope with its impact at local level. Some members, particularly on the 'left' of the POEU, had always been critical of productivity bargaining.[116] But their criticisms were taken up more generally by 1968, when it was claimed that the pay was not fully compensating for the intensification of work that was taking place under productivity agreements. The pressure arising from the latter was compounded by the introduction of 'Management by Objectives' techniques at first-line supervisory level which resulted in additional pressure on the workforce. Fears were also being expressed that productivity agreements were leading to unemployment, although within telecommunications the labour force was expanding. These views were reflected in increasingly hostile conference motions.

The increased pressures at branch, area and regional level also created a demand for more FTOs and lay officials. The NEC was opposed to an increase in FTOs or a devolution of FTOs to regional or area level. Some branches also felt that such a change would further impinge on their autonomy. The NEC did agree, however, to the proposal from the membership that branch representatives should be chosen by the branch and established in each workplace. These developments too aroused mixed feelings among some branches. Some branch officials saw the representatives as a threat to their own position and influence, whereas others welcomed them as an addition to their own power and facilities.

Thus by the end of the period under study, the productivity strategy was coming under considerable criticism. There was also a growing uneasiness among those who valued the occupational basis of POEU organization at the erosion of the powers of the branches in favour of new structures within the union. The fears of such groups were not totally without foundation, for the leadership, if not the membership at large, was convinced that by the end of the period the existing occupational divisions enshrined within the constitution were no longer wholly appropriate or effective. The occupational distinctions between 'internal' and 'external' engineers were becoming increasingly blurred as a result of technical changes and the new flexibility introduced under the productivity agreements. A more co-ordinated approach was therefore required at area level to match the strengthened, developed management structure under the new Post Office corporation.

Like the TGWU, the POEU leadership seized upon productivity bargaining as a means of pursuing broader ends, although with totally different objectives in mind. In the case of the POEU it was seen as a means of maintaining maximum flexibility in negotiations in a period of incomes policy and in the comparatively rigid civil service context. But in order for flexibility to be compatible with the other objective of integrating the various grade levels and occupational groups within the POEU, it had to be done within a centralized framework. By seizing the initiative early it prevented management from initiating moves that might have split the union. Having taken the decision the leadership proceeded to sell it hard, and secured the adaptation of the union machinery to accommodate it. However, towards the end of the 1960s protests began to emerge and modifications in the policy and its outcomes were accordingly made.

In the *NUM*, as in UCATT, the issue of centralized versus decentralized bargaining was closely bound up with political factions within the union. The establishment of a centrally determined standard day wage in the coal industry has been an objective of the NUM since 1946. The union was opposed to regional differentials and piecework systems on the grounds of equity. It was also envisaged, particularly by the 'left' within the NUM, that a day wage structure would focus attention on the need to secure by national action a satisfactory basic wage.[117]

The NUM began to achieve its objectives with the National Power Loading Agreement (NPLA) of 1966. This replaced the previous pit and district agreements and carried a commitment that there would be one uniform national rate by 31 December 1971.

Some areas of the NUM, however, predominantly the high-productivity ones, were not in favour of a centralized day wage structure. For example, Nottinghamshire miners, who were among the best paid in Britain (in 1947 earnings were approximately 15 per cent above the national average, and in 1966 the area's shift rates were the second highest in the country), voted overwhelmingly against the introduction of the NPLA. Nottinghamshire, one of the least militant areas of the NUM, not surprisingly, favoured local rather than national negotiations. As R. G. Searle-Barnes noted,

in much of the Nottinghamshire Union's history there is an awareness that they could obtain locally by peaceful methods terms more favourable than could be achieved by militant action nationally and it is the more remarkable that the Union leadership were so often prepared to sacrifice local advantage for national solidarity. It has always been the dilemma of the Union in Nottinghamshire that they were ever likely to gain least and lose most from national negotiations and national agreement.[118]

The rationalization of the wages structure was achieved in the belief that once the rationalization was completed real progress could be made towards restoring the mineworkers as a whole to a more favourable relative earnings position. Rationalization, however, while producing a common level of earnings, actually demanded the greatest sacrifices from the areas that were most highly paid.

After 1960 coalmining consistently lagged behind the all-industry rate of increase in average earnings. The change in 1957–58 from a shortage to a surplus of fuel was traumatic in its effects. While the all-industry increase in average earnings was 22.1 per cent between 1956 and 1960, in mining it was 8 per cent. In 1967 the miners' average earnings were still 107 per cent of the manufacturing average, but by 1971 this had declined to 93 per cent.[119] As the NUM argued before the Wilberforce Inquiry, miners' earnings should have increased, if anything, in relation to the average because of their acceptance of a markedly reformed pay structure, a reference to the introduction of the NPLA in 1966, and their active co-operation in sustained increases in productivity. Instead, as a result of the NPLA, all miners lost out and the originally high-pay, high-productivity areas lost out most (see Table 44).

The general discontent of the miners at this state of affairs was expressed in the election swings 'leftward' over the period, including the election of Lawrence Daly as general secretary. The strategy was also reviewed. During the 1960s the union had accepted lower wage increases on the assumption that it would prevent further pit closures. Yet the decline in wages and pit closures had proceeded together. The union therefore considered ways of increasing wages so that those miners remaining would do so on a reasonable wage. The NUM thus switched to a militant industrial strategy under the influence of Lawrence Daly and others long before the oil crisis vastly increased their strategic bargaining power.

Although the new leadership mobilized the whole union behind industrial action to achieve better national settlements, this did not imply a full commitment by all areas to the centralized strategy lying behind the action. Indeed, the

Table 44 *Differential decline in real incomes of areas of the NUM*

Area	Increase in rate of pay, 1966– Jan. 1972	Position in earnings league, 1966	Decline in pay rate at constant (1966) prices
	%		%
Scotland	33.3	12	–1.8
Northumberland	23.4	8	–9.1
Durham	33.3	12	–1.8
Yorkshire	21.2	7	–10.7
Lancashire	18.5	3	–12.7
Cumberland	33.3	12	–1.8
North Wales	33.3	12	–1.8
Nottinghamshire	15.3	2	–15.0
North Derbyshire	18.5	3	–12.7
Leicestershire	26.1	11	–7.0
Cannock Chase	25.8	10	–7.3
North Staffs	30.0	9	–4.2
South Staffs & Shropshire	33.3	12	–1.8
Warwickshire	20.3	5	–11.3
South Wales	33.3	12	–1.8
Kent	11.7	1	–17.7
South Derbyshire	20.4	6	–11.2

Source: J. Hughes and R. Moore (eds.), *A Special Case? Social Justice and the Miners* (Penguin 1972), pp. 16 and 29.

fact that they had suffered disproportionately from centralization hardened the attitudes of the high-productivity areas such as Nottinghamshire, Lancashire and Derbyshire against centralization as a policy.

The two opposing views on the value of the national day wage structure and centralized negotiations in general were brought to the forefront again in the 1974 discussions on productivity agreements. A particular point of contention was whether productivity should be measured nationally or locally. The left were opposed to pit-based productivity schemes. They were concerned that they might reintroduce the unfairness inherent in the pre-1966 piecework system (although the productivity schemes were devised to take account of different pit potentials). Most importantly, however, the left thought that they would jeopardize the national cohesion and strength that the miners had built up since the introduction of the NPLA; indeed, it could be said that this was their primary objective in pursuing centralization. In contrast, the Nottinghamshire area, together with other areas that would benefit from a pit-based scheme, were in favour of the NCB's locally based productivity schemes.

During the 1960s, the aim of centralization, long cherished by certain elements in the leadership, particularly on the 'left' for the reasons outlined above, happened to coincide with the desire of the management to achieve a centralized and standardized structure. Moreover, the sacrifices that this entailed interacted with the 'left's' aims of boosting the national standard rate and thereby prepared the ground for the major strikes of 1972 and 1974.

However, this was not a permanent line-up of internal and external forces. The management in 1974 was already considering various forms of local bonus, and the union's higher earning areas were similarly in favour of local productivity deals. The latter's influence in 1974 was not sufficient to change the union's policy at that juncture, but they did succeed in their attempts to introduce local productivity incentives in 1977.

NUBE has traditionally been committed to centralized collective bargaining. This strategy is partly conditioned by the preferences of the employers and the staff associations, who have always pressed for the maximum degree of devolution to the domestic level. After 1968, however, there was increasing internal pressure for the devolution of bargaining. Prominent in voicing these demands were the Trustee Savings Bank staff (98 per cent organized in NUBE, but having only one representative on the Executive). They differed from the majority of NUBE members in banking in that they had secured recognition much earlier and had never had to face the opposition of internal staff associations. Indeed, the EC member from the TSB raised the whole question of 'internalism' in *NUBE News*. He argued that the staff associations had gained strength in the past from their appeal to 'internalism' and that NUBE must cater for this as well as for a broader union consciousness. He concluded the article by suggesting that, whether NUBE merged with the internal staff associations or not, it must change its traditional structure in favour of one that acknowledged the legitimate demands for greater 'internalism'. Such views were anathema to certain sections in the union, however, who opposed the introduction of various aspects of 'internalism' on the grounds that it could lead to company domination.

This ideological division influenced not only decisions on centralization/ decentralization of negotiations but also the question of diffusion through lay participation in negotiations. Hence, although the union gradually extended the use of 'seconded representatives' and 'office representatives', already common in the internal staff associations and ASTMS, this was opposed by many branches. For example, a motion submitted by the South Wales Area Council at the 1972 Conference opposed the concept of 'seconded representatives' paid for by the banks, which they described as a form of company unionism. The motion was lost, but the South Wales area has continued to submit motions on the point and to insist on representation by fully independent and professional union staff.

Financial constraints, however, prevented any expansion of the FTO complement. Indeed, as in the case of other unions in the study, NUBE found the increased use of 'seconded representatives' and 'office representatives' a useful way of tackling the increased work load at domestic level without having the financial burden of employing its own officials to do it.

Thus, in addition to the external constraints of other unions, staff associations and employers, the NUBE leadership has to contend with conflicting views within its own membership. Some members wanted to adopt the forms of local representation found in the external organizations with which NUBE was in competition; other members, with a long experience of opposition to these very organizations,[120] were clearly antagonistic towards any structural alterations that would not help NUBE differentiate itself from its competitors.

Summary and conclusions

The overall pattern of change in bargaining structure among the unions studied has been a move towards greater dispersal of decision-making on each dimension examined. Only one union, the NUM, has moved in the opposite direction, from a highly devolved collective bargaining system to one that became increasingly centralized, although it still remains reasonably diffused because of a high degree of accountability to the membership. UCATT similarly attempted to strengthen its national negotiations but with less success than the NUM.

The degree of dispersal has differed, however, between unions. The TGWU was the only union to produce a total transformation on both dimensions – decentralization and diffusion of power. Power to bargain in the AUEW(E) was already diffused, but steps were taken during the period to decentralize formally what was already largely *de facto* decentralized. NUPE shows many similarities to the TGWU in its attempt to disperse power from the top, but differs from the AUEW(E) and TGWU in being a public service union in an area in which negotiations are still predominantly centralized. The other public sector unions, including the POEU, also retained centralized negotiations.

All the unions in the sample except the NUM experienced a greater scope for bargaining and an increased workload at local level, but their response to that workload varied. In all unions the number of shop stewards increased, but only in the TGWU was this accompanied by a national reduction in the ratio of FTOs, to members. In most of the other unions an increase in shop stewards was accompanied by an increase, although not of the same order, in full-time officials.[121]

Change in each of the unions examined was influenced by certain configurations of the external environment. Slichter, Healey and Livernash have outlined the context in which national-level negotiations on standard rates of pay are likely to be most appropriate.

Wage standardization requires substantial union organisation throughout an industry with reasonably homogeneous product and process, or throughout a self-contained competitive segment of an industry. Mention should be made of the many environmental variations that are significant in this connection – national as contrasted with local product markets, large-scale as contrasted with small-scale operating units, large multi-union companies as contrasted with small companies, locational stability as contrasted with locational fluidity, industries with many diverse products as contrasted with industries with fairly simple product structures, various degrees of price competition in product markets, hourly method of pay contrasted with piece rates . . . single union representation as contrasted with rival union representation, complex variations in union jurisdiction relative to product markets, and so forth.[122]

The level at which collective bargaining takes place within a union is therefore to a lesser extent than some of the other dimensions we have discussed within the discretion of the individual union. For collective bargaining to take place at all there must be a minimum degree of consent on the part of the employer and the latter have a considerable part to play in determining the level at which it takes place. Moreover, unions are often in a multi-union bargaining unit which again sets limits on their independence. Nor is the content of bargaining, another major determinant of the level at which bargaining takes place, wholly under union control. The impact of incomes policy and the productivity bargaining associated with it during the period under study have been major determinants of the levels at which bargaining takes place. On the question of lay participation and control, this is more within the direct control of each union; even so, the practices of other unions in a bargaining unit, the attitude of employers on recognizing and granting facilities to shop stewards and the policies of the state have also had a considerable influence.

Within these broad parameters, however, the reactions of different unions and their ability to change to meet the new situations confronting them have varied quite significantly. In the case of UCATT the leadership, it could be argued, pursued a centralizing strategy almost wholly inappropriate to the content and context of bargaining within which it operates. In this case, internal factors played an important part in determining the leadership's policy, but they are under considerable pressure from the major opposition group within the union to change direction, and a degree of accommodation between the two alternative strategies is beginning to emerge. In contrast, the TGWU's new leadership reinforced, in the late 1960s, the tendency to decentralization and diffusion implicit in productivity bargaining. The pressures for such change within the TGWU were evident long before the accession of Jones. He could, as general secretaries in the TGWU had done previously, merely have made the minimal concessions required to dampen down pressure from within. Instead he positively encouraged devolution.

In the GMWU, on the other hand, although they were under some internal pressure from members, particularly in areas such as the car industry where they were working alongside TGWU members, they did not enthusiastically embrace the decentralization and diffusion of union bargaining structures. It was not until the pressures exploded in the Pilkington strike that decisions were taken at the centre to encourage such developments, especially after the accession of Basnett. However, unlike the TGWU, where the general secretary could take the lead and ensure compliance among FTOs lower in the hierarchy, in the GMWU the regional secretaries continued to exercise their own discretion in the implementation of such policies. It was the gradual accession of regional secretaries who were in sympathy with the new developments, and who supported the election of Basnett and worked with him to change the GMWU policies in this field, who were most crucial in changing the GMWU.

In the AUEW(E) because power in collective bargaining, as in other aspects of policy-making, is so diffused and FTOs closely accountable to the membership through the process of periodic election, the leadership has less power both in determining policy and in ensuring that policies once decided are fully implemented. Nevertheless, the replacement of Carron by Scanlon did have a crucial impact on negotiations for a new engineering procedure. On the other hand, Scanlon and the Progressives were unable to secure full compliance in their attempt to decentralize all substantive negotiations with the engineering employers to the domestic level.

In the case of NUPE the leadership went far beyond the pressure of purely external factors or of internal membership pressure in attempting radically to change the degree of lay participation in the bargaining process. NUPE could, like the POEU, have retained productivity bargaining within the centralized bargaining framework and continued to rely on FTOs to pursue negotiations. Like the TGWU, however, the leadership took a conscious decision to take advantage of the opportunity that productivity bargaining gave to diffuse bargaining by reducing the dependence of members on FTOs. No doubt in this case, as in the case of the TGWU, economic considerations combined with ideological beliefs to secure the adoption of such a policy.

The POEU, too, took initiatives beyond those demanded by the bargaining content and context. Indeed, although it took advantage of external pressures to engage in productivity bargaining and of the change to corporation status to strengthen its own independent bargaining strategy, it strongly resisted attempts by the employers to devolve bargaining to the area and domestic level in the interests of maintaining the integrity of its own secession-prone organization.

In the case of the NUM and NUBE there are deep divisions within each organization over the question of decentralization and diffusion, reflecting differences of both ideology and circumstance among the membership. Thus, although certain changes that have taken place reflect the influence of external change agents, they also reflect the dominance of particular interests within the membership. In the case of the NUM, the differences of view over bargaining strategy reflect the difference of interest between the high-productivity and traditionally high-earnings areas and those in the less productive areas, and broadly, although not uniformly, coinciding with these the right and left within the union. In NUBE the division is between those who would like to see a greater degree of domestic negotiation and those who see any move in that direction as the adoption of 'internalism', long opposed as characteristic of the internal staff associations. In many unions, therefore, one could not easily predict the direction in which collective bargaining policy will go simply from an analysis of the context in which the unions operate.

9 The conditions of change in trade unions

The aims of the chapter

This chapter has three related objectives which are explored in successive sections. The first aims to summarize and explore our findings in respect of the factors affecting change. This enables us to draw certain conclusions about the agents of change and the change processes. In broad terms it may be said that this section concerns the past and the conclusions that may be drawn from its analysis.

The section that follows is centrally concerned with speculation about the future. There we consider how far it may be said that the study has uncovered certain trends or patterns of change which could form the basis for subsequent developments. We also discuss alternative patterns of change and the factors that seem most likely to affect them.

The final section contains a number of conclusions which may be said to be action-oriented. In effect, we ask what practical lessons may be drawn from our findings by various interested parties such as trade unionists, employers, governments and students of the subject.

The conditions of change

The extent and areas of change

We set out to study the extent to which changes of significance had taken place in all the main dimensions of union activity in our sample. It proved easy enough to classify these under three main heads: changes affecting (1) union government, (2) job territories and (3) job regulation.

In the case of union government we noted two distinct forms of change. The first was towards decentralization and diffusion. This happened in both non-bargaining and bargaining channels of internal decision-making in some unions. The process was taken furthest in the TGWU, where regional secretaries were encouraged to expand their influence at the expense of national officers and an additional layer of government was introduced at the district level. At the same time greater reliance was placed on lay representation and the development of workplace-based forms of participation. This resulted in a shift of the balance of influence from full-time officers to lay activists – especially shop stewards – at the district and local level. It could be argued that, simultaneously, the influence of the general secretary, relative to other national and district full-time officials, initially increased as a result of the process. (Certainly this appeared to be the case during the greater part of Jones's leadership.)

Similar decentralizing tendencies affected NUPE. Once again, special arrangements were made to make the union more responsive to rank-and-file pressures – noticeably in the internal processes of decision-making in the bargaining field. Greater reliance was also placed on the development of lay representation and increased workplace participation. Thus in both the TGWU and NUPE there was a more or less determined attempt to break with established traditions and decision-making processes in the interest of decentralization and diffusion.

There were also moves towards greater degrees of horizontal diffusion of decision-making in several other unions, namely ASTMS, the AUEW(E), NALGO, the NUT and to a lesser extent the GMWU. For the most part these were on a *de facto* rather than *de jure* basis, often involving the development of factionalism. Although the AUEW(E)'s introduction of postal ballots was the result of a *de jure* change. It should also be noted that in the case of ASTMS and the AUEW(E) the scope for radical vertical dispersal was limited: their systems of government were, particularly in the bargaining channels, already highly decentralized.

On the other hand the trend towards greater decentralization was by no means universal. There was little sign of it in the POEU and UCATT. The POEU successfully sought to retain central control of decision-making in the bargaining and non-bargaining fields. Most notable of all, the leadership of the newly formed UCATT were able to effect a degree of centralization in both fields. Indeed, the ASW used the formation of UCATT to embody this objective in the rules of the new organization.

In the area of job territory change similarities and differences between unions were more complex. The main similarity was that virtually all unions in the sample, with the exception of the NUM and the special case of the newly formed UCATT, enjoyed some degree of natural growth – usually a rate in excess of the overall rate of increase in union membership. On the other hand, there were marked differences between unions in this respect, and when one takes into account the impact of mergers on growth the differences between unions were more striking.

Once again it is possible to group a number of unions together, in respect of both their experience and policies in relation to natural growth and their attitudes to mergers. The record of the TGWU was similar to that of NUPE, or NALGO, so far as natural growth is concerned. Its nearest model in the merger race was undoubtedly ASTMS. All these unions exhibited rates of growth far in excess of the national average – often in competition with well established rivals. All four could claim to have grown at relatively high rates across the broad expanse of their membership, although ASTMS was the most adventurous in their attitude towards the extension of job territories. Contrasting with the performance of these innovative and expanding unions we may set the record of four others – UCATT, the NUM, the AUEW and the GMWU. The first two faced a membership challenge that was broadly similar – although they responded in very different ways. In the case of UCATT the member unions that combined to form this merger were all subject to serious membership decline. Yet largely as a result of the formation of UCATT they managed to reverse this trend and initiate a period of modest growth. In this sense the leadership of the ASW, which took the lead in promoting and carrying through the merger, reacted to the problems that faced them in a positive and innovative way; indeed, in this respect there is a parallel with the role played by their general secretary and the leadership provided in the TGWU by Jones. Both men sought to impose a relatively well thought out strategy on their very different organizations with some degree of success. So far as UCATT is concerned, the contrast with the passive response of the NUM is striking.

But the more complicated records of the AUEW and GMWU are no less interesting. Apart from the Foundry Workers, the unions that combined to form the AUEW faced membership stagnation, rather than membership loss. So far as membership growth was concerned, they lacked the campaigning zeal and positive approach of the TGWU, ASTMS or NUPE. Partly for this reason we termed their merger 'consolidatory' – to mark it off from the defensive aims of the unions who formed UCATT and the aggressively expansionist plans of the TGWU and ASTMS.

In this respect the policies of the AUEW may be said to be closer to those of the GMWU – although the latter organization failed to produce the basis for further growth as a result of any type of merger. What it did enjoy was a modest degree of natural growth, which was above the national average but concentrated in the two regions where a more positive approach was adopted by local leadership. Once again, the contrast with the more generally expanding and growth-conscious TGWU is pertinent, since both unions occupy broadly similar job territories.

In the area of job regulation we drew a distinction between changes in character and modifications of existing structure. In the case of the first we noted a general growth in militancy and a greater readiness to accept the need for industrial action as a conscious element in union strategy. (In the case of NALGO this involved a change in union rules and provision for a strike fund.)

In this respect the most notable developments were those that weakened the traditional parochialism and insularity of unions like the NUT and NALGO, ending in their decisions to affiliate to the TUC. Analogous developments were also found in NUBE, and they may have affected the readiness of several small organizations to merge their identity with ASTMS.

So far as changes in the structure of job regulation are concerned we identified two divergent tendencies. Once again, the TGWU appeared as the most developed example of a decentralizing and diffusing organization, introducing a wide range of changes intended to encourage local bargaining by shop stewards and other lay representatives. They also sponsored moves away from industry-wide wage bargaining. At the other extreme of this spectrum we found the NUM, which pioneered and carried through a similarly radical move in the opposite direction, involving the abandonment of workplace bargaining over wages and the introduction of a much more centralized bargaining system.

In between these two extremes can be placed every other union in our sample, with NUPE a notable addition to the devolutionist camp and UCATT the most determined centralizer after the NUM.

Among the remaining decentralizers the AUEW(E) is possibly the most interesting. Here the most important development was the determination of the leadership, under Scanlon, to end the industry-wide disputes procedure in its existing form. But in some ways more significant was the attempt to pursue industry-wide objectives via local initiatives, including strike action. It was concluded that one reason for the failure of this policy was the degree of decentralization that already existed in AUEW(E)'s decision-making structure; in effect, Scanlon lacked the means to secure compliance or co-operation at local level. Also worth noting, on the devolutionist side, was the typical enthusiasm for local bargaining by lay representatives shown in the two growth areas of the GMWU; once again, the policies adopted in the North East and Scotland resembled those of the rival TGWU, rather than the rest of the union.

Finally, among the organizations that remained committed to centralization, it is worth noting the position of the POEU. In this case a traditional resistance to devolution was maintained in the face of employer pressure and inducement – in the form of productivity payments. The result was union acceptance of productivity bargaining, in a form that was compatible with the maintenance of industry-wide job regulation. In some ways it is possible to argue that there is a parallel here with the initiative of the ASW leadership.

In conclusion, we have uncovered several contrasting patterns or trends of change against a very general background of membership growth and increasing militancy. First, there were widespread moves towards greater degrees of decision dispersal. This often affected both union government and job regulation and involved deliberate attempts to raise the level of lay participation. Second, alongside developments of this kind there were counter-moves, in a minority of organizations, towards greater degrees of centralization and concentration in the areas of union government and collective bargaining. Third, there were widely different attitudes towards natural growth and merger growth, with the majority of organizations tending towards more positive policies as the period proceeds.

Before concluding this section it is worth stressing one general point. It should not be forgotten that from the viewpoint of particular unions and their leaders the changes that we have sought to analyse under three different headings were usually seen as part of an interrelated or common pattern of development. Indeed, in many instances national leaders felt that they were striving to implement policies that were mutually reinforcing.

Thus unions like the TGWU, ASTMS or NUPE pursued dispersal in the area of union government, for reasons that were clearly related to their aims in respect of job regulation and union growth. In effect, they believed that taken together these policies would result in membership satisfaction and expansion.

Conversely, at the other end of the spectrum, and at the beginning of our period, national leadership in the GMWU saw no need to change their governmental processes, partly because they were thought to be compatible with existing growth and bargaining objectives. In much the same way it could be argued that the NUM's lack of interest in expanding beyond the boundaries of its traditional job territory helped to ensure that its desire to move to a more centralized form of bargaining was a practical possibility.

But it is also clear that there was a common theme running through the aims of the leaders of UCATT – especially those leading the old ASW. They argued that moves towards more centralized forms of government and job regulation were interdependent. Indeed, these objectives determined the scope for job-territory change – since mergers were sought only among unions who were prepared to subscribe to such aims.

It can even be suggested that the leaders of the consolidatory AUEW shared related objectives. At least they were all looking for a loose alliance, which would enable their own organizations to pursue their somewhat disparate bargaining and growth objectives under a common umbrella. In this case the very absence of well defined and united objectives in two of the main areas of change came to determine the degree and type of change that was possible in the third.

The processes of change

It will be remembered that in this study we have sought to maintain a distinction between those factors influencing change that could be regarded as exercising their influence through factors that were *external* to a given union, and those rooted in *internal* developments. In this section we seek to summarize what has been discovered about the role and relative importance of external and internal factors, as a prelude to drawing certain general conclusions about change agents and the process of change.

The role of external factors

So far as external factors are concerned we may be said to have discovered the influence of five rather different factors: the economic environment; factors directly affecting the composition of the labour force; management and employer attitudes and policies; government attitudes and policies; the attitudes and policies of other unions and the TUC. Let us see what can be decided about the influence of each of these in turn.

So far as the economic environment is concerned we need to note that for the most part our period was one of declining employment opportunities, rising inflation and relatively low levels of economic growth. It has often been claimed that such an environment has contributed towards the general changes in union character that we sought to analyse in Chapter 7, including the rise in militancy and the breakdown in parochialism that helped push unions such as the NUT and NALGO into the TUC. Our study confirms this judgement, especially if one takes into account the impact of the economic environment on government attitudes and policies, which are considered in more detail below. On the other hand, it is clear that general influences of this kind cannot go far in explaining the different degrees of militancy and aggressiveness shown by different unions in similar or identical situations – for example the contrasting record of the TGWU, NUPE and the GMWU in various parts of the public sector.

One problem in assessing the relative importance of external factors that affected the composition and size of the labour force is that it is not easy to discern their general direction. Clearly there were a number of technological and market factors that combined to produce significant and sharp reductions in particular sections of the labour force – most notably in coal mining, docks and foundries. For the most part they had a negative impact on union membership in the unions affected and played their part in inducing job territory and bargaining change. On the other hand, technological and market factors in other parts of the labour market resulted in a growth of recruitment opportunities – most clearly in respect of white-collar workers, women and certain higher skilled groups. These may also be said to have influenced the adoption of new growth objectives, further job territory aims and even modifications in existing government structures – most notably in unions like the TGWU, NUPE and ASTMS.

Yet once again we have to note that the responses that individual unions made to such external agents of change differed widely. On the one hand labour-only sub-contracting threatened the established construction unions with membership collapse, producing the relatively centralized and concentrated UCATT. On the other hand leadership in the TGWU pioneered formal changes aimed at further decentralization and diffusion in virtually all its trade groups. And both these different positive responses are to be contrasted with the largely inactive national leadership of the NUM and the GMWU, in the face of similar threats and/or opportunities.

In the case of employer and management attitudes and policies very few claims for influence need to be entertained outside the area of bargaining change, so long as it is agreed that the influence of government in seeking to uphold the conditions of its own incomes policy, by pressurizing public sector employers, is best considered under a subsequent heading. This apart, it is clear that in manufacturing industry many of the larger firms or corporations took the lead in sponsoring moves away from national bargaining during the late 1960s and early 1970s. Others sought to negotiate more extended forms of plant bargaining, alongside changes in payment systems and structures. Yet even here these management initiatives were significantly helped (or hindered) by the attitude of particular unions – for instance the enthusiasm of the TGWU as against the more mixed approach of the GMWU. It also needs to be recorded that in banking management objectives were frustrated by union and staff responses, while in the case of the Post Office the objection of the POEU to all forms of local productivity bargaining effectively prevented decentralization.

To assess the relative importance of government as an agent of change one needs to consider the impact of government initiatives in three rather different areas: incomes policy, general legislation affecting trade unions, and the consequences of the 1964 Act which eased the legal requirements for union mergers.

In the case of incomes policy we have already noted its general impact on the rise of militancy during our period. This is impossible to measure but was strongly stressed by all those we interviewed at the time. More specific, and more easy to observe, was the special influence that government attempts to enforce their incomes policy guidelines had on the size and scope of industrial action in particular parts of the public sector – most notably in respect of several white-collar groups who undertook industrial action for the first time in our period. We have also noted that, in the case of the NUT and NALGO, government attitudes to pay bargaining were a major factor in overcoming rank-and-file resistance to TUC membership, although even here it should be remembered that they needed to be complemented by other 'favourable' internal developments, including important changes in national leadership, membership composition and long-standing activist campaigns.

Furthermore, the common guidelines and enforcement mechanisms of successive waves of incomes policy produced widely different degrees of reaction and resistance in different unions and groups. If one seeks to explain these differences one is inevitably drawn into an assessment of the importance of differences in union traditions, leadership styles and constitutions – for example in the case of the reaction of the miners in 1972 and 1974, or the very different responses of UCATT and the TGWU to the 1972 construction dispute.

But if the overall importance of incomes policy is not easy to assess and allocate, what can be said of the effect of general legislation, such as the 1971 Industrial Relations Act? The first point to be made is surely that the 1971 Act was intended to make a significant impact on each one of our major areas of change. Union government was to be formalized and centralized through the device of 'registration'. (In particular, it was envisaged that the conditions of registration would require unions to specify in some detail the ways in which industrial action was to be authorized and controlled.) It was also claimed that the legal support that registered unions would enjoy in their attempts to gain recognition from recalcitrant employers would have a significant impact on union growth. Indeed, the provisions of the Act implied that the body established to encourage the spread of recognition would attempt to do this in a way that contained and prevented inter-union rivalry and competition. In this way, the supporters of the Act could claim that it was a 'reformist' measure, designed to tackle the complex of overlapping job territories that were criticized by the Donovan Commission and other would-be reformers of the British system of industrial relations.[1] It was also hoped that the act would transform trade union bargaining behaviour, causing unions to accept legally enforceable collective agreements and the need to discipline members involved in 'unconstitutional' strike action.[2]

We saw that in the event all these hopes came to nothing, largely because the great majority of unions refused to register and virtually all the employers they dealt with decided not to take advantage of unions' increased legal vulnerability. They also agreed to continue to sign collective agreements that had no force in law.

But it was not only because trade unions and employers did their best to avoid the provisions of the Act that it had little or no impact. As the authors of the definitive study of its impact on the British system of industrial relations point out, the government itself invoked its right to insist on a pre-strike ballot on only one occasion, with the result that the size of the pro-strike majority 'further weakened its confidence in the wisdom of its own legislation'. And they conclude:

It was widely believed by the managers and the trade unionists whom we interviewed that, from the end of 1972 onwards, the Government wanted to avoid, as far as possible, the use of the controversial parts of the Act by management or individuals. Some managers told us that the DE has actively discouraged any use of the Act's collective bargaining provisions.[3]

After the election of a new government in 1974 the Industrial Relations Act was repealed and replaced by the Trade Union and Labour Relations Act (TULRA) and the Employment Protection Act (EPA). As part of the Social Contract between the Labour government and the TUC they were designed to be much more acceptable to trade unionists in general and union general secretaries in particular. Partly as a result, union attitudes to incomes policy improved for several years – although towards the end of the government's period of office there were notable disputes over the enforcement of government norms in the public sector. Meanwhile, what can be concluded about the direct effects on the TULRA and the EPA on our three major areas of change?

First, neither sought to sponsor change on the scale of 1971.[4] There was no intention to change any established relations in the field of union government, for example, and it can be argued that in the case of most aspects of job regulation the central aim of the TULRA was to secure and protect a return to the *status quo ante*, as it was seen by the TUC.[5] Yet there was one aspect of the EPA that was intended to foster further membership growth and advance by promoting union recognition. In this way it could be argued that the EPA had similar job territory objectives to those of the 1971 Act.[6] However, at the time of writing, as the result of the combined effects of employer resistance and judicial interpretation, it cannot be said that this part of the EPA has had more than a trifling impact on union growth.[7] We conclude that, so far as the changes we have to explain are concerned, the direct effect of both the TULRA and the EPA are no more significant than the 1971 Act.[8]

There remains the role of the 1964 Trade Union Amalgamations Act to be considered. It seems to us that this did have a lasting impact on job territory change; for it made it possible for the leadership of unions like ASTMS, the ASW and the TGWU to arrange 'suitable marriages' with smaller organizations without having to gain the direct consent of their own rank and file. This enabled them to concentrate on providing the officers of minor unions with an attractive package of inducements and incentives, to gain their support for a proposed transfer of engagements. At the same time the 1964 Act lowered the degree of consent required where ballots were still needed.

As we argued in Chapter 6, it is not a coincidence that most of the mergers we studied followed the 1964 law. We doubt whether many of them could have been carried through without it. Certainly the expansionary achievements of unions like ASTMS and the TGWU would have been much less impressive if they had needed to ensure 50 per cent polls and 20 per cent majorities among their own members before small unions could be absorbed.

Yet it must be stressed once again that the external agency of the 1964 Act in no way determined the shape and distribution of the merger movements it precipitated. It merely removed existing legal obstacles and provided all unions with indiscriminate and equal opportunities for growth and development.

What did influence the direction and approach of particular unions was our fifth external factor: the attitudes and policies of other unions and the TUC. As we saw, the TUC did its best to encourage a positive reaction to the 1964 Act, by inaugurating innumerable inter-union conferences and meetings. It is reasonable to argue that this helped to focus union attention on the opportunities presented to unions by the new legal rules. Several defensive mergers can be traced back to discussions conducted with the help of the 'good offices' of the TUC. On the other hand, we also noted that in several of the mergers studied events took a quite different shape to that first mooted by TUC officials – most notably in the case of UCATT. There the leaders of the unions involved explored several other alternatives before deciding on their own tailor-made amalgamation. And for the most part these possibilities were developed and explored by means of bilateral contacts of a highly personal character, and they owed more to the internal needs and judgements of a few general secretaries than to the initiatives of Congress House.

But they were also increasingly influenced by the activities of rival unions. Indeed, it is clear that as the 1960s advanced more and more unions became aware of the policies and 'predatory' strategies of a relatively small number of their expansionist neighbours. Among our sample the most obvious impact was felt in the GMWU, but it is also clear that both the AUEW merger and the decision to form UCATT were influenced by external developments of this kind.

Thus we may say that the job territory objectives of unions like ASTMS and TGWU came to exert a growing and disproportionate influence on their would-be rivals. In effect, their well publicized successes appeared to both narrow the scope for further advance and demonstrate what could be done if sufficient attention was paid to the problem.

It is now possible to summarize what we have discussed about the role of external change under four heads. First, as might be expected, external factors appear to have had least influence over changes in internal union government. In some instances broad movements in occupational or industrial balance have affected the composition of union membership. This may well have had an effect on rank-and-file demands and leadership responses. Of course, one obvious external influence at work on union government has been the preferences of employers in respect of decentralized collective bargaining. Yet even here, as we noted, the attitudes and preferences of union leaders were more important and crucial than those of employers. Much depended on how far they wished to encourage or resist proposals for bargaining change.

Second, so far as job regulation itself is concerned, something can also be claimed for the initiatives of government against a background of economic stagnation and inflation. In general terms it can be said that influences of this kind helped to generate rising degrees of militancy – most notably in the public sector. Yet once again these general influences were accompanied by widely differing degrees of resistance and response in different unions and groups.

Third, there can be little doubt that it has been in the area of job territory change that British unions have been most affected by external factors. In the first place, managerial, technological and market factors have combined to present all unions with changes in the composition and scope of their traditional job territories. Indeed, some organizations have been threatened with near bankruptcy and eventual extinction as a result of a combination of events of this kind. Others have benefited in a passive way from the natural expansion of established job territories. A few have been able to exploit opportunities arising out of job territory change in ways that have transformed their situation. In this objective they have been greatly assisted by the more relaxed legal provisions of the 1964 Act. Indeed, so far as the reform of union behaviour is concerned, this modest and uncontroversial Act may be said to have exerted much more lasting and significant impact than the combined effects of the IRA, the TULRA and the EPA. In the second place, both merger search and natural growth have been influenced by the external prodding of the TUC and the still more important example of a small number of committed expansionist unions.

Nevertheless, the fourth and final conclusion we may draw from this discussion of the role of external factors must surely be that they tend to present themselves to trade unions in ways that allow for a number of alternative responses. Thus, even in the critical area of job territory change unions appear to be free to respond to similar degrees of challenge and opportunity in ways that vary through a wide spectrum, from the notably restrictive and passive NUM to the intermediate GMWU and on to the unusually expansionist ASTMS. It therefore seems reasonable to conclude that in our period the external agents of change did little more than present British unions with extra problems to solve. To assess how they have gone about deciding appropriate responses, and to consider what may be said to be the keys to relative success, we need to turn to a discussion of what may be concluded about the role of internal factors.

The role of internal factors

Internal factors may be broadly divided into two groups: those that relate to the attitudes and policies of particular union groups, and those that concern the influence of particular decision-making structures – most notably the provisions of the union rule book.

We need to consider first the influence of two related groups – the mass membership and the minority of lay activists. They need to be considered together if only because the influence of the former was for the most part given focus and form by the activities and demands of the latter. We have noted instances where union membership, in alliance with lay activists, did affect each one of our areas of change, but it seems that their influence can be observed most readily in the field of job regulation.

It will be remembered that it was largely as a result of rank-and-file pressure that significant changes took place in the bargaining strategy of several unions – most notably in the public sector. In more general terms it was argued that differences in rank-and-file reactions and activist pressure were part of the reason for differences in the extent to which the two general unions moved towards bargaining decentralization and diffusion. In this respect we noted that the TGWU had come to terms with the demands of several traditionally militant groups, in particular dockers and London busmen. They were already used to enjoying relative bargaining autonomy, and were likely to have insisted on further decentralization if this had not been a central plank of union policy by the late 1960s. By contrast, the GMWU's membership contained more than its fair share of traditionally moderate and relatively inactive groups – such as those in gas, water supply and several other public service occupations. This was one reason why leadership in the GMWU was under less pressure to adopt militant attitudes to incomes policy.

It is less easy to discern the extent and nature of rank-and-file influence on systems of internal union government, largely because changes that affect them were for the most part also sponsored and encouraged by particular sections of the national leadership. Thus in unions like the TGWU, NUPE, NALGO and the GMWU the changes that resulted in more participative systems of consultation were all initiated by either national or local leadership. They certainly went much further in the TGWU and NUPE because national leadership believed them to be important. On the other hand, intelligent leaders at every level may be expected to respond to pressure from below. And in each case, where changes were introduced it is possible to argue that local and other specialist needs were being taken into account by the national leaders.

But perhaps it is most difficult to assess the relative influence of the mass membership in unions like the NUM and AUEW(E). For here factionalism has developed to a point where there are two clearly defined alternative government parties and they operate in a more or less unified way at every level of union government. This was seen most clearly in our account of the AUEW(E)'s move to secure postal voting. As we saw, this fundamental change in the unions' decision-making process had profound consequences for the balance of power within the AUEW(E), but this does not mean that it makes sense to regard the result as a victory of the lower levels of membership over the national leaders.

Of course it is true that one consequence of postal voting has been an extension of the democratic process, in the form of an increase in the number of members who vote in elections. But it does not follow from this that day-to-day decisions taken within the union are becoming more decentralized or diffused. On the contrary, if the result were to be 'one party', it would be possible to argue that for all practical purposes administrative and executive power has become much more centralized and concentrated in the majority leadership group on the executive. This may well be what the AUEW(E) needs at this stage of its development, but it is hardly an example of a rank-and-file revolt.

So far as job territory change is concerned, the role of rank-and-file pressure would seem to be less positive than it has been in the area of job regulation. Yet its influence is much easier to assess than it was in respect of union government change. For example, we noted that in general terms the craft members of the craft unions acted as a restraining influence on the recruitment and merger ambitions of their national leaders – especially where their plans were likely to involve the enrolment of the lesser skilled or rival craft groups. In contrast to this, the leaders of unions like the TGWU or ASTMS were much freer to advance into new and untried job territories. It also seems reasonable to suggest that the NUM's passive acceptance of massive and continued membership decline was not unrelated to the traditional insularity of miners.

On the other hand, it cannot be argued that in any of the unions we studied natural membership growth, or the extension of job territory via mergers, became a popular cause. There were no rank-and-file campaigns similar to those of the 1920s designed to achieve 'one union for engineers'. Conscious and deliberate job territory change took the form it did largely as a result of the ambitions and policies of national leaders. At their most significant, other groups only acted as barriers to some avenues of change.

This brings us to our general conclusions on the overall impact of national leaders on the process of change itself. It seems to us that evidence so far presented suggests that they have been by far the most important internal group. Indeed, we would go further and suggest that in the case of three types of change they have exercised a dominant influence.

Their first area of dominance is obviously merger change. Given that several external factors combined to produce both the need for mergers and the means to achieve them, all the mergers we studied became practical possibilities only because a more or less united national leadership decided to engage in a systematic process of merger search. They were also required to conduct successful overtures, negotiations and settlements with other merger partners. Whatever was agreed, they had to sell to other interested parties – in the case of minor unions via the medium of a ballot. Moreover, the suitability of potential merger partners was in the end largely decided by the personal and strategic requirements of the dominant leadership group. And in several instances the attitudes and competence of a single general secretary were crucial.

The second area of obvious dominance concerns internal union government, especially the carrying through of formal change and administrative innovation. Once again, only a relatively united leadership at national level could take the action required to carry through change of this kind. They were needed to make a case at rules revision conferences; they decided appropriate boundary changes and overcame local resistances. If interested parties such as local full-time officials had to be persuaded, induced or coerced, this was seen as a task for national officials – especially general secretaries. And once again, the direction and form of change was greatly affected by the views that particular national leaders took of their strategic requirements and power position.

The third aspect of change, where we would argue that the role of national leadership appears to have been only slightly less dominant, concerns job regulation. Here, it is true, employer preferences and membership demands were sometimes quite important; we have even argued that in some instances governments must share a measure of responsibility. But we also said that these factors failed to account for the notable differences between unions in respect of their response to common developments of this kind. And it seems to us that they can very largely be explained by reference to the aims, beliefs, prejudices, and even the life experience of particular union leaders. This was perhaps the most evident within the GMWU, where we saw that two regional secretaries adopted atypical attitudes towards the role of shop stewards which brought them closer to the views of Jones (TGWU) than to those of their own general secretary. But it can also be seen in the contrasting attitudes and achievements of, say, Jenkins (ASTMS) and Smith (UCATT). And once again, the views they took were not entirely unconnected with their own political and strategic requirements.

However, we readily concede that, in respect of other types of change, such as changes in rates of natural growth and changes in union 'character', the relative importance of national leadership is nowhere near as pronounced. For example, membership has increased and union character has changed without any action on the part of national leadership (although even here we have to note that particular leaders – notably Jones and Jenkins – did successfully pioneer a drive for higher rates of achieved growth).

All in all, it seems to us that one of the central conclusions to emerge from this study is that, so far as change is concerned, a very great deal depends on the attitudes, objectives and calibre of general secretaries or their equivalents. A union that is led by a conservative or lazy general secretary, who is content to accept the traditional view of the organization's scope, aims and structure, will launch few initiatives designed to achieve conscious and deliberate change. Yet desire to innovate and influence events, and even an abundance of energy, will not usually be sufficient to overcome the forces of inertia, prejudice or interest. There also has to be above-average political skill, and not a little courage. We argue below that the importance of leadership in this sense has been overlooked in most previous writing about trade unions. At this stage we need to consider the role of the major constraint that operates on even the most dynamic and effective general secretary. This is our final internal factor affecting change: the decision-making structure.

In so far as change involves positive action on the part of the national leadership, they obviously must act through the union's decision-making structure. In so far as they are aware of membership demands for change, or preferences in favour of the *status quo*, they are largely dependent on the union's network of officers, committees and conferences to keep them informed about the limits of the possible. It is therefore important to ask how far the study enables us to assess the importance of different kinds of decision-making structures in facilitating or inhibiting change. In this respect it is best to begin with differences in constitutional arrangements, as set out in union rule books.

Four conclusions may be drawn from the study. First, the record suggests that receptivity to change is higher where the rules provide that decisions are relatively highly centralized and concentrated, especially where they can be influenced and controlled by the national officials. In this respect it helps if full-time officers are appointed and controlled by the general secretary. It does not help if officials are elected by and responsible to local groups or sections of the membership, or if they are selected and controlled by regional officials. It may assist change if the decision-making process is bifurcated, so that a high degree of bargaining diffusion can be combined with the retention of administrative and financial centralization. It will not help if the national leadership has to gain the agreement from a number of largely autonomous bodies with different functions – especially if national leadership is excluded from their deliberations.

Second, whatever the extent of decision dispersal, it helps if the powers given to the national leadership under the rules can be exercised with flexibility and discretion. This is partly a matter of how far the rules provide for general or reserve powers, as against a detailed prescription of the formal limits of leadership authority. Third, it helps if existing rules can be changed and adapted to fit new circumstances. Rigid procedures that involve calling special 'rules revision' conferences are unlikely to help would-be reformers.

Finally, the record shows that much depends on the existence and strength of factions. These can alter the way in which the formal provisions of the rules are interpreted. They may also provide the basis for opposition to leadership initiatives. Unions without organized factions are likely to be more easy to influence, but once factionalism exists rival factions will tend to dictate the scope and direction of change. And if factions are developed to the point where they form the basis for national parties, much will depend on how far a single party emerges that can command a majority at all the important levels of a decision-making structure.

The processes of change

It is now possible to bring together some of our main conclusions concerning the processes of change in the past. With the aid of two further diagrams we aim to summarize the conditions of change, although in presenting the processes in this way we are clearly simplifying their interaction. In Figure 12 we illustrate the relative importance of external and internal change agents in relation to each one of our change areas. The five external agents lie across the top of the diagram; across the bottom we have placed the two significant internal groups affecting change. The *degree* of influence exerted by each change agent is suggested by the *width* of the arrows linking it to one area or another.

A number of general conclusions emerge. First, it appears that the factors precipitating change in the area of union government are relatively less complex than is the case in other areas. In effect, national leadership has been heavily involved in all major changes, although it has been reacting to other factors, such as the demands and aspirations of the membership. Second, job territory change emerges as the result of a rather more complex interplay of change agents. Here at least three external factors have been of importance, although once again action has been required by national leadership if conscious and deliberate change was to be carried through. So far as merger change is concerned, the diagram suggests that government action (in the form of the 1964 Act) has been crucial – yet it is possible to regard this as a 'once for all' release of restrictions rather than a positive incentive to change it. Once again, the role of national leadership is strongly marked.

Third, so far as job regulation change is concerned, Figure 12 suggests a very different pattern of influences affecting the two kinds of change involved. In respect of bargaining structure, the role of national leadership is again seen to be of importance, although there are other agents at work, most notably the policies of employers and government and shop stewards. In contrast to this, the importance of national leadership is less marked in respect of union character change; this is seen as least likely to be subject to influences under leadership control.

A fourth conclusion relates to the relative importance of different change agents on change in all its forms. One is struck by the relatively wide ambit of government influence, as against the more narrow claims advanced for the impact of employers or the TUC. Yet if one sets aside what may be seen as the 'special case' of the 1964 Act, the diagram illustrates once again the relative importance of internal variables in general and national leaders in particular. This point comes out with even more emphasis in the explanation of Figure 13 to which we now turn.

This diagram is designed to illustrate the barriers to change arising out of

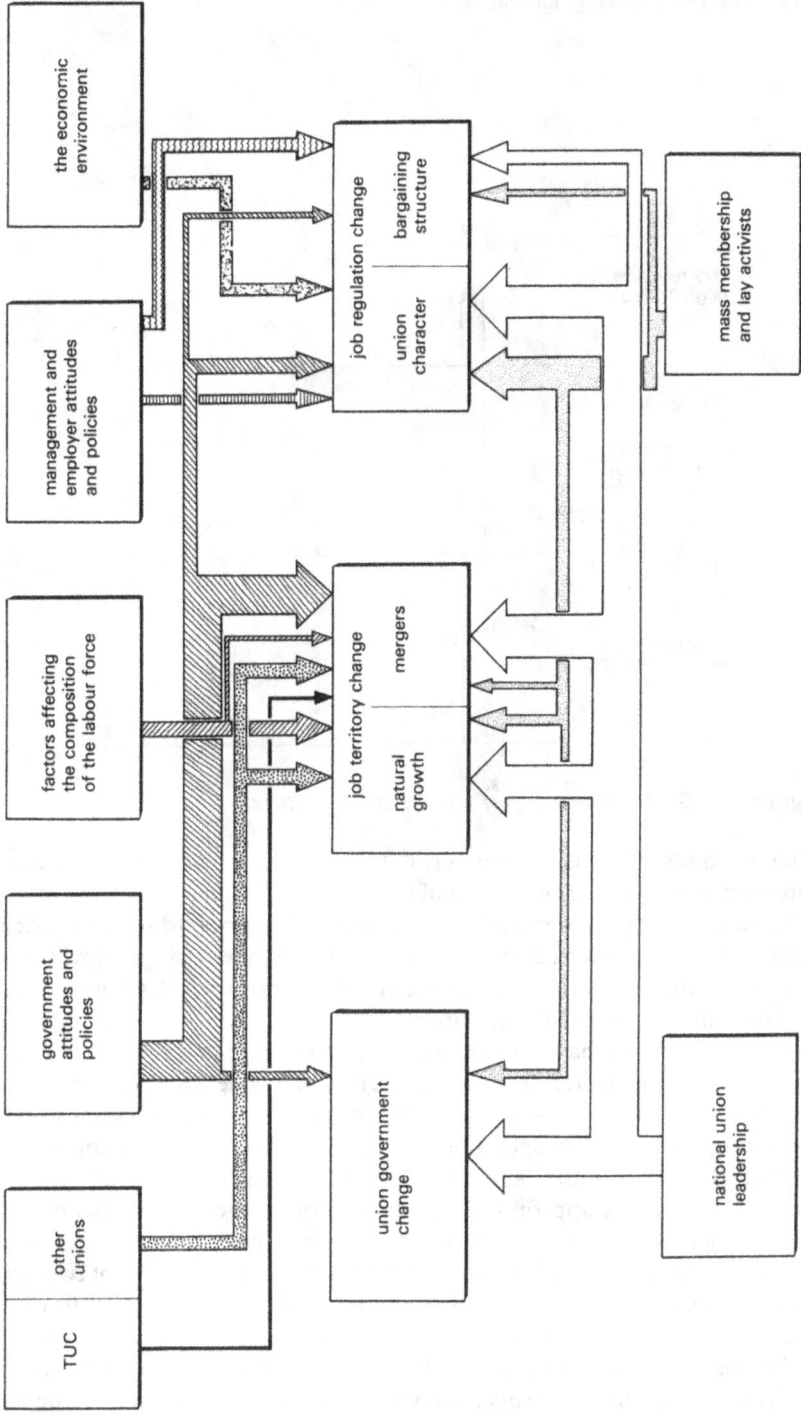

Figure 12 *Factors affecting change*

Internal agents of change

the economic
environment

management and
employer attitudes
and policies

factors affecting
the composition
of the labour force

government
attitudes and
policies

other
unions

TUC

job regulation change

bargaining
structure

union
character

mass membership
and lay activists

job territory change

mergers

natural
growth

union government
change

national union
leadership

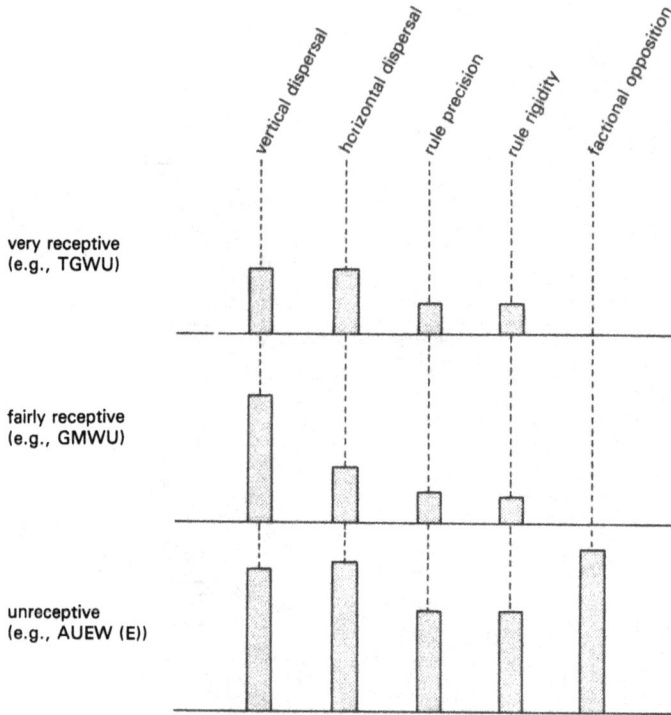

Figure 13   *Decision structures: receptivity to change*

different kinds of decision structures. The five main obstacles, or sources of resistance, are listed across the top of the diagram. On the vertical axis are three different examples of union decision structures, ranged according to the extent to which their constitutions and procedures help or hinder change. It will be seen that the 'receptive' union at the top has little decision dispersal, a low level of rule precision and no factional opposition.

In conclusion, we may say that the process of change in trade unions emerges from our study as the result of the interaction of a wide variety of external and internal factors. Yet relatively few of these can effect change, in the terms set out in our original model, by operating directly on specific areas of change – that is, without the intervention and commitment of existing national leadership working through the appropriate decision-making structures. Thus, apart from received membership growth and loss and a number of changes in membership character, significant and lasting change depends on the existence of two critical pre-conditions: first, a more or less united leadership committed to change; second, a decision-making structure that is sufficiently receptive to change to enable the leaders to get their way. For the most part the more innovative and skilful leaders in our sample operated within structures of this kind, although this was not always the case. Fortunately, from the viewpoint of change, the more receptive structures were usually blessed with leaders who wished to use them. But it is as well to remember, as we turn from our consideration of the past to speculation about the future, that this also need not always be the case.

Future patterns of change

This section considers how far the study has uncovered trends of change that could form the basis for informed speculation about the future. It is argued that, while the pace and direction of change is not sufficiently predictable to enable us to discern any general or predominant trends, it is reasonable to suggest several alternative patterns. It is also possible to predict the likely role to be played by a number of key change agents.

The influence of external factors

We turn first to the likely impact of external influences: what kind of problems and opportunities are they likely to present to unions and their members?

At first glance the simplest external factor to assess would seem to be future size and composition of the labour force. It is generally agreed that demographic developments will increase the size of the available labour force over the next ten years, particularly as a result of an increase in school-leavers, a reduction in the rate of retirement and a rise in female activity rates. Indeed, informed commentators suggest that by the late 1980s the combined effect of these factors should increase the available labour force by about two million.[9] In itself this development could provide the basis for a substantial further increase in union membership growth.

But this need not be the case. Unions organize among the actual labour force – in other words, those employed on full-time work. Whether the actual labour force increases depends, for the most part, on the level of economic activity – most importantly on the sustainable level of growth. Once again, informed commentators are agreed that unless growth rates can be raised to 3 per cent or more in most of the years in the decade, the size of the actual labour force will fall during the 1980s.

Moreover, once one considers projected changes in its occupational and industrial balance it seems only reasonable to assume significant membership loss. For it is the well organized parts of the labour force that are expected to decline; while the less well organized occupations and industries should stabilize or expand. Thus the share of manufacturing in total employment is bound to fall, even if unemployment declines. At the same time, there will be a continued increase in the proportion of the labour force providing social, professional and miscellaneous services. Even within manufacturing there will be a decline in heavy industry, as against a measure of stabilization in areas like food manufacture. Most important of all, from the viewpoint of membership growth, it seems safe to predict that there will be no repetition of the rise in public sector employment, which did so much to assist unions like NUPE and NALGO in the early 1970s.

Yet can we conclude from trends of this kind that in overall and relative terms most British unions will face the prospect of inevitable membership decline? Surely most of the unions in our sample will still try to continue to grow by positive initiatives designed to offset their received decline? After all, there are still islands of non-unionism in the public sector – for example among para-medicals and government industrials. Small-scale manufacturing industry is not yet fully unionized, neither is construction. Most important of all, there are still members to be won in services such as insurance, banking and finance; even in manufacturing, private sector management is virtually non-unionized. In other words, the potential available for achieved growth is still greater than the likely worst total of received membership loss. This means that, although we can conclude that factors affecting the future composition and size of the labour force do not favour trade unions, what actually happens to union membership will depend on the continued impact of many other change agents, which we discuss further below.

On the record of the past, the next most important external factor is undoubtedly government. And in the light of our study we need to consider what can be said about the possible impact of future legislation and incomes policies. At the moment of writing a Conservative administration has introduced a number of legislative proposals to modify the working of the TULRA and the EPA. The most important are intended to make secondary picketing unlawful and to provide additional compensation for workers who lose their job as a result of a closed shop; it also allows actions for breach of commercial contracts. It is too early to judge the full extent of trade union resistance to these measures, or to decide the likely long-term reactions of employers. Yet it is difficult to believe that in themselves proposals of this kind will have more far-reaching effects than the still more sweeping and ambitious provisions of the 1971 Act. We feel safe in concluding that what is enacted will have little or no impact on existing systems of union government, although it might well affect union–government relations, bargaining behaviour and union character.

A possible exception to this verdict might seem to be the proposals to facilitate the use of secret ballots in certain elections, calling and ending strikes and rules revision decisions, by offering to provide public funds to cover their cost. We only examined the impact of ballots on union elections in the AUEW(E). On the basis of this study it can be suggested that, if this legislation leads to the more extended use of postal ballots in union elections, it could have an impact on the balance of power in a number of unions along the lines of the postal ballot in the AUEW(E). But for this to happen the ruling majority in each union would have to sponsor a move towards postal balloting – and this would usually require a change of existing rules. After the experience of the AUEW(E) this would be done only where it was clearly in the interest of the prevailing majority; and for the most part we may assume that 'left-wing' factions and groups would tend to oppose moves of this kind. On balance, we feel that an enabling statute of this kind is unlikely to have a major impact on existing systems of union government.

It is worth noting that the present government have quite abandoned more radical attempts to 'reform' union government by changes in union rule books via the device of 'registration'. They have also not adopted a formal incomes policy – a public commitment to specific pay norms or criteria. At the moment of writing pay movements are to be kept within 'responsible' limits by less direct methods, for example high interest rates and tight cash limits. Once again it may be argued that it is too early to say what the results will be, but we feel we are justified in asserting a note of scepticism at this point.

As H. A Clegg has recently argued, 'for the last seventeen years the country has not been without some form of incomes policy for more than a few months at a time', although incoming governments have invariably tried to avoid early commitments to formal pay norms. As he also demonstrates, the problem has been that alternative policies, including high interest rates and cash limits, have not arrested the pace of wage inflation with sufficient speed or effectiveness; so that sooner or later one government after another has felt the need to supplement them by more direct methods. At which point Clegg concludes: 'The relevant question, therefore, is not whether Britain will soon see the last of incomes policy, but whether the future will bring another series of short lived or one lasting policy.'[10]

This prognosis seems to us to be broadly correct, although we see no need to speculate on how far the present government is likely to be able to move beyond short-term expedients to more sustained policies. What we feel we can assume, in the light of the study, is that in one form or another government intervention in the name of pay restraint is likely to exercise a continued influence on union–government relations. Clearly, any return to specific pay norms is likely to impact most immediately on the public sector, where even the more indirect models of expenditure cuts and tight cash limits have helped to produce resistance and the threat of industrial disputes.

It seems to us that when developments of this kind are combined with TUC opposition to the legislative amendments to the TULRA and the EPA, we are justified in assuming a return to the kind of union–government relationships that existed under the 1970–74 Conservative government – namely, growing antagonism, mitigated by the need to reach periodic settlements in respect of outstanding disputes.

How far this climate will induce further modifications in union character, both in the public and the private sector, we consider further below; but clearly much will depend on how far the government's economic policies in general are seen to be successful.

This brings us to the impact of changes in the economic environment. Is it possible for us to say anything at all about developments in this area? We feel this can be done only on the basis of three alternative assumptions; and it should be understood that we are not suggesting that anything in our study enables us to decide which of them is the most plausible.

The first assumption may be described as the 'optimistic scenario'. On this assumption the plans of the government for higher levels of investment, efficiency and output are achieved or surpassed. At the same time the world economy moves out of depression into sustainable expansion. As a result the government is able to encourage and allow rising real wages and levels of employment.

Given the record of the 1960s and the evidence of the study, it does not seem reasonable to conclude that in themselves developments of this kind will result in more modest union demands, more receptive and accommodating employers and a consequent decline in union militancy. As we saw, the growth in militancy took place in periods of relatively high employment and growth – at least in relative terms and in the light of subsequent developments. The factors that combined to produce these modifications of union character, especially those that resulted in a greater readiness of public sector workers to become involved in various forms of industrial action, seem likely to persist – even if the economy does attain levels of prosperity that rival and surpass the early 1960s.

Of course, the optimistic scenario may make it possible to avoid many prolonged and bitter disputes, involving attempts to hold down real wages while reducing employment levels still further. It should also provide the basis for more acceptable compromises and more lasting settlements of disagreements. All the same, it seems only reasonable to assume that it will continue to be accompanied by a relatively high level of industrial conflict.

The question is whether or not this tendency is likely to change – and if so in what way – on the basis of our second assumption: a pessimistic scenario. On this view the economy fails to recover, and government policy involves an attempt to secure progressive reductions in real wages against a background of ever rising unemployment.

Of course, it is argued by advocates of monetarism that sooner or later an economic prospect of this kind induces a major change in worker attitudes; as a result union wage targets become more 'realistic' and industrial disputes less likely to occur. In effect, it is argued, if the labour market is sufficiently depressed for long enough, union character is significantly changed on a more or less permanent basis. We may term this change a move towards 'defensive moderation'.

In the light of this study, however, we are sceptical of the notion of defensive moderation as a universal or lasting feature of British trade unionism. This is not to deny that many unions may revise their strategies in the light of a prolonged depression – and we further consider the alternatives open to them below. Many of them may indeed become more moderate, in the same sense that they will be ready to settle for terms and conditions far below those thought to be attainable in earlier periods. But it does not follow from this that there will be a decline in the level of overt conflict – especially in the public sector.

One problem would be that even a general depression is likely to have a differential impact on the power position of different groups and unions. As in the past, some would remain convinced that their position was unassailable, either because the demand for their product remained high or because the services they provided were essential and irreplaceable. We argue below that many groups in the public sector are in such a position, and that it is likely to have an increasingly important influence on the character of their organizations.

At the moment we are only concerned to stress that we see no reason to suppose that groups of this kind would not continue to fight to defend their job security, and even to maintain and improve their real income position – if need be at the cost of substantial and protracted industrial disputes. It also seems only reasonable to suggest that, while many groups in more vulnerable positions may come to modify their expectations, this need not bring them in easy and immediate reach of management limits or government objectives. Much will depend on the pace at which revisions are taking place on different sides of the bargaining table; there may still have to be some form of overt struggle, if only to determine the changing parameters of what will be an increasingly uncertain bargaining situation.

Our third assumption is that both the extremes described above are somehow avoided. Rising real wages and lower levels of unemployment are not attained on any sustainable basis; yet the level of economic activity does not decline to the point where it could be expected to induce a major change in worker expectations and demands. In this case we would also expect to see the continuation of a relatively high level of union militancy and industrial action – without much improvement in union government relations – along the lines of our optimistic scenario.

We therefore conclude that, so far as we can see, there is little reason to expect developments in the economic environment to reverse the trend towards higher levels of overt conflict. The only exception to this prognosis would seem to be either a return to the kind of union–government agreement that formed the basis for the Social Contract of the mid-1970s or a still more dramatic attempt at a statutory incomes policy, along the lines of the Conservative government of 1972. We return briefly to these possibilities in a later section.

There are two other external influences, which are likely, to judge from the study, to be of less importance: employers and the TUC. In the case of employers, the main impact may well be on the rate of achievable growth – especially in respect of private sector management. The work of Bain and others shows that in the field of white-collar recruitment the degree of employer hostility is significant.[11] It also has been important in deciding which union obtained early recognition – carrying with it the opportunity to service new members and the right to represent them to management.

Much may depend on whether or not private employers prefer to encourage the unionization of management by established unions – partly to avoid conflict with them, and partly to prevent further inter-union disputes. What they may prefer instead is to encourage the claims of what are thought to be more moderate specialist organizations, for example the Engineers and Managers Association or the United Kingdom Association of Professional Engineers. If this turns out to be their view, and they are successful, it is likely to have a negative impact on the rate of achievable growth in several of the unions in our sample, including ASTMS, the TGWU, the GMWU and TASS, although, of course, these specialist organizations could later merge with one of the established unions.

On the record of the past one might expect employers to have some influence on the direction of future bargaining developments. This may well be the case, if a significant number of multi-plant combines decide that they wish to encourage the enterprise-wide bargaining. On the other hand, we find it very difficult to decide how far employers in general will wish to introduce other bargaining changes, such as for example a further move away from industry-wide bargaining. This is largely because the study suggests that employer attitudes in this matter are likely to be significantly affected by their reaction to the detailed content of particular incomes policies. Since we have already decided that it is impossible to say anything about these in advance, we turn to the likely role of the TUC.

In the past we have accorded the TUC a modest role in facilitating and encouraging the post-1964 merger movement. It would seem that this role has largely been completed. For the most part potential merger partners are now well aware of their options; how they adjust to each other will depend on the responses that their leaders make to their perceived organizational requirements and internal political necessities. We consider a number of alternative scenarios in the section below on future union leadership.

However, it has been suggested that if union–government relations deteriorated sufficiently the TUC might be required to play a more significant role than any it has played in the past in the area of job regulation. It could find itself responsible for the co-ordination, or even the conduct, of widespread industrial action designed to oppose and change various aspects of government policy, say, in respect of public sector wages or statutory wage control. It is true that the experience of the 1970–74 period suggests that such common approaches and responses would not be easy to develop and sustain; but in the light of certain aspects of the campaign against the 1971 Industrial Relations Act this possibility seems at least worthy of inclusion at this point.

The influence of internal factors

From the viewpoint of trade unions the pattern that emerges from the above review is hostile and uncertain: more problems than opportunities, and little prospect of easy gains. What are the likely responses of unions and their members to such an environment? We turn first to the role of activists and the rank and file.

It seems reasonable to assume that in most unions trends towards decentralization and diffusion will continue. Recent studies indicate that the number of shop stewards and other lay activists are continuing to rise – much faster than either union membership or the number of full-time officials. Indeed, an authoritative and recent estimate indicated that the number of 'full-time' shop stewards is now considerably higher than the number of full-time officials.[12] There are also indications that the network of lay committees, both formal and informal, continues to proliferate.[13] In such a context we may surely assume that the trend towards more participative bargaining styles, and a greater reliance on lay decision-taking, is likely to continue – particularly in unions like NUPE and the TGWU, but in many other organizations as well.

One is prompted to ask how far developments of this kind are likely to affect the growth and development of factionalism? It has been argued above that dispersed systems of union government encourage the development of factions, although some unions, like the TGWU and NUPE, have so far managed to avoid them. Is it reasonable to suppose that if present trends continue this will be the case in, say, five years' time? In this respect it is worth noting certain very recent developments in the TGWU, which were touched on in our study.

It will be remembered that in this union administrative and executive influence was exercised by the national full-time leadership by means of an informal alliance between the general secretary and lay members of his Executive. This alliance enabled the general secretary to dominate the business at the biennial delegate conference, control the appointment and use of local and regional officials and carry through a series of bargaining and administrative initiatives involving action at every level in the union. But indications were also given of how the policy of decentralization and diffusion was contributing to the emergence of a more independent and autonomous Executive. Given autonomy, the possibility has emerged of significant and lasting conflict between the general secretary and the majority on the Executive, especially in respect of the appointment of senior officials.

It is arguable that if this trend develops the conditions will have emerged for the development of a form of factionalism. Indeed, it might be argued that, once the traditional system of dependence and patronage is clearly replaced by one based on independence and opposition, stable government would re-emerge only if factionalism developed to the point where it became party government.

And in this sense an analogy could be drawn with the present position of the AUEW(E). As we saw in the study, one of the essential functions of party government in the AUEW(E) was that it made possible some form of national leadership, given a rule book that disperses decisions to an almost unworkable degree. As a result the present leadership of the union can hope to commend itself to a like-minded majority at every major level of decision-taking – but most importantly at the level of the Executive Council. One way of highlighting some of the most recent problems of national leadership in unions like TGWU and NUPE is to pose the question, Is there a case for these organizations seeking to develop certain features of the decision-making structures of unions like the AUEW and/or the NUM? And if there is, how likely is a development of this kind in the near future?

Of course it might well be argued that if this were to happen the disease would be worse than the cure. Two-party systems, in their more developed sense, are largely confined to unions where they are buttressed and reinforced by the need to conduct regular elections for all full-time officials at every level of the organization. This could be said to be too high a price to pay for stable party government. In any case it may, in the end, prove possible to combine more independence for the executive with a measure of administrative control for the general secretary – given a high calibre of leadership and a general desire to maintain unity. Clearly, much will depend on the atmosphere and temper of rank-and-file opinion. Can we say anything about possible developments in this respect, as a result of our study?

Once again, we must take refuge in alternative scenarios. We have already argued that external factors are likely to provide unions in general, and public sector unions in particular, with a relatively hostile environment. We have also said why they will contribute to a continuation, and even an increase, in union militancy. The result will be that union leaders may expect to be presented with requests and demands for support in an increasingly uncertain situation – in defence of both income standards and jobs.

One way of dealing with pressures of this kind, in unions where decentralization and diffusion has been introduced or encouraged, is by the adoption of still more participative styles of leadership. Thus. members who are making the most militant demands, or are in the mood for industrial action in the context of a national claim, may find themselves encouraged to decide their own responses. In other words central control over the use and deployment of industrial sanctions will be further relaxed, to the point where it takes very different forms and degrees in respect of different membership sections and groups.

In the recent past there have been indications that a number of important unions – most notably those involved in industrial action in local government and the NHS – have been moving in this direction. As a result, much industrial action has become more fragmented, partial and diffused in its impact. In particular, the conventional 'all-out' stoppage, involving a total and indefinite refusal to work, has tended to be avoided in favour of a locally determined mixture of overtime bans, one-day strikes, 'working to rule' and refusals to handle particular categories of work.

One possible scenario would be if this kind of industrial action became the norm, at least in the public sector; partly because it enables activists and rank-and-file members to decide their own response to particular disputes, and partly because it appears to be more flexible and graduated, so that it need not involve the total denial and collapse of essential public services.

No doubt there will be those who denounce behaviour of this kind as an abnegation of union leadership. Doubtless some union leaders – who continue to operate within relatively centralized and concentrated decision-making structures – will seek to resist movements of this kind in their own organizations. It may also turn out, in the not-so-long run, to be a high-risk strategy – involving substantial financial consequences in terms of strike pay and a tendency to escalate. All we are suggesting here is that, given the likely pressures on many union leaders, it represents at least one policy option. Which brings us to the question of the policy options facing national union leadership in general.

In the model of change we saw that national leadership exercised a predominant influence over the responses made to major problems and opportunities in each one of our areas of change. The model also indicated that those operating within receptive structures ought to be able to respond more quickly to challenge. Unfortunately, it does not follow from this that one can predict future responses in any detail. We also noted that in the past a great deal has depended on the capacities, intentions and character of individuals. Even if we were foolish enough to make sweeping personal judgements on the likely future performance of all leading officers in the major unions, the conclusions advanced would be largely unprovable. There would also still be no way of deciding the identities and characteristics of their successors.

Yet there are several areas of possible change where the options open to national leaders merit informed speculation. It seems to us that these can best be approached via a consideration of alternatives in the field of job territory change; for here the options are much easier to predict and analyse, and the success of different leaders depends on what one assumes about their future response to change in other areas.

To begin with, it is surely reasonable to suppose that, given the absence of easily available natural growth, the post-1964 merger movement will quicken and extend. So far as the smaller unions are concerned, there are over 250 with less than 1000 members. Most of them organize in areas of stagnant or declining membership. It seems to us that most of them will survive only at the cost of rapid absorption into larger organizations.

At the other end of the scale come the thirty-nine unions with over 50,000 members, eleven of which were included in our study. Taken together they cover about 88 per cent of all union members. It seems to us that it is here that we will discover potential merger partners for most small unions that manage to survive into the 1990s. What is it possible to say about the merger objectives of the larger unions? From the viewpoint of their merger potential, they can best be considered in three groups.

The first consists of the twenty or so unions whose membership is confined to the public sector – the civil service, local government, education, the Health Service and the nationalized industries. In the anticipated climate of public sector retrenchment and expenditure cuts, the three and a half million trade union members covered by unions in this group would appear to be prime candidates for defensive or consolidatory mergers – especially those who are members of the ten or so unions with a membership less than 100,000.

In terms of its size and diversity NALGO might be thought to be in the strongest position to make an expansionist bid for one or more of these organizations, although it must be noted that the majority of unions involved actually organize in areas where NALGO's leadership has no direct experience and a very small membership. In this respect it is arguable that there is more support for a consolidatory merger between the CPSA and the SCPS and a defensive merger involving the remainder of the non-industrial civil service. Similar alliances are discernible among teachers, or in respect of the NHS.

In other parts of the public sector there is probably less scope for amalgamations. In some nationalized industries – for example mining and iron and steel – there is already one dominant union organized on industrial lines. In others, such as railways and the Post Office, several well entrenched organizations guard their independence and show little desire for change.

But there are more possibilities among our second group of unions; those with more than 50,000 members whose job territories are largely confined to the private sector. There are about ten of these unions, organizing in fairly narrow sections of private industry – for example clothing, textiles, baking, agriculture, printing and paper. Taken together the unions in this group represent about a million workers, who, with some notable exceptions are for the most part in poorly paid, under-organized and declining trades. In most cases the merger movement of the 1960s had produced one or two major unions, but there remains considerable scope for further consolidation. In some trades the major union is still surrounded by numerous small craft groups. In the well organized printing and paper industry there have also been a number of relatively minor amalgamations, but the attempt to merge two of the three largest unions – SOGAT and NATSOPA – had to be unscrambled during the early 1970s, partly for personal reasons.

And so we come to our third and final group, which is the most important of all from the viewpoint of future merger activity. This consists of the ten unions with more than 50,000 members, most of which organize in both the public and the private sector. The bulk of them have developed job territories across a wide spectrum of British industry, and naturally enough they include the five largest unions in our sample: the TGWU, the GMWU, the AUEW, ASTMS and UCATT. Alongside these are five other unions with similar 'intermediate-open' (see page 67 above) scope for recruitment, whose membership is as follows:

EETPU	420,000
USDAW	441,000
APEX	151,000
ASBSBSW	128,000
NUSMWCHDE[14]	75,000

These ten unions represent between them more than 50 per cent of organized workers, or just over six million trade unionists. It seems evident that the merger ambitions and plans of their leaders will largely determine the future structure of the British trade union movement. What can we say about the options and opportunities open to them in the light of our study?

First, we may surely assume that only four of the ten have the organizational resources and membership base to operate as natural aggressors in a major merger battle: the AUEW, ASTMS, the TGWU, and the GMWU. The crucial question is which of these is likely to develop the most merger potential – both in relation to the six remaining intermediate-open unions and in respect of the wider trade union movement.

At first glance the leadership of the AUEW might seem to be in the best position. At least three of the smaller organizations listed above are similar in origin – ex-craft unions, with similar histories, traditions and rule books (the EETPU, the ASBSBSW and the NUSMWCHDE). Like the AUEW, they organize and recruit within the engineering industry and know its procedure and agreements.

However, we discovered in the study that structural similarities and membership consanguinity are not self-evident and sufficient arguments in merger discussions. It is even more important to be able to offer an attractive 'deal' to the established leadership in the minor merging union. In this respect it helps if one's own decision-making structure is flexible, receptive and reasonably centralized on the non-bargaining side.

But our study demonstrated that from this viewpoint the national leadership of the AUEW are in a relatively weak position. They are also divided among themselves and are not agreed about the terms on which their existing alliance can continue. In some ways the present leaders of the AUEW(E), who wish to form future alliances on the basis of a common rule book, might be thought to be better placed if they could escape from the confines set by one of their present merger partners, the 'left-wing' leadership of TASS. It has been argued that, if TASS were to decide to separate itself from the present federal structure of the AUEW, the way would be clearer for the emergence of a more widespread and genuine amalgamation of craft and ex-craft unions extending beyond engineering (including unions such as UCATT, and the bulk of the organizations in the TUC's Group 8: Iron and Steel and Minor Metal Trades).

But for this to happen the national leadership of the AUEW(E), who would need to take the lead in such a merger movement, would have to be prepared to develop and carry through their own constitutional modifications. These would need to include some provision for occupational and/or trade autonomy, within the context of a common rule book. But they would also want to concern themselves with the consequences of any likely mergers on their own political position. And this would almost certainly involve preservation and extension of the present arrangements for postal ballots. Several potential merger partners might find it difficult to accept terms of this kind.

For all these reasons we would argue that both ASTMS and the TGWU are in a rather stronger starting position in the merger race. Both unions' decision-making systems might have been designed to facilitate merger 'deals'. In both cases the leadership has considerable experience of accommodating the wishes of a variety of merger partners. What can we say about their relative handicaps?

ASTMS starts with the advantage of impressive earlier form in the promising areas of non-TUC staff associations; particularly insurance, commerce and banking. It would also claim to be the natural home for the bulk of the unions in the TUC's Group 17: Professional, Clerical and Entertainment. (Included in this group are other intermediate-open unions like APEX and the broadcasting and television unions.) Other white-collar organizations that might reasonably be regarded as natural merger partners for ASTMS would appear to include both the NUJ and even the EMA. (In both instances ASTMS already recruits alongside these organizations, and would claim to be gaining in relative importance.) In general terms it may be said that, if ASTMS were able to carry through a merger movement of this scope, it would virtually double its present membership – i.e. move to a base of one million members.

Clearly the main difference between ASTMS and the TGWU is that the latter can hope to advance across a somewhat broader front – that is, into adjacent job territories affecting both manual and non-manual workers. So far as manual workers are concerned the most obvious opportunities for future TGWU initiatives would seem to be outside the territories of other intermediate-open unions (for example in the TUC's Group 3: Transport Workers), mainly concentrating on the non-railway unions. But they might also hope to attract one or more of the less financially stable and rather 'closed' unions in areas such as clothing, textiles, baking or agriculture.

So far as intermediate-open unions are concerned, the most promising medium-term target for the TGWU would seem to be USDAW, given the fact that its traditional base in the co-operative movement is rapidly declining. The possibility of a 'monster' merger between the TGWU and GMWU is a matter best considered after we have discussed the relative position and form of the GMWU.

Given their record among white collar groups, the leaders of the TGWU would naturally claim that they could hope to at least match the performance of ASTMS in this area. This may well be the case so far as manufacturing industry is concerned, outside the area of middle-level and higher management. In this respect the most important struggle may well be over the future of APEX. If ASTMS were able to effect an early amalgamation with APEX the balance of advantage in manufacturing would clearly tip in their direction, but even on this basis it can be said that the immediate merger potential of the TGWU is likely to be somewhat larger than ASTMS.

Of course, relative growth potential would be transformed if the leaders of the TGWU would come to terms with their 'sister' general union. Which brings us to the future chances of the GMWU in the merger race.

The first point to make is that on past form the GMWU's immediate position is even weaker than that of the AUEW. It lacks the penumbra of smaller unions with similar origins and structural features. Yet its own admixture of regionalization and horizontal concentration allied to an absence of occupational autonomy has helped to make it an even less attractive merger partner in the past. It also has the disadvantage of being in more or less open competition with the larger, and more constitutionally attractive, TGWU – often from a subordinate position at the bargaining table.

On the other hand, the GMWU could argue that it was in a relatively strong medium-term position, on several grounds. In the first place, it could hope to merge with one or two reasonably sized organizations in the public sector, for example CoHSE, the Firemen and even the Greater London Council Staff Association. Second, given a modest degree of occupational autonomy, it still hopes to be able to attract one or more of the ex-craft unions with which it shares common bargaining rights – most notably the EETPU. Third, the leaders of the GMWU might well argue that in time their apparently impregnable 'right-wing' image will make them the natural allies of other 'right-wing' leadership groups – those who more or less control unions as diverse as UCATT, USDAW and NALGO. But these are little more than hopes and speculations. At the moment of writing it must be said that the merger prospects for the GMWU are at least as dim as those facing the present leadership of the AUEW(E).

Yet it does not follow that the future leaders of the GMWU will wish to abandon their present independence and autonomy, merely to enable their own organization to be engulfed by an organization that is more than twice its size. There are no compelling reasons why they should enter what would be at best a consolidatory and at worst a defensive merger – least of all in association with an increasingly diffused and fragmented TGWU leadership. Indeed, there seems to be little reason why any of our four surviving predators should wish to merge with each other in the foreseeable future. On the contrary, they are likely to remain on the scene – whatever else changes – searching for minor partners, who can be more easily absorbed into an existing or barely modified government structure, in ways that are unlikely to threaten existing alliances and power groups.

In this respect, it might be argued, the prospect for British trade union structure is not altogether unlike Orwell's vision of 1984. There, it may be remembered, a series of battles for supremacy ends in the emergence of three super-states – Eurasia, Oceania and Lastasia – each unable, or unwilling, to overcome or absorb the other; each content to co-exist, in a state of containable conflict, mitigated by periods of unity and co-operation in the face of a common threat.

But we have speculated enough about the future; it is time to draw together what has been written in this section. There would seem to be four features common to all the alternatives we have considered. First, all indications suggest that British trade unions are likely to be presented with the need to change within the context of a relatively hostile external environment – for instance a labour market containing threats to existing job territories, little or no opportunities for received growth, legislative changes that threaten assumed immunities, continued government intervention in wage bargaining and the public sector, and so on – all taking place against the background of an economy that is at best recovering and at worst falling further behind its major competitors.

Second, given this context, much is likely to depend on the reactions and policies of particular employers. Thus in the vital area of job territory change the level of achieved growth in particular unions is likely to be significantly influenced by how far employers resist the unionization of middle- and lower-level management by established TUC affiliates – as against non-TUC staff associations, or 'mavericks' like the EMA. Then again, in the wider area of job regulation, the attitudes of employers will influence the future scope and levels of collective bargaining, just as their readiness to make use of new laws will largely determine how significant they are for union government and bargaining behaviour.

Third, given all these developments, there seems no reason to suggest a diminution in the pattern of increasing militancy that was a general feature in the period of our study – particularly amongst activists and union members in the public sector. There were also good reasons for supposing that this tendency would be accompanied by a continuation, and even an extension, of membership participation and lay involvement in the areas of union government and job regulation (although this does not mean that there will not be counter-moves towards greater centralization and concentration affecting particular unions). These may well be accompanied by some increase in the scope and degree of factionalism.

Finally, and as in the past, the ability of individual unions to respond to these challenges and problems will continue to depend on the action, or inaction, of national leaders and their supporting groups. This will remain true even if factionalism does develop in unions where it has so far been absent – most notably in the TGWU. For factionalism does not make leadership any less necessary: only rather more/demanding and difficult. In any case, we do not know enough about the roots of factionalism to enable us to be dogmatic about the conditions under which it can be combined with able and effective leadership. This is a problem we return to briefly in our final section below.

Lessons for interested parties

What conclusions can we derive from the study that are likely to be of value to various interested parties? We must first divide the latter into two broad groups: practitioners and serious students of the subject. But practitioners need to be further sub-divided into trade unionists and the rest – governments, employers and those that seek to influence their behaviour.

Governments and employers

From the viewpoint of non-unionist practitioners six conclusions might be thought to be of interest. First, our study suggests that they should not assume that British unions are unchanging, passive and fossilized institutions. On the contrary, they emerge as fairly effective survivors, able to meet the challenge of external threat and internal pressure at least as well as other comparable institutions.

The problem has been that the changes they introduce to meet challenges have not always been those that non-unionist practitioners expected, or planned, should occur. This is partly because effective change involves leadership initiative, and union leaders are internally oriented in their perceptions of what is required. Thus our second conclusion is that possible changes tend to be viewed as opportunities or threats to internal leadership positions. What leaders try to do is reconcile the need for change with their own security and established power base.

Third, in deciding on the most appropriate response to make to a challenge, some leaders have far more room for manoeuvre than others. They also differ greatly in the resources at their disposal. For these reasons similar forms of external pressure are likely to produce a wide variety of internal responses (or non-responses). Fourth, even the more powerful and influential union leaders are likely to be increasingly constrained by the further development of a number of recent trends in union character and behaviour – in particular, the spread of more participative forms of decision-making and the growth of rank-and-file militancy. Fifth, there are reasons to suggest that a number of leaders will find themselves operating within a climate of increasingly fragmented factionalism – including, in some instances, the need to move towards systems of 'party government'. Nevertheless, and this would be our final practical conclusion, a great deal will continue to depend on the personality, capacity and overall drive of particular union leaders, especially those who come to lead the larger organizations in intermediate and open job territories.

The most obvious general lesson to be learnt from all these conclusions is that non-union practitioners who hope to change established patterns of union behaviour need to know much more than they have usually done about the specific concerns, capacities and priorities of important union leaders; otherwise what they intend is likely to continue to produce negligible or counter-productive results. One way of summarizing this point is to suggest that outsiders should beware of policies and initiatives that assume that most leaders, at most times, have more or less the same needs and similar degrees of influence. Policies based on generalizations about how the 'trade union movement' is likely to react are often a cloak for ignorance. (They may even indicate that the speaker is just not interested in the internal perceptions and priorities of actual union leaders.)

This lesson is of equal relevance to leaders of employers' associations, who may wish to alter established bargaining levels, as it is to a plant manager, who could be trying to gain agreement for a new pay structure; but it seems to us that it is most frequently neglected by governments of all kinds. For our study suggests that in the past successive governments have been frustrated because they failed to anticipate how their various initiatives were likely to make an impact on union thinking and behaviour at national level and below.

For example, in the area of legal regulation they have not appreciated that it is much easier to release unions than contain them. Thus the 1964 Act, which made mergers easier, was influential – because it helped union leaders to do what they wish to do. By contrast, the 1971 Act was relatively unimportant – because it tried to get them to restrain their members, by using ineffective and implausible sanctions. (But then, the 1974 legislation turned out to be just as powerless to change certain aspects of employer behaviour – most notably in respect of union recognition.)

More generally, the study also confirms that union leaders tend to adopt a sectional view of government policies and the likely impact of these on their own organization. And if significant aspects of any government's policies are thought to threaten established modes of leadership behaviour – especially in relation to activists, or union finance – the result is bound to be general hostility.

All this is not to imply that governments are not entitled to pass what laws they like, even if they do seem to threaten the peace of important members of the General Council. But those who frame and suggest policies of this kind need to realize why they are bound to be resented and resisted. Governments should, in other words, understand that they have a finite sum of goodwill at their disposal. It cannot be in their interests to waste this in pursuit of unachievable and unimportant objectives.

On the other hand, politicians might well reply that the study also indicates that the co-operation and goodwill of the most influential of union leaders is unlikely to count for much against a rising tide of membership resentment directed at the government – especially in respect of its role as employer. We have already stressed that this is the aspect of union behaviour that is least amenable to national direction and control; for union leaders a choice between antagonizing the members and falling out with politicians is not really a choice at all.

Trade unions

On the assumption that many of these truths are evident enough to union leaders themselves, we may ask whether the study suggests any further lessons for them. We consider that there are at least three. The first relates to the fact that union leaders are often insufficiently aware of the differences between their own decision-taking structure and that of other unions. Of course they may admit that in many ways 'we are not like the AEU', or even that 'they do things differently in the General and Municipal'. What is not fully appreciated, in our experience, is just why this should be so – and how difficult it would be to change the situation. As a result there is often a lack of forbearance and a readiness to assume that 'what we can get away with in our organization ought to be possible in Peckham Road, or Thorne House'.

We would therefore suggest that union leaders do not always know all they should about the specific concerns and priorities of their union colleagues, or would-be rivals. Yet factors of this kind have upset more than one amalgamation search, just as they have led to misunderstandings and difficulties in areas like multi-union bargaining.

Second, union leaders should consider how far they may be able to profit from each other's achievements – not least in the field of union government. Of course our study does not suggest that there is any ideal 'model' for union government; nor does it support the advocates of particular structural reforms. On the other hand, one of its continuing themes has been that there are a number of constitutional features, or devices, that help in solving common problems – for example the device of bifurcation, or the introduction of provisions for group autonomy. We fully see why some unions have not embodied these features in their own constitutions; we are not convinced that national leadership has always examined the advantages that might accrue if they did.

Finally, the study prompts us to ask whether union leaders have always considered sufficiently carefully the medium- and long-term consequences of some of the changes they have sought to introduce – in particular, the maximum possible devolution of bargaining decisions, combined with the simultaneous encouragement of all forms of lay participation. It could be that in the end the structure of decision-taking that emerges will turn out to be incompatible with the retention of significant degrees of power and influence at the centre – even in respect of more or less routine administrative and financial decisions. This could result in large and potentially powerful unions attempting to operate without the unifying presence of effective national leadership in any important area. Given the general scenario painted of the next ten years or so, we are not convinced that this is the decision-making structure that major British unions require to meet the challenge of the 1980s.

Students of the subject

The lessons to be derived from the study for students of trade unionism can be considered under two heads: implications for terminology, and areas for further research. In the case of terminology we would argue that the notion of decision dispersal is a more useful way of classifying types of union government and the process of union decision-making than traditional concepts such as notions of degrees of 'participation', alternative forms of 'democracy' or tendencies towards 'oligarchy'.

We believe that the notion of decision dispersal, along both the vertical and the horizontal continuum, is more precise and feasible. It also enables more significant distinctions to be marked. Above all, it is more 'neutral', in that it does not imply that any given degree of dispersal is to be preferred or aimed at as an end in itself.

But we would also argue that the distinctions we introduced into the classification of job territories are an advance on previous terminologies – the notions of diversity and exposure and the division of union attitudes towards growth which we described as positive or passive. So far as merger search is concerned we would also claim that it is important to know why a given union embarks on merger activity – whether it is motivated by defensive, consolidatory or expansionist objectives. We claim that if our terminology is adopted students of the subject can finally abandon the traditional and confusing labels of 'general', 'craft', and 'industrial unionism' – which fit almost no unions and misleadingly combine existing job territories with future membership objectives.

When the notions of diversity and relative exposure are combined with the related notion of decision dispersal they provide the basis for a more meaningful system of classification than H. A. Turner's attempt at a 'morphology' of trade unionism based on his division between 'open' and 'closed' unions. Using this classification, Turner sought to establish a connection between degrees of 'openness' and forms of union government. Thus relatively open unions, such as the TGWU and the GMWU, were said to be likely to exhibit the characteristics of 'popular bossdom', while more exclusive organizations, such as the AEU, were labelled 'aristocracies'.[15] But Turner also sought to establish a causal relation-ship between degrees of 'closure' and methods of job regulation. He argued that unilateral regulation would be found in more or less closed groups, whereas open organizations would tend to concentrate on collective bargaining.

We would argue that our study demonstrates that these classifications are of doubtful utility, and are subject to more and more exceptions, in the contemporary situation. The unions we studied were never quite closed, or entirely open, in Turner's sense; they adopted policies towards new job territories that had little or nothing to do with their earlier degree of exclusiveness or form of government. Of course, in very general terms there was a move towards more 'open' attitudes of recruitment, but this only served to limit still further the applicability of Turner's distinction. Most important of all, our largest union, the TGWU, became progressively less and less like its closest rivals in terms of Turner's morphology – less and less of a 'popular bossdom': while the Engineers, remaining a 'craft' aristocracy, in terms of involvement in decision-taking, became more and more dependent on an unofficial party system that has no place in Turner's morphology. We also found no correlation between degrees of exclusiveness and forms of job regulation, as he suggests.

In short, we discovered that many different factors combined to influence the distribution of power and the forms of decision-taking in different unions. It is true that Turner sometimes mentions other factors, but he invariably attributes the major weight to the occupational composition of the membership, which he relates back to his basic distinction between open and closed organizations. For all these reasons we suggest that a typology based on particular features of membership composition and traditional attitudes towards job territory change cannot function as a short-cut to an understanding of union behaviour. An adequate typology must find room for different systems of decision-taking and styles of leadership. It should also be based on an understanding of the fact that those who take most decisions in a union are usually primarily influenced by internal political considerations.

Turning to the implications of our study for further research, it is convenient to make a distinction between established studies and work in neglected areas. So far as established studies are concerned we should mention two important areas where recent work by leading students of the subject can be said to be in need of reconsideration as a result of our findings. The first concerns the studies of G. S. Bain and his associates in the field of union growth;[16] the second relates to the role of collective bargaining, developed by H. A. Clegg in a recent study.[17]

Bain's theory of aggregate union growth is a complex one, most clearly set out in his most recent econometric analysis, *Union Growth and the Business Cycle*. From our point of view the feature of his theory most open to challenge is the extent to which Bain relies on what we would term external factors to explain union growth – rates of change in prices, wages and unemployment, along with the impact of changes in government attitudes and even legislation.[18] This emphasis on external agents is accompanied by criticism of previous writers who are said to have neglected quantitative techniques – including those, like Shister, who allotted a significant role to union leadership.[19]

Bain's data are drawn from many different countries and his time spans are much longer than ours – sometimes stretching back into the nineteenth century. More importantly, his methodology is totally different and his concentration on the quantitative necessarily means that his results and inferences cannot easily be compared with ours. Nevertheless, we find it impossible to accept the clear implication in much of his work that unions are relatively powerless to affect the aggregate level of unionization by positive and deliberate action. Above all, we cannot square his verdict on the role of union leadership with our evidence. As he puts it, 'union leadership is dependent upon and constrained by the same socio-economic forces which motivate or enable workers to join trade unions. As such it is very much a secondary or derivative determinant of aggregate union growth.'[20]

The evidence of our study is that unions are able to 'achieve' a substantial increase in membership through their own efforts. We also cannot agree that several of Bain's external factors work in the unselective way he suggests – at least not at our level of analysis. For example, he considers that inflation acts as a general inducement or 'threat' – driving workers into unions to protect standards, and making employers more willing to recognize them. We would rather emphasize the different ways in which inflation can affect particular unions – most obviously UCATT, which found it difficult to maintain services or increase subscriptions in a period of rising prices. But in contrast to UCATT we would cite the experience of NALGO, where inflation contributed to a more aggressive bargaining and recruitment policy; or the TGWU, where it helped to strengthen the case for relying on servicing by shop stewards, because they were relatively cheap. Yet in other unions – for instance the GMWU – inflation was easily absorbed, and appears to have made little impact on attitudes to growth for some considerable time.

Similarly, Bain argues that the rate of growth in money wages has an overall or 'credit effect' on union membership – since would-be members credit unions with general money increases, and so hurry to join them. This may happen in some instances, but our research indicates that in respect of UCATT, for example, higher money wages actually undermined unionization. Most building workers came to feel that in periods of rapidly rising prices they did not need organization and were better placed if they sought to negotiate individual 'lump' contracts with non-union employers. It was not until the leadership of UCATT became convinced of the need to undertake militant action to combat this process that membership stabilized.

In sum then we would argue that our studies throw doubt on how far macro-statistical analysis can provide a full explanation for the complex of factors that affect union growth, both at the level of trade union movement as a whole and in relative terms. As Bain admits, in his latest contribution to the subject, his is a theory that stresses both the 'propensity and the opportunity to organise'.[21] What it fails to do is find sufficient room for the determination and the will to organize, and the critical role of leadership.

What we think is needed, at this stage, is not a more developed or refined analytical framework, including further macro-variables,[22] but a study that seeks to combine our kind of evidence with Bain's kind of data – perhaps carried out at an intermediate level, where it is possible to distinguish between the relative impact of internal and external factors in contrasting situations.

In the area of collective bargaining our study most clearly challenges those who assert that variations in bargaining structure are the key to differences in union behaviour. This influential viewpoint, which was to some extent implicit in much of the work of Allan Flanders, has recently been most clearly argued in H. A. Clegg's interesting work, *Trade Unionism under Collective Bargaining: A Theory Based on Comparisons in Six Countries.*

Clegg concludes that the 'evidence from six developed affluent Western democracies' indicates that, where collective bargaining is the 'predominant' method of job regulation, 'its dimensions account for union behaviour more adequately than any other set of explanatory variables can do'. It follows that differences in union density, structure, government and strike incidence are largely 'explained' by Clegg by reference to appropriate differences in the extent, level and scope of collective agreements. And since bargaining structure itself is seen as largely a function of the 'structure and attitudes of employers' associations and management', Clegg's view of the causal factors influencing union behaviour is even more 'externally rooted' than that of Bain.[23] It is also just as much at variance with the implications of our study.

Once again, it is not easy to compare our evidence with his. Clegg roams over even longer time periods, and he moves from country to country. He is also largely concerned to explain why union density is lower in America than elsewhere; why German unions are more centralized than British unions; why some countries have more strikes than others, and why so many trade union structures appear to lack logical cohesion. His short answer is that the forms taken by collective bargaining in each country seem to be the most plausible single reason for the differences he observes; but it is difficult to reconcile this broadest of explanatory brushes to our own empirical findings at a much lower level of aggregation.

We can only say that we remain unconvinced. It may well be that in very general terms the extent to which bargaining makes an impact on the lives of members and would-be members affects union membership figures. It is plausible to suggest that centralized systems of bargaining encourage and perpetuate centralized systems of union government. It is self-evident that, where bargaining is sufficiently decentralized and fragmented, strike action is inclined to take a similar form. But it does not follow from all this that these are the only factors involved; or even the most important. (Certainly Bain would not agree that this was the case in respect of union growth.)

As we have seen, the membership achievements of unions in very similar bargaining situations vary significantly – for reasons that have nothing to do with bargaining structure. Many unions would find it impossible to even try to match their government procedures with their bargaining arrangements; if only because they are party to hundreds of different bargaining systems. This must be the case in respect of all large, intermediate or open unions (for example the TGWU, ASTMS, the AUEW(E) and the GMWU). Whatever may account for their differences in decision dispersal, this cannot possibly be the result of a myriad of conflicting pressures deriving from the indirect impact of thousands of very similar collective agreements. Of course, in our evidence the simplest explanation for differences is to be found in the power structures specified in constitutions, but even this is only the beginning of a total explanation. Similarly, on our evidence relative militancy and its forms are influenced by many other important considerations – most notably, in recent years, by changes in membership levels and composition and the actions of national government.

But perhaps it is in respect of what Clegg suggests about the determinants of bargaining structure that our study is most in conflict with his theory. He roundly asserts that 'In most instances the answer is that the structure and attitudes of employers' associations and management are the main influences.'[24] We can only say that we have not found this to be so. On occasion particular unions, such as the POEU, have successfully resisted management aims and policies in this area. In other cases, for example the TGWU, they have imposed their will on managements who were disinclined to accept change in any form. But for the most part change has been jointly determined, and the union's role has usually been crucial in effecting successful change.

Once again we conclude that what is needed is further research to decide how far the findings of this study can be integrated in a more extended theory of trade unionism as such. Clegg may be right to assume that variations in the scope and form of collective bargaining help to explain variations in union behaviour over a very wide area; in that sense there may well be no other 'single set of variables' that compared with bargaining structure in its overall impact. But even if further research establishes that this is the case, it will not follow that in any single aspect of union behaviour bargaining structure provides the essential 'key' to differences between unions – especially since, in the British context, so many different unions face very similar bargaining structures. Once again we need further research, which focuses on internal as well as external factors, and does not confine itself to the cross community level.

Having reviewed the impact of our findings on two established areas of research, we turn to consider how far the study may be said to suggest further areas of research of a more pioneering kind. Three obvious examples spring to mind, one from each of our major areas of change.

First, there is clearly a need for further study of the roots of decision dispersal and the probable consequences of further moves in this direction on other aspects of union behaviour. Not enough is known about the relationships between established leadership and the rank and file in a period of rapid decision dispersal – either horizontally or vertically. Personally we doubt how far existing leadership styles can survive too great a degree of decision dispersal – especially if dispersal is sufficiently advanced on the bargaining side. There may also be a link here with degrees of factionalism and its forms. For example, is there a natural connection between decentralization and diffusion and the growth of faction even in unions where officers are not elected by membership ballot? Earlier in this chapter we sought to suggest that this might well be the case. What we are suggesting now is that our tentative but plausible suggestion should be examined and explored by focusing on a study of the processes of decision dispersal in a number of unions where there have been significant moves in this direction already.

Second, there is also a need to investigate further the links between decision allocation and systems of job regulation in general. Without subscribing to the view that all aspects of union behaviour are determined by collective bargaining requirements, there are obviously areas where what happens in the field of job regulation interacts on other aspects of union activity. One such area is the impact of bargaining decentralization and diffusion on the growth of rank-and-file pressure. As we saw, in those unions that encouraged decision dispersal there tended to be a rapid development of powerful and coercive pressures on national leadership. Is it possible that, faced with pressures of this kind, some leaders will seek to buttress their own authority by sponsoring a return to more centralized systems of bargaining? Or will they react by developing more formal and structured procedures for obtaining the considered views of the rank and file as a whole, say, by the sponsorship of membership ballots? Or will they seek to develop their own unofficial party system to counter the new rank-and-file pressure? Once again it could be relatively easy to select a number of unions in contrasting bargaining situations whose behaviour in this respect could be studied with profit.

Finally, in the field of job territory change there is clearly a need to know more than we do about the roots of merger search and the effects of mergers on union behaviour. We have suggested that a combination of constitutional, political and leadership factors tend largely to determine the direction of merger search and its relative chances of success. But there is much still to be discovered about the relative importance of these factors in different circumstances. If we knew more than we did about these influences the future structure of the British trade union movement might be more easy to predict. There is certainly a case for introducing questions concerning job territory change into studies of other areas of change. Thus one may ask how far it will continue to be possible for leaders of bifurcated unions such as the TGWU to reserve for themselves an area of discretion in respect of merger searches against the background of a much more powerful and interventionist executive.

Similarly, changes in union character and militancy are bound to have some impact on the direction of merger search. Already, as we have seen, it is possible to speculate about the emergence of a relatively 'non-militant' federation or group under the leadership of the relatively non-radical GMWU.

If we can be allowed one final and extremely speculative generalization about the possible future pattern of British trade union development which we think emerges from our study, and which cries out for further investigation, it would be as follows. It could be that the pressure for cumulative decision dispersal, which may well be the single most important trend now desirable in some large British unions, is likely to produce two alternative leadership reactions. These may be termed, for the purpose of investigation, *accommodation* and *resistance*. In unions where the dispersal process is already too advanced to be resisted leadership may indeed have no alternative but to accommodate. This may well involve quite new processes of decision-taking: slower, more formal and doubtless very difficult to accommodate to present notions of the role of union leadership (especially those notions dear to the hearts of politicians, economists and others with little recent experience of the day-to-day problems of union leaders). On the other hand, where prospects of this kind are foreseen by established national leaders and they have not become irreversible, a decision may be taken to resist. In other words, these leaders will seek to avoid, so far as possible, forms of bargaining and procedures of government that seem likely to shift their own organizations past the point where further resistance is impossible.

It would be foolish to believe that leaders who resist will always fail in what they set out to do. Much will depend on how far they are prepared to sponsor modifications of their own in the field of decision allocation, rather than insist, at all times, on the maintenance of the *status quo*. Much will also depend on the external environment of the trade union movement during the next decade or so. We have given our reasons for suggesting that in the uncertain climate of the 1980s cumulative decision dispersal may not be quite what the British trade union movement needs: if this truly is the case then we do not doubt that it will not be what it gets. For as we have sought to show, British trade unions can adapt to most things if they have to do so – although they are likely to interpret the challenges facing them on their own terms. Above all, they are survivors.

Appendix   Classification of motions submitted to the Engineers' NC, 1973

The following gives some idea of how Table 10 on page 115 was drawn up by showing the manner in which the 517 motions submitted to the 1973 NC were subdivided.

Of these 517 motions, 246 were classified as industrial, 189 as political and 82 as industrial/political.

The 246 industrial motions included 28 on 'Wages and Conditions'; 5 against productivity bargaining; 14 on holidays; 7 on 'Shorter Working Week'; 12 on 'Apprentices and Youths'; 9 on equal pay – suggesting union action in industry; 2 on CSEU; 4 on supervisory members; 6 on overtime and night shift pay; 4 on the Temporary Relaxation Agreement; 2 on the Procedure Agreement; 83 on specific industrial agreements, for example on electricity supply; 3 on income tax and tool allowances; and 67 miscellaneous items such as guaranteed week, lay-offs, redundancies and severance pay, EEF/CSEU agreements, tri-partite agreements, etc. Obviously some of the above have political overtones, for instance the pay claim debate during a period of incomes policy, but as there were separate motions attacking a wage freeze as such, the wages and conditions motions, which are similar to previous wages and conditions motions outside incomes policy periods, were put into the industrial bracket.

Of the 189 political motions, 5 were dealing with the Labour Party and proscription; 16 on the EEC; 22 on some aspect of nationalization; 34 on old age pensions; 13 on the Housing Finance Act; 9 on support for the *Morning Star, Tribune* and *Labour Weekly*; 28 on foreign policy; 7 on racialism and intolerance; and the remaining 55 on such things as social security acts, free school milk, family allowance, the environment and pollution.

It was difficult to separate the industrial/political motions from the other two categories, but the main type of motion in this field was influenced by the union's reaction to government involvement in industrial relations. For instance, of the 82 motions classified as industrial/political, 40 were on some aspect of the IRA and/or NIRC and 25 were on wage freeze or incomes policy topics, which leaves only 17 on such issues as legislation for greater safety at work, compensation for industrial diseases, etc.

Notes and references

Chapter 1 The scope and nature of the study

1 B. Russell, *History of Western Philosophy* (Allen & Unwin), p. 14.
2 See S. Perlman, *A Theory of the Labour Movement* (Macmillan 1928).
3 See H. A. Turner, *Trade Union Growth, Structure and Policy* (Allen & Unwin 1962).
4 See J. Hughes, *Trade Union Structure and Government*, Donovan Commission Research Paper no. 5 (HMSO 1967) for the first discussion of the notion of the 'natural growth pattern' of British trade unions.

Chapter 2 Methodology and model

1 C. Wright Mills, *The Sociological Imagination* (New York: Oxford University Press 1959), p. 72.
2 All the minor case studies were completed by others. The NUPE information has been obtained from R. Fryer *et al.* who have been working on a study of that union at Warwick University. The rest were carried out by postgraduate students in association with the project.

Chapter 3 Areas of change

1 These figures and those that follow are taken from Robert Price and George S. Bain, 'Union growth revisited: 1948–74 in perspective', *British Journal of Industrial Relations*, vol. 14, no. 3 (November 1976), pp. 339–55.
2 Although white-collar union membership grew by 33.6 per cent between 1948 and 1964, it did not keep pace with the growth in employment, and consequently white-collar union density declined over this period. After 1964, however, the growth of white-collar unionization was greater than that of white-collar employment and consequently there was an increase in white-collar density.
3 See R. T. Buchanan, 'Merger waves in British unionism', *Industrial Relations Journal*, vol. 5, no. 2 (Summer 1974), pp. 37–44.
4 *Royal Commission on Trade Unions and Employers' Associations, 1965–1968: Report*, Cmnd 3623 (HMSO 1968), p. 96.
5 The analysis that follows has been put forward by Michael Silver in 'Recent British strike trends: a factual analysis', *British Journal of Industrial Relations*, vol. 11, no. 1 (March 1973), pp. 66–104.
6 ibid., p. 97.
7 ibid., p. 75.
8 ibid., p. 98.

9   Ralf Dahrendorf, *Class and Class Conflict in Industrial Society* (Routledge & Kegan Paul 1963), p. 268.

10 *Royal Commission on Trade Unions and Employers' Associations.*

11 Allan Flanders, *Industrial Relations: What's Wrong with the System?* (Institute of Personnel Management 1965), p. 25.

12 ibid., p. 31.

13 See, for example, Shirley Lerner, 'The future organisation and structure of trade unions' in B. C. Roberts (ed.), *Industrial Relations: Contemporary Problems and Perspectives* (Methuen 1964), pp. 101–13.

14 In examining the system of government of the AEU and AUEW(E) or Engineers, changes in the title owing to amalgamations did not necessarily coincide with alterations in the system of union government. An attempt will however be made to use the right title where it is of any significance for government of the union.

15 The ASW was the major union involved in forming UCATT in 1971 following its merger with ASPD in 1970. The system of government of the ASW very much influenced the government adopted by UCATT, but there were some quite significant changes arising from the merger and these will be referred to in the text.

16 H. A. Turner, *Trade Union Growth, Structure and Policy* (Allen & Unwin 1962).

17 Sidney and Beatrice Webb, *Industrial Democracy* (Longmans 1901).

18 R. Michels, *Political Parties* (Glencoe, Ill.: Free Press 1911).

19 S. M. Lipset, M. Trow and J. Coleman, *Union Democracy: The Internal Politics of the International Typographical Union* (Glencoe, Ill.: Free Press 1956).

20 See, for instance, R. Martin, 'Union democracy: an explanatory framework' *Sociology*, vol. 2 (1968) and J. D. Edelstein and M. Warner *Comparative Union Democracy* (Allen & Unwin 1975)

21 TGWU Rule Book, rule 7, clause 4.

22 See, for instance, TGWU BDC (1953), minute 92.

23 The GMWU and NALGO called their intermediate geographic areas 'districts' in the early 1960s but in size they were the equivalent of other unions' regions and hence are given this title for the purpose of making useful comparisons across unions.

24 GMWU Report of the 53rd Congress (1968).

25 See T. J. Connelly, *The Woodworkers 1860–1960* (Amalgamated Society of Woodworkers 1960).

26 J. B. Jefferys, *The Story of the Engineers* (Lawrence & Wishart 1945), p. 72.

27 Connelly, pp. 110–11.

28 See Chapter 7 for a detailed description of bargaining in these unions.

29 See *Industrial Relations Review and Report* (July and December 1972).

30 TGWU Rule Book (1968), rule 4 (6).

31 GMWU Report of 53rd Congress (1968), pp. 323–4.

32 The ASW's membership in 1960 was still overwhelmingly craft, and although craft membership in the AEU was approximately 50 per cent some 95 per cent of members contesting election to full-time officer positions in the union between 1945 and 1975 were skilled workers.

33 A. Bullock, *The Life and Times of Ernest Bevin*, vol. 1 (Heinemann 1960), p. 205. Bevin was the founding father and first general secretary of the TGWU.

34 The appeals body was a later addition for some unions, including the GMWU, which introduced one under the influence of the Industrial Relations Act 1971; see GMWU Report of 60th Congress (1975), Appendix 2, p. 519.

35   See Bullock for comment on the formation of the TGWU.
36   See TGWU Report, 17th BDC (1957), minute 23.
37   See TGWU Report, 15th BDC (1953), minute 74.
38   See for example TGWU Report, 20th BDC (1963), minute 88.
39   See TGWU Report, 22nd BDC (1967), minute 63, and Report of 23rd BDC (1969), minute 43.
40   See TGWU Report, 18th BDC (1959), minutes 55 and 56.
41   ASTMS Rule Book, rule 24 (6).
42   See *Socialist Worker* 11 May 1974 and 10 August 1974 for a leading IS member on internal politics of ASTMS and his own dismissal from the NEC.
43   See, for instance, *The Times* (22 September 1976) for comment on the vote on ASTMS NEC against nationalization of banking and insurance, which owed much to the insurance section's opposition to the proposal.
44   This arrangement was changed in January 1975. The General Council was then disbanded and the National Executive Committee (now called Executive Council) was enlarged. This does not basically alter the above argument, as all regional secretaries are now on the new EC plus twenty lay delegates and the general secretary. It would appear that the new structural changes had no impact on the GMWU's general system of government which is dominated by the general and regional secretaries.
45   See GMWU Rule Book, rule 13.
46   See 'Cameron Report', *Report of Court of Inquiry into Trade Disputes at the Barbican and Horseferry Road Construction Sites in London*, Cmnd 3396 (HMSO 1976).
47   See *Morning Star* (21 June 1976) and *The Times* (14 July 1976) on these events.
48   AUEW Engineering Section, rule 2 (16).
49   See Chapter 4 for an examination of the two-party system.
50   See I. Richter, *Political Purpose in Trade Unions* (Allen & Unwin 1973), pp. 100 and 156–8.
51   See pp. 41–2 and Figure 3 for an explanation of the significance of the different levels and shadings used in the diagram.
52   See, for instance, G. S. Bain and L. Elsheikh, *Union Growth and the Business Cycle* (Basil Blackwell 1976); and Bain and Price.
53   For details of the membership trends of various unions see Table 2, p. 32.
54   Turner, p. 248.
55   NUBE was accepted back into the TUC in 1975.
56   The proportion of all teachers organized in unions of one kind or another was 81 per cent in 1950, 75 per cent in 1967 and 83 per cent in 1973.
57   Some of the decline in the proportion organized by the NUT is accounted for by the expansion of the further education sector where the NUT does not actively recruit. This is reflected in the growth of the Association of Teachers in Technical Institutions (now amalgamated with the Association of Teachers in Colleges and Departments of Education to form the National Association of Teachers in Further and Higher Education, NATFHE) from 2 per cent of the total in 1960 to 9 per cent in 1973.
58   The Joint Four comprise the Association of Head Mistresses (AHM), the Association of Assistant Mistresses (AAM), the Assistant Masters' Association (AMA) and the Incorporated Association of Headmasters (IAHM).
59   For example, G. S. Bain, *The Growth of White Collar Unionism* (Oxford University Press 1970).
60   Turner, p. 244.

61 H. A. Clegg, *Trade Unionism under Collective Bargaining* (Basil Blackwell 1976), p. 10. By 'structure' in this context Clegg is referring to membership scope.

62 In 1924 and 1943 the TUC Conference proposed that reports be prepared on closer working between unions. Similar demands were renewed in the late 1950s and early 1960s. In 1959 Congress carried a resolution calling for greater co-ordination between unions, and in 1962 it was agreed that 'it is time the British trade union movement adapted its structure to modern conditions. It instructs the General Council to examine and report on the possibility of re-organising the structure of both the TUC and the British trade union movement with a view to making it better fitted to meet modern industrial conditions'. It was felt at this time that the wave of mergers in big business, which produced 'a greater concentration of industry', and that 'the development of modern techniques' called for a compensating rationalization of union structure.

63 Connelly, p. 4.

64 Connelly, p. 84.

65 Thirty-three per cent of AUBTW's membership was non-craft, compared with less than 10 per cent in the ASW.

66 Jefferys, p. 208.

67 It is difficult to be more precise because skilled workers are not classified as such. The union collects statistics only by section, and since many craftsmen have over the years since 1926 opted for Section V rather than for the more expensive and craft exclusive Section I, the latter no longer reflects their full numbers. Bearing this caveat in mind, the proportion of members in Section I declined from 37.4 per cent in 1940 to 31.9 per cent in 1960 and 25.3 per cent in 1970.

68 Those newly eligible for membership in 1942 included: methods engineers; development engineers and rate fixers; progress chasers; marine surveyors and engineers' surveyors; inspectors and all other engineers who were indisputedly connected with production and whose technical ability has fitted them for the posts that the engineering industry itself has.created.

69 The agreement was:
   (1) all professionally qualified scientific workers; all laboratory workers and all scientific workers in the chemical industry to be organized by AScW;
   (2) all supervisory grades other than those in (1) to be in ASSET;
   (3) technicians not engaged on production to be organized by the AScW;
   (4) all technicians in production to be organized by ASSET;
   (5) mutual recognition of those already organized in the wrong grades.

70 For details see S. W. Lerner, *Breakaway Unions and the Small Trade Union* (Allen & Unwin 1961).

71 'Internal' post office engineers are those employed in the construction, installation and maintenance of equipment and apparatus inside the telephone exchanges, as distinct from 'external', who are employed in the construction and maintenance of external line plant.

72 R. M. Blackburn, K. Prandy and A. Stewart, 'White-collar associations: organisational character and employee involvement', in *Proceedings of a SSRC Conference Social Stratification and Industrial Relations* (SSRC September 1968), p. 88.

73 Allan Flanders, *Trade Unions* (Hutchinson 1965), p. 76.

74 Clegg, p. 116.

75 Turner, p. 364.

76 V. L. Allen, 'The paradox of militancy', in Robin Blackburn and Alexander Cockburn (eds.), *The Imcompatibles: Trade Union Militancy and the Consensus* (Penguin
   1967), p. 251.

77 See W. Craik, *Sydney Hill and the National Union of Public Employees* (Allen &
   Unwin 1968), p. 85.

78 R. Fryer, A. Fairclough and T. Manson, *Organisation and Changes in the National
   Union of Public Employees* (Department of Sociology, University of Warwick;
   August 1974), p. 36. National Committees mentioned in the quotation were not
   introduced until after 1960.

79 In the national local government committee the situation is somewhat different, in
   that the Metropolitan District is entitled to four representatives, and the Eastern and
   North Western Districts, both of which cover the territory of two provincial Whitley
   Councils, are each entitled to two representatives.

80 Beatrice Webb, 'English teachers and their professional organisation', *New Statesman*, vol. 5 (September 1915).

81 The Main Committee settles the salaries of teachers in primary and secondary
   schools, while other committees (formally autonomous, but in practice subordinate
   to the Main Committee) settle the salaries of teachers in further education. In 1965,
   following the Remuneration of Teachers Act, the DES entered the Burnham
   Committees on the Management side.

82 These advisory committees include: Primary Schools; Middle Schools; Secondary
   Schools; Special Education; University Departments and Colleges of Education;
   Teaching Staff in Community Homes; Inspectors, Organisers and Advisory Officers
   of LEAs; Retired Teachers; Young Teachers; Teachers' Centres.

83 The majority of UCATT members are in the construction industry and were thus
   covered by the NFBTO. The percentage of the membership of each of the constitu-
   ents of UCATT who were affiliated to the NFBTO is given below.

	Total membership	Affiliated to NFBTO	% in NFBTO
ASW	191,620	121,856	64
ABT	2,000	900	45
ASPD	74,064	60,011	81
AUBTW	82,112	78,272	95
UCATT total	349,796	261,039	75

84 Donovan Research Paper no. 7, *Employers' Associations* (HMSO 1967), p. 34.

85 ibid.

86 Clive Jenkins, 'My Strategy', *Industry Week* (30 January 1970), p. 8.

87 'There are a great number of positive advantages associated with the pattern of
   national bargaining, and to recognise the benefits of a measure of local bargaining
   does not invalidate them. It must be remembered that national bargaining represents
   the primary function of national trade unions. In other words it expresses the
   common factor, the common interest which exists among the membership involved.'
   Trade Unionism (Trades Union Congress 1966; evidence to Donovan Commission),
   p. 51.

88 ibid., p. 88.

89 Trades Union Congress, p. 88.

90   See Table A, p. 14, Table B, p. 15 and Table C, p. 16 in the Donovan Report.
91   See, for example, V. Feather, 'The Royal Commission's Analysis: A Trade Union Appraisal, *British Journal of Industrual Relations*, vol. 6, no. 3 (November 1968), p. 339; and H. A. Turner, 'The Royal Commission's Research Papers', *British Journal of Industrial Relations*, vol. 6, no. 3 (November 1968), p. 351.
92   Donovan Report, pp. 36–7.

Chapter 4   Changes in internal government

1   See Chapter 3, pp. 37–60, for a description of unions' systems of government around 1960.
2   See pp. 27–30.
3   TGWY Report, 22nd BDC (1967), minute 58.
4   See pp. 128–30.
5   TGWU proposed amendments to rule 9, Appendix V to GEC Minutes, February 1968.
6   TGWU 4th Rules Conference (1968), minute 12.
7   TGWU proposed amendments to rule 9, Appendix V to GEC Minutes, February 1968.
8   J. L. Jones, *The Right to Participate: Key to Industrial Progress* (TGWU 1970).
9   From interviews with regional secretaries.
10   It should be pointed out that in all these and other internal government changes Jones was assisted and supported by his deputy general secretary, Urwin, who shared to a great extent with Jones the general secretary's duties.
11   See Chapter 3 for a brief description of the methods used in the TGWU.
12   See V. L. Allen, *Trade Union Leadership* (Longman 1957), pp. 280–8.
13   TGWU 4th Rules Conference (1968), minute 25.
14   See Chapter 8 for a more comprehensive examination of development in the bargaining channel of government.
15   TGWU Report, 17th BDC (1957), minute 102.
16   A. Bullock, *The Life and Times of Ernest Bevin* (Heinemann 1960), p. 192.
17   See *Report of Inquiry into the Locally Determined Aspects of the System of Payment and Earnings Opportunities of Registered Dock Workers in the Port of Liverpool (including Birkenhead)* (HMSO October 1967).
18   See D. F. Wilson, *Dockers* (Fontana 1972), pp. 82, 195–6.
19   Wilson, *Dockers*.
20   J. Jones polled 334,125 votes to the next candidate's vote of 28,335. There were ten candidates.
21   J. Jones in C. Levinson (ed.), *Industry's Democratic Revolution* (Allen & Unwin 1974), p. 257.
22   TGWU's assistant general secretary's Report to the GEC (1968).
23   See p. 208.
24   In a letter to the authors.
25   ibid.
26   See for example, L. Wootton, 'Parties in union government: the AESD', *Political Studies*, vol. 9 (June 1961). This describes the factionalism in the forerunner of TASS in the late 1950s.
27   AUEW 'Instrument of Amalgamation', p. 6.

28 See Table 10, p. 115.

29 The nature and organization of the two parties in the Engineers is examined later in the chapter.

30 It was stated in interview that if the seven Foundry delegates had been given a free vote they would have split 6 to 1 *for* the Social Contract and thus reversed the Joint Conference decision to 36–33 in favour of supporting the Social Contract.

31 See 'Insight', no. 17 (1975). This is an unofficial paper which supports the moderates in the Engineering Section of the AUEW.

32 See the *Sunday Times* (21 December 1978).

33 See *Financial Times* (11, 15 and 17 September 1975).

34 See *Financial Times* (11 September 1975).

35 As stated in the High Court, Duffy *v.* AUEW, 24 September 1975 before Mr Justice Cantley.

36 See pp. 101–2 for comment on the precedent setting Foundry Workers' action when they mandated delegates against the Social Contract in 1975.

37 See pp. 112–13 below for how the president lost his casting vote at the NC.

38 See R. Undy, 'The electoral influence of the opposition party in the AUEW Engineering section, 1960–1975', *British Journal of Industrial Relations*, vol. 17, no. 1 (March 1979), which included an examination of the Engineers' opposition party's electoral activity. Some of the material used in that article is reproduced in this section of the chapter.

39 These and other descriptions were used in interview by members of the Engineers to describe the two parties. The left were, for instance, referred to as Marxists, Communists, fundamentalists, broad left, etc., while the right was known as the establishment, revisionists, anti-communists, Labour loyalists.

40 See 'IRIS' (March 1959).

41 These are president, general secretary, two assistant general secretaries and seven executive councillors.

42 AEU Rule Book (1960 and 1970), rule 2 (10).

43 See the *Morning Star* (12 March 1975), which carried a picture of the various papers used by the Labour Group, many of them being produced on a regional basis.

44 If there is no overall majority on the first ballot the two candidates with the highest votes progress to the second and final ballot.

45 See 'IRIS' (April 1962 and July 1962). The candidates named by 'IRIS' as having left-wing support, that is, Ambrose and Wright, both reached the second ballots.

46 That is, elections in which the total electorate vote and which involve the posts of president, general secretary, assistant general secretaries and national organizers.

47 See AEU NC Report (1960).

48 See *AEU Journal* (July 1966).

49 ibid., p. 273.

50 'IRIS' argued that factory-based branches, approximately 500 of the Engineers' 2500 branches, could wield a totally disproportionate influence in elections when the average vote was between 6 and 11 per cent.

51 See Undy, 'Electoral Influence', for a breakdown of voting in these two elections.

52 Average branch vote was 11 per cent or fifty votes.

53 This is the usual range of postal ballot voting but it is a percentage of those voting who are on the register and therefore marginally overstates the actual percentage of total membership voting.

54 This body is the NC under another name.
55 See 'IRIS' (February 1968), news survey, 'Voting in union elections'.
56 The NC is convened as the Rules Revision Committee every five years.
57 See the AEF Engineering Section Report of the Rules Revision meeting (1970) and 'AUEW(E) postal ballots', 'IRIS' (April 1973).
58 The *Financial Times* (17 February 1975).
59 'Engineering News and Views' (February 1975).
60 It looked from this election as if Boyd (moderate) would defeat the progressives' candidate, Wright, quite comfortably in the second ballot for general secretary. Two incumbent progressives also lost their jobs in the October elections.
61 See *Morning Star* (14, 19 and 20 March 1975).
62 See Incomes Data Services Ltd, Brief 70 (October 1975).
63 *The Times* Law Report (12 June 1975).
64 See pp. 188–203 for a detailed discussion of the AUEW merger.
65 Of the seven alterations the formation and composition of: (a) one EC, president and general secretary was proposed, covering (b) one National Conference, (c) one Rules Revision Committee, (d) one Final Appeals Court, (e) one financial structure, (f) one common method of choosing full-time officials, (g) guarantee of the continuance of the four sections under one EC.
66 See I. Ritcher, *Political Purpose in Trade Unions* (Allen & Unwin 1973).
67 See Appendix for a description of how the motions were allocated to the categories.
68 See *UCATT Journal* (January 1976) for branch voting on the seventy-seven rule revision questions.
69 UCATT *Viewpoint* (February 1976).
70 *The Times* (3 November 1975).
71 Motion 68, Perivale Branch, London Region, Report of 58th Congress (1973), pp. 317–21.
72 GMWU Report of 59th Congress (1974).
73 This was a sub-committee of the General Council and in fact dealt with most business, thus reducing the General Council to a rubber-stamping role in decision-making.
74 A. Utting, a Communist Party member, won the Division 3 seat with 10,014 votes to the next candidate's 6881 votes. There were five candidates in the elections.
75 See P. Ferris, *The New Militants* (Penguin 1972).
76 'NALGO Action Group [NAG] News' (August/September 1972).

Chapter 5   Change in job territory: natural growth

1 See G. Bain and F. Elsheikh, *Union Growth and the Business Cycle* (Basil Blackwell 1976) and G. Bain and R. Price, 'Union growth and employment trends in the United Kingdom 1964–70', *British Journal of Industrial Relations*, vol. 10, no. 3 (November 1972), pp. 325–9.
2 See J. Hughes, *Trade Union Structure and Government*, Donovan Commission Research Paper 5 (HMSO 1967).
3 See Table 5, p. 67.
4 ibid.
5 See Bain and Price.
6 Figure 1, p. 28.

7 Local Government, Food Drink and Tobacco, and Engineering.

8 From an interview with a past official of the GMWU.

9 By Professor H. Clegg and Warwick University Industrial Relations Research Unit.

10 Certainly their position was relatively much stronger than their opposite number in the Midlands. Here the TGWU's Region 5 officers inherited a relatively strong position in both engineering and local government, partly as a result of an earlier amalgamation with the Midlands-based Workers' Union.

11 Unfortunately, direct employment–membership comparisons cannot be made for these regions as they differ significantly from the Department of Employment's statistical regions, but comparisons with centres of employment can be made and these show no major changes in employment that could account for the changes in membership.

12 The trade groups were reorganized in 1969. This regrouping makes any comparison across trade groups before 1969 of little, if any, value.

13 TGWU Report, 23rd BDC (1969), minute 43.

14 This was the year mentioned by regional secretaries as the start of the check-off campaign to reduce the incidence of lapsed membership.

15 TGWU *Record* (December 1973).

16 TGWU *Record* (February 1974).

17 Estimated from returned postal questionnaires sent to the TGWU's district offices.

18 The remaining membership of the Engineers was mainly composed of apprentices and superannuated members.

19 The number discounted includes those with associate membership and joint membership with the ATTI. Associate membership is non-paying student membership without voting rights, and ATTI became a virtually autonomous organization maintaining a separate existence in this period and can therefore also be discounted when considering trends in NUT membership.

20 See Chapter 3, p. 67.

21 See G. S. Bain, *The Growth of White Collar Unionism* (Oxford University Press 1970).

22 R. Price and G. S. Bain, 'Union growth revisited: 1948–1974 in perspective', *British Journal of Industrial Relations*, vol. 14, no. 3, pp. 339–55.

23 ASTMS Officers Handbook, p. 1.

24 *Public Service* (March 1972), p. 7.

25 UCATT 1974 Delegate Conference.

26 See Chapters 3 and 7 for a further examination of change in NALGO's character.

27 *Viewpoint* (September 1972).

28 Centralized in the case of the non-bargaining channel of this bifurcated union.

29 ASTMS evidence to the Donovan Commission: *Report* (HMSO 1968) p. 2247.

30 See Table 20, p. 139.

31 Bain; Bain and Price; and Bain and Elsheikh.

32 Bain, p. 183.

33 Bain and Elsheikh, p. 117.

Chapter 6   Change in job territory: mergers

1 See H. A. Clegg, *General Union in a Changing Society* (Basil Blackwell 1964), ch. 4.

2 See J. B. Jefferys, *The Story of the Engineers* (Lawrence & Wishart 1971), p. 191.

3 See Jefferys, pp. 192–4.

4   See R. Postgate, *The Builders' History* (National Federation of Building Trade Operatives 1923), p. 395.

5   See G. D. H. Cole, *The World of Labour* (Bell 1913), p. 266.

6   See J. D. M. Bell in A. Flanders and H. A. Clegg, *The System of Industrial Relations in Great Britain* (Basil Blackwell 1967), p. 150.

7   The AUBTW National Delegate Conference, 1970 *Annual Report*, p. 102.

8   ibid. (the union's accountant).

9   *ASPD Journal* (July 1966), p. 4.

10 *UCATT Journal*, Annual Report on Finance (1972).

11 G. Smith in *UCATT Journal* (April 1972), p. 192.

12 *ASPD Journal* (March 1969), p. 1.

13 See G. Latta, 'Trade union finances', *British Journal of Industrial Relations*, vol. 10, no. 3 (November 1972), pp. 392–411.

14 See *Department of Employment Gazette* (December 1976).

15 *Report of the Committee of Inquiry under Professor E. H. Phelps-Brown into Certain Matters concerning Labour in Building and Civil Engineering*, Cmnd 3714 (HMSO 1968).

16 See, for instance, *Financial Times* (23 March 1973). The 400,000 estimated appeared to originate in an unpublished NEDC report.

17 NFBTO Conference Report (1969), p. 6.

18 From UCATT's Research Department.

19 Firms with over 1200 employees. There were eighty-five firms over this size in 1968, employing 20 per cent or 272,000 operatives.

20 AUBTW NDC Report (1970), p. 157.

21 This information was gathered during interviews.

22 A NEDO calculation reported in R. Taylor, 'Can the lump be abolished', *Socialist Commentary* (January 1974).

23 *Report of the Committee of Inquiry under Professor E. H. Phelps-Brown*, Research Supplement, p. 66.

24 ibid., p. 114–15.

25 R and D Paper, Ministry of Public Building and Works, 'Modernisation of Construction Industry', November 1967.

26 NFBTO Conference Report (1969).

27 See ASW Conference Report (1968), p. 45.

28 See *ASPD Journals* (May and October 1968).

29 AUBTW 2nd Quarterly Report (1970).

30 TUC Report (1962).

31 TUC Report (1963).

32 AUBTW Conference Report (1970), p. 166.

33 See *NUFTO Record* (May 1970).

34 Later NUFTO and the ASWcM merged to create FTAT on a trade group basis.

35 G. Smith, *National Building* (June 1971), p. 180.

36 AUBTW 41st Conference Report (1970), p. 196.

37 ibid., p. 199.

38 ASW/ASPD Rules Revision Voting (1970), 'A Proposed New Constitution for your New Society'.

39 NAOP National Delegate Conference (1967), p. 88.

40 ibid., p. 94.

41 ibid.
42 See, for instance, 'Building Workers' Charter', vol. 1, no. 5 (1970).
43 See, for instance, *ASPD Journal* (July 1969).
44 *ASPD Journal* (June 1967).
45 NAOP National Delegate Conference (1967), p. 93.
46 In the extensive rules revision of 1976, the regional secretaries became elected officers of the union.
47 UCATT Rules 1972; rules 24, 26 and 29.
48 UCATT Rules 1972; rule 24, clauses 20–22.
49 In the 1976 rule changes it was agreed further to reduce the EC to a seven-man executive by 1981. The composition in 1981 would be three ASW, two ASPD and two AUBTW.
50 NAOP National Delegates Conference (1967), p. 91.
51 AUBTW 2nd Quarterly Report (1968).
52 ASW Report of 22nd Conference (1968), pp. 44–5.
53 See Jefferys, p. 260.
54 ibid., p. 208.
55 ibid., p. 194.
56 AUFW Annual Delegate Meeting Report (1965).
57 AUFW Annual Delegate Meeting (1960), p. 108.
58 AUFW Annual Delegate Meeting Report (1961), p. 83.
59 AUFW Annual Delegate Meeting Report (1966), p. 88.
60 Calculations were made using the 1961 Census and the 1971 Census of 1 per cent economically active. The occupations used in the calculations were: 021 Smiths & Foreman, 032 App's Eng's and Allied Trades, 036 Welders, 037 Turners, 038 M/C Toolsetters, 039 M/C Tool Operators, 040 Toolmakers and Tool fitters, 041 Motor Mech's and Auto Engineers, 042 Maintenance Fitters, 043 Fitters and Erectors, 047 Press Workers and Stampers, 048 Metal Workers nec, 049 Watch and Chronometer, 050 Precision Instrument Makers, 052 Coach Repairers, 053 Inspectors Metal and Elect, 054 Other Metals, 108 Engineers Labourers nec.
61 These calculations were also made from Census reports. For the AUFW they include: 020 Moulders & Coremakers, 023 Fitters and Metal Drawers and 109 Labourers in Foundries, 'Other Employees and out of Employment' male and female.
62 Using Census figures.
63 AUEW Engineering Section, NC Report (1973).
64 G. S. Bain, *The Growth of White Collar Unionism* (Oxford University Press, 1970), p. 34.
65 Figure given in interview by a DATA national official.
66 A CEU national officer in interview.
67 AUFW 17th Annual Delegate Conference (1962), p. 21.
68 ibid., p. 20.
69 ibid.
70 See H. J. Fyrth and A. Collins, *The Foundry Workers* (AUFW 1959), p. 310.
71 ibid., p. 311, quoting from 'Amalgamation: Report of Meeting of Trade Unions in the Engineering Industry', 29 February 1956, p. 19.
72 AScW Annual Council Report (1967).
73 *AEU Journal* (January 1966).
74 From an interview with an ex-NUVB national officer.

75   The following comments on the merger negotiations rely almost exclusively on material gathered in interviews.
76   This was tentatively suggested in the *AEU Journal* (January 1966).
77   An official of the Scottish Brassturners, Fitters & Instrument Makers Association, D. Tonner, lost his position in the AEU in elections following a merger between the two unions.
78   See, for instance, the 1972 'National Agreement [for] Outside Steelwork Erection and Steam Generating Plant Erection Agreements'.
79   This was one of DATA's points in its ten-point amalgamation programme.
80   TASS used the AUEW in 1973 to press its claim for the right to represent all staff workers within the amalgamated union. See *TASS News* (October 1973).
81   See Jefferys, ch. 9.
82   Quoted in article, 'Trade unions take the offensive in the City', *Financial Times*, 18 May 1970.
83   'Amalgamation: the decision is yours', *AScW Journal* (September 1967), p. 18.
84   ibid.
85   ibid.
86   See A. Bullock, *The Life and Times of Ernest Bevin* (Heinemann 1960), vol. I, chs. 8 and 9.
87   TGWU Report, 22nd BDC (1967), Minute 58.
88   Speech given to the Industrial Society Conference on 7 June 1974 by Claude Smith, secretary, Midland Bank Staff Section of ASTMS.
89   An interview with the authors.
90   *Financial Times* (18 May 1970).
91   See J. Hughes, *Trade Union Structure and Government*, Donovan Commission Research Paper no. 5, Part 1: 'Royal Commission on Trade Unions and Employers Associations' (HMSO 1967), p. 53.

Chapter 7   Changes in the character of job regulation

1   C. T. B. Smith, R. Clifton, P. Makeham, S. W. Creighton and R. V. Burn, *Strikes in Britain: A Research Study of Stoppages in the UK* (HMSO 1978).
2   This analysis of public and private sector trends is taken from Andrew McLeod, 'Pay in the public sector' (unpublished paper, Nuffield College, Oxford 1974).
3   R. J. Liddle and W. E. J. McCarthy, 'The Impact of the Prices and Incomes Board on the reform of collective bargaining', *British Journal of Industrial Relations*, vol. 10, no. 3 (November 1972), p. 417.
4   The percentage of strikes involving administrative workers increased from an average of 5.8 per cent of strikes in 1966–69 to 8.2 per cent of strikes in 1970–73.
5   For details see D. Volker, 'NALGO's affiliation to the TUC', *British Journal of Industrial Relations*, vol. 4, no. 1 (March 1966), p. 61.
6   ibid.
7   See *Public Service* (February 1962).
8   Contained in its consultative paper, *NALGO in the 70s* (NEC 1972), p. 13.
9   Because of inflation it was agreed to raise the contribution to £100,000 p.a. in 1966 and £250,000 p.a. in 1970.
10 *Public Service* (July/August 1961), p. 2.

11   ibid.
12   *Public Service* (July 1966), p. 6.
13   ibid.
14   Information about industrial action in NALGO is derived from reports of the Emergency Committee's proceedings in *Public Service* and from interviews with district officers at local level.
15   *Public Service* (October 1969), p. 1.
16   *Public Service* (January 1970), p. 1.
17   Of 66,153 ballots 33,323 were returned. Of these 45 per cent (23 per cent of the total) were for a total ban on overtime, and 34 per cent (17 per cent total) for selective strikes on full pay, and 13 per cent (6 per cent total) on part pay.
18   *Public Service* (February 1974), p. 20: three in five voted in the ballot. Of these 63 per cent were in favour of an overtime ban, 60 per cent voted for refusal to work with agency staff, 49 per cent selective strikes on full pay, 37 per cent selective strikes without pay, and 40 per cent a one-day token strike.
19   Pay norms were expressed in percentage rather than cash terms; major weight was thrown on the 'productivity' criterion; and comparability, which was a traditional component of public service pay, was specifically eschewed.
20   For details see pp. 307–8.
21   See *inter alia* G. S. Bain, *The Growth of White Collar Unionism* (Oxford University Press 1970) and V. A. Ellis, 'Some sociological dimensions of unionisation among technical and supervisory employees' (unpublished PhD Thesis 1971).
22   See NBPI, *Second General Report, July 1966 to August 1967* Cmnd 3394 (HMSO 1947), paragraph 47.
23   NBPI, *Pay and Conditions of Industrial Civil Servants*, Cmnd 4351 (HMSO 1970).
24   See G. A. Dorfman *Wage Politics in Britain 1945–67* (Charles Knight 1974), p. 113.
25   The other organizations represented were: NALGO, the Institution of Professional Civil Servants, the Association of Officers of Executive Councils and Pricing Committees, the British Gas Staff Association, the Confederation of Health Service Employees, the LCC Staff Association, the Metropolitan Water Board Staff Association and the Association of Scientific Workers. Those organizations sending observers included: the Central Council of Bank Staff Associations, NUBE, the British Dental Association, the BMA, the Engineers' Guild and Royal College of Nursing.
26   *The Schoolmaster* (1 September 1961), p. 346.
27   NALGO, 'NALGO in the '70s', submitted by the National Executive Council to the 1972 Annual Conference, p. 9. The Emergency Committee is a sub-committee of the NEC.
28   Although the composition of the NEC still does not reflect the occupational composition of the union at large. In 1971 the respective proportions were:

	% NEC members	*% members as whole*
Senior officer* grades and above	71.09	20.87
Below senior officer grades	28.11	76.88
Retired		5.25

* Senior officers are defined as those on £2000 p.a. and above in 1971.

29 Source: Alex Spoor, *White Collar Union – 60 Years of NALGO* (Heinemann 1967), Appendix.

30 The definition of chief officer is somewhat arbitrary and includes chief officer of small as well as very large units of local government. Moreover, the figures for the NEC includes some honorary officers, such as honorary solicitors, whose positions have tended to be occupied by personalities with long service and who tend therefore to be in high-ranking occupations.

31 'IRIS News' (April 1973), p. 5.

32 For example, a 'Reform Movement' existed in the Electricity section in the mid-1960s, and in 1972 'Public Service' reported a 'ginger group' in the health service which claimed to represent Regional Hospital Board Staff and which was bringing in officers from other unions to address NALGO members. Communist-based action groups have also operated in the past, at least at branch level, but there is no evidence that any concerted effort had been made by Communists to gain office in NALGO.

33 P. Ferris, *The New Militants* (Penguin 1972).

34 Much of the information in this section is derived from A. Boys, 'The changing union: a study of the National Union of Teachers, 1960–74' (unpublished MA thesis, University of Warwick).

35 Since its inception in 1870 its first major objective was the 'control of entrance to the profession and teachers' registration'; see A. Tropp, *The School Teachers* (Heinemann 1957), p. 113. In a recent prospectus on 'what the union stands for' the NUT cited as an objective 'the establishment of a Teaching Council with powers to provide self-government for the profession'.

36 *The Teaching Council*, an NUT discussion document, pp. 8–9.

37 The call for NUT affiliation was first raised in the 1890s. It reappeared in 1917 and in 1920 and was rejected by the executive. It was debated in conference in 1939 but was not again until 1965.

38 See 'Affiliation to the Trades Union Congress', a statement submitted to the 1966 NUT conference.

39 The union first used strike action in 1907 when it financed striking teachers in West Ham who were opposed to locally imposed wage cuts. Local strike action appeared again in the 1950s in the Durham closed shop dispute.

40 The offer amounted to an increase of $6\frac{1}{2}$ per cent on the basic scale. In round figures, it provided a scale rising from £650–£1250 compared with a claim for £775–£1375. It contained several inducements. Younger teachers were satisfied with its provisions for 'booster' payments in the fourth and fifth years of teaching. It abolished the distinction between second and third year trained teachers and provided for a review if the economic situation changed rapidly.

41 The Management Panel subsequently went to arbitration unilaterally.

42 *The Teacher* (12 March, 1968).

43 *The Teacher* (2 February, 1969).

44 *The Teacher* (21 February, 1969).

45 In 'Rank and File', no. 6, it was argued that local associations should take the initiative in setting up local strike funds and committees for strike action along with the NAS.

46 NUT Annual Report (1970), p. 81.

47 Public support for the teachers' claim was identified as essential. The Executive allocated £20,000 for this purpose. Advertisements were placed in *The Guardian* and

The Times with undeniable effect: 'a decisive impact, secured widespread publicity, and were well worth the £4,000 they cost. Subsequently the development of the union's publicity campaign secured massive, and in general, very favourable publicity in press, radio and television': a summary in the Executive Report for 1970, p. 51.

48 At this time it was difficult to differentiate between 'official' action and unofficial action.

49 *The Teacher* (28 November 1969).

50 An opinion poll published in the *Evening Standard*, carried out by the Opinion Research Centre, showed that the public not only supported the teachers' claim but thought that it was too modest.

51 *The Teacher* (7 February 1970); see also V. Burke, *Teachers in Turmoil* (Penguin 1971), pp. 91–4.

52 *The Teacher* (9 January 1970).

53 This action included 7000 teachers in Birmingham, Southwark and Waltham Forest. Referenda in those areas revealed 80 per cent support for indefinite strike action.

54 The Assistant Masters' Association, which had originally advocated such action, dissociated itself from the NUT recommendation.

55 Executive press release, 4 March 1970.

56 The recommended basic scale would rise from £1250 to £2200 by ten annual increments, replacing the existing scale of £980 to £1720 by fourteen increments.

57 NUT Campaign Brief no. 7 (7 December 1970), p. 20.

58 *The Teacher* (12 March 1971) outlined the Executive's reasons for opposing arbitration in the following terms:

   1) The objectivity of any arbitration machinery had been brought into question in the light of Hugh Clegg's removal from the chairmanship of the Civil Service Arbitration Tribunal.

   2) The arbitration procedure under the Remuneration of Teachers Act 1965 contained the following serious drawbacks to 'objectivity': (a) the Minister could fix a global sum; (b) DES representation during negotiations restricted freedom of negotiation; (c) the Secretary of State for Employment chose two of the three members of the arbitrating panel; (d) economic considerations can and do enter into negotiations; (e) even though an arbitration award may prove acceptable to the teachers the Minister has power to override that award.

59 An Executive amendment to strike action that the London teachers' case would be better served by a mass lobby was defeated by 23 votes to 7. The three phases of strike action were: Phase I – strike for three days by 1357 members in 97 schools; Phase II – 3146 members in 211 schools; Phase III – 2532 members in 225 schools.

60 The membership had been urged to vote 'yes' on three questions: would they support withdrawal of labour for (i) one day? (ii) up to two weeks? (iii) more than two weeks? *The Times* reported one Executive member as having stated that 18,000 supported (ii) and 16,000 supported (iii).

61 *The Teacher* (14 June 1974).

62 Pay Board, *London Weighting,* Advisory Report no. 4; Cmnd 5660 (HMSO 1974).

63 Reported in *The Teacher* (19 April 1974).

64 NUT Annual Report (1974), p. 54.

65 See pp. 221–3 and pp. 230–4 for comment on these factors.

66 C. J. Margerison and C. K. Elliott, 'A predictive study of the development in teacher militancy', *British Journal of Industrial Relations*, vol. 8, no. 3 (November 1970). The

survey was based on 315 completed questionnaires sent to teachers (excluding head-masters) in a northern urban area (see p. 413).

67 *Report of the Committee of Inquiry into the Pay of Non-University Teachers* (Houghton Report), Cmnd 5848 (HMSO 1974).

68 ibid., p. 13. The baseline 1965–6 = 100 was chosen because (1) 1965 was just before the start of government incomes policies; (2) it coincided with the change in teachers' negotiating machinery; (3) it gave a sufficient time span to demonstrate trends. The standardization by age was to take account of the influx of young teachers into primary and secondary schools and of the older age structure in further education.

69 Presidential address to Conference, 1963, reported in NUT Annual Report (1964), p. 90.

70 From a speech by Alex Baker (Executive) to Annual Conference; reported in *The Teacher* (26 April 1963).

71 R. D. Coates, *Teachers' Unions and Interest Group Politics: A Study in the Behaviour of Organised Teachers in England and Wales* (Cambridge University Press 1972), p. 105.

72 Although there may have been no direct relationship between NAS militancy and inclusion in Burnham, it appeared to be significant. Having pressed politically for representation on Burnham without success, the NAS had turned to more direct action. At its 1961 conference the NAS voted for 'militant action' to protest against NAS exclusion from Burnham, for an independent inquiry into teachers' salaries, and the 'gross underpayment of schoolmasters'. A series of local strikes followed, in each of which members from a single school were withdrawn for a day.

73 The increase was put at 9000 members: *The Teacher* (12 April 1968).

74 Reported in *The Times* (31 January 1974).

75 NUT Memorandum on Affiliation (1966), p. 56.

76 The ATTI in 1967 and the NAS in 1968.

77 For example see Ronald Manzer, *Teachers and Politics* (Manchester University Press 1970), p. 148: 'the activist political structure of the Union can distort the attitude of the rank and file and plunge the leadership into pursuit of impossible goals'.

78 Ronald Gould echoing the words of the NAS's general secretary in *The School-master* (17 March 1961). For example, the Sustentation Fund, which could be used to finance strike action, stood at £1,358,600 in 1961 – just about £6 per head. Until 1968 the union also had a Salaries Campaign Fund, which had always stood at a relatively small amount. The rules also gave power to raise levies when necessary.

79 'Technical' strike action involved formal resignation but continuing teaching, while the 'industrial' strike involved a complete withdrawal of services in breach of teachers' contracts of employment.

80 This principle had been established only in 1961.

81 Speech by delegate to Annual Conference 1963.

82 Delegate speech at same conference. Strike action was also referred to as 'organizational suicide'.

83 *The Teacher* (26 April 1963).

84 NUT Annual Report (1968), p. 124.

85 Report of the 1968 Conference in *The Teacher* (12 April 1968). The amount contained in the sustentation fund over the period under study was:

	£		£
1960	1,509,534	1967	1,720,588
1961	1,358,600	1968	1,767,740
1962	1,356,383	1969	1,748,145
1963	1,423,834	1970	2,120,463
1964	1,499,454	1971	2,670,655
1965	1,580,491	1972	3,029,303
1966	1,664,685	1973	2,882,946

86 The Executive intended to do this by stating that any action to be taken was to be decided by the Executive member for each area in consultation with regional officials.

87 *The Teacher* (21 March 1969).

88 Although it appeared to be lost on a show of hands, a card vote resulted in a majority in favour of an interim claim, of 25,000 votes.

89 'Rank and File', no. 9, p. 4.

90 *The Teacher* (16 April 1971).

91 *The Teacher* (2 March 1973).

92 The motion ran:

> the Union salary policy should be based on the principle of the rate for the job of teaching in the classroom . . . the present salary structure, which divides class teachers into different categories and offers great incentives to the teacher to leave the classroom to undertake administrative duties, is against the interests of both teachers and the education service. Conference demands, therefore, that future salary claims should be diverted towards achieving (a) a substantially improved starting salary of £1,800; (b) a reduction in both the number and size of differentials; (c) a steady reduction in the number of separate scales; (d) eventual establishment of a single scale for all teachers. [*The Teacher*, 22 February 1974]

93 Burke, p. 29.

94 Thus, in 1969 the NUT executive was composed of thirty-seven head teachers and one deputy head.

95 Report of the Young Teachers' Conference in 1972 in *The Teacher* (6 October 1972).

96 See *The Teacher* (1 and 8 December 1972).

97 Report of the Executive meeting in *The Teacher* (23 February 1973).

98 'Rank and File', no. 7 (1969).

99 The two Executive members were Beth Stone (elected for District 27 – outer London) and Dick North (elected for District 26 – inner London). In 1973 Beth Stone was refused Executive papers for allegedly leaking information in breach of the Executive's confidentiality code.

100 The original strike clause required an affirmative vote by five-eighths of the *total* membership before strike action was taken by any section of the membership. The new clause, on the other hand, made provision for strikes in sections of the industry where a ballot need be taken only of those concerned and requires a simple majority of those entitled to vote.

101 With 5100 members, NUBE organized approximately 70 per cent of Welsh bank employees and the proportion was even higher in the South Wales area.

102 The agreement consisted of average overall increases in the basic pay of bank clerks aged 16–21 of 7 per cent for men and 10.9 per cent for women, average overall in-

creases in minimum retirement salaries amounting to 7 per cent for men and 17.4 per cent for women, and also an increase in minimum salaries for bank managers of 6.8 per cent. The agreement was designed to establish a closer alignment of pay between banks and to take a step towards the introduction of equal pay.

103 NBPI Reports no. 6, *Salaries of Midland Bank Staff*, Cmnd 2839 (HMSO 1965); no. 34, *Bank Charges*, Cmnd 3292 (HMSO 1967); no. 106, *Pay in the London Clearing Banks*, Cmnd 3943 (HMSO 1969); and no. 143, *Hours and Overtime in the London Clearing Banks*, Cmnd 4301 (HMSO 1970).

104 In 1941 the bank employers offered BOG joint recognition with the internal staff associations, but the proposal was rejected by a special delegate meeting of the guild. For them a joint staff side as proposed by the employers 'would have been tantamount to admitting that the Guild had to get the approval and consent of internalism before it could talk to employers'; *The Bank Officer* (February 1942).

105 'One thing is clear,' he said, 'that there is great room for improvement in the relations of all parties concerned, and I venture to think and say that, in the interests of the industry as a whole, there is need for action to secure that improvement.' He concluded, optimistically, that, 'provided firm agreements could be reached on what are "national" as opposed to "internal" issues', and provided that claims to exclusive representation (from NUBE) were departed from, 'the history of the recent past gives some encouragement for the belief that it should be possible to obtain acceptance of the principle of joint negotiation in respect of these national or general issues': Cameron Report – 'Report of the Inquiry by the Hon. Lord Cameron, DSC, QC, into the Complaint made by the National Union of Bank Employees on 12 March 1962 to the Committee on Freedom of Association of the International Labour Organization, Cmnd 2202 (HMSO 1963), paras. 325, 329 and 333.

Chapter 8 The structure of decision-making in job regulation

1 See R. Undy, 'The devolution of bargaining levels and responsibilities in the TGWU, 1965–75,' *Industrial Relations Journal*, vol. 9, no. 3 (Autumn 1978). Some of the material used in that article is reproduced in this section of the chapter.

2 TGWU evidence to the *Royal Commission on Trade Unions and Employers' Associations, 1965–68*, Cmnd 3623 (HMSO 1968), para. 45.

3 Verbatim report of the TGWU Biennial Delegate Conference (1969).

4 See NBPI Report no. 63, *Pay of Municipal Busmen*, Cmnd 3605 (HMSO 1968), p. 1.

5 See TGWU *Record* (June 1967).

6 Scamp Report.

7 The TGWU has the second largest membership in the CSEU.

8 The NJICs listed in Table 42 are not comprehensive. They include only those that were of some importance for the TGWU while also corresponding with the NES's categorization by industrial agreement. The NJICs quoted, however, do cover approximately 44 per cent of the TGWU membership.

9 TGWU Annual Report (1970), p. 69.

10 The information on lay representatives is drawn from information gathered from questionnaires: 200 questionnaires were sent to district officials in Regions 1, 2, 3, 4,

5, 6, 7, 8 and 9, and 62 usable replies were received. Some replies were informative on certain questions and not on others.

11 See M. Mellish, *The Docks after Devlin* (Heinemann 1972), pp. 126–33.

12 TGWU Report, 14th BDC (1951), minute 86.

13 *Report of a Committee of Inquiry into Certain Matters Concerning the Port Transport Industry*, Cmnd 2734 (HMSO 1967) (The Devlin Report), para. 287.

14 Jack Jones, in C. Levinson (ed.), *Industry's Democratic Revolution* (Allen & Unwin 1974).

15 Changes in the composition of high-level negotiating committees were identified in interviews or from other sources.

16 Jones in Levinson, p. 250.

17 This comment was made during interview.

18 See *Sunday Times* (23 March 1969) and F. Silverman, 'The 1969 Ford strike', in *Trade Union Register 1970*.

19 TGWU Report (1972), p. 172.

20 TGWU Report (1970), p. 158.

21 TGWU Report (1966), p. 102.

22 H. Urwin, *Plant and Productivity Bargaining* (TGWU 1970), p. 4.

23 ibid.

24 Devlin Report and Scamp Report.

25 NBPI Reports nos. 1 (1965), 48 (1967), 94 (1968), 29 (1967), 49 (1967), 50 (1967), 63 (1968), 91 (1968), 92 (1968), 103 (1969), and 105 (1969) respectively.

26 The most famous of these were the Fawley productivity agreements documented in Allan Flanders, *The Fawley Productivity Agreements* (Faber and Faber 1964). But there were several others, for example the British Oxygen Company Ltd, Imperial Chemical Industries Ltd, the Electricity Supply Industry, Alcan Industries Ltd.

27 NBPI Report no. 123, *Productivity Agreements*, Cmnd 4136 (HMSO 1969), p. 3.

28 TGWU Annual Report (1970), p. 101.

29 NBPI Report no. 36, p. 36.

30 Royal Commission on Trade Unions and Employers' Associations, *Productivity Bargaining* (HMSO 1967), p. 29, para. 132.

31 Urwin, p. 4.

32 TGWU Report, 17th BDC (1957), minute 103, 'Consultation with Membership'. In 1957 a motion calling for more lay representation on 'all bodies on which the union is entitled to representation' was also defeated; minute 102.

33 TGWU Members' Handbook, p. 49 (our emphasis).

34 In 'Union in Action', p. 9, it says: 'The shop steward is the key figure in carrying out the TGWU's policy for high wages and effective organisation. Our plans . . . depend upon workshop representatives who are able to take the initiative and play a positive part in negotiations with management.'

35 TGWU Third Rules Conference (1962), minute 52.

36 An exception to this can be found in the docks when the loss of members in Northern Docks in the 1960s led the union to consider altering its structure.

37 TGWU Report, 23rd BDC (1969), minute 29.

38 J. L. Jones, *Trade Unionism in the Seventies* (TGWU 1970).

39 Jack Jones, Levinson, p. 266.

40 ibid. (Jones's emphasis).

41 It is not intended when citing Jones alone as the architect of change to overlook the

role played by Urwin. In a number of interviews FTOs stressed Urwin's role. As the two appear to have acted in concert, however, no attempt is made to distinguish between their activities.

42 Jack Jones, in Levinson, pp. 257 and 266.
43 Verbatim report of TGWU Biennial Delegate Conference (1969).
44 NBPI Report no. 92, *Pay and Conditions in the Building Industry*, Cmnd 3837 (HMSO 1968).
45 Derived from earnings and time rates in the *Department of Employment Gazette*.
46 See *Report of the Royal Commission on Trade Unions and Employers' Associations, 1965–68* (Donovan Report), Cmnd 3623 (HMSO), ch. 3.
47 T. J. Connelly, *The Woodworkers 1860–1960* (ASW 1960), p. 35.
48 NBPI Report no. 92, *Pay and Conditions in the Building Industry*.
49 *ASPD Journal* (September 1967).
50 Most of this information is from interviews with FTOs.
51 V. G. Munns and W. E. J. McCarthy, *Employers Associations: The Result of Two Studies*, Donovan Commission Research Paper no. 7 (HMSO 1967).
52 ibid.
53 *Financial Times* (23 March 1973).
54 G. D. H. Cole, *The World of Labour* (Bell 1913), p. 266.
55 W. Haber and H. Levinson, 'Labour relations and productivity in the building trades' (1956); cited in *Industrial Relations*, vol. 11, no. 8 (October 1972).
56 Cameron Report.
57 'The most conservative estimate is that at least £10 million is still lost every year through the lump.' *The Guardian* (26 March 1976).
58 *UCATT Journal* (July 1974).
59 In 1975 1049 of the 14,000 firms in the National Federation of Building Trade Employers had registered, although the signatories represented 60 per cent of those employed in the construction industry; see *The Guardian* (11 February 1975).
60 1974 UCATT Conference Report.
61 Quoted in the *New Statesman* (11 August 1972).
62 It was estimated that 'In June of '74 the guaranteed weekly earnings for craftsmen will have increased from £20 to £32, a rise of £12 or 60 per cent.' *Viewpoint* (the UCATT Journal) (1972).
63 These ran foul of the government's counter-inflation policy in October 1973.
64 Figures derived from union district reports.
65 Figures quoted by a member of the EC.
66 'Report for the GMWU on the workload and functions of full-time officers', p. 12.
67 The figures for FTOs include the general secretary, NIOs and regional officials.
68 Extract from the 'Special report on union reorganisation: union reorganisation on an industrial basis', (1968).
69 Figures from a report to the Economic Committee of the Executive Council for NUPE (October 1975); quoted in R. Fryer, A. Fairclough and T. Manson, 'Does the trade union branch matter? Some evidence from the National Union of Public Employees' (unpublished paper, Department of Sociology, University of Warwick 1975).
70 Much of the information in this section derives from R. Fryer, A. Fairclough and T. Manson, 'Organisation and change in the National Union of Public Employees' (unpublished paper, Department of Sociology, University of Warwick August 1974).

71 Quoted from the discussion pamphlet circulated to the members by the Executive Council, 'New ways for NUPE', in W. Craik, *Sydney Hill and the National Union of Public Employees* (Allen & Unwin 1968).

72 Fryer, Fairclough and Manson, 'Organisation and change in NUPE'.

73 According to the Warwick survey in 1974 (Fryer, Fairclough and Manson, 'Organisation and change in NUPE', p. 12) over a third (38 per cent) of NUPE's stewards had held office for a year or less, almost half (46 per cent) of them have never been members of another union where they might have experienced shop steward roles of one kind or another, and of those who had only a quarter (23 per cent) had held some office in the union such as steward or branch secretary.

74 Branch officials, particularly branch secretaries, had traditionally been the lay officials who carried out any negotiating activities not conducted by FTOs. After the introduction of shop stewards their role continued, often handling those issues that shop stewards could not handle alone.

75 For example, the NBPI and the White Paper, *In Place of Strife*, were critical of the 1922 engineering procedure.

76 The Foundry Workers were already amalgamated with the Engineering Union but retained their autonomy within the CSEU.

77 Fryer, Fairclough and Manson, 'Organisation and change in NUPE', p. 17.

78 I. Richter, *Political Purpose in Trade Unions* (Allen & Unwin 1973), p. 97.

79 *Memorandum of Agreement between EEF and CSEU including Agreed Points for Guidance*, p. 4.

80 NPBI Report no. 29, *The Pay and Conditions of Manual Workers in Local Authorities, the National Health Service, Gas and Water Supply*, Cmnd 3230 (HMSO 1967).

81 *Report of the Independent Committee of Inquiry under Sir Jack Scamp into the Trade Union Side's Claim of April 1970*. (NJIC for Local Authorities Services 1970), p. 14.

82 *Financial Times* (9 and 16 May 1973).

83 Fryer, Fairclough and Manson, 'Organisation and change in NUPE', p. 11.

84 *AUEW(E) dispute benefit, 1962–72*

Year	Dispute benefit	Year	Dispute benefit
1962	£72,665	1967	£ 114,709
1963	78,274	1968	297,245
1964	92,845	1969	445,646
1965	94,905	1970	605,094
1966	69,905	1971	1,609,442
		1972	2,636,356

The particularly high figures for 1971 reflect action in protest at the Industrial Relations Act and those in 1972 reflect the decision to support workplace bargaining in pursuit of the national pay claim when the union was faced with an impasse at national level.

Thus the EEF recorded in their annual review for 1972–73 that '160 strikes took place in support of domestic submissions of the claim and 1,966,868 days were lost.'

85 Minutes of evidence, p. 34; our emphasis.

86 The lack of urgency on the part of the AEU was demonstrated by the fact that between 1961 and 1967 the union made no serious formal approach to the EEF regarding major changes in the agreement.

87 The *status quo* clause reads:

> Where an employer takes a decision which is within the framework of an existing agreement or an established practice there shall be no obligation upon the employer to postpone the implementation of that decision until agreement has been reached or the procedure has been exhausted. On the other hand, where an employer takes a decision which means established practice, and the worker concerned objects to that decision, the employer shall be obliged to reach agreement or exhaust the procedure before implementing the decision.

88 In addition to containing an acceptable *status quo* clause it also secured the objective of shortening the disputes procedure. Under the new procedure grievances would be taken up first inside the plant, where a written procedure should be devised containing as many stages as the participants agree to be appropriate. The second stage would be an external conference of local union officials sitting with shop stewards, and should be held within seven days of application. The procedure would then have been exhausted, instead of going to national level. The reforms were expected to shorten the time taken from nine or ten months to a few weeks.

89 *Financial Times* (7 April 1972).

90 The thirteen-point claim included £6 per week increase in the basic craft rate, substantial general increases for others, longer holidays and shorter hours.

91 See *Industrial Relations Review and Report*, no. 36 (July 1972) and no. 45 (December 1972).

92 *Industrial Relations Review and Report*, no. 36 (July 1972), p. 3.

93 *Financial Times* (18 April 1972).

94 Extract from the *Special Report on Union Reorganisations: Union Reorganisation on an Industrial Basis* (1968).

95 A detailed account of the strike at Pilkingtons has been given in Tony Lane and Kenneth Roberts, *Strike at Pilkingtons* (Collins/Fontana 1971).

96 *Report of the Court of Inquiry under Professor John C. Wood into a Dispute between Pilkington Brothers Ltd. and Certain of their Employees* (HMSO 1970).

97 *Final Report of the NEC Sub-Committee into the Affairs of the 91 Branch (Pilkington's St. Helens) Liverpool, North Wales and Irish Region* (unpublished 1970/1).

98 The GMWU leadership had been willing to remove 'militant' members from the union, as in the case of the Savoy Hotel dispute in 1948 and the Ford, Halewood, dispute in 1969.

99 With the possible exception of such coherent groups as the ambulance men, who threatened secession, and the dustmen.

100 Fryer, Fairclough and Manson, 'Organisation and change in NUPE', p. 18.

101 ibid.

102 ibid., p. 25.

103 A form of productivity scheme was in fact introduced after the period covered by our study, although it did not involve a return to the pre-1966 piecework-based system.

104 Indeed, bargaining between the Post Office and the POEU had included some productivity elements long before the term 'productivity bargaining' became fashionable. Moreover, the union had continually sought recognition for the increasing technical complexity of members' work. These developments came to a head in 1963 when the POEU composed a 'value of work claim' which introduced productivity into the pay equation. The POEU continued to press for productivity-based negotiations and it was they who initiated new discussions with the Post Office in 1960.

105 For example at the 1967 Conference, motion 206 from West Cornwall read: 'To give, as soon as possible, consideration to the appointment of Regional Secretaries or officers of the Union on a full-time basis, particularly in view of the forthcoming changes in Post Office management'.

106 John Hughes and Roy Moore (eds.), *A Special Case? Social Justice and the Miners* (Penguin 1972), p. 34.

107 The proposals provided for the payment of bonuses for production above 75 per cent of a standard agreed locally after work study. Underground workers, apart from face workers, and surface workers would be paid 50 per cent of a face worker's average bonus earnings on an agreed area basis.

108 'Seconded representatives' are seconded from their normal work in the institution concerned and continue to be paid by the bank. Their function is largely to act as an assistant to the full-time officer in negotiations and organizational work in their institution. They also often act as secretary to their National Advisory Committee.

109 Select Committee on Nationalized Industries, The Post Office, First Report, vol. II (HMSO 1967), p. 106.

110 Civil service pay is determined primarily by 'fair comparisons' with equivalent grades outside. Major reviews until 1974, however, did not take place every year, and therefore central pay settlements (CPSs) were negotiated for all grades not in pay research that year based on general movements of pay outside. The Civil Service Pay Agreement 1974 provided for annual pay research-based increases and therefore the need for CPSs ceased.

111 For example, at the 1963 Conference a move was made to replace PRU by wage claims based on technical knowledge, skills, productivity, and the profits of the Post Office and pursued by industrial action where necessary, and on that occasion it was only narrowly defeated by 32,608 votes to 34,895.

112 Thus in 1967 they received the normal pay research settlement because the government honoured the agreement. In 1968 they obtained 6 per cent when the norm was 3 per cent. In 1969 they received 10 per cent although they had to hold a one-day strike to obtain it, and in 1970 just before the election they received 12 per cent.

113 The Select Committee on Nationalized Industries reporting on the Post Office in 1967 demonstrated the considerable room for growth in telecommunications and on p. 105 indicated how the engineering grades were expected to benefit most from the growth of telecommunications:

Telecommunications staff

	March 1966	March 1971	% change
Engineering (incl. apprentices)	93,000	104,000	+12
Clerical	19,000	15,000	–21
Operating	55,000	48,000	–13

114 The most recent of these had been the secession of the skilled 'internal' telephone engineers in 1945 to form the Engineering Officers (Telecommunications) Association (EOTA).

115 In 1968 the POEU negotiated a 6 per cent increase and in 1970 a 12 per cent increase based on productivity and other considerations across the board.

116 See, for example, J. Higgins, 'Fawley revisited', *POEU Journal* (February 1965). Further articles also followed from J. Higgins and others; e.g. J. Higgins, 'Even handed justice', *Live Wire* (Metropolitan West Branch POEU, June 1969); J. Higgins and D. Rattery, 'Pay and incomes policy', *POEU Journal* (May 1966).

117 See Hughes and Moore, pp. 17–18 for further comment on the NUM's bargaining objectives.

118 R. G. Searle-Barnes, *Pay and Productivity Bargaining: A Study of the Effect of National Wage Agreements in the Nottinghamshire Coalfields* (Manchester University Press 1969), pp. 19–20.

119 Hughes and Moore, p. 25.

120 This comment applies only to the internal staff associations, not to ASTMS.

121 This does not imply that the TGWU as a consequence had a very low ratio of FTO to members: with a ratio of 1:3834 (1976) it was more amply serviced than the AUEW(E) (1:6402), the POEU (1:7380), the NUT (1:5468), was similar to the GMWU (1:3809), and less well serviced than UCATT (1:2000), and ASTMS (1:3400).

122 S. H. Slichter, J. H. Healey and E. R. Livernash, *The Impact of Collective Bargaining on Management* (Washington, DC: Brookings Institution 1960), p. 607.

Chapter 9 The conditions of change in trade unions

1 Donovan Report (*Royal Commission on Trade Unions and Employers' Associations, 1965–68*, Cmnd 3623 (HMSO 1968), ch. 10.

2 See W. E. J. McCarthy and N. D. Ellis, *Management by Agreement* (Hutchinson 1974) for a general discussion of the aims of the 1971 Act in relation to trade union behaviour. Also B. Weekes *et al.*, *Industrial Relations and the Limits of the Law* (Basil Blackwell 1975).

3 Weekes, p. 228.

4 Of course we are concerned here with the *collective* aims of both acts. It is not denied that the EPA significantly extended the legal rights of individual workers, and this had had some impact on the services provided by trade unions. It is also evident that the TULRA has affected the operation and form taken by the closed shop – see B. Weekes, 'The law and practice of the closed shop', *Industrial Law Journal* (December 1976).

5 That is to say, the aim was to facilitate the continuance of non-legal collective agreements against a framework of statutory protection which allowed unions to employ their customary forms of industrial action. In this sense the objective was a legal framework similar to that which union leaders believed they had achieved before a line of cases in the 1950s and 1960s undermined this assumed protection.

6 Of course the EPA's job territory objectives were less 'reformist' than the Industrial Relations Act in the sense that this time there were no specific provisions designed to discourage inter-union competition (i.e. along the lines of the 1971 provisions relating to 'sole' bargaining units.) Also, use of Section 11 of the EPA was open to all 'independent' unions; it was not confined to those who were prepared to accept the internal changes involved in the 1971 procedure for 'registration'.

7 Thus the 1978 Report of the Advisory Conciliation and Arbitration Service concludes: 'As a direct result of the operation of the legislation some 48,000 workers were covered by collective bargaining arrangements by the end of 1978. The Service

had no evidence of the indirect effects which legislation may have had, for example, on employer attitudes to trade union recognition.'

8   It also seems reasonable to reach much the same verdict in respect of two other 'Social Contract' laws – the Health and Safety at Work Act, and the Sex Discrimination Act. We came across no evidence that they had any significant effect on any of our areas of change in the period under review – which is not to say anything about their effect in general – i.e. so far as individual rights and management practices are concerned.

9   See the 1978 *Review and Plan of the Manpower Services Commission* (HMSO, November 1978). Also 'New projections of the future of the Labour Force', *Department of Employment Gazette* (June 1977).

10   H. A. Clegg, *The Changing System of Industrial Relations in Great Britain* (Basil Blackwell 1979), p. 378.

11   G. S. Bain, *The Growth of White Collar Unionism* (Oxford University Press 1970).

12   See Clegg, pp. 41–53; also William Brown (ed.), *Warwick Survey of Workshop Relations* (unpublished study, University of Warwick) and cited in that work.

13   Clegg, *The Changing System of Industrial Relations in Great Britain*, pp. 41–53.

14   The NUSMCHDE's Conference voted in October 1979 for merger with the AUEW. Its members voted on the issue in January 1980.

15   H. A. Turner, *Trade Union Growth, Structure and Policy* (Allen & Unwin 1962), pp. 289–91.

16   See Bain; also G. S. Bain and Elsheikh, *Union Growth and the Business Cycle* (Basil Blackwell 1976); and articles by Bain, Elsheikh and R. Price in the *British Journal of Industrial Relations* (November 1976 and March 1978).

17   Clegg, *Trade Unionism Under Collective Bargaining*.

18   See particularly Bain, *The Growth of White Collar Unionism*, and *Trade Union Growth and Recognition* (HMSO 1967).

19   Bain and Elsheikh, *Union Growth and the Business Cycle*, p. 21.

20   ibid., p. 23.

21   Bain and Elsheikh, 'Trade union growth: a reply', *British Journal of Industrial Relations* (March 1978), p. 99.

22   For this reason our study would not support the largely methodological and abstract criticisms of R. Richardson in 'Review article', British Journal of Industrial Relations, vol. 15, no. 2 (July 1977).

23   Clegg, p. 10.

24   See Clegg p. 10, where the case is argued in terms of bargaining having 'its best chance of being effective when it operates at the points where managerial decisions are taken and employers' associations reach their collective conclusions'. But of course this assumes that it is *employers* who want bargaining to be effective, rather than trade unions. Many trade unionists would doubt this. They might well wish to argue that in practice employers often refuse to bargain at the most 'effective' or productive level. On this analysis trade unions need to exert pressure to secure the right to bargain at what they regard as the right level.

Bibliography

Books

Allen, V. L., *Trade Union Leadership*, London: Longman 1957

Allen, V. L., 'The paradox of militancy', in Robin Blackburn and A. Cockburn (eds.), *The Incompatibles: Trade Union Militancy and Consensus*, Harmondsworth: Penguin 1976

Bain, G. S., *Trade Union Growth and Recognition* (Royal Commission on Trade Unions and Employers' Associations Research Paper no. 6), London: HMSO 1967

Bain, G. S., *The Growth of White Collar Unionism*, London: Oxford University Press 1970

Bain, G. S., and Elsheikh, L., *Union Growth and the Business Cycle*, Oxford: Basil Blackwell 1976

Bullock, A., *The Life and Times of Ernest Bevin*, London: Heinemann 1960

Burke, V., *Teachers in Turmoil*, Harmondsworth: Penguin 1971

Cameron Report: see *Report of a Court of Inquiry by the Hon. Lord Cameron. . . .*

Clegg, H. A., *General Union in a Changing Society*, Oxford: Basil Blackwell 1964

Clegg, H. A., *The System of Industrial Relations in Great Britain*, Oxford: Basil Blackwell 1976.

Clegg, H. A., *Trade Unionism under Collective Bargaining: A Theory Based on Comparisons in Six Countries*, Oxford: Basil Blackwell 1976

Clegg, H. A., *The Changing System of Industrial Relations in Great Britain*, Oxford: Basil Blackwell 1979

Coates, R. D., *Teachers' Unions and Interest Group Politics: A Study in the Behaviour of Organised Teachers in England and Wales*, Cambridge University Press 1972

Coles, G. D. H., *The World of Labour*, London: Bell 1913

Commission on Industrial Relations, *Facilities Afforded to Shop Stewards*, Cmnd 4668, London: HMSO 1971

Connelly, T. J. *The Woodworkers 1860–1960*, London: Amalgamated Society of Woodworkers 1960

Craik, W., *Sydney Hill and the National Union of Public Employees*, London: Allen & Unwin 1968

Dahrendorf, R., *Class and Class Conflict in Industrial Society*, London: Routledge & Kegan Paul 1963

Devlin Report: see *Report of a Committee of Inquiry into Certain Matters Concerning the Port Transport Industry*

Donovan Report: see *Royal Commission on Trade Unions and Employers' Associations 1965–68*

Dorfman, G. A., *Wage Politics in Britain, 1945–67*, London: Charles Knight 1974

Durcan, J. W., McCarthy, W. E. J., and Redman, G., *Strikes in Britain*, London: Allen & Unwin forthcoming

Edelstein, J. D., and Warner, M., *Comparative Union Democracy*, London: Allen & Unwin 1975
Ellis, V. A., 'Some sociological dimensions of unionisation among Technical and supervisory employees', unpublished Ph.D thesis, University of Leeds 1971

Ferris, P., *The New Militants*, Harmondsworth: Penguin 1972
Final Report of the NEC Sub-Committee into the Affairs of the 91 Branch (Pilkington's St Helens Liverpool, North Wales and Irish Region, unpublished 1970/1
Flanders, A., *The Fawley Productivity Agreements*, London, Faber & Faber 1964
Flanders, A., *Industrial Relations: What's Wrong with the System?*, London: Institute of Personnel Management 1965
Flanders, A., *Trade Unions*, London: Hutchinson 1965
Flanders, A., and Clegg, H. A., *The System of Industrial Relations in Great Britain*, Oxford: Basil Blackwell 1967
Fryer, R., Fairclough, A., and Manson, T., 'Organisation and change in the National Union of Public Employees', unpublished paper, Department of Sociology, University of Warwick 1974
Fryer, R., Fairclough, A., and Manson, T., 'Does the trade union branch matter? Some evidence from the National Union of Public Employees', unpublished paper, Department of Sociology, University of Warwick 1975
Fyrthm, H. J., and Collins, A., *The Foundry Workers*, Manchester: AUFW 1959

Hughes, J., *Trade Union Structure and Government* (Donovan Commission Research Paper no. 5), London: HMSO 1967
Hughes, J., and Moore, R., (eds.), *A Special Case? Social Justice and the Miners*, Harmondsworth: Penguin 1972

Jackson, M. P., *Labour Relations in the Docks*, Farnborough: Saxon House 1973
Jefferys, J. B., *The Story of the Engineers*, London: Lawrence & Wishart 1971
Jones, J. L., *The Right to Participate: Key to Industrial Progress*, London: TGWU 1970
Jones, J. L., *Trade Unionism in the Seventies*, London: TGWU 1970

Lane, Tony, and Roberts, K., *Strike at Pilkingtons*, London: Collins/Fontana 1971
Lerner, S. W., *Breakaway Unions and the Small Trade Union*, London: Allen & Unwin 1961
Levinson, C. (ed.), *Industry's Democratic Revolution*, London: Allen & Unwin 1974
Lipset, S. M., Trow, M., and Coleman, J., *Union Democracy: The Internal Politics of the International Typographical Union*, Glencoe, Ill.: Free Press 1956

McCarthy, W. E. J., and Ellis, N. D., *Management by Agreement*, London: Hutchinson 1974
Macleod, A., 'Pay in the public sector', unpublished paper, Nuffield College Oxford 1974
Manzer, R., *Teachers and Politics*, Manchester University Press 1970
Mellish, M., *The Docks After Devlin*, London: Heinemann 1972
Michels, R., *Political Parties*, Glencoe, Ill.: Free Press 1911

Munns, V. G., and McCarthy, W. E. J., *Employers Associations: The Result of Two Studies* (Donovan Commission Research Paper no. 7), London: HMSO 1967

National Board for Prices and Incomes (NBPI)
  Reports
   1   *Road Haulage Rates* (Interim), Cmnd 2695, London: HMSO 1965
   6   *Salaries of Midland Bank Staff*, Cmnd 2839, London: HMSO 1965
  29   *The Pay and Conditions of Manual Workers in Local Authorities, the National Health Service, Gas and Water Supply*, Cmnd 3230, London: HMSO 1967
  34   *Bank Charges*, Cmnd 3292, London: HMSO 1967
  36   *Productivity Agreements*, Cmnd 3311, London: HMSO 1967
  40   *Second General Report, July 1966 to August 1967*, Cmnd 3394, London: HMSO 1967
  48   *Charges, Costs and Wages in the Road Haulage Industry*, Cmnd 3482, London: HMSO 1967
  49   *Pay and Conditions of Service of Workers in the Engineering Industry*, Cmnd 3495, London: HMSO 1967
  50   *Productivity Agreements in the Bus Industry*, Cmnd 3498, London: HMSO 1967
  63   *Pay of Municipal Busmen*, Cmnd 3605, London: HMSO 1968
  91   *Pay and Conditions in the Civil Engineering Industry*, Cmnd 3836, London: HMSO 1968
  92   *Pay and Conditions in the Building Industry*, Cmnd 3837, London: HMSO 1968
  94   *Productivity Agreements in the Road Haulage Industry*, Cmnd 3847, London: HMSO 1968
 103   *Pay and Productivity in the Car Delivery Industry*, Cmnd 3929, London: HMSO 1969
 105   *Pay of General Workers and Craftsmen in Imperial Chemical Industries Ltd*, Cmnd 3941, London: HMSO 1969
 106   *Pay in the London Clearing Banks*, Cmnd 3943, London: HMSO 1969
 123   *Productivity Agreements*, Cmnd 4136, London: HMSO 1969
 143   *Hours and Overtime in the London Clearing Banks*, Cmnd 4301, London: HMSO 1970
 146   *Pay and Conditions of Industrial Civil Servants*, Cmnd 4351, London: HMSO 1970

Pay Board, *London Weighting* (Advisory Report no. 4), Cmnd 5660, London: HMSO 1974
Perlman, S., *A Theory of the Labour Movement*, London: Macmillan 1928
Postgate, R., *The Builders' History*, London: National Federation of Building Trade Operatives 1923

Report of the Inquiry by the Hon. Lord Cameron, DSC, QC, into the Complaint made by the National Union of Bank Employees on March 12th, 1962 to the Committee on Freedom of Association of the International Labour Organisation, Cmnd 2202, London: HMSO 1963
Report of a Committee of Inquiry into Certain Matters Concerning the Port Transport Industry (the Devlin Report), Cmnd 2734, London: HMSO 1967
Report of a Court of Inquiry into Trades Disputes at the Barbican and Horseferry Road Construction Sites in London (the Cameron Report), Cmnd 3396, London: HMSO 1967
Report of Inquiry into the Locally Determined Aspects of the System of Payments and

Earnings Opportunities of Registered Dock Workers in the Port of Liverpool (including Birkenhead) (the Scamp Report), London: HMSO 1967

Report of the Committee of Inquiry into the Pay of Non-University Teachers (the Houghton Report) Cmnd 5848, London: HMSO 1974

Report of the Committee of Inquiry under Professor E. H. Phelps-Brown into Certain Matters concerning Labour in Building and Civil Engineering, Cmnd 3714, London: HMSO 1968

Report of Court of Inquiry under Professor John C. Wood into a Dispute Between Pilkington Brothers Ltd. and Certain of their Employees, London: HMSO 1970

Report of the Independent Committee of Inquiry under Sir Jack Scamp into the Trade Union Side's Claim of April 1970, London: NJIC for Local Authorities Services 1970

Richter, I., *Political Purpose in Trade Unions*, London: Allen & Unwin 1973

Roberts, B. C., (ed.), *Industrial Relations: Contemporary Problems and Perspectives*, London: Methuen 1964

Royal Commission on Trade Unions and Employers' Associations, 1965–68: Report (the Donovan Report), Cmnd 3623, London: HMSO 1968

Royal Commission on Trade Unions and Employers' Associations, Productivity Bargaining (Donovan Commission Research Paper no. 4), London: HMSO 1967

Scamp Report: see *Report of Inquiry into the Locally Determined Aspects of the System of Payments and Earnings Opportunities of Registered Dock Workers*

Searle-Barnes, R. G., *Pay and Productivity Bargaining: A Study of the Effect of National Wage Agreements in the Nottinghamshire Coalfields*, Manchester University Press 1969

Select Committee on Nationalised Industries, *The Post Office*, London: HMSO 1967

Slichter, S. H., Healey, J. H., and Livernash, E. R., *The Impact of Collective Bargaining on Management*, Washington, DC: Brookings Institution 1960

Smith, C. T. B., Clifton, R., Makeham, P., Creighton, S. W. and Burn, R. V., *Strikes in Britain: A Research Study of Stoppages in the UK*, London: HMSO 1978

Special Report on Union Reorganisation: Union Reorganisation on an Industrial Basis, GMWU internal report 1968-9

Spoor, Alec, *White Collar Union – 60 Years of NALGO*, London: Heinemann 1967

Trades Union Congress, *Trade Unionism*, London: TUC 1966

Tropp, A., *The School Teachers*, London: Heinemann 1957

Turner, H. A., *Trade Union Growth, Structure and Policy*, London: Allen & Unwin 1962

Urwin, H., *Plant and Productivity Bargaining*, 2nd ed., London: TGWU 1970

Webb, S. and Webb, B., *Industrial Democracy*, London: Longmans 1901

Weekes, B., *et al.*, *Industrial Relations and the Limits of the Law*, Oxford: Basil Blackwell 1974

Wilson, D. F., *Dockers*, London: Fontana 1972

Wright Mills, C., *The Sociological Imagination*, New York: Oxford University Press 1959

Articles

Bain, G. S., and Price, R., 'Union growth and employment trends in the United Kingdom, 1964–70', *British Journal of Industrial Relations*, vol. 10, no. 3 (November 1972)

Blackburn, R. M., Prandy, K., and Stewart, A., 'White-collar associations – organisational character and employee involvement', *Proceedings of a SSRC Conference on Social Stratification and Industrial Relations* (September 1978)

Buchanan, R. T., 'Merger waves in British unionism', *Industrial Relations Journal*, vol. 5, no. 2 (Summer 1974)

Elsheikh, F., and Bain, G. S., 'Trade union growth: a reply', *British Journal of Industrial Relations*, March 1978, p. 99

Feather, V., 'The Royal Commission's analysis: a trade union appraisal', *British Journal of Industrial Relations*, vol. 6, no. 3 (November 1968)

Higgins, J., 'Fawley revisited', *POEU Journal*, February 1965

Higgins, J., 'Even handed justice', *Live Wire* (Metropolitan West Branch POEU), June 1969

Higgins, J., and Rattery, D., 'Pay and incomes policy', *POEU Journal*, May 1966

Jenkins, Clive, 'My strategy', *Industry Week* (30 January 1970), p. 8

Latta, G., 'Trade union finances', *British Journal of Industrial Relations*, vol. 10, no. 3 (November 1972)

Liddle, R. J., and McCarthy, W. E. J., 'The impact of the Prices and Incomes Board on the reform of collective bargaining', *British Journal of Industrial Relations*, vol. 10, no. 3 (November 1972)

Margerison, C. J., and Elliott, C. K., 'A predictive study of the development in teacher militancy', *British Journal of Industrial Relations*, vol. 8, no. 3 (November 1970)

Martin, R., 'Union democracy: an explanatory framework', *Sociology*, vol. 2, no. 2 (May 1968)

Price, R., and Bain, G. S., 'Union growth revisited: 1948–1974 in perspective', *British Journal of Industrial Relations*, vol. 14, no. 3 (November 1976), pp. 339–55

Richardson, R., 'Review article', *British Journal of Industrial Relations*, vol. 15, no. 2 (July 1977)

Silver, M., 'Recent British strike trends: a factual analysis', *British Journal of Industrial Relations*, vol. 11, no. 1 (March 1973), pp. 66–104

Silverman, F., 'The 1969 Ford strike', *Trade Union Register 1970*, Nottingham: Spokesman

Taylor, R., 'Can the lump be abolished', *Socialist Commentary* (January 1974)

Turner, H. A., 'The Royal Commission's research papers', *British Journal of Industrial Relations*, vol. 6, no. 3 (November 1968)

Undy, R., 'The devolution of bargaining levels and responsibilities in the TGWU, 1965–75', *Industrial Relations Journal*, vol. 9, no. 3 (Autumn 1978)

Undy, R., 'The electoral influence of the opposition party in the AUEW Engineering Section, 1960–1975', *British Journal of Industrial Relations*, vol. 17, no. 1 (March 1979)

Volker, D., 'NALGO's affiliation to the TUC', *British Journal of Industrial Relations*, vol. 4, no. 1 (March 1966)

Weekes, B., 'The law and practice of the closed shop', *Industrial Law Journal* (December 1976)

Wootton, L., 'Parties in union government: the AESD', *Political Studies*, vol. 9 (June 1961)

Newspapers, union journals, etc.

Financial Times
The Guardian
Morning Star
Sunday Times
The Times

Department of Employment Gazette
Employment and Productivity Gazette
IDS Brief
Industrial Relations Review and Report
Ministry of Labour Gazette

New Statesman
Socialist Worker

AEU Journal
AScW Journal
ASPD Journal
AUEW(E) Journal
GMWU Journal
NUFTO Record
POEU Journal
Public Service NALGO journal)
The Record (TGWU journal)
The Teacher (NUT journal)
TASS News
UCATT Journal
Viewpoint (UCATT paper)

'Building Workers Charter' (UCATT unofficial publication)
'Engineering News and Views' (AUEW(E) unofficial publication)
'Engineering Voice'
'Industrial Relations Information Service' ['IRIS'] News'
'Insight' (AUEW(E) unofficial publication)
'NALGO Action Group News' (NALGO unofficial publication)
'Rank and File' (NUT official publication)
'Voice of the Unions'

Index

For Product Safety Concerns and Information please contact our EU
representative GPSR@taylorandfrancis.com
Taylor & Francis Verlag GmbH, Kaufingerstraße 24, 80331 München, Germany

www.ingramcontent.com/pod-product-compliance
Lightning Source LLC
Chambersburg PA
CBHW070539270326
41926CB00013B/2150